Obfuscated C
and
Other Mysteries

Don Libes

John Wiley & Sons, Inc.
New York • Chichester • Brisbane • Toronto • Singapore

Senior Acquisitions Editor: *Diane Cerra*
Associate Managing Editor: *Janice Weisner*
Assistant Editor: *Terri Hudson*

Library of Congress Cataloging-in-Publication Data

Libes, Don, 1958-
    Obfuscated C and Other Mysteries / Don Libes
        p.   cm.
    Includes bibliographical references (p.   ) and index.
    ISBN 0-471-57805-3 (Book/Disk : acid-free paper)
    1. C (Computer program language)   I. Title.
  QA76.73.C15L53 1993
  005.13'3--dc20   92-17028

Printed in the United States of America
10 9 8 7 6 5 4 3 2 1

To Donn Fishbein
who introduced me to C and UNIX and forever warped my mind . . .

and to Penny Peticolas
who tried her best to unwarp it.

Contents

Preface—The Good, the Bad, and the Ugly

The Good

There are many good introductory C programming books, and a few good expert-level books. This book aims between them. If you already have some C programming under your belt and are interested in exploring further, this book is for you.

This book is composed of essays originally published in a number of magazines, as well as some new essays. Each essay introduces practical techniques for the C programmer. All of the essays are based on problems encountered in the real world. Rather than covering C feature-by-feature, however, these essays describe how to make and build things—real things—with C.

As these essays were published in magazines, it is difficult to get copies of them now; yet I continually get requests from people who have seen them, not saved the magazines, and now badly want another copy—hence, this collection.

The essays are presented in increasing order of complexity. In the beginning they are very straightforward. Toward the end, they become quite challenging. Feel free to skip the first few chapters if they are too simple for you. You'll find something intriguing soon enough.

The Bad

The book also contains an evil (or humorous, depending on your point of view) side. Half of the book contains programs that won the Obfuscated C Code Contest, an annual ritual in which the C community makes light of itself by purposely using the language in the most obscure ways possible. These programs are reproduced here—for the first time—*with explanations*.

At first sight these programs may seem irrelevant to everyday programming. Whereas some of them might never have been created were it not for the contest, quite a few draw on actual examples of coding styles that one encounters when debugging or modifying other people's code. Although no one wants to admit to having written such code, everyone has seen it. The fact is, even the best programmers occasionally write tricky code that is quickly forgotten and then left undocumented until some unlucky saps come along to fix things, and finds themselves in a swamp. Even worse, the code may appear on the surface to do one thing but in reality do something entirely different. (How many times have you found a comment that did not correctly describe the code beside it?)

Many of the programs are remarkable for the amount of logic squeezed into such a small space. Quite a few use very interesting algorithms or were prepared themselves by very interesting algorithms. Many of these programs have become useful as torture tests in compiler suites, and they will undoubtedly force you to expand your own mind when you study them. And admittedly, some are just downright insane and only good for laughing at and making fun of.

Although a few of them are easy to understand, some require substantial expertise, so you will find something to challenge you no matter how many years of C programming you have under your belt.

As with the rest of the essays in the book, the obfuscated C chapters appear in order of increasing complexity. This coincides with the chronological order in which they appeared. To win the contest nowadays requires surpassing all previous obfuscation. The obfuscated chapters are mixed in with the other chapters, not for further obfuscation, but rather to give you a break. After studying and finally making sense of the most outrageous code, you'll be warmed up, open, and receptive to *my* code! (You might even think it's better written than it really is.) And after several chapters of education, you'll be ready for some more fun.

The Ugly—Standard C vs. Classic C

Standard C is the common name for the C standards promulgated by ANSI, ISO, and NIST (which are all technically identical)[1]. Before the ANSI standard passed in late 1989, there was no official standard. Yet C was implemented on hundreds of different computers and operating systems allowing a high degree of source code portability. Based primarily on *K&R1* and one particularly well-known implementation (the UNIX Portable C Compiler), this pre-Standard C was effectively standardized, although as more and more implementations appeared its definition became more and more vague. Today it is popularly called *Classic C*.

For the most part, Classic C is a subset of Standard C. For example, Standard C defines many more library functions than Classic C does. Standard C also codifies more guarantees, such as what mathematical properties hold upon overflow. On the other hand, Standard C does break some Classic C code. For example, varargs was modified and it is painful to code portably to both the old and new styles.

Writing strictly conforming Standard C guarantees that your programs are portable to any Standard C compiler. While this sounds great, actual practice is quite disheartening. For instance:

- Not everyone has Standard C compilers. This is especially a problem for obsolete CPU lines. There is little incentive for vendors to modernize software in these environments.

- Whereas C is well defined, environments are not. For example, Standard C says nothing about device drivers or file systems. The standard won't save you from all of the differences between DOS and UNIX.

- There are very few interesting strictly conforming programs. The fact is, most real programs use extensions or violate the standard outright. In their intended environments, these programs work just fine.

---

1. Abbreviations not defined in the text can be found by referring to the Index.

Although Standard C is an admirable achievement (and has been endorsed by many people), it is not perfect, nor does it render older compilers completely anachronistic. Indeed, many Classic C compilers are debugged and highly optimized and will remain so. While some Standard C features (e.g., prototypes) are very useful, others (e.g., trigraphs) are of interest to a very small, specialized community. Some changes (e.g., to stdarg.h) actually complicate portability.

In the past, good programmers were cognizant of most of the guarantees made by Classic C compilers, and stayed away from shaky ground. Standard C does not lessen this responsibility. A programmer must be just as careful when programming as before. The good thing about Standard C is that the programmer's responsibilities are much more clearly stated, and guaranteed behavior of compilers is now explicit.

When striving for maximal portability with minimal effort, I forsake many of the new features of Standard C. Because Classic C is for the most part a subset of Standard C, it is possible to produce programs that are indeed portable to all C compilers. With few exceptions, the code in this book is portable to both Classic and Standard C. In some cases, I describe Standard C features that solve a problem not otherwise possible with Classic C.

This necessarily sacrifices some advantages of pure Standard C. On the other hand, the resulting code is portable to a much larger set of computers. In actual practice, it is a good idea to write code that dynamically uses these features when and only when they are supported, but the resulting code can be very difficult to read. Naturally, I've tried to avoid this unless I'm specifically drawing attention to it. C standardization is discussed further in the final chapter.

Prototypes

Prototypes are defined by Standard C and are supported by some Classic C compilers. I have chosen to make use of them here just as I do in practice. (The real advantage of prototypes is during software development. There is no particular advantage in program presentation such as in this book.)

To do this, I define the header `proto.h` as follows. The encompassing `#ifndef` `PROTO_H` prevents the file from being processed twice.

```
#ifndef PROTO_H
#define PROTO_H
#if __STDC__==1 || PROTOTYPES_EXIST
#define PROTO(A)   A
#else
#define PROTO(A)   ()
#endif /* has prototypes */
#endif /* PROTO_H */
```

By including this header, you can get the benefit of prototypes when using a compiler that supports them, and you are not penalized when using a compiler that does not support them. For example, you could create a header `foo.h` that declares some complex function headers such as:

```
/* foo.h */
#include "proto.h"

char bar PROTO((void));
char **foofunc PROTO((struct gorp *,char *(*)));
```

The extra set of parentheses enclosing the entire argument list allows the arguments to disappear when compiling in an environment without prototypes.

The definitions in your `.c` files must use the old syntax. Standard C allows this (so long as parameters have "widened" types). Unfortunately, there is no easy trick to using the new-style declaration there. Fortunately, it doesn't matter. When running in a prototype-supporting environment, the compiler will report if your declarations don't match your definitions.

A couple of other things I'll sneak in to `proto.h` are declarations to portabilize `malloc` and friends. I'll explain these as I use them later.

```
#if __STDC__==1
#include <stdlib.h>
#include <stddef.h>
typedef void *Generic;
typedef size_t Size;
#else
typedef char *Generic;
typedef int Size;
Generic malloc PROTO((unsigned));
Generic realloc PROTO((Generic,Size));
Generic calloc PROTO((Size,Size));
void free PROTO((Generic));
#endif /* _STDC__==1 */
```

Disk

All the source in this book is provided in a machine-readable form on the enclosed DOS-compatible disk. Unless otherwise noted, the contents of the disk are in the public domain. You may use the contents as you wish, although the authors would appreciate credit if you use their code.

I've also added a few extra goodies to the disk (since there was a little space left over) that you will enjoy, including Steve Summit's list of "Frequently Asked Questions" (with answers, of course) from Usenet, and Stan Brown's list of "Identifiers to Avoid." Steve's list has been compiled from experts' definitive answers to the most commonly asked questions about C. Stan's list nicely complements the C Standard by documenting every identifier the Standard reserves. The list also documents where each identifier is defined in the standard, thereby unintentionally functioning as a very useful index.

Typography

Text is set in Times Roman. Terms being defined are *italicized*. `Small boldface Courier` is used for C code as well as files, hostnames or literal I/O. Straight quotes (' or ") are used when they are literally part of the C characters or strings. Curly quotes ('' or "") are occasionally used to distinguish literal text from surrounding text if it might not otherwise be obvious.

Acknowledgments

Thanks to Phil Nanzetta, Steve Clark, Sarah Wallace, Dave Oskardmay, and Bryan Catron for proofreading much of the text in this book when it first appeared as separate columns. Thanks to Ed Barkmeyer, who was always willing to discuss the material with me. I apologize for taking up so much of his time doing so.

A number of people helped proofread or offered information that I've used in the text. Thanks to Chris Schanzle, John Rodkey, Paul Grahm, Donn Fishbein, Martin Minow, Guy Harris, Joe Yao, Dan Kegel, and Henry Spencer. Lennie (my mother) and Susan (my sister) read the manuscript cover-to-cover and corrected many of my grammatical atrocities.

Many thanks to Steve Summit, Rex Jaeschke, Doug Gwyn, Stephen Friedl, and John Ogilvie, who supplied numerous corrections and suggestions that greatly improved the book overall. They found subtle errors in code that I had been using for many years, and gave me many excellent suggestions on content and style as well. I apologize to each of them for having to correct so many mistakes.

Thanks to all the Obfuscated C authors. I admire your creativity, and thank you for explaining your programs when I couldn't. Thanks to Landon Curt Noll and Larry Bassel for giving permission to use their `Makefile`s supplied on the disk and, more importantly, for putting in all the effort of judging the contest every year.

Thanks to my parents, Sol and Lennie, who published *Micro/Systems Journal*, and to Robert and Donna Ward at *The C Users Journal* for providing forums in which I could write about C. Thanks to Howard Hyten at *CUJ* for editorial assistance. All of them provided substantial proofreading as well and I thank their readers for keeping me on my toes.

Thanks to copyeditor Shelley Flannery and proofreader Ellen Daniels. The enthusiasm of Wiley's editors was a real pleasure; Diane Cerra, Terri Hudson, and Janice Weisner greatly eased the final difficult and demanding effort required to put everything in its place and make it look so good.

Finally, thanks to Susan Mulroney who put up with me during this project, and provided support in just about every way. I'm yours again (at least until the next book).

## CHAPTER 1

Implementing Variably-Sized Arrays

If you've ever written generic subroutines that operate on arrays, you've probably run across the problem of trying to pass arrays of arbitrary sizes. For example, suppose we would like to have a routine that prints out matrices. We might try:

```
print_array(array)
int array[][];
```

The C compiler doesn't accept this. (Mine prints out "null dimension".) This is because arrays are stored without information such as the number of rows and columns. Well, then let's try adding the size of the array to the parameters.

```
print_array(array,r,c)
int array[r][c];
```

The C compiler rejects this also, saying "constant expected". Array sizes must be constant in C. What a pain!

There are several ways of getting arbitrarily-sized arrays, however. One way is to do the addressing yourself. With the help of a macro, this solution is readable.

```
#define MAT(x,y)    mat[(x)*c + (y)]

print_matrix(mat,r,c)
int *mat;
int r, c;
{
    int i, j;
    for (i=0; i<r; i++) {
        for (j = 0; j < c; j++) {
            printf("%d ",MAT(i,j));
        }
        putchar('\n');
    }
}
```

Now, we can declare the matrix and call our routine as follows:

```
int matrix[ROWS*COLUMNS];

print_matrix(matrix,ROWS,COLUMNS);
```

2 • Implementing Variably-Sized Arrays

The main drawback to this solution is that it is time-expensive. Each time you reference the array, a multiplication is performed. To access every member in the array requires ROWS×COLUMNS multiplications. The other drawback is that MAT requires that the number of columns be available, which I've passed implicitly through the variable c. This limits its usefulness in manipulating several different-sized arrays simultaneously.

You may never have realized that it isn't necessary to perform those multiplications, simply because it seems inherent in figuring out matrix element addresses. However, if we are willing to sacrifice some storage we can avoid the multiplication.

What we do is calculate the addresses for the base of each row once and store them in a separate (one-dimensional) array. Then we can get to any element simply by adding the column offset to the base address of the appropriate row.

For example, a 5×3 matrix would require an auxiliary five-element array, called a *row vector*. Each element of the row vector is an address of the first of three elements of the array.

As we can get to every element of the matrix through the row vector, there is no need to pass the array itself. So the first argument becomes the row vector. (It is still called mat, though.)

Now print_matrix looks like this:

```
print_matrix(mat,r,c)
int *mat[];     /* row vector: array of pointers to ints */
int r,c;        /* rows and columns */
{
      int i, j;

      for (i=0; i<r; i++) {
            for (j=0; j<c; j++) {
                  printf("%d ", mat[i][j]);
            }
            putchar('\n');
      }
}
```

This type of array takes a little more work to set up:

```
int *matrix[ROWS];   /* row vector */
int i;

/* now initialize each pointer in the row vector */
for (i = 0 ; i < ROWS ; i++ ) {
    /* allocate space for the columns */
        matrix[i] = (int *)malloc(COLUMNS * sizeof(int));
    }

print_matrix(matrix,ROWS,COLUMNS);
```

This technique has the disadvantages that it takes up a little more space than a true array and it requires initialization. If you create a subroutine to do this for you, consider dynamically allocating the row vector also.

But the advantages are many. It is faster than multidimensional arrays because less multiplication is performed to address it. Each row can have a different number of elements. For example, it can be used to implement a symbol table that requires storing different length strings in an array or keeping an open hash table. Another advantage is that these arrays can be created dynamically. All of these advantages extend to higher-dimensioned arrays (resulting in even more time savings).

Non-Zero-Based Arrays

C provides arrays that are indexed beginning from 0. Sometimes this is inconvenient. For example, some algorithms are more easily stated in terms of arrays indexed from 1. There are a number of common tricks to achieve this as if it was built into the language; however, none of them are completely portable. They will probably work on your machine, but Standard C doesn't guarantee it.

Here is one such technique, which uses a second declaration to map your logical index into the true location. Declare an array of **SIZE** ints that can be indexed beginning at **BASE** (where **SIZE** and **BASE** are macros for the real values you want) as follows:

```
int array_fake[SIZE];
#define array(x) (array_fake[(x)-BASE])
```

For example, if **SIZE** is 32 and **BASE** is 5, you can write **array(5)** and this will refer to the first element in the array (or **array_fake[0]**). You can set this up to work with row vectors as well.

## CHAPTER 2

Writing a Translation Program

In this chapter, I discuss building a translation program that is in the style of a filter. I mean to be educational rather than practical, so I have forsaken completeness and will instead concentrate on ideas and program readability. My intent is that you should be able to take what I've given you here and build on it.

A filter is a program that reads its input, performs some translation upon it, and writes that translated output. Surprisingly, a great many programs follow this simple paradigm. My example will be a program to "decipher" WordStar document files. Even if you have never used WordStar, you'll still benefit from this chapter—the lessons apply to many tasks. Indeed, I no longer use WordStar, but recently I needed to use the text from a bunch of old WordStar files. In fact, I don't even have a copy of WordStar anymore, so I had to go looking at the raw files in order to get at the text.

If you've ever printed a raw WordStar document file on your screen (without going through WordStar), you will have already noticed that there is more in the file than just the text. If you haven't, try it. You will notice that most of the text appears, but some of the characters are wrong and there are a lot of nonprintable characters embedded in the file.

All the information is there, but WordStar uses the high-order bit in each byte for information as well as including extra bytes for print control characters. Unfortunately, MicroPro will not give out the format specification of its WordStar document files, but don't let that dissuade you. It's not that difficult to decipher.

I can't cover all the goodies in WordStar here, so I've restricted myself to the things you are most likely to see. Following my lead, it should not be hard to extend what I've given you.

If you want to probe your own files, try examining them with a debugger or binary editor so that you can see the binary values alongside the ASCII characters. This is what I found:

- Some characters have their most significant bit (MSB) on. This is used to denote several things (see below).

- Like all MS-DOS text files, lines are terminated with cr-lf (carriage return, linefeed) sequences (ASCII 0D 0A).

- Dot commands (e.g., ".op") appear in the file verbatim.
- Blanks with the MSB set are *soft*, meaning they have been added automatically by WordStar to pad out the line.
- ASCII 1F indicates a soft hyphen, automatically added by WordStar for automatic hyphenation.
- Linefeeds with the MSB set are soft, having been added automatically. *Hard* linefeeds (MSB clear) denote the end of a paragraph.
- WordStar print control characters (e.g., control-B) appear in the file verbatim.
- Tabs do not appear in the file, but are stored as blanks.
- All other characters appear as their ASCII values in the file. Characters, at the ends of words in paragraphs that have been justified, have their MSB set.

Assuming that we want to transfer this file to another computer system, we usually must change the file so that it looks like an ordinary text file. This means that we have to do things such as trimming the high-order bits and removing the WordStar-dependent directives like the dot commands and the print-control characters.

At the end of this chapter is a program I've written that handles the basic problems of converting WordStar document files to raw text. The more esoteric features aren't covered. However, given this start, you should be able to easily add the code to handle any additional features.

You can also customize this program to your application. With some simple changes, this program could be used to generate `troff`, TEX, or any format as output. The conventions I have chosen to use actually mimic `wsconv`, an anonymous public-domain program from the PC/BLUE software library. I'll briefly go through some of the more interesting parts of the program, referring to source lines by the numbers running down the left-hand side of the program listing.

The program is written in the style of a typical UNIX filter. It copies its standard input to its standard output with appropriate modifications. Internally, the program sits in a loop, reading one character at a time. (Buffering is left to the standard I/O package.) Based on the character attributes and the current state, the character is printed and/or the state is changed.

By reading from the standard input and writing the standard output, the program avoids any need for dealing with filenames. Options, too, are skipped here. (See p. 35 in Chapter 6 for an example of how to handle options.)

Lines 13–17: `CONTROL` is defined and used. This macro generates control character values given the corresponding letter. (ASCII is assumed throughout.)

Lines 19–26: The conventions for handling WordStar print control characters are defined. For example, an underlined string will print out as `<_string_>`. (Some typesetters actually understand this convention.)

Line 28: Anything declared as `Bool` should have only the value `TRUE` or `FALSE`. This is purely a programming convention since `Bool` is `typedef`ed to `int`.

Lines 32–45: These define several state variables that will be used to make decisions along with the next character. In a simple state-machine-style program like this one it makes perfect sense, but larger programs probably call for a different approach.

Lines 53–56: Our first problem is turning off the eighth bit on all characters. The variable `msb_was_set` remembers whether the bit was set.

Lines 57–61: WordStar terminates lines with a cr-lf sequence. If our system terminates lines with a newline (like a UNIX system), we can just discard the carriage-return. (This is required for Standard C text streams.) If a hyphen added by a justify operation is encountered, we attempt to remove it by delaying line wrap until we see the real end of the current word.

Lines 62–64: I have chosen to ignore dot commands. They can be handled here without any problems.

Lines 65–75: Spaces come in two flavors: soft and hard. Hard ones are real, but soft ones have been added by a justification operation. Tabs are denoted by hard spaces, so we'll try to undo them, too. I assume eight-column tab stops.

Line 79: The start of a dot command is recognized here.

Lines 82–85: These handle WordStar print control characters. `do_wscntrl` does the work; `wscntrl` just recognizes the characters.

Lines 86–88: These remove all the other WordStar control characters we are too lazy to correctly handle.

Lines 89–104: If the character has not been handled at this point, it has to be text, so it is just passed through. If we are at the beginning of a word, we also perform the translation of spaces back to tabs here by calling `space_out`.

Lines 109–132: These define `space_out`. This function takes a source and destination column and prints out the least number of tabs and spaces to move the cursor to the destination column. For a good exercise, try writing `space_out` yourself before looking ahead. It's short but tricky!

Lines 154–183: These define `do_wscntrl`. This translates control character directives into printable versions.

Source Code

The line numbers are *not* part of the source code. I have added them to make it easier to describe what line I'm referring to.

```
1    #include <stdio.h>
2    #include <ctype.h>

4    #define TRUE          1
5    #define FALSE         0
```

```
7      #define LF               '\n'
8      #define CR               '\r'
9      #define SOFT_HYPHEN      0x1f /* inserted to break words */
                                     /* at eol */

11     #define TABSIZE          8

13     #define CONTROL(x)       (1 + (x) - 'A')
14     #define BOLD             (CONTROL('B'))
15     #define SUPERSCRIPT      (CONTROL('T'))
16     #define SUBSCRIPT        (CONTROL('V'))
17     #define UNDERSCORE       (CONTROL('S'))

19     #define BOLD_BEGIN        "<<<"
20     #define BOLD_END          ">>>"
21     #define UNDERSCORE_BEGIN "<_"
22     #define UNDERSCORE_END    "_>"
23     #define SUBSCRIPT_BEGIN   "<<"
24     #define SUBSCRIPT_END     ">>"
25     #define SUPERSCRIPT_BEGIN"<^"
26     #define SUPERSCRIPT_END   "^>"

28     typedef int Bool;
29     Bool wscntrl();      /* true if arg is WS control char */
30     int column;          /* column to output next character */

32     Bool superscript = FALSE;    /* if we are superscripting */
33     Bool subscript = FALSE;      /* if we are subscripting */
34     Bool bold = FALSE;           /* if we emboldening */
35     Bool underscore = FALSE;     /* if we are underscoring */
36     Bool msb_was_set;  /* if char had most significant bit set */
37     Bool soft_space = FALSE;     /* if we are between words */
38         /* and have seen a soft space, but no other spaces */
39     Bool soft_hyphen = FALSE;    /* if we are in the middle */
40         /* of a word that was hyphenated by WS */
41     Bool dotcmd = FALSE;/* if we in the middle of a dot cmd */
42     Bool wrap_soon = FALSE;      /* if we should wrap as */
43         /* soon as we get to the end of the current word */
44     int spacerun = 0;   /* number of spaces seen in a row */
45     void space_out(), newline(), do_wscntrl(); /* utility fns */

47     int
48     main() {
49         int c;           /* last character read */
50         while (EOF != (c = getchar())) {
51             /* look at single characters */

53             /* remember if most significant bit set */
54             if (msb_was_set = 0x80 & c) {
55                 c &= 0x7f;    /* turn off most sig. bit */
```

```
 56                    }
 57                    if (c == CR) continue;    /* LF always follows */
 58                    if (c == LF) {
 59                        if (soft_hyphen) {
 60                            wrap_soon = TRUE;
 61                        } else newline();
 62                    } else if (dotcmd) {
 63                        /* throw away chars while in a dot cmd */
 64                        continue;
 65                    } else if (c == ' ') {
 66                        /* ignore blanks with msb - they are soft */
 67                        if (msb_was_set) {          /* a real space */
 68                            soft_space = FALSE;
 69                            spacerun++;
 70                            column++;
 71                            if (wrap_soon) {    /* wrap now! */
 72                                newline();
 73                                wrap_soon = FALSE;
 74                            }
 75                        } else soft_space = TRUE;
 76                    } else if (c == SOFT_HYPHEN) {
 77                        /* handle hyphens with msb - they are soft */
 78                        soft_hyphen = TRUE;
 79                    } else if (c == '.' && column == 0) {
 80                        /* text processing directive */
 81                        dotcmd = TRUE;
 82                    } else if (wscntrl(c)) {
 83                        /* placeholder to handle WS print control */
 84                        /* chars e.g. ^S (underscore), ^B (bold) */
 85                        do_wscntrl(c);
 86                    } else if (iscntrl(c)) {
 87                        /* unknown control character - ignore */
 88                        continue;
 89                    } else { /* normal character */
 90                        /* if we encountered a soft space, stick */
 91                        /* in at least one space */
 92                        if (soft_space) {
 93                            spacerun = 1;
 94                            column++;
 95                            soft_space = FALSE;
 96                        }
 97                        if (spacerun) {      /* beginning of word */
 98                            /* calculate tabs/blanks to lay down */
 99                            space_out(column - spacerun, column);
100                            spacerun = 0;
101                        }
102                        putchar(c);
103                        column++;
104                    }
105        }
```

```
106        return 0;
107    }

109    /* print out least number of spaces and tabs to move us */
110    /* from "oldpos" to "newpos" */
111    void
112    space_out(oldpos,newpos)
113    int oldpos;    /* old position */
114    int newpos;    /* new position */
115    {
116        int spaces, tabs;  /* number of spaces/tabs to print */
117        int i;

119        if (oldpos >= newpos) return;/* no space in between */

121        /* first calculate tabs */
122        tabs = newpos/TABSIZE - oldpos/TABSIZE;

124        /* now calulate spaces */
125        /* if old&new follow same tab stop, use simple diff */
126        if (tabs == 0) spaces = newpos - oldpos;
127        /* if not, then it's remainder from nearest tab stop */
128        else spaces = newpos % TABSIZE;

130        for (i = 0; i < tabs; i++) putchar('\t');
131        for (i = 0; i < spaces; i++) putchar(' ');
132    }

134    /* true if WordStar control character */
135    Bool
136    wscntrl(c)
137    int c;
138    {
139        return ((c == BOLD) ||
140            (c == UNDERSCORE) ||
141            (c == SUPERSCRIPT) ||
142            (c == SUBSCRIPT));
143    }

145    void
146    newline()
147    {
148        if (!dotcmd) putchar('\n');
149        column = 0;
150        spacerun = 0;
151        dotcmd = FALSE;
152    }
```

```
154  void
155  do_wscntrl(c)
156  int c;
157  {
158       switch (c) {    /* print control character */
159       case BOLD:
160            if (bold) printf(BOLD_END);
161            else printf(BOLD_BEGIN);
162            bold = !bold;
163            break;
164       case UNDERSCORE:
165            if (underscore) printf(UNDERSCORE_END);
166            else printf(UNDERSCORE_BEGIN);
167            underscore = !underscore;
168            break;
169       case SUBSCRIPT:
170            if (subscript) printf(SUBSCRIPT_END);
171            else printf(SUBSCRIPT_BEGIN);
172            subscript = !subscript;
173            break;
174       case SUPERSCRIPT:
175            if (superscript) printf(SUPERSCRIPT_END);
176            else printf(SUPERSCRIPT_BEGIN);
177            superscript = !superscript;
178            break;
179       default:
180            /* unknown - ignore for now */
181            break;
182       }
183  }
```

## CHAPTER 3

The 1984 Obfuscated C Code Contest

In much of this book, I discuss C programming techniques by providing examples that are educational. In other words, code is readable, easily modifiable, portable, modular, well-commented, structured, etc. I like to think of such well-written code as "elegant." Such programs should be a pleasure to read. However, not everyone writes beautiful code, and I would be remiss in my duties as an educator to ignore that fact.

Normally I don't consider it worthwhile to publish "ugly" or unreadable code, but there are some examples that one can actually learn from (much as I learned that a red flame was hot by sticking my hand in it).

Thus, it is with much pleasure that I present the results of the 1984 Obfuscated C Code Contest[1] (later years can be found in later chapters). The goal was to write the most obscure C program within the rules (see p. 137 in Chapter 17). The contest was run by Landon Noll, who collected the entries and then wondered about how much thought each author must have put into destroying an otherwise good piece of code. Landon said,

> The contest was motivated by reading the UNIX source code to the Bourne
> shell (/bin/sh). I was shocked at how much simple algorithms could be
> made cryptic, and therefore useless, by a poor choice of code style. I asked
> myself, "Could someone be proud of this code?"

Following are the top four entries from the 1984 contest. Please read them carefully. If you think you understand one, you've probably glanced at it too quickly. These programs are the most bizarre examples of C code that I've ever seen. (Yes, they're much worse than any UNIX sources.) Amazingly, they all work.

They're not just good for a laugh. Each one is good for hours of study. Not only do they show you what *not* to do, but they teach you how to deal with very strange code. And you can actually learn some of the finer points of C by studying these very unusual programs.

Listed after each program is a description (it isn't obvious) and/or an analysis. I encourage you to study the program before turning to the description or analysis. Try to figure out what it does and how it does it.

---

1. The name was later changed to "*International* Obfuscated C Code Contest," but I will omit "International" in all further references for the sake of consistency.

(Dis)Honorable Mention

Anonymous

```
int i;main(){for(;i["]<i;++i){--i;}"];read('-'-'-',i+++"hell\
o, world!\n",'/'/'/'));}read(j,i,p){write(j/p+p,i---j,i/i);}
```

This entry was submitted anonymously, probably because, as one of the judges remarked, the author was "too embarrassed that they could write such trash, I guess."

Analysis

Analysis of this program is fairly straightforward. Indenting to follow its internal structure yields:

```
int i;
main()
{
      for (;i["]<i;++i){--i;}"];read('-'-'-',
                             i+++"hello, world!\n",'/'/'/'));
}

read(j,i,p)
{
      write(j/p+p,i---j,i/i);
}
```

The control expression of the `for` appears at first to be `i` indexed by a double quote. Actually, the double quote begins a string that terminates at the next double quote. So what originally looked like code is really just a literal string. But what is the meaning of `i` indexed by a string? Array indexing is defined in terms of pointer arithmetic. In particular, `a[b]` is equivalent to `*(a+b)`. Since addition is commutative, this can be written as `*(b+a)`, which can then be rewritten `b[a]`. Thus, `a[b]` is equivalent to `b[a]`. What does this mean for the program?

Another curious thing is the expression `'-'-'-'`, which is the first argument to `read`. It can be read as the value of the hyphen subtracted from the value of another hyphen. The value of any character is its ASCII encoding, but the exact number is irrelevant as any number subtracted from itself is 0. Thus, this is an obscure way of providing the constant 0. Similarly, the expression `'/'/'/'`, which appears later in the program, is an obscure way of providing the constant 1.

Rewriting the `for` as a `while` and applying the other transformations yields:

```
int i;
main()
{
      while ("]<i;++i){--i;}"[i]) {
            read(0, i+++"hello, world!\n", 1);
      }
```

```
}

read(j,i,p)
{
     write(j/p+p, i---j, 1);
}
```

It may look odd (get used to it), but a literal string is being indexed just as it appears. This actually has some uses in real code, but here it is just controlling the loop. As i increments (via two of the three plusses in the read argument) each time through the loop, the next character in the literal string is selected and compared against zero to decide whether the loop should continue. Each character has a non-zero value, except for the null after the last character. The null has a zero value and when it is accessed and tested, the loop (rewritten as a while for readability) terminates.

There are fourteen characters in the string—thus, read will be called fourteen times. (i will be initialized to 0 implicitly.) Note, however, that this program's implementation of read consists of one call to write! Since the third argument of write is 1, read is actually *writing* a single character each time it is called. The second argument of read passes the string "hello world!\n" with one character dropped off the front each time. Here's a version with the function renamed appropriately:

```
int i=0;
main()
{
     while (i<14) {
          write1char(0, "hello, world!\n"[i++], 1);
     }
}

write1char(j,i,p)
{
     write(1,i,1);
}
```

I've simplified the arguments as much as possible. One remaining silliness is that the second argument to write1char is of type int while what's really passed is a pointer to a char. If it had been declared correctly, the original definition of read would have done pointer division! As is, this program may fail to run on systems where sizeof(int) != sizeof(char *). But if you are sufficiently lucky, this program ends after having printed:

```
hello world!
```

Third Place Award

Mike Laman <ncr-sd!dsi!laman>
Decom Systems Inc.
Carlsbad, California

```
a[900];     b;c;d=1    ;e=1;f;    g;h;O;     main(k,
1)char*     *l;{g=      atoi(*     ++l);      for(k=
 0;k*k<      g;b=k      ++>>1)     ;for(h=     0;h*h<=
g;++h);     --h;c=(    (h+=g>h    *(h+1))     -1)>>1;
while(d     <=g){       ++O;for    (f=0;f<    O&&d<=g
;++f)a[     b<<5|c]     =d++,b+    =e;for(     f=0;f<O
&&d<=g;     ++f)a[b    <<5|c]=    d++,c+=     e;e= -e
;}for(c     =0;c<h;    ++c){      for(b=0     ;b<k;++
b){if(b     <k/2)a[    b<<5|c]    ^=a[(k      -(b+1))
<<5|c]^     =a[b<<5    |c]^=a[    (k-(b+1     ))<<5|c]
;printf(    a[b<<5|c   ]?"%-4d"   :"      "   ,a[b<<5
|c]);}      putchar(   '\n');}}   /*Mike      Laman*/
```

When I first saw this program, I assumed that the author worked for NSA and had encrypted it. In fact, it is a real piece of code and the compiler had no problem whatsoever digesting it. Nevertheless, the author was obviously poking fun at the compiler's complete disregard for whitespace between language tokens. I suppose the author should be given some credit for commenting his code (see the lower right-hand corner).

When run with the argument, 33, it produces the following spiral of numbers:

```
26   25   24   23   22   21
27   10    9    8    7   20
28   11    2    1    6   19
29   12    3    4    5   18
30   13   14   15   16   17
31   32   33
```

Analysis

After rearranging the code and renaming things, I decided the code might have originally looked as follows:

```
int a[900], f;

int c;         /* current column */
int r;         /* current row */
int max;       /* max number */
int dir = 1;   /* 1 for inc, -1 for dec */
int O = 0;     /* max in current pass */
int cur = 1;   /* current number */
```

```
main (cols,argv)
char **argv;
{
    max = atoi (*++argv);
    for (cols = 0; cols * cols < max; c = cols++ >> 1);
    for (rows = 0; rows * rows <= max; ++rows);
    --rows;
    r = ((rows += max > rows * (rows + 1)) - 1) >> 1;
    while (cur <= max) {
        ++O;
        for (f = 0; f < O && cur <= max; ++f)
            a[c << 5 | r] = cur++, c += dir;
        for (f = 0; f < O && cur <= max; ++f)
            a[c << 5 | r] = cur++, r += dir;
        dir = -dir;
    }

    for (r = 0; r < rows; ++r) {
        for (c = 0; c < cols; ++c) {
            if (c < cols / 2)
                a[c << 5 | r] ^= a[(cols - (c + 1)) << 5 | r]
^= a[c << 5 | r] ^= a[(cols - (c + 1)) << 5 | r];
            printf (a[c << 5 | r] ? "%-4d" : "    ",
                a[c << 5 | r]);
        }
        putchar ('\n');
    }
}
```

The program allocates a 900-element array and then uses it as if it were a 2D-array. Each column index of the matrix is generated by doing a shift left (<<5), thus allowing a maximum of 32 elements in each row.

The program starts by finding the lengths of the actual matrix it will produce as output. The simplest way to do this is to take the square root of the original argument. The author does this very cleverly by simply testing every single number beginning at 0 and increasing by 1, until the square exceeds the target with the following code:

```
for (rows = 0; rows * rows <= max; ++rows) ;
```

In the while loop, the program places the numbers in order in their proper positions. The original 900-element array may be much bigger than necessary, but the program ignores this and uses a corner of it. In reality, the corner is spread out all over the place because the columns are offset from each other by 32.

At the bottom of the loop, the assignment:

```
e = -e;
```

is used to change the direction in which the array is accessed. In the example above, the numbers 3, 4, 5, 6, and 7 are laid down in increasing addresses. Then e's sign is flipped and the indices count down as 8, 9, 10, 11, 12 and 13 are written. One assignment writes the rows while the other writes the columns.

The remaining loop actually reads back through the array and writes the output, one row at a time. The particularly long line in the middle of that loop simply swaps the values of the first and second operands using a series of X-ORs.

```
a[c << 5 | r] ^= a[(cols - (c + 1)) << 5 | r] ^= a[c << 5 | r] ^=
a[(cols - (c + 1)) << 5 | r];
```

Second Place Award

Dave Decot <decot@hpisod2.hp.com>
Hewlett-Packard
Cupertino, California

```
#define x =
#define double(a,b) int
#define char k['a']
#define union static struct

extern int floor;
double (x1, y1) b,
char x {sizeof(
     double(%s,%D)(*)())
,};
struct tag{int x0,*x0;}

*main(i, dup, signal) {
{
  for(signal=0;*k * x * __FILE__ *i;) do {
   (printf(&*"'\"",x);      /*\n\\", (*((double(tag,u)(*)())&
                                             floor))(i)));
      goto _0;

_0: while (!(char <<x - dup)) {      /*/*\*/
       union tag u x{4};
 }
}

while(b x 3, i); {
char x b,i;
  _0:if(b&&k+
  sin(signal)               / *     ((main) (b)-> x0));/*}
  ;
}

*/}}}
```

Analysis

As far as I can tell, this program does just what it appears to do, which is absolutely nothing. Nonetheless, the fact that it even compiles is a shock. This program was the first one I ever saw that demonstrated such odd practices as radical changes of semantics before and after macro substitution, playing games with comment delimiters, and totally meaningless redefinitions of library and system call names.

In case you are wondering, no, this is not legal Standard C. In fact, none of the programs so far have been. Don't hold your breath for the next ones, either.

First Place Award

Sjoerd Mullender <sjoerd@cwi.nl>
Centrum voor Wiskunde en Informatica (Inst. for Math. and CS)
Amsterdam, Netherlands

Robbert van Renesse <rvr@cs.cornell.edu>
Cornell University
Ithaca, New York

```
/* Portable between VAX11 && PDP11 */
short main[] = {
    277, 04735, -4129, 25, 0, 477, 1019, 0xbef, 0, 12800,
    -113, 21119, 0x52d7, -1006, -7151, 0, 0x4bc, 020004,
    14880, 10541, 2056, 04010, 4548, 3044, -6716, 0x9,
    4407, 6, 5568, 1, -30460, 0, 0x9, 5570, 512, -30419,
    0x7e82, 0760, 6, 0, 4, 02400, 15, 0, 4, 1280, 4, 0,
    4, 0, 0, 0, 0x8, 0, 4, 0, ',', 0, 12, 0, 4, 0, '#',
    0, 020, 0, 4, 0, 30, 0, 026, 0, 0x6176, 120, 25712,
    'p', 072163, 'r', 29303, 29801, 'e' };
```

This is one of my favorite contest winners of all time. It was submitted by both authors when they were students (both held bachelor's degrees in mathematics at the time) at Vrije Universitait (Free University) in Amsterdam.

Author's Analysis

"When this program is compiled, the compiler places the array somewhere in memory, just like it places any compiled code somewhere in memory. Usually, the C startup code (crt0.o) calls a routine named main. The loader fills in the address in the startup code, but, at least on the old systems where this program ran, it doesn't know that the main in this program isn't code but data!

"When the program is run, the C startup code transfers control to the location main. The contents of the array just happen to be machine instructions for both a PDP-11 and a VAX.

"On the VAX, the routine main is called with the calls instruction. This instruction uses the first (2-byte) word of the called routine as a mask of registers that are to be saved on the stack. In other words, on the VAX the first word can be anything. On the PDP, the first word is a branch instruction that branches over the VAX code. The PDP and VAX codes are thus completely separate.

"The PDP and VAX codes implement the same algorithm:

```
for (;;) {
    write(1, "   :-)\b\b\b\b", 9);
    delay();
}
```

"The result is that the symbols :-) move over the screen. delay is implemented differently on the PDP, where we used a nonexistent system call (sys 55), and on the VAX where we used a delay loop.

"My co-author, Robbert, and I had earlier written a similar program for an assignment on the PDP-11. Along came the first Obfuscated C Code Contest, and we decided that we should write a program like this, but make it run on two different architectures. We didn't think long about what the program should do, so it does something very simple.

"We started with writing the PDP code in assembler. We both knew PDP-11 assembler, so that was no problem. The assembler code we came up with is as follows:

```
pdp:
        mov     pc,r4
        tst     -(r4)
        sub     $9,r4
        mov     r4,0f
        mov     $1, r0
        sys     4; 0:0; 9
        mov     $1000, r2
1:
        sys     55
        sob     r2, 1b
        br      pdp
```

"This is not the code we originally wrote, but it is the code that we ultimately used in the program. The string to be printed is shared by the VAX and the PDP code and is located between the two sections. First, the program deals with figuring out the address of the string. Then the program counter is saved in a scratch register. Since the program counter points at the second instruction, we subtract 2 from the scratch register in the second instruction. Then we subtract the length of the string and store the result in the location with label 0. This has to do with the calling sequence of system calls on the PDP. Following the sys instruction is the system call number (4 for write), the address of the buffer (pointed to by label 0), and the length of the buffer (9). The file descriptor is in register r0. The rest of the code implements a delay loop. In each iteration, a nonexisting system call (55) slows things down.

"We assembled this program and extracted the machine code from the resulting object file. We used this code in the VAX part. Since neither of us was fluent in VAX assembly, we wrote the VAX code in C and massaged the compiler output. The VAX assembly program that we came up with is as follows:

```
vax:    .word 0400 + (pdp - vax) / 2 - 1
1:
    pushl   $9
    pushal  str
    pushl   $1
    calls   $3,write
    cvtwl   $32767,r2
2:
    decl    r2
    jneq    2b
    jbr     1b

write:  .word 0
    chmk    $4
    ret

str:    .ascii "  :-)\b\b\b\b"

pdp:    .word 4548, 3044, 58820, 9, 4407, 6, 5568, 1, 35076,
    0, 9, 5570\, 512, 35117, 32386, 496
```

"The first word (after the label **vax**) is the PDP branch instruction. PDP branch instructions are octal 400 + the distance divided by 2. The string that both the PDP and VAX programs use is after the **str** label, and the PDP code is after the **pdp** label.

"On the VAX, the program pushes 9 (the length of the string), the address of the string and 1 (the file descriptor) on the stack and calls **write**. Since we didn't know the exact calling sequence for system calls, we just copied the source for the **write** system call stub into our program. After **write** finishes, the program executes a delay loop, after which it jumps back to the start of the program.

"We assembled this program, and extracted the machine code from the object file. After this we only had to convert the machine code to ASCII and write a little bit of C to glue everything together. We wanted to use different formats for each constant in the resulting array, and we wanted to choose the format randomly. So we wrote a program to choose an appropriate format at random. The program we wrote for that follows. This program actually also extracted the machine code from the object file.

```
#include <stdio.h>
#include <a.out.h>

main(argc, argv)
char **argv;
```

```
{
    register FILE *fp;
    register short pos = 0, c, n;
    register char *fmt;

    if (argc != 2) {
        fprintf(stderr, "Usage: %s file\n");
        exit(1);
    }
    if ((fp = fopen(argv[1], "r")) == NULL) {
        fprintf(stderr, "%s: can't open %s\n", argv[0],
argv[1]\);
        exit(2);
    }
    fseek(fp, (long) sizeof(struct exec), 0);
    printf("/* portable between VAX and PDP11 */\n\n");
    printf("short main[] = {\n");
    for (;;) {
        if (pos == 0) printf("\t");
        c = getc(fp) & 0377;
        if (feof(fp)) break;
        n = getc(fp) << 8 | c;
        switch (rand() % 5) {
        case 0:
        case 1:
            fmt = "%d"; break;
        case 2:
            fmt = "%u"; break;
        case 3:
            fmt = "0%o"; break;
        case 4:
            fmt = "0x%x"; break;
        }
    if (32 <= n && n < 127 && (rand() % 4)) fmt = "'%c'";
        printf(n < 8 ? "%d" : fmt, n);
        printf(",");
        if (pos++ == 8) {
            printf("\n");
            pos = 0;
        }
        else printf(" ");
    }
    printf("};\n");
}
```

"As can be seen, there is a slight preference for decimal, and also a character format is sometimes used, but only if the data is a printable ASCII character.

"When we ran this program, we were almost completely satisfied with the result. The only problem we had was that the program had chosen an octal representation for the first word. Since everybody knows what a PDP-11 branch instruction looks like (everyone knows that the traditional magic word for an executable, 0407, is a PDP-11 branch), we changed that to decimal. After checking the size of the resulting program we saw that it was one byte too long. The limit was 512 bytes, and our program was 513 bytes. So we changed the word `and` in the comment to `&&`."

## CHAPTER 4

Implementing Sets with Bit Operations

Sets with a small number of elements are easily implemented by bit operations in many languages. The C keyword `enum` allows the programmer to use sets directly without worrying about the implementation. However, `enum`s are inappropriate for large sets, and many Classic C compilers never supported `enum`. In any case, the implementations I will present allow more general uses than `enum`s provide.

Using bit operations, we can implement sets capable of operations such as union, intersection, difference, assignment, membership, equality, and size. The ordering relation can also be implemented, although strictly speaking this is not a set operation.

Small Sets

A simple example of the use and implementation of a set is in the BSD 4.1 UNIX `select` system call. `select` takes parameters that represent sets of file descriptors. Since the number of files that a process could have open in that system is 20, the set of file descriptors is easily represented by a 32-bit integer. Each bit, then, designates a file descriptor.

For example, if the set has an integer value of 25 decimal (or 11001 binary) the file descriptors referred to are 4, 3, and 0 because the bits in the 4, 3, and 0 positions are on. In this example, the index of the bit is exactly the value of the file descriptor. However, this need not be the case. What is important is the small number of elements.

For sets like the one above, which have no more elements than the number of bits in a single datum like an `unsigned int`, we can use the following constructs for set operations:

```
unsigned int set1, set2, set3;
set3 = set1 | set2;        /* union */
set3 = set1 & set2;        /* intersection */
set3 = set1 & ~set2;       /* difference */
```

To declare a set, define it as an `unsigned int` (or whatever integral type you choose). I highly recommend using a `typedef` to make things more readable. Macros can also be used for the set operations themselves. For example:

```
#define UNION |
set3 = set1 UNION set2;
```

To define a one-element set, use the macro `elt` with a small index representing the index of the element.

```
#define elt(x)          ((unsigned)1<<(x))
```

The `member` macro returns 1 or 0 depending on whether an element is in the set or not.

```
#define INTERSECT        &
#define member(s,x)      (0 != ((s) INTERSECT elt(x)))
```

`min_elt` returns the smallest index in a set (or -1 if the set is empty). These examples should be enough for you to write any other set operation you need using this representation.

```
int min_elt(x)
int x;
{
     int i;

     /* first check if set is empty */
     if (x == 0) return(-1);
     for (i=0; member(x,elt(i)); i++) ;
     return(i);
}
```

Big Sets

This is fine for sets with a small number of elements but what about larger universes? For example, if we are writing a device driver for a disk, we must maintain the sets of disk cylinders that are queued to be read and written. A list of cylinders is a prime candidate for representation by a bit vector. The only real difference is that such a set is probably bigger than the number of bits in any data type on your machine.

Suppose we have 100 cylinders and our largest data type is a 32-bit `long`. Then we would need four `long`s to get at least 100 bits for the cylinders ($3*32 < 100 <= 4*32$). To get 100 bits, we can declare an array of `long`s. `bigset` is a macro that does exactly that.

```
#define bigset(name,bits)    struct {\
            int number;             /* of subsets */\
            SUBSET data[1 + ((bits)-1)/BITS_PER_SUBSET];\
        } name = {1 + ((bits)-1)/BITS_PER_SUBSET}
```

This macro expands to a structure declaration. The structure defines an array of SUBSETs large enough to hold the set. We also define the number of SUBSETs in `number`, so that we won't have to pass lengths as extra arguments into our set routines. SUBSET can be defined to be whatever is convenient for you. I always use unsigned long because the longer the type, the faster the routines will execute. For folks who watch every bit, shorter types will waste less space (by leaving less unused bits at the end of the set array).

Here are the necessary macros to finish off bigset. CHAR_BIT is defined by some environments including Standard C.

```
#ifndef CHAR_BIT
#define CHAR_BIT          8
#endif
#define SUBSET            unsigned long
#define BITS_PER_SUBSET   (CHAR_BIT * sizeof(SUBSET))
```

Now we can declare sets for 100 cylinders to be read and written as:

```
bigset(readcyls,100);
bigset(writecyls,100);
```

In order to pass these sets as parameters, we'll have to define a type for that. We can't use bigset because it defines a class of structures; the following type suffices. A length of 1 serves as a placeholder, acknowledging that the C compiler doesn't care about the length since nothing follows the data element.

```
struct bigset_param {
    int number;
    SUBSET data[1];
};
```

Most of the standard set operations (union, intersection, assignment, etc.) look very much the same. A single loop performs its respective operation on an entire SUBSET at a time. Here is the code for union. Notice that it expects a pointer to a bigset_param.

```
void
bigset_union(s1,s2,s3)    /* s1 = s2 U s3 */
struct bigset_param *s1, *s2, *s3;
{
    int i;
    for (i=0;i<s1->number;i++)
        s1->data[i] = s2->data[i] UNION s3->data[i];
}
```

bigset_print (below) prints a representation of a set using 1's and 0's. It uses an extra inner loop to print out each bit. Think about how this might help you rewrite our earlier version of min_elt to work on big sets.

```
void
bigset_print(s)
struct bigset_param *s;
{
    int i, j;
    for (i=0;i<s->number;i++) {
        for (j=0;j<BITS_PER_SUBSET;j++) {
```

```
            putchar(s->data[i] INTERSECT elt(j)?'1':'0');
        }
    }
}
```

Here is some code for turning on an individual bit by its index.

```
void
bigset_set(s,i)      /* turn on element i in set s */
struct bigset_param *s;
int i;
{
    s->data[i/BITS_PER_SUBSET] |= elt(i%BITS_PER_SUBSET);
}
```

Of course, you should declare all these routines in a header along with SUBSET and other definitions. The routines need a cast in order to make the compiler ignore the mismatch between the structure generated by bigset and the formal parameter bigset_param. This makes the header a bit more complicated. Here's what would appear in it for the bigset_print function.

```
void bigset_print PROTO((struct bigset_param *s));
#define bs_print(s) bigset_print((struct bigset_param *)&s)
```

At the same time, I've added an & to make the call even more convenient. Declarations of the other functions are similar. Here is some code using these routines.

```
bigset(readcyls,100);
bigset(writecyls,100);
bigset(activecyls,100);

main()
{
    /* request cylinders 1 and 10 to be read */
    bs_set(readcyls,1);
    bs_set(readcyls,10);

    printf("cylinders to read: ");
    bs_print(readcyls);
    putchar('\n');

    /* request cylinder 4 to be written */
    bs_set(writecyls,4);
    printf("cylinders to write: ");
    bs_print(writecyls);
    putchar('\n');

    /* find out cylinders requiring action */
    bs_union(activecyls,readcyls,writecyls);
    printf("cylinders requiring I/O: ");
    bs_print(activecyls);
    putchar('\n');
```

```
        }
```

Optimizations

You should now be able to finish the rest of the routines. If you are interested, you might experiment with different implementations to see whether there is any difference in speed. Here are some ideas:

- Convert `bigset_set` to a macro.

- Use pointers instead of array references in the loops.

- Convert divisions to shifts. Convert mods to bitwise ANDs. (This can be done only because we are working with powers of two.) For example, `x/BITS_PER_SUBSET` for `BITS_PER_SUBSET == 32` can be written `x>>5` (since 5 is log 32 base 2).

## CHAPTER 5

Context-Independent Macros

Macros provide a means of textual substitutions in the source code at compile-time. Most people get along fine with an intuitive idea of how they work, but occasionally stumble over anomalies.

These anomalies come from the C preprocessor's limited understanding (less than ours) of C. For example, while the preprocessor knows not to perform substitutions inside of quoted strings, it doesn't prevent changes in operator bindings, as the following example shows:

```
/* weight of battery and components */
#define ACID_WEIGHT      5
#define COVER_WEIGHT     1
#define BATTERY_WEIGHT   ACID_WEIGHT + COVER_WEIGHT
                         /* WRONG! */

    /* compute total weight of 10 batteries */
    total_weight = 10 * BATTERY_WEIGHT;
```

In this example, the assignment turns into a computation of `10*5+1`. This is evaluated as `(10*5)+1`, not `10*(5+1)` as the programmer presumably intended. The problem is that an operator (`+`) inside the macro was of lower precedence than one (`*`) outside the macro.

The opposite problem can also occur. If your macro takes parameters, it is possible that a parameter that is an expression can be interpreted incorrectly. For example, if the expression 5+3 is substituted for **x** in the macro value **x*100**, the result will be 305 rather than the intended 800.

A simple guideline to avoid these headaches is: always parenthesize macro parameters. If the macro definition contains an expression, parenthesize that as well.

It is rare that this ability of the preprocessor to change bindings is what is desired, although it is used occasionally (and typically produces obfuscated code). See the previous chapter for some classic examples!

Unfortunately, the preprocessor can complicate things even further because it has the same effect on statements that it has on expressions. This is a much more troublesome problem because the indentation that we use is completely ignored by the C compiler. While we understand the control of the program at a glance because of the indenting of the code, it can be misleading when, in reality, the program has a completely different structure.

For example, suppose we are writing code that assumes that a tree pointer is valid. By assuming this, the code can be simplified. Yet we also want to protect against the possibility that an actual programming error earlier might cause us to be handed an invalid tree. We would like to be able to say something like:

```
tree_check(treeptr,"some relevant error message");
```

This will generate code to validate the tree when the program is run. If the tree isn't valid, a message will print stating that "`some relevant error message - tree invalid`".

By implementing `tree_check` as a macro, it is possible to get the desired effect. While it can be done as a function as well, I will show later how a macro lets us conveniently skip the checks once we are satisfied the program is completely debugged. (Array bounds checking is another good use for this technique.)

The actual checking of the tree is done by the function `tchk`, which returns 0 if the tree is valid or 1 if not. Further details of `tchk` are not relevant here. It could do any number of things, such as checking that the tree is balanced or something similar. Using `tchk`, a simple definition for `tree_check` is:

```
#define tree_check(tree,msg) \
    if (tchk(tree)) printf("%s - tree invalid\n",msg)
```

Look at this macro very carefully. You should notice two things.[1] The first is that we have put parentheses around `tree`. You should be able come up with an example where `tree_check` would not perform correctly if we left the parentheses out. Also, take note that there is no terminating semicolon at the end of the `if` statement. This allows us to use the macro as if it were a function call, that is, to terminate it with a semicolon at the point of usage.

Now suppose we have the following piece of code:

```
if (a > b) tree_check(tree, "eh?");
else c = 5;
```

This is what happens after the macro is expanded:

```
if (a > b)
    if (tchk(tree)) printf("%s - tree invalid\n","eh?");
    else c = 5;
```

The `else` has bound with the wrong `if`! Not only will this function behave incorrectly, but the C compiler will not complain about it. It will compile just fine. These kinds of errors can be very hard to find, because the block and control bindings of the program don't match the indentation level. The C compiler pays no attention to indentation, while humans treat it "religiously."

---

1. Well, three. For simplicity, I've sent diagnostics to `stdout`. In reality, `stderr` is a much better place.

The problem has occurred because our macro looks like a function call but doesn't behave like one. Because the macro is only a textual substitution, it is free to rebind itself with any part of the program that the control structure syntactically warrants. If `tree_check` had been a function, this would never have happened (and sometimes this is your only recourse).

One way to stop this rebinding is to make the `if` statement into its complete cousin. For example:

```
#define tree_check(tree,msg) \
    if (tchk(tree)) printf("%s - tree invalid\n",msg); \
    else
```

Notice the `else` just hanging off the end? This prevents another `else` from binding with the `if`. Remember that we are assuming that the user will terminate the macro use with a semicolon so that the `else` will be followed immediately by a semicolon (or more precisely, with a null statement). Unfortunately, if you forget the semicolon, you will have more trouble since the following statement will be sucked up as the statement to be executed in the `else` clause (again without errors or warnings of any kind)!

Well, then, why don't we just put the whole thing in a pair of braces? This seems like a good idea because it makes the macro into a complete C statement. You can also declare local variables and have other control structures such as loops in the macro.

Unfortunately a problem arises in the following code fragment:

```
if (expr) tree_check(tree,"...");
else ....
```

which turns into:

```
if (expr) {
    if (tchk(tree)) printf("%s - tree invalid\n","...");
};
else ....        /* SYNTAX ERROR */
```

What happened is that `tree_check` is replaced by a block, but the block is followed by a semicolon. This semicolon came from the user adding it to the end of the macro. It now terminates the `if` prematurely.

Is there anything that will do the job? The answer is yes, but it's not exactly pretty. (You won't hit yourself on the head and say "Why didn't I think of that?") The following macro does the job:

```
#define tree_check(tree,msg)  do {\
    if (tchk(tree)) printf("%s - tree invalid\n",msg);\
                        } while (0)
```

This is very similar to the previous case where we enclosed the macro in a block. The difference is that this one requires a semicolon to make it into a syntactically correct and complete statement. The block is sealed from misinterpretation through rebindings, and it will be executed once and only once. Although it may seem like an unusual way to do it, every (reasonable) compiler will optimize the statement so that the extra test is not performed.

I particularly like this macro because if the user inadvertently leaves off the semicolon, the C compiler will complain. On the other hand, the compiler won't complain with a macro like this:

```
#define tree_check(tree,msg)  if (1) {\
      if (tchk(tree)) printf("%s - tree invalid\n",msg);
                            }
```

For people who absolutely have to have the shortest macro, no matter how much readability is sacrificed, here it is:

```
#define tree_check(tree,msg)  if ((tchk(tree) ; \
      else printf("%s - tree invalid\n",msg);
```

It is particularly ugly, because (1) the test is reversed, which can be a little confusing, and (2) there is a null "then" clause due to the semicolon immediately following the expression, which is easy to miss.

I'm not encouraging you to use these last two macros. Rather I'm pointing out that you may see things like this when reading C source, and you should be able to understand them when you see them.

Note that in each macro above, you can replace the **printf** by a block of statements.

It is sometimes useful to have an **if** statement embedded in an expression (rather than a statement). This can be done with the following macro:

```
#define tree_check(tree,msg)    (tchk(tree) || printf(....))
```

although this is not that useful because you can't have local variables and looping control structures. However, it is occasionally called for.

The reason to implement **tree_check** as a macro is that once you have debugged your program, you can turn off the checking in the final version without doing any editing of your source. Do this by storing **tree_check** and any other debugging macros in your tree definition header as follows:

```
#ifdef TREE_DEBUG
#define tree_check(tree,msg)  if (1) {\
      if (tchk(tree)) printf("%s - tree invalid\n",msg);\
                            }
#else
#define tree_check(tree,msg)
#endif DEBUG
```

By defining **TREE_DEBUG**, the checks will generate real code. Once you are satisfied with your code, you can avoid the overhead of the checks without having to change any code by recompiling without **TREE_DEBUG** being defined.

## CHAPTER 6

Parsing Command-line Arguments—Getopt

One of the stumbling blocks every C programmer encounters is figuring out how to access the command-line arguments within a program.

By convention, initial control of a program is given to the function `main`, which can declare parameters `argc` and `argv`. `argc` and `argv` are a strange albeit useful representation of what was on the command line that invoked the program.

`argv` is an array of strings (or more precisely, pointers to `char`). Each string is one of the tokens of the command with which the program was invoked. (A token is necessarily defined by the operating system, but is usually a group of characters delimited by whitespace.) The first token is just the name of the program and hence, `argv[0]` is not usually examined. (In fact, the program name is very difficult to divine on some systems, and the C Standard explicitly says there is no guarantee that `argv[0]` contains anything meaningful.) `argc` is the number of pointers in `argv` not including the trailing `NULL` pointer. This layout provides the ability to pass a variable number of arguments to a program. However, this layout is unwieldy when one considers it in relation to how command-line arguments are used in a typical program, particularly if it follows traditional UNIX conventions.

For example, command-line arguments are often single-character flags that may or may not have a following value that may or may not be separated by whitespace. Ugh. Flags with no values may appear consecutively in one `argv` string. Some programs are generous and allow all of these argument-passing styles and more. Other programs are more idiosyncratic and will only accept, for example, arguments that are separated by whitespace. Worst of all are programs that insist on having the arguments in a particular order.

Writing argument parsing routines is always a headache. You have to think of all the ways a user could reasonably enter the input and expect it to be accepted. Archetypal `argv` parsing consists of a `while` loop to look at each argument, enclosing a `switch` that actually determines what code is executed for the different argument flags. Finally, there may be a loop to pick any remaining arguments, such as filenames. Such archetypal code also usually has bugs in it, since it is confusing to write code that can handle all of these possibilities.

There have been several efforts to clean up the user interface. Some of them are quite innovative (and would break existing programs). For example, one suggestion has been to use "+" as well as "–" as a flag prefix. To compile with optimization, you might say `cc +opt` and to compile with no optimization, `cc -opt`.

Others are not as earth-shattering, but useful nonetheless. Included in this chapter is the source code to *getopt*, an argument parser that I will show you how to use. This code was first introduced in UNIX System III and later put in the public domain by AT&T to encourage uniformity and consistency in the way arguments are formed from one UNIX command to another.

I have seen different versions of `getopt`—this one is based on the version given out at the 1985 UNIFORUM conference in Dallas. I have made minor modifications in it, although the result still conforms to the AT&T specification. I also added comments that describe the logic and each of the variables so you can understand the code itself. Oddly, the AT&T manual page describing `getopt` is licensed, so I will describe in my own words how to use it.

`getopt` will make your programs simpler for other people to use—they will not have to learn yet another interface. `getopt` is not hard to use inside your programs. It has a well-defined interface and is portable to any C compiler that uses these `argc/argv` conventions.

Calling Getopt

Each time `getopt` is called, it returns the next argument from the command line. Additionally, it sets a number of external variables (such as the argument value). If you need to reference these, be sure to include `extern` declarations for them.

`getopt` takes three arguments. The first two are the `argc` and `argv` arguments that were received by `main`. The third argument is a string containing the characters that are used as argument flags. A character followed immediately by a colon indicates that the flag takes a value. (Hence, ":" cannot be used as a flag character.) For example,

```
getopt(argc,argv,"i:n:ab")
```

indicates that the program takes flag arguments of `i`, `n`, `a` and `b` and that the `i` and `n` flags will have values immediately after them. Flags are restricted to one character. For example,

```
program -i 12 -n hello -a
```

would be parsed correctly by the above `getopt` call; 12 is the argument to the `i` flag, "`hello`" is the argument to the `n` flag, and `a` has no argument. (`b` is not used in this call.) On the command line, flags need not have any space separating them, as long as the first character of each token of flags is a hyphen. For example, we could rewrite the above call as:

```
program -ai 12 -n hello
```

Before calling `getopt` from a C program, it is necessary to have some definitions, which I usually store in the header `getopt.h`. It looks like this:

```
#ifndef GETOPT_H
#define GETOPT_H
#include "proto.h"          /* define PROTO */

int getopt PROTO((int, char **, char *));
extern char *optarg;        /* current argv string */
extern int optind;          /* current argv index */
extern int optopt;          /* option character */
extern int opterr;          /* getopt prints errors if 1 */
#endif /* GETOPT_H */
```

The calling code includes `getopt.h` and then calls `getopt`. A typical program fragment follows:

```
#include "getopt.h"

...
{
    char optchar;
    ....
    while (EOF != (optchar =
         getopt(argc,argv,"i:n:ab"))) {
         switch (optchar) {
         case 'i':
              i_flag = TRUE;
              i = atoi(optarg);
              break;
         case 'n':
              n_flag = TRUE;
              n = optarg;
              break;
         case 'a':
              a_flag = TRUE;
              break;
         case 'b':
              b_flag = TRUE;
              break;
         }
    }
    /* the rest of the arguments are */
    /* files, so pick them up, too */
    for (;optind < argc; optind++) {
         ... = fopen(argv[optind],"...");
    ...
    }
}
```

Notice that the flags that have values pick up their string values in `optarg`. The `i` flag converts its string argument to an integer by the call `atoi(optarg)`.

To complete the documentation of `getopt`, here are some other things you should know about it. When all the flags have been scanned, `getopt` returns `EOF`. The token "`--`" may also be used to terminate `getopt` processing. It is not necessary for the user to supply this as a token, although it is useful when you want to specify a file named, say, "`-f`"! (It is not a very smart idea to have filenames that look like flags.) When "`--`" is scanned, `getopt` returns `EOF`.

After `EOF` is returned there may be more data on the command line (such as files). `optind` is the index of the next `argv` string after the last token successfully read by `getopt`. A single hyphen also terminates processing, but unlike a double hyphen, the single hyphen is left to be consumed by the application. This is traditionally used as a shorthand to indicate that the standard input should be read instead of a file.

'`?`' is returned when an unknown flag is encountered, or a flag that requires a value does not have one. Thus, you should include a case for '`?`' (or `default` will do) that prints out the standard calling sequence to indicate that the user has called your program incorrectly. It is possible to get the actual incorrect flag that the user specified by examining the external character variable `optopt`.

If the value of `opterr` is 1, `getopt` will print error messages about unexpected arguments or missing argument values (as well as returning '`?`'). If `opterr` is preset to 0, no messages will be printed.

The `getopt` code assumes the existence of `strchr`. Some Classic C systems call this `index`. If you don't have either, you can easily write it yourself. `strchr` takes arguments of a string and a character, in that order. It returns a pointer to the first occurrence of the character in the string. If the character does not appear in the string, `NULL` is returned.

Source Code—getopt.c

```
/* optarg - parse command-line arguments */
/* Author: AT&T */

#include <stdio.h>

#define ERR(s, c)    if(opterr){\
    char errbuf[2];\
    errbuf[0] = c; errbuf[1] = '\n';\
    fprintf(stderr, argv[0], (unsigned)strlen(argv[0]));\
    fprintf(stderr, s, (unsigned)strlen(s));\
    fprintf(stderr, errbuf, 2);}

extern int strcmp();
extern char *strchr();
extern int strlen();
```

```
int   opterr = 1;      /* getopt prints errors if this is on */
int   optind = 1;      /* token pointer */
int   optopt;          /* option character passed back to user */
char *optarg;          /* flag argument (or value) */

int   /* return option character, EOF if no more or ? if problem */
getopt(argc, argv, opts)
int   argc;
char **argv;
char *opts;                  /* option string */
{
      static int sp = 1;   /* character index in current token */
      register char *cp;   /* pointer into current token */

      if(sp == 1)
          /* check for more flag-like tokens */
          if(optind >= argc ||
             argv[optind][0] != '-' || argv[optind][1] == '\0')
                 return(EOF);
          else if(strcmp(argv[optind], "--") == 0) {
                 optind++;
                 return(EOF);
          }
      optopt = argv[optind][sp];
      if(optopt == ':' || (cp=strchr(opts, optopt)) == 0) {
          ERR(": illegal option -- ", optopt);
          /* if no chars left in this token, move to next token */
          if(argv[optind][++sp] == '\0') {
                 optind++;
                 sp = 1;
          }
          return('?');
      }

      if(*++cp == ':') {/* if a value is expected, get it */
          if(argv[optind][sp+1] != '\0')
                 /* flag value is rest of current token */
                 optarg = &argv[optind++][sp+1];
          else if(++optind >= argc) {
                 ERR(": option requires an argument -- ", optopt);
                 sp = 1;
                 return('?');
          } else
                 /* flag value is next token */
                 optarg = argv[optind++];
          sp = 1;
      } else {
          /* set up to look at next char in token, next time */
          if(argv[optind][++sp] == '\0') {
```

```
                /* no more in current token, so setup next token
*/
                sp = 1;
                optind++;
        }
        optarg = 0;
    }
    return(optopt);/* return the current flag character found */
}
```

CHAPTER 7

Not Cast in Concrete

Intuitively, a cast converts a value of one type to another. The syntax of a cast is a type name in parentheses followed by the expression to be cast. For example, to produce a null character pointer, zero is cast as follows:

```
(char *)0
```

To paraphrase *K&R2* (p. 42), *a cast has the same effect as an assignment to a variable of the casted type.* Internally, this means that a value's bit pattern may change due to a cast. Some casts actually increase or decrease the number of bits used in representing the value.

If you don't want the bit patterns to change, you probably want to use a `union`. A practical example of this is the problem of comparing an IEEE-style floating-point number against infinity. Since infinity is represented as a specific bit pattern rather than a number, there is no way to specify infinity in the natural notation of the type. One solution is to declare a `union` of a `float` and an integer long enough to store the infinity bit value, and then use the integer type and the bitwise operators when testing for infinity.

General Guidelines

If you find yourself always casting a variable before using it, you should probably reexamine your declaration, and ask yourself why it isn't declared as the casted type to begin with. In general, casts are unnecessary when variables are declared appropriately. However, there are valid reasons for casting and I will discuss the major ones.

Pointer Conversions

The first one I want to discuss is the `NULL` problem. Assuming that `NULL` is defined as 0, the following is valid:

```
char *broiled = NULL;
```

Assignment implicitly converts the right-hand side to the type on the left-hand side, but you still need an explicit cast for pointer types. The only exception is the null pointer (as I've shown above) and `void *` pointers. These are special and do not require casts.

If a function has not been declared with a prototype (always the case with Classic C), such conversions do not take place during calls to that function. Because of that, the following function call is incorrect:

```
function_takes_pointer_arg(NULL)    /* WRONG */
```

There are two problems with this call. They stem from the fact that without prototypes, C does not check function calls against actual function interfaces. So if NULL is defined as 0, the statement will have the compiler pass an int-sized zero.

The first problem is that the size of the pointer that the function expects may be different than the space required to hold an int. If the pointer is larger, extra bits accessed will have garbage values in them. Either way, following arguments will not be accessed correctly. Redefining NULL as, say, (char *)0 or 0L will not help, because pointers to different types are not guaranteed to be the same size.

The second problem is that the machine's internal null pointer may use a non-zero bit representation. Then, even if sizeof(pointer) == sizeof(int), the values won't match unless C does the conversion. The cast will do this conversion correctly.

If you are writing in Classic C, or there is a chance your code may be ported to such an environment (or you are passing arguments in the variable part of a variable-length argument list), *always cast NULL or 0 when passing it as a pointer argument*. To play it safe, do it all the time—then you won't even have to wonder about these possibilities.

An alternative to passing 0 or NULL in the first place is to declare a null value for each type. For example, if you use a type foo_t created with typedef, you could pass NULL_FOO to any function with the following #define:

```
typedef ... foo_t;
#define NULL_FOO ((foo_t *)0)
```

It is a matter of taste whether you think this makes code more readable, but it leaves open the possibility that you can easily change your own representation of a null foo. It also enables the compiler to complain if you accidentally use the wrong level of indirection.

Casting to Void and Void *

In Classic C, two functions that always require casts are malloc and free. (A cast is actually unnecessary when allocating character arrays, but it won't hurt!) malloc returns space guaranteed to be properly aligned for any object type, declared as returning char *. Just as the results of malloc are always cast, similarly the argument to free should be cast back to char *. In Standard C, malloc and free use void * instead of char * and the casts are not necessary. For portability between the two environments, cast explicitly. (Ironically, void * was invented specifically for the purpose of avoiding having to do this!)

If you use both Standard C and Classic C, you face the problem of whether to write `void *` or `char *`. A common practice is to create a new type name for the purpose of isolating the dependency.

```
#ifdef __STDC__
typedef void *Generic;
#else
typedef char *Generic;
#endif
```

Note that `void *` is not magic. For instance, you can't cast an integer to a function just because you stuck `(void *)` in the assignment. `(void *)` only works on values that were assignment-compatible to begin with. Although this may not seem to buy much, it is necessary for guaranteeing the correct operation of functions like `malloc` and `qsort`, which support data of any type.

Because of `malloc`'s guarantee, it is acceptable to recast its result to any pointer type. However, recasting of arbitrary pointers may lose information, depending on a machine's memory alignment rules. Even worse is what happens if you explicitly violate memory alignment restrictions. I unthinkingly did this while writing a program on a Motorola 68000. I was reading variably-sized objects out of a buffer that I was managing myself. Occasionally I would get a fault while reading a two-byte integer. The code looked something like this:

```
char *bufptr = buffer;
two_byte_integer = *(int *)bufptr;      bufptr += 2;
one_byte_integer = *(char *)bufptr;     bufptr += 1;
two_byte_integer = *(int *)bufptr;      /* WRONG! */
```

The condition was set up because there was no padding between elements in the buffer and some of the elements were an odd number of bytes in length. The 68000 requires that word loads and stores be aligned on even-byte boundaries, and I was violating this, hence the bus fault.

I am too embarrassed to admit the number of days it took me to figure out what was going on. Unfortunately, my code wasn't nearly this simple. Other things combined to mislead me, including (1) porting it to a VAX (which doesn't have word alignment restrictions), causing the problem to "disappear" and (2) the debugger I was using cleverly faked the odd-address access and executed the request by doing two loads without telling me that! Remember that when you cast a pointer, you are assuming responsibility for pointer compatibility.[1]

Another thing to avoid is assigning to the result of a cast. For example, the code:

```
((int *)bufptr)++;
```

might be construed as a way to temporarily increment a character pointer by `int`-sized jumps. But it really doesn't make sense, because the result of a cast is not an

---

1. According to Henry Spencer, "If you lie to your compiler, it will get its revenge."

addressable chunk of memory (*modifiable lvalue* in Classic C, or *object locator* in Standard C). You can't get back to `bufptr` after the cast. Instead, do it as:

```
bufptr = (char *)(1 + (int *)bufptr);
```

For an entirely different purpose, any value may be cast to `void`. Normally, this is used only to state that you are discarding the return value of a function. This is especially common in functions like `sprintf`, which returns a value that is not normally of interest, even for checking errors.

```
sprintf(....);
(void) sprintf(....);
```

Either form is acceptable C, but pedantic tools such as `lint` will complain "`sprintf returns a value which is ignored`" unless you tell it that you are intentionally ignoring it by use of the `void` cast.

The last example of when to ignore information is the rule *if you can't handle an error, you shouldn't be checking for it*. This might apply in:

```
(void) fprintf(stderr,"panic: cannot recover ...");
```

After all, if the call to `fprintf` fails, what should the program do?

Function Casting

Pointers to functions may be cast using the same rules as other casts. While function casting is rather unusual, a common technique is the following (extracted from the header `signal.h` on many UNIX systems):

```
#define SIG_ERR  (void (*)())-1
```

This definition of `SIG_ERR` coerces –1 to be of type "pointer to function returning nothing." It's hard to imagine what –1 might do if called as a function. In fact, it is never actually called; –1 is cast that way only so that it can be checked as a return value against `signal`, which is defined to return—you guessed it—"pointer to function returning nothing." What `signal` is saying when it returns –1 is that you have handed it an "erroneous signal," hence the name "`SIG_ERR`." Incidentally, this definition is not portable, but UNIX systems make sure that it works anyway.

Arithmetic Conversions

More typical uses of casts appear in arithmetic expressions (which includes character manipulation). The most common reason is the need to use a library call such as `sqrt`, which is defined for `double`s, but you have an `int`. In that case, the following suffices:

```
double sqrt();
int x, y;
x = (int)sqrt((double)y);
```

Here we have cast twice, first to promote `y` to the type required by `sqrt`, and second to convert the `double` returned by `sqrt` to an `int`. The latter cast isn't necessary, but it serves as a reminder that there was a truncation (or "demotion") from a `double` to an `int` and accuracy was lost. Sometimes this is exactly what is wanted. Sometimes this is an error, since a `double` can store much larger numbers than an `int`.

H&S warns that some C implementations incorrectly handle casts intended to reduce the size of a value. For example, assume that an `int` is 32 bits and a `short` is 16 bits.

```
(int)(short)0x12345678;
```

On these broken implementations, the value of the expression is 0x12345678 rather than 0x5678, which is what it should be due to the truncation. For portability, avoid using casts for truncation and instead use assignments or explicit masking instructions.

Casts to Avoid Sign Propagation

Operations that propagate the sign bit can be rectified by casting from a signed to an `unsigned` type. For example, shifting signed `int`s can propagate sign bits. Avoid this by specifying variables `unsigned` or casting them to `unsigned` in expressions.

Standard C clarifies what happens when `unsigned` values become too large—they are converted to signed values. This preserves the value, but as a large negative value. This can be a problem if you compare it with another value. Although this was not historically well-defined, it was common for compilers to preserve `unsigned`-ness rather than value. Use casts when doing such comparisons.

Some compilers treat `char`s as `signed` unless they are explicitly declared `unsigned`. Arbitrarily declaring all `char`s (or any other types) `unsigned` is a mistake, however, because you may pay a significant performance penalty for using it instead of plain `char`.

Casts to Avoid Numeric Overflow

It is occasionally useful to cast operands to larger types to avoid overflow. For example:

```
double z;
int x = INT_MAX;

z = x + x;          /* overflow */
z = x + (double)x;  /* ok */
```

The first attempt at the addition fails because the addition of two `int`s is an `int`, which is not large enough for the result. The second attempt works because the addition of an `int` and a `double` is a `double` that is large enough for the result. (Of course, this doesn't guarantee accuracy. The `double` may not be able to store all the significant digits.) This example doesn't depend on the result being assigned to a `double`. The result of the addition expression is the problem. You must always be careful to check whether your intermediate results need such a cast, even if you know that the final result fits.

Documenting a Coercion that Will Occur Anyhow

Occasionally, it is useful to use a cast as documentation that a conversion is going to take place. This might not be clear otherwise.

In unprototyped function calls, for example, `char`s and `short`s are promoted to `int`s, and `float`s to `double`s. Therefore, the following calls are equivalent even though they don't appear to be if you aren't familiar with the automatic promotion of arguments in C function calls. (It was certainly a surprise to me, when I first heard it!)

```
float f = 522.9347;
char c = 'Z';

function(f,c);
function((double)f,(int)c);
```

Certain other operations also cause automatic conversions, which are sometimes usefully pointed out by putting in redundant casts. These include returning values from functions, assignments, and some miscellaneous arithmetic and logical operations.

## CHAPTER 8

The 1985 Obfuscated C Code Contest

Chapter 3 (p. 13) described the idea of obfuscated C and presented the results of the 1984 Obfuscated C Code Contest. This contest is run annually by Landon Noll, who collects C code that is so awful to read, it is actually funny. Viewed in the right light, you might even call it educational. (For more background see the earlier chapter.)

The original contest limited entries to 512 bytes. This was raised to 1024 bytes for the entries shown here, and raised higher in following years. Obviously the contest judges will bend the rules in order to recognize outstanding obfuscation wherever it is found. So, if you absolutely can't get your program shorter than 1025 bytes, don't worry about it. Or if your one-year-old refused to include a single comment in the piece of code she banged out one day by rolling her head across the keyboard, but it proves Fermat's last theorem, send it anyway. I'm sure the judges will give it its fair due. After all, it can't be any worse than much of the C code that we've seen, and who knows, it might even end up as an essential part of the next release of the operating system.

Best Small Program

Jack Applin <neutron@hpfcls.fc.hp.com>
Hewlett-Packard
Fort Collins, Colorado

Robert Heckendorn

```
main(v,c)char**c;{for(v[c++]="Hello, world!\n)";
(!!c)[*c]&&(v--||--c&&execlp(*c,*c,c[!!c]+!!c,!\
c));**c=!c)write(!!*c,*c,!!**c);}
```

Analysis

On a first quick glance at this 128-byte program for obvious clues, I picked out the functions `write` and `execlp`. `write` is obvious, but `execlp` was worrisome. `execlp` is a UNIX function that overlays the current program with another. I hoped the program wasn't calling this!

Indenting the program didn't help much. Neither did switching the formal variables to `main`, suggestively but misleadingly named `v` and `c` for `argc` and `argv`. Both of these transformations are done below:

```
main(c,v)
char **v;
{
    for (c[v++] = "Hello, world!\n)";
            (!!v)[*v] &&
            (c-- || --v && execlp (*v, *v, v[!!v] + !!v, !v));
        **v =! v)
        write (!!*v, *v, !!**v);
}
```

A quick glance at the original program might mislead you into thinking that the `for` has an empty statement, but if you look closely, you will see that the right parenthesis is inside double quotes and does not match the earlier left parenthesis! In fact, the `write` in the last line of the program is the statement part of the `for`. In between is the control expression.

To make the program simpler to read, I massaged the `for` into a `while`, and broke up the control expression into separate statements.

```
main (c, v)
char **v;
{
    c[v++] = "Hello, world!\n)";
    while (1) {
        if (!(!!v)[*v]) break;
        if (!(c--) && !(--v && execlp (*v, *v, v[!!v] + !!v,
                                                        !v))) break;
        write (!!*v, *v, !!**v);
        **v = !v;
    }
}
```

At this point, I realized that `execlp` was indeed being called, apparently with some program generated within the program itself.

The first statement assigns a pointer to the string `"Hello..."` to a spare part of the `argv` structure (spare because it is defined to initially hold a null pointer). This is tested by the first statement of the `while` to see whether the string is empty—well, almost; it stops one short of the paren at the end of the string trying to throw you off the track. Eventually, the loop terminates. The `!!` notation is an obfuscated way of writing 0 if the argument is 0, and 1 if the argument is non-zero. We can see this used in the first and third argument of the `write` statement. Thus, one character (the first character of `v`) is being written to the standard output on each call.

On each call? Yes, initially the `&&` short-circuit skips `execlp` and writes an H, but the second time through the loop, `c` is 0, and thus the right side of `&&` executes.

`execlp` takes the program name to be executed as its first two arguments, and this is exactly what is passed, by first decrementing v. The third argument is the string to be printed, and `v[!!v]` gets back to that. `!!v` (or 1) is added to drop off the leading character.

Now the program is invoked again, but with an argument. The assignment in the first statement ends up being ignored because it will end up in `v[2]`, rather than `v[1]` like the first time. The rest of the program executes as before, first writing a character and then reinvoking itself. The result is that the program calls itself anew to print out every single character in the string (not including the right parenthesis):

```
Hello, world!
```

Most Obscure

Lennart Augustsson <augustss@cs.chalmers.se>
Chalmers Institute of Technology
Gothenburg, Sweden

```
#define p struct c
#define q struct b
#define h a->a
#define i a->b
#define e i->c
#define o a=(*b->a)(b->b,b->c)
#define s return a;}q*
#define n (d,b)p*b;{q*a;p*c;
#define z(t)(t*)malloc(sizeof(t))
q{int a;p{q*(*a)();int b;p*c;}*b;};q*u n a=z(q);h=d;i=z(p);i->a=u
;i->b=d+1;s v n c=b;do o,b=i;while(!(h%d));i=c;i->a=v;i->b=d;e=b;
s w n o;c=i;i=b;i->a=w;e=z(p);e->a=v;e->b=h;e->c=c;s t n for(;;)o
,main(-h),b=i;}main(b){p*a;if(b>0)a=z(p),h=w,a->c=z(p),a->c-
>a=u,
a->c->b=2,t(0,a);putchar(b?main(b/2),-b%2+'0':10);}
```

When run, this program prints

```
10
11
101
111
1011
1101
10001
10011
10111
11101
11111
100101
(and on and on)
```

These are the primes in binary.

Author's Analysis

"This program started its life as a nice lazy functional program. It goes something like this:

```
let rec
    filterm p (a.b) =
        if a % p = 0 then
            filter p b
        else
            a . filterm p b

and from n = n . from (n+1)

and sieve (a.b) = a . sieve (filter a b)
in
    sieve (from 2)
```

"This is the sieve of Eratosthenes in a standard lazy setting. The first translation into C yields:

```
#include <stdio.h>
#define closure struct Xclosure
#define list struct Xlist

struct Xclosure {
    list * (*f)();
    int a1;
    closure *a2;
};

struct Xlist {
    int hd;
    closure *tl;
};

#define NEW(t) ((t *)malloc(sizeof(t)))

list *from(n) {
    list *l;
    l = NEW(list);
    l->hd = n;
    l->tl = NEW(closure);
    l->tl->f = from;
    l->tl->a1 = n+1;
    return l;
}

list *filterm(p, l)
closure *l;
```

```
{
     list *x;
     closure *t;

     t = l;
     do {
          x = (*l->f)(l->a1, l->a2);
          l = x->tl;
     } while(x->hd % p == 0);
     x->tl = t;        /* NEW(closure) */
     x->tl->f = filterm;
     x->tl->a1 = p;
     x->tl->a2 = l;
     return x;
}

list *sieve(z, l)
closure *l;
{
     list *x;
     closure *t;

     x = (*l->f)(l->a1, l->a2);
     t = x->tl;
     x->tl = NEW(closure);
     x->tl->f = sieve;
     x->tl->a2 = NEW(closure);
     x->tl->a2->f = filterm;
     x->tl->a2->a1 = x->hd;
     x->tl->a2->a2 = t;
     return x;
}

print(l)
closure *l;
{
     list *x;

     for(;;) {
          x = (*l->f)(l->a1, l->a2);
          printf(" %d", x->hd);
          l = x->tl;
     }
}

main()
{
     closure *s;

     setbuf(stdout, NULL);
```

```
        s = NEW(closure);
        s->f = sieve;
        s->a2 = NEW(closure);
        s->a2->f = from;
        s->a2->a1 = 2;
        print(s);
}
```

"Nothing remarkable happens here, it's just taking care of evaluation order, etc.

"The precise obfuscation steps have been lost to history but some key points are:

- Rename all things to **a**, **b**, **c** or **d**, and functions to **u**, **v**, **w**, and **t**.

- Change the print routine to be **main**. **main** called as a print routine is distinguished by a (nonportable) single negative argument.

- Use **,** instead of **;** at some places.

- Especially obfuscated is "**x?y,z:w**" (in **main**). This violates *K&R1* precedence rules, but is accepted by Standard C and most Classic C compilers.

- Introduce **#defines** for the most common character combinations without any consideration of their meaning (e.g., **s**).

- This gave me a program that was 513 characters long. The final step to get it to 512 was to change the output base to 2 instead of 10. This also made the output more obscure."

Worst Abuse of the C Preprocessor

G. L. Sicherman <gls@hrmso.att.com>
AT&T Bell Laboratories
Middletown, New Jersey

```
#define C_C_(_)~' '&_
#define _C_C(_)('\b'b'\b'>=C_C>'\t'b'\n')
#define C_C _|_
#define b *
#define C /b/
#define V _C_C(
main(C,V)
char **V;
/*   C program. (If you don't
 *   understand it look it
 */  up.) (In the C Manual)
{
    char _,__;
    while (read(0,&__,1) & write((_=(_=C_C_(__),C)),
    _C_,1)) _=C-V+subr(&V);
}
```

```
subr(C)
char *C;
{
    C="Lint says "argument Manual isn't used." What's that
    mean?"; while (write((read(C_C('"'-'/*"'/*"*/))?__:__-_+
    '\b'b'\b'|((_-52)%('\b'b'\b'+C_C_('\t'b'\n'))+1),1),&_,1));
}
```

As the program suggests, lint does complain (among others things) that:

> line 11: warning: argument Manual unused in function main

Nonetheless, after a silent compilation, the program performs a Caesar substitution of its input. *Caesar substitution* is a transliteration of text where each letter is replaced by another letter a fixed distance (in this case 13 letters) later in the alphabet. It is also called rot (for "rotation") or rot13. For example, "Obfuscate" is encoded as "Boshfpngr".

Author's Analysis

"My first reaction to the announcement of the Second Obfuscated C Code Contest was annoyance at having missed the first one. My second reaction was that a C program could be grossly obfuscated by making the preprocessor insert comments in it, if that were possible.

"On experimenting with the Reiser preprocessor, I found that if I used macro substitution for the slash in /*, the preprocessor would still strip the comment; but if I used macro substitution for the asterisk, the preprocessor would not catch it. The trick of using a two-sided comment delimiter to increase obscurity is borrowed from Charles E. Pearson, who used to write Pascal production code with

> (*) COMMENTS THAT LOOKED LIKE THIS. (*)

"I chose rot13 for a starting program because it was useful and, so far as I knew, had not been used in previous contests.

"I defined c as the comment delimiter in honor of the language, and because main(C,V) looked natural enough to trip up most people at the outset. The block comment is another bit of misdirection. It looks like merely an unhelpful comment where most people would expect no comments, but the third line is not part of the comment! After the preprocessor strips the block comment, the compiler balances the c after main(with the c in the third line, making the actual declaration main(Manual). This accounts for the cryptic message from lint.

"Many modern preprocessors complain about using the v macro with no argument; the one I used in 1985 accepted it silently. The hidden trick is that v expands to another macro call with only a left parenthesis, so the preprocessor scans ahead to find a matching right parenthesis! The mishmash of double quotes, single quotes, and comment delimiters in line 21 is necessary to introduce parentheses to match those in the v macros without unbalancing the parentheses in the preprocessor output. The 'subroutine' only appears to contain nested strings and a two-line string. Actually the preprocessor matches the first two double quotes, then two *single* quotes, and so on. The compiler proper never sees most of this code, but if you tamper with any of it, either the preprocessor or the compiler is sure to complain.

"When you pass the program through `cpp` (twice!) and reformat it, it exhibits only routine arithmetical and logical obfuscation and confusing operator precedence:

```
main(Manual)
{
    char _,__;
    while (read(0,&__,1) & write((_=(_=~' '&__,
    -('\b'*'\b'>=_|_>'\t'*'\n'))?__:__-_+
    '\b'*'\b'|((_-52)%('\b'*'\b'+~' '&'\t'*'\n')+1),1),&_,1));
}
```

"Of course, this program works only on UNIX-compatible systems using ASCII."

Strangest-Looking Program

Ed Lycklama <sun!suncan!klg!ed>
KL Group
Toronto, Canada

```
#define o define
#o ___o write
#o ooo (unsigned)
#o o_o_ 1
#o _o_ char
#o _oo goto
#o _oo_ read
#o o_o for
#o o_ main
#o o__ if
#o oo_ 0
#o _o(_,__,___)(void)___o(_,__,ooo(___))
#o __o
(o_o_<<((o_o_<<(o_o_<<o_o_))+(o_o_<<o_o_)))+(o_o_<<(o_o_<<(o_o_<
<o_o_)))
o_(){_o_ _=oo_,__,___,____[__o];_oo _____;_____:___=__o-
o_o_;_____:
_o(o_o_,____,__=(_-o_o_<___?-o_o_:___));o_o(;__;_o(o_o_,"\-
b",o_o_),__--);
_o(o_o_," ",o_o_);o__(--___)_oo
_____;_o(o_o_,"\n",o_o_);_____:o__(_=_oo_(
oo_,____,__o))_oo _____;}
```

This program not only looks odd, but it acts odd, too! When run, it reads input and rewrites the output so that it appears to be moving across the line from left to right.

Analysis

Cracking the program was not very hard, although it used some new forms of obfuscation worth noting. In particular, the `#define o define` allowed further macros to be defined very obscurely. This is definitely not portable!

After macro preprocessing, several lines had expressions of the form `(1<<((1<<(1<<1))+(1<<1)))+(1<<(1<<(1<<1)))`, which is a roundabout way of specifying 80. Also, the o's disappeared, leaving variables (and labels) composed entirely of underscores.

A more readable version of this program appears below and can barely be seen to do just what I described in the first paragraph (although the gotos obscure it even further).

```
main () {
        char __ = 0,_____,_____,_____[80];
        goto _____;
_____: _____ = 79;
_____: write(1,_____,(_____ = (__-1<_____?__-
1:_____))));
        for (; ____; putchar('\b'), ____--);
        putchar(' ');
        if (--_____) goto _____;
        putchar('\n');
_____: if (__ = read(0,_____,80)) goto _____;
}
```

Most Well-Rounded Confusion (Grand Prize)

Carl Shapiro <carl@otto.lvsun.com>
Teleguide
Henderson, Nevada

```
#define P(X)j=write(1,X,1)
#define C 39
int M[5000]={2},*u=M,N[5000],R=22,a[4],l[]={0,-1,C-1,-1},m[]={1,-
C,-1,C},*b=N,*d=N,c,e,f,g,i,j,k,s;main(){for(M[i=C*R-1]=24;f|d>=b
;){c=M[g=i];i=e;for(s=f=0;s<4;s++)if((k=m[s]+g)>=0&&k<C*R&&l[s]!=
k%C&&(!M[k]||!j&&c>=16!=M[k]>=16))a[f++]=s;if(f){f=M[e=m[s=a[rand
()/(1+2147483647/f)]]+g];j=j<f?f:j;f+=c&-16*!j;M[g]=c|1<<s;M[*d
++=e]=f|1<<(s+2)%4;}else e=d>b++?b[-1]:e;}P(" ");for(s=C;--s;P(
"_"))P(" ");for(;P("\n"),R--;P("|"))for(e=C;e--;P("_"+(*u++/8)%2)
)P("| "+(*u/4)%2);}
```

When run, this program generates a maze. As if the program itself wasn't obfuscated enough, the explanation will be: I was not able to decipher the program, nor was Carl able to send me an explanation. At the same time, another winner offered to skip explaining his own original winning entry if he could provide a substitute for Carl's program with an explanation. Of course, he had to rewrite Carl's program first, so although it does the same thing, it looks completely different and works in an entirely different way. Is that clear? No? Good. Here it is:

John Tromp <tromp@cwi.nl>
CWI
Amsterdam, Netherlands

Author's Analysis

"I have a long history of writing maze-generating programs. The first I ever saw must have been one in a book containing listings of Sinclair ZX-Spectrum programs. As I remember, it didn't make a whole lot of sense.

"That was before I knew about recursion. As I became familiar with the notion, I had little trouble writing my own maze generator, taking care of the stacky bits with a simple array. Later still I suffered quite a few headaches from converting the program to Z-80 assembler for speed's sake. Developments of the program have since been directed by availability of output devices. On occasion I took a long train ride to a friend with an ink-jet printer to produce mazes in all different colors.

"I perceived two problems with that method of generating mazes. First, the mazes produced were hardly random, having very long corridors with very few junctions. This made solving the mazes a bit too easy, in my opinion. Second, the generator had to allocate memory for the entire maze. This limited the length of the mazes I could print. Being rather obsessed with mazes, I wasn't satisfied with a *mere* four meters worth of maze.

"This got me thinking about generating mazes on the fly, line by line, without having to remember much information. That way, you could conceivably just start printing a maze, and tell it to somehow finish it nicely as you notice the printer running out of paper.

"My submission is an obfuscated version of a program I wrote to generate mazes in this way. The central data structure is a collection of circular doubly linked lists, the elements of which correspond to the maze cells of one row of the maze. More precisely, each list contains the cells of the current row that are connected by a path in the already-generated part of the maze above the current row. Thus the lists form a partition of the cells in the current row; each cell is contained in exactly one of these lists. The doubly linked lists are stored in the arrays L (for left) and R (for right). For a set of cells $i_1, i_2, ..., i_k$ (from left to right) that are all connected in the part of the maze above the current row, $R[i_1] = i_2$, $R[i_2] = i_3$, ..., and $R[i_k] = i_1$. Similarly for the left pointers.

"How do we make use of this data structure? For each new row of the maze, we visit all its cells from left to right, and for each one decide whether it should be connected to its right neighbor (the next cell visited) and whether it should be connected to its neighbor below (in the next row). We would like the decision to be as random as possible, but at the same time, we want the resulting maze to be what is formally known as a spanning tree. That means that there should be exactly one path between any two cells in the maze, a highly desirable property of mazes. Since this property prohibits cycles, connections which would result in a cycle will have to be avoided. It also requires all cells to be connected, so certain vital connections will have to be enforced. It turns out that the prohibition of connections is an issue only for right-connections, while the enforcement of connections is an issue only for down-connections.

"Our data structure is ideally suited to testing either condition and for the necessary updates. Here's what we do at cell i with right neighbor i'.

"Note that i' = i-1 in the algorithm but I want to avoid the apparent confusion. Also, no update of the data structure is required when omitting a right-connection or when making a down-connection. Also, a cell takes over the identity of its down-neighbor after the second decision.

"To decide on a right-connection, check if i equals L[i']; if so then a right-connection is prohibited as it would create a cycle. Otherwise, flip a (slightly biased) coin. To make the connection, we join the two lists by the following operations:

```
R[L[i']]=R[i] ; L[R[i]]=L[i'] ; /* link L[i'] to R[i] */
R[ i ]= i' ; L[ i']= i   ; /* link   i   to   i' */
```

"We will later print a '.' (right-connection) or a '|' (no right-connection), after we print the character for the presence/absence of a down-connection.

"To decide on a down-connection, check if i equals L[i]; if so then this cell is alone in its list and a down-connection is enforced to keep it connected to the rest of the maze. Otherwise, flip a (slightly biased) coin.

"To omit the connection, we take the cell out of its list by the following operations:

```
R[L[i]]=R[i] ; L[R[i]]=L[i] ; /* link L[i] to R[i] */
R[ i ]= i ; L[ i ]= i   ; /* link   i   to i  */
```

"We now print a blank (down-connection) or underscore (no down-connection), followed by the character for the presence/absence of a right-connection.

"A trick is used to make sure that the last cell, j, in a row does not try to connect to its nonexisting right neighbor. We ensure that the test for equality of j and L[j'] always succeeds by creating a dummy cell for j' and setting L[j'] to j. (In the algorithm j=1 and j'=0.)

"To finish the maze, a special last row is created in which some right-connections are enforced to ensure the connectedness of the entire maze. The workings of the corresponding piece of code are not hard to understand given the above, and are left as an exercise for the reader.

"Here is the gist of the unobfuscated code:

```
main()
{
  L[0] = scanf("%d",&H); /* reads height and sets L[0] to 1 */
```

```
for (E = 40; --E; L[E] = R[E] = E)
  printf("._");                        /* close top of maze */
printf("\n|");
while (--H)                            /* more rows to do */
{ for (C = 40; --C; printf(M))         /* visit cells left to right */
  {if (C != (E=L[C-1]) && 6<<27<rand())/* do right-connect ? */
    { R[E] = R[C];                     /* link E */
      L[R[C]] = E;                     /* to R[C] */
      R[C] = C-1;                      /* link C */
      L[C-1] = C;                      /* to C-1 */
      M[1] = '.';                      /* no wall to the right */
    }
    else M[1] = '|';                   /* wall to the right */
    if (C != (E=L[C]) && 6<<27<rand()) /* omit down-connect? */
    { R[E] = R[C];                     /* link E */
      L[R[C]] = E;                     /* to R[C] */
      L[C] = C;                        /* link C */
      R[C] = C;                        /* to C */
      M[0] = '_';                      /* wall downward */
    }
    else M[0] = ' ';                   /* no wall downward */
  }
  printf("\n|");
}
M[0] = '_';                            /* close bottom of maze */
for (C = 40; --C; printf(M))           /* bottom row */
{ if (C != (E=L[C-1]) && (C == R[C] || 6<<27<rand()))
  { L[R[E]=R[C]]=E;
    L[R[C]=C-1]=C;
    M[1] = '.';
  }
  else M[1] = '|';
  E = L[C];
  R[E] = R[C];
  L[R[C]] = E;
  L[C] = C;
  R[C] = C;
}
printf("\n");
}
```

"Obfuscation starts by getting rid of the comments and whitespace, nesting assignments, and other minor things. To shorten the program further, we integrate the last row loop into the main one. The test for omitting the down-connection should always succeed on the last row, so we simply extend this test to `C!=(E=L[C]) && 6<<27<rand() || !H`. The main loop then becomes:

```
M[1] = C!=(E=L[C-1]) && 6<<27<rand() ?
        L[R[E]=R[C]]=E,L[R[C]=C-1]=C,'.' : '|';
```

```
*M = C!=(E=L[C]) && 6<<27<rand() || !H ?
        L[R[E]=R[C]]=E,L[C]=R[C]  =C,'_' : ' ';
```

and we notice a lot of similarity between the right and down cases. Once we get the idea to loop on a variable, say z, from 1 to 0, we quickly arrive at the following huge improvement (in obfuscation):

```
for (Z=1; Z>=0; Z--) {
    M[Z] = C!=(E=L[C-Z]) && 6<<27<rand() || !H&!Z ?
        L[R[E]=R[C]]=E,L[R[C]=C-Z]=C,"_."[Z] : " |"[Z];
}
```

"Due to the enormous amount of functionality captured in these few lines, it is already amazingly hard to comprehend them without knowing their evolution. This code is shortened further by reversing the string constants and their index z, thus allowing z to be lifted from the entire assignment. Also, the inequality is replaced by a subtraction, a technique discovered and used by many OCCC authors:

```
for (Z=1; Z>=0; Z--) {
    M[Z] = Z[C-(E=L[C-Z]) && 6<<27<rand() || !H&!Z ?
        L[R[E]=R[C]]=E,L[R[C]=C-Z]=C,"_." : " |"];
}
```

(The L[C-Z] will later be replaced by the more obfuscated C[L-Z]. Restricting the obfuscation to only this occurrence of L hopefully adds to the mystery.)

"The program now has three nested loops, one over the rows of the maze, one over the cells within this row, and one over the two directions in which connections can be made:

```
while (--H) {
    for (C=40; --C; printf(M)) {
        for (Z=1; Z>=0; Z--) {
        }
    }
    printf("\n|");
}
```

"With yet another trick, we will fold them all into one big loop! From the point of view of the innermost loop, z toggles between 1 and 0; when it goes from 0 to 1, then M must be printed and c must be decremented; when c becomes 0, then \n| must be printed, c must be reset to 39 and H must be decremented. This can be expressed by the following code:

```
if (Z == 0) printf(M);
if ((C-=Z=!Z) == 0) {
    printf("\n|");
    C = 39;
    H--;
}
```

which can also be further obfuscated as

```
Z || printf(M);
(C-=Z=!Z) || printf("\n|"), C = 39, H--;
```

"Other notable obfuscations at this point were to (1) spell MAZE, (2) 'sign' the program with the author's initials, and (3) give the impression of a copyright symbol (not to be taken seriously). Also, by making all variables of the type char * (except the maze height which is made the argument of main), we avoid the need for declaring ints, saving another four characters. We thus arrive at the following arguably minimal-length program for generating arbitrary length mazes:

```
char*M,A,Z,E=40,J[40],T[40];main(C){for(*J=A=scanf(M="%d",&C);--
E;J[E]=T[E]=E)
printf("._");for(;(A-=Z=!Z)||(printf("\n|"),A=39,C--);Z||print-
f(M))M[Z]=Z[A-(E=A
[J-Z])&&!C&A==T[A]|6<<27<rand()|||!C&!Z?J[T[E]=T[A]]=E,J[T[A]=A-
Z]=A,"_.":" |"];}
```

"The only issue that remains to be considered is aesthetics. While the above code nicely emphasizes the minimality of the code, it's not particularly pleasing to the eye. We could do with a better layout.

"After some thinking, an ingenious idea struck me. The layout of the code should resemble a maze. Not just any maze, but one whose very structure contains yet another reference to mazes! I first started experimenting with layouts where the internal walls of the maze would spell the word MAZE, but I somehow failed to be satisfied. Then I tried the other possibility of having the corridors spell MAZE. Since this requires less internal wall structure, it allows for a much better impression of the four letters spelling MAZE.

"Below is the program in its final layout. Note how the two decrement operators suggest an entry and exit to the maze!

```
char*M,A,Z,E=40,J[40],T[40];main(C){for(*J=A=scanf(M="%d",&C);
--         E;           J[         E]        =T
[E   ]=  E)  printf("._");  for(;(A-=Z=!Z)  ||  (printf("\n|"
)   ,   A   =           39              ,C            --
)   ;   Z   ||    printf   (M    ))M[Z]=Z[A-(E   =A[J-Z])&&!C
&   A   ==              T[                          A]
|6<<27<rand()|||!C&!Z?J[T[E]=T[A]]=E,J[T[A]=A-Z]=A,"_.":" |"];}
```

"What's more, running the UNIX command "tr " -}" "0 "" (which substitutes 0's for blanks and changes everything else to blanks) exposes the hidden message:

```
0000000000000   000000000000000   0000000000000000   0000000000000000
  000   00   000                 00                00   00
0000 000 0000 000000000000000   0000000000000000   0000000000000000
0000 000 0000   0000         000   000                000
0000 000   0000000000000   000000000000000000000000000000000000
```

"Let me conclude with the observation that the number of references to MAZE in the program equals the letter count of this word. Namely:

- the variables spell MAZE,
- the program generates MAZEs,
- it has the layout of a MAZE,
- whose corridors spell MAZE."

## CHAPTER 9

Garbage In

This chapter discusses some common problems when reading input.

scanf

`scanf` does the opposite of `printf`. Well, sort of.

`scanf(format,arg1,arg2,...)` reads the standard input (typically, the keyboard) interpreting characters according to `format`. The results are stored in the locations pointed to by `arg1`, `arg2`, etc. `sscanf` is just like `scanf` except that it reads from the string given as its first argument rather than the standard input. For example:

```
char name[20], first_word[20];
int age;
double iq;
char string[] = "Don 10 4.5 foobar"

sscanf(string,"%s %d %lf %s", name, &age, &iq, first_word);
```

assigns the string `Don` to `name`, 21 to `age`, 4.5 to `iq`, and `foobar` to `first_word`. Like `printf`, there are three different variations of `scanf`. Besides `scanf` and `sscanf`, there is `fscanf`, which reads from a stream specified by its first argument.

One of the big differences between `scanf` and `printf` is that arguments to `scanf` must be *pointers* to storage. Look back to the example and you will see `&age` rather than `age`. If you think about it, you will realize this is necessary. In order to have a subroutine store anything into `age`, its address must be passed. Since array names are automatically converted to pointers, they need no `&`.

The most common error using `scanf` is to forget the `&`. Typically, an uninitialized integer is used as a pointer, resulting in an address fault. In an unprotected operating system such as MS-DOS, a random area of memory will be destroyed.

```
int integer;

scanf("%d",integer);       /* WRONG - need & */
```

The second most common error is a format type mismatch. Because pointers are passed, there is no automatic argument "widening," so there is a real distinction between `char`, `short`, and `int`, or between `float` and `double`.

`scanf` is also confusing because it *only reads until the format is satisfied*. Interactively, this can lead to problems such as:

```
for (i=0;i<MAX;i++) {
    printf("enter number %d: ",i);
    scanf("%d",&number[i]);
}
```

If the user presses return without entering a number, perhaps expecting help or to be prompted again, `scanf` will keep trying to read and not return, so the poor user gets no response. Or if more than an integer is entered, input past the integer will be read by a *later* `scanf`.

Changing the format to `"%d\n"` forces `scanf` to find the returns, however this causes a new problem. `scanf` treats returns equivalent to whitespace. *Whitespace* is defined as any number of spaces, tabs and returns (or newlines). Therefore, the user now has to type a return and the *next* integer (and return) in order to terminate the whitespace! This is ridiculous.

One solution is to follow every `scanf("%d"...)` by code (i.e., `gets`) to eat up the following newline. A better solution is to use `fgets`, and *then* parse the string using `sscanf` (after checking for an empty line). This way you get control back on an empty line and you always read whole lines. Do not assume that a newline terminates each buffer. In this way, you will correctly handle the line whether or not it is terminated with a newline (or was just too long).

Even if you are just reading the standard input, `fgets` is preferred to `gets`, because with `gets`, long input lines can overflow the user-supplied buffer. Also, don't forget to check the return value from `fgets`. If `NULL` is returned, the end of file was detected, and you should ignore anything in the buffer.

With old Standard I/O libraries, there is one drawback to using this approach over the original `scanf`. If `scanf` cannot interpret the input according to the format, it will leave the pointer where things stopped making sense. This is not possible with `fgets` and Classic `sscanf`. However, Standard C defines the `%n` format that places the number of characters scanned thus far into the integer pointed to by the corresponding argument. Thus, in Standard C implementations, it is possible to reparse data starting exactly from where the problem occurred.

Just for the record, none of these tips (or formatted I/O in general) works on binary data. If you need to read a binary file, you should be use `fread` and explicitly open the stream in binary mode. (On UNIX, text and binary streams are identical. On other systems, the Standard-C "b" mode flag for `fopen` is essential for binary streams. Alas, there is no portable way to access the three standard streams as binary.

Handling Arbitrarily Long Lines

But what if you don't know how long input lines can be? What if there are no limits on the length of the input, and yet you would like to be able to store each line in a buffer?

That is a common problem, and here is a subroutine that solves it. `big_fgets` is just like `fgets` except that it only takes one argument, a pointer to a `FILE`. `big_fgets` returns the address of `malloc`'d memory with the next line from the file. When you are done with it, don't forget to `free` it! Like `fgets`, `big_fgets` returns `NULL` upon end of file, and preserves newlines.

```c
#include <stdio.h>
#include "proto.h"   /* define malloc and friends */
#define GROW_BY 256

char *big_fgets(fp)
FILE *fp;
{
    int c;
    Size string_length = 0;        /* including NULL */
    Size buffer_length;
    char *buffer, *new;

    if (!(buffer = malloc(buffer_length = GROW_BY)))
            return(NULL);

    while (EOF != (c = getc(fp))) {
        buffer[string_length++] = c;
        /* if no more space in buffer for more */
        /* chars, increase the size of the buffer */
        if (string_length >= buffer_length) {
            buffer_length += GROW_BY;
            if (!(new = realloc(buffer,buffer_length))) {
                free((Generic)buffer);
                return(NULL);
            }
        }
        if (c == '\n') break;
    }
    /* check for EOF */
    if (string_length == 0) {
        free((Generic)buffer);
        return(NULL);
    }
    buffer[string_length++] = '\0';
    /* Now that we know what size the string is, */
    /* make do with a smaller buffer */
    new = realloc(buffer,buffer_length);
    return(new?new:buffer);
}
```

The basic idea of `big_fgets` is that string space is allocated from memory in multiples of `GROW_BY` bytes. If more space is needed, the old buffer is `realloc`'d by another `GROW_BY` bytes. Clearly, a careful choice of `GROW_BY` can be important in terms of efficiency.

Waiting for Input that May Never Come

The opposite problem of handling lines that are impossibly long is handling lines that are impossibly short. In other words, what happens if nothing is waiting to be read? Unless you make other arrangements, a request for input will not return until characters are available.

If you are reading from a keyboard, `fgets` will return upon encountering newlines no matter what length you specify. Almost all systems have a way of disabling this line buffering so that requests for input return as soon as any characters are available. However, it is still possible to wait forever if no characters have been entered.

There are no system-independent ways of solving this problem; however, by creating modular subroutines it is possible to be reasonably portable. In addressing this problem, the first issue is that there are several styles of checking for availability of input. Few systems implement all of them in their full generality.

Polled Input

Polling for input means that the program explicitly checks for input at certain times. It further implies that if no input is waiting, the program does something else rather than waiting for input to arrive.

BSD UNIX variants and many PC C compilers support an `ioctl` (`FIONREAD`) that allows one to check for the number of characters pending. In CP/M, there is a BIOS call (`CONST`) that tells you if characters are waiting. In DOS, there is a BIOS call that plays the same role. Many compilers provide special functions such as `kbhit` (Microsoft, Borland) that return true or false depending on whether a character is waiting. In each of these cases, the style of solution is to check whether characters are waiting before issuing the blocking `read`.

Alternatively, the behavior of `read` may be changed so that it does not block if no characters are waiting. UNIX System III, System V and modern BSD UNIX (4.2 or later) support non-blocking reads. In the case that no characters are waiting, read returns `-1`, while `errno` is set to `EWOULDBLOCK`. Non-blocking I/O is set up with `fcntl`. The parameters are typically system-dependent. Here is an example from 4.2 BSD:

```
fcntl(fd,F_SETFL,FNDELAY);
```

A more sophisticated technique, supported directly by fewer systems, is reading with timeouts. System III, System V, and BSD UNIX support this kind of I/O. If the indicated time passes without the `read` being satisfied, the `read` returns. Reading with timeouts of less than one second can be done via `ioctl` on System III and V and through `select` on BSD UNIX. Modern versions of UNIX System V also provide `poll`, which is analogous to `select`. Timeouts of greater than one second can be done portably between all UNIX systems with the following code:

```
1          signal(SIGALRM,alarm_handler);
           cc = -1;
3          if(setjmp(context)) {
4               errno = EINTR;
           } else {
6               alarm(5);        /* timeout after 5 seconds */
7               cc = read(fd,buffer,count);
8               alarm(0);        /* turn off alarm */
           }

    alarm_handler(sig)
    int sig;
    {
           ...
15         if (cc == -1) longjmp(context,1);
           else /* go back to setjmp and skip over read */
               return;

    }
```

Briefly, this code does the following:

- On line 1, `signal` registers a function to be called in the event of an "alarm clock" signal occurring.

- On line 3, `setjmp` "remembers" where we are and what we are doing so that we can jump back to this point later. The first time we are here, `setjmp` returns 0. In this case, `alarm(5)` (line 6) sets up an interrupt five seconds from now. This signal will interrupt the `read`, so that we can get control. In particular, the function registered at line 1 will be called when this happens.

- On line 7, `read` begins. If `read` returns normally, we go to line 8 and turn off the alarm. However, if five seconds go by and `read` has not completed, the alarm signal occurs and `alarm_handler` is called. `longjmp` (line 15) resets the stack to the way it looked at line 3 and we find ourselves returning from `setjmp`. What is returned is the second argument of `longjmp`. Since the second argument of `longjmp` is 1, we go to line 5 and set the appropriate variables to make it look as if `read` has completed abnormally.

- If `read` completes and the alarm goes off anyway (before we have a chance to turn it off), `cc` is changed so that `alarm_handler` is called but it just returns.

This is a good example of using `setjmp/longjmp` for a non-local `goto`. If you have never used these functions, let me point out the unusual side effect of `longjmp` to "unwind" the stack. In this case, it caused us to "forget" that we were executing a `read`. I will talk more about `setjmp/longjmp` and show other useful applications of them later (see p. 151 in Chapter 18).

Interrupt-Driven Input

Polling for input is often inconvenient. Polling can also be inefficient. For example, if you are monitoring dozens of devices that do I/O infrequently but have to be serviced quickly when input occurs, you are going to waste a lot of time checking for input. The potential exists to miss servicing a device because you are busy checking others. A better solution might be to generate an interrupt when characters arrive.

In BSD UNIX, this is done by calling `fcntl` to arm the device driver. When input arrives, a `SIGIO` signal is generated, starting a user-selected routine for catching such signals (set up with `signal`). Here is an example from 4.2 BSD:

```
void (*sigio_handler)();

signal(SIGIO,sigio_handler);
fcntl(fd,F_SETFL,FASYNC);
/* direct signals to this process */
fcntl(fd,F_SETOWN,SIGIO);
```

When using this approach, there is a real problem with what to do in the interrupt handler. Data shared with the application body must be properly interlocked, usually by temporarily blocking `SIGIO`, or data structures may become logically inconsistent due to being changed by the interrupt handler. Basically, this approach has all of the problems of concurrent programming without sufficient support for it. With *great care*, it can be made to work reliably. (See p. 335 in Chapter 35 for an example.)

In DOS or CP/M there are no system-independent primitives with which to request interrupt-driven I/O. Under DOS, it is possible to write a device driver or interrupt handler, although it will not necessarily be portable from one version of DOS to another.

As an example, consider DOS. Interrupt 9 of the BIOS is called on every keystroke. Thus, it is possible for the user to install a keyboard interrupt handler by placing its address in the appropriate interrupt table entry. Typically, your interrupt handler will want to pass on characters it is not interested in handling by calling the original keystroke interrupt handler. The program must also clean up after itself at termination by restoring any interrupt vector entries that have changed.

Note that interrupt handlers must terminate with an `IRET` (RETurn from Interrupt) rather than a `RET`. Since the C compiler will generate `RET`s, if you wish to write the interrupt handler in C, you must code a small piece of assembler to do an `IRET`. Of course, you can't call *it* because this will generate a return, also!

One solution is to write an assembler routine `c_interrupt` that decides whether to jump to the old interrupt handler, or the new C interrupt handler. If the C function is invoked, it returns to `c_interrupt` when it completes. `c_interrupt` then concludes with an `IRET`.

Conclusion

Rather than providing the volumes of information that this material deserves, I have attempted to touch all bases. I have discussed portable techniques for getting input, and have briefly mentioned a few nonportable tricks for avoiding non-blocking input from some archetypal operating systems. With what I have presented here, you should be able get input in many ways and have a good feeling for what other possibilities exist.

## CHAPTER 10

Keeping Track of Malloc

`malloc` and `free` provide a simple general-purpose memory allocation package. `malloc(size)` returns a pointer to a block of at least `size` bytes. When the user is finished with the block, `free(p)` returns the `malloc`'d storage pointed to by `p`.

`malloc` and friends are quite easy to use. They do have some pitfalls, however, and we'll look at one of them in this chapter, along with a solution.

The motivating problem with `malloc` is this: Once a user has `malloc`'d a piece of memory, it is the responsibility of the user to eventually return the memory (via `free`). If the user is finished with the memory, and "forgets" about the pointer (by overwriting it, perhaps) instead of calling `free`, garbage is created.

The reason this is known as *garbage* is that no one, not the user (through data structures) nor the system (through `malloc`), is responsible for this data. It is inaccessible for the remainder of the life of the current program.

Although garbage collectors (routines that comb through memory looking for garbage) have been written in C environments, their use is very specialized. C itself has no provision for garbage collection. The reason is because, in general, it is impossible to look at memory and tell whether you are looking at data, pointers, or garbage. It all looks the same.

Because of this, we must be very careful when allocating memory. In order to keep track of dynamically allocated storage, we typically have two alternatives.

- We must create a function that "knows" how to free our complex data structures, or
- We must keep track of dynamic allocations in such a way that we don't forget to `free` them when done.

Let us take an example structure that can be combined recursively to build up a tree.

```
struct node {
    struct node *left;
    struct node *right;
} *a, *b, *c, *d, e, *f;  /* Note: "e" is not a pointer */
```

Imagine now that we made the appropriate calls to `malloc` and the correct assignments so that we built a tree (below). Although the picture doesn't show it, you can assume that e and f point to other things, as well.

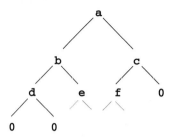

Now suppose we are finished with the tree, and we would like to `free` all the nodes in it. Since the tree has a very simple structure, it would be easy to create a function that simply freed nodes in a post-order traversal. (We will discuss later why it has to be post-order.)

However, notice that node `e` was statically allocated. It would be a mistake to `free` node `e` (since `free` is only valid for `malloc`'d data). Unless we add some information to the node structure as to whether it was allocated dynamically or statically, it will be impossible to decide whether to `free` the node or not.

Now this is a very simple tree, and it is easy to write a tree-walk function, but now suppose you have many different types of trees, linked lists, and other data structures. You must write a `free`-like function for each of these and you must change it when you change any of the tree data structures or construction functions.

The alternative is to allocate memory in such a way that a record is kept automatically of which nodes depend upon other nodes.

I have written an allocator that does exactly this. It can be used to allocate any data structure, and you do not have to modify your data structure. Like `malloc`, one call is used for allocations and one call for deallocations.

These routines are as simple to use as `malloc` and `free`, and further, are compiler- and machine-independent since they call `malloc` and `free` to do the real allocation and deallocation.

Key_malloc

The three user-callable functions in this package are defined by the header `key_malloc.h` below.

```
#ifndef KEYMALLOC_H
#define KEYMALLOC_H

#include "proto.h"   /* define PROTO, Generic, malloc, etc */

Generic key_malloc PROTO((Generic key, Size size));
struct km_link *key_free PROTO((Generic data_or_key));
void key_change PROTO((Generic key, Generic data));


#endif /* KEYMALLOC_H */
```

`key_malloc(key,size)` behaves like `malloc(size)` except that a key must be supplied. This key is used to group allocations together. The key may be any pointer.

In order to return `key_malloc`'d memory, the buffer pointer is passed to `key_free`. If this pointer is also a key, any memory `key_malloc`'d with that key is `key_free`'d.

For example:

```
a = (struct node *)key_malloc((Generic)0,SIZE);
a->left = (struct node *)key_malloc(a,SIZE);
a->right = (struct node *)key_malloc(a,SIZE);
a->left->left = (struct node *)key_malloc(a->left,SIZE);
a->left->right = (struct node *)key_malloc(a->left,SIZE);
a->right->left = (struct node *)key_malloc(a->right,SIZE);
a->right->right = NULL;
```

Here we are building up a tree with the root `a`. When we are finished with the tree, we return all storage with:

```
key_free(a);
```

Now we may begin to see the power and elegance of this approach.

Although I didn't mention it earlier, the definition of `key_free` implies that it recursively descends through the tree. Anything freed is in turn treated as a key to free further buffers. Because we built the tree in such a way that each node depends upon its parent node, the tree can be freed with a single call. Notice that **NULL** nodes will not be `key_free`'d because they were not `key_malloc`'d to begin with. And if you attach statically allocated nodes to the tree, they won't be freed either.

If we had created the tree with `malloc`, not only would we have to understand the exact structure of the tree, *and* know whether the nodes were dynamically or statically allocated, but we *must* free the tree in a post-order traversal.

Why Post-Order?

You must be careful not to free a node before freeing its children, because `malloc` does not guarantee that once data is freed, it is not overwritten. In particular, if we wanted to free a very small tree, `a`, with only a left and right node, the following code fragment (pre-order) is not portable:

```
/* INCORRECT */
free(a);
free(a->left);        /* reference to unknown data */
free(a->right);       /* reference to unknown data */
```

In-order traversal has similar problems. Instead, traversal must be post-ordered:

```
/* CORRECT */
free(a->left);
free(a->right);
free(a);
```

The problem with the first example is that `free(a)` relinquishes the memory that `a` points to and yet, in the next line, `a->left` refers to that memory. This is not portable. (It may work on some systems when the moon is in the right phase.)

`free` makes no guarantees that we can continue to reference freed storage. We might expect that the memory remains undisturbed until the next `malloc`, but this expectation is naive. Indeed, many implementations of `free` will modify memory returned to them immediately (typically using the first few bytes as a pointer to the next element in a linked list of unallocated buffers).

Looking back at `key_free`, we are assured by its definition (and looking in the source below) that when it deletes a node (say, `x`), any nodes that depend upon that node (`x`) will be deleted first. Thus:

```
key_free(a);
```

recursively frees (in the correct order) any `key_malloc`'d data that depends upon `a`.

Any storage that was `key_malloc`'d may be `key_free`'d explicitly at any time. Thus, it is possible to do partial `key_free`s, such as:

```
/* free right half of tree */
key_free(a->right);

/* build it back up again */
a->right = (struct node *)key_malloc(a,SIZE);
a->right->left = NULL;
a->right->right = NULL;

/* free entire tree */
key_free(a);
```

A function you may find helpful with `key_malloc` and `key_free` is `key_change`. `key_change(newkey,buffer)` allows a part of the tree to be saved from garbage collection by associating the named buffer with a new key. For example, if we create the tree `a`, as above, we may want to save the right branch but destroy the rest of the tree. We can do that as follows:

```
key_change((Generic)0,a->right);   /* or any other key */
key_free(a);
```

Because `a->right` is no longer keyed to `a`, neither it and nor its children will be deallocated when the rest of `a` is. Of course, we must save the value of `a->right` somewhere, or else we will not be able to access it ourselves!

New and Key_new

An aid to using `malloc` and `key_malloc` are the macros below:

```
#define new(type) ((type) *)malloc(sizeof(type))
#define key_new(key,type) \
            ((type) *)key_malloc(key,sizeof(type))
```

Calls to `malloc` such as:

```
nodeptr = (struct node *)malloc(sizeof(struct node));
nodeptr = (struct node *)
                key_malloc(key,sizeof(struct node));
```

can now be rewritten in a much simpler form:

```
nodeptr = new(struct node);
nodeptr = new_key(key,struct node);
```

This makes code much more readable, while making it less likely that you will use the wrong cast or forget the cast entirely. You can see this technique used in the code at the end of this chapter.

Extensions

Before concluding this chapter, I would like to mention an obvious extension. Create a function called, say, `key_end`. Upon being called, `key_end` will print out all buffers that have not been freed, which we can simplistically call "garbage." A nice implementation would print out not only their addresses but also their sizes, their contents (interpreted into printable form if necessary), and the line numbers where memory was allocated. This last piece of data could be gathered by setting up a macro such as:

```
#define key_malloc(key,size) key_malloc1(key,size,__LINE__)
```

where `key_malloc1` does the real work. (`__LINE__` is a symbol automatically defined for just this purpose.) This would be great for debugging!

Conclusion

I have presented several functions that allow the user to easily manage dynamically allocated memory. `key_malloc` and friends are oriented toward hierarchical structures (such as trees) where one is constantly building up structures and tearing them down again.

`key_malloc` runs on top of `malloc` and introduces both a small space and time overhead on top of what `malloc` already consumes. However, the effect of these functions is to relieve the programmer of writing many utility functions and keeping track of every `malloc`.

There are many opportunities for refinement in the ideas presented here. Generalized graphs can be supported with reference counts. Circular data structures typically require true garbage collection. Both of these are fascinating topics; their implementation and study can provide the programmer with tremendously powerful tools and knowledge.

Source Code—key_malloc.c

```c
#include <stdio.h>
#include "key_malloc.h"

/* The following km_link structure is used to build up a singly
linked list.  Each link in the list points to one malloc'd item as
well as the key it depends upon.  Thus, it is a simple operation
to scan during a key_free to find all the links and their data
that should be freed.
*/

static struct km_link {
     Generic data;  /* pointer to malloc'd memory for user */
     Generic key;   /* pointer to what it depends on */
     struct km_link *next;    /* next km_link */
} *first_km_link = 0;    /* initially empty list */

static struct km_link *delete_km_link();

#define new(type) (type *)malloc(sizeof(type))

Generic
key_malloc(key,size)      /* returns data or 0 if none left */
Generic key;
Size size;
{
     struct km_link *link;

     if (!(link = new(struct km_link))) return(0);
     if (!(link->data = malloc(size))) {
          free((Generic)link);
          return(0);
     }
     link->key = key;

     /* insert link into linked list of km_links in no */
     /* particular order.  Easiest is in front of list. */
     link->next = first_km_link;
     first_km_link = link;

     return(link->data);
}

void key_change(key,buffer)
Generic key;
Generic buffer;
{
     struct km_link *link;
```

```
    for (link = first_km_link;link;link=link->next) {
        if (link->data == buffer) {
            link->key = key;
            return;
        }
    }
    fprintf(stderr,"key_change: no buffer with that key\n");
}

struct km_link *
key_free(key)
Generic key;    /* may be both data and a key */
{
    struct km_link *link;
    struct km_link *next = 0;

    /* look for nodes dependent upon key */
    for (link=first_km_link;link;) {
        if (key != link->key) link = link->next;
        else link = key_free(link->data);
    }

    /* if key was also key_malloc'd, free it (and its link) */
    for (link=first_km_link;link;link=link->next) {
        if (key == link->data) {
            next = delete_km_link(link);/* remove from list */
            free(key);              /* free the (now) data */
            free((Generic)link);/* free link */
            break;
        }
    }
    return(next);
}

/* remove this link from the linked list of km links */
static struct km_link *  /* return next valid link */
delete_km_link(p)
struct km_link *p;
{
    struct km_link **link;

    for (link = &first_km_link;*link;link = &(*link)->next) {
        if (*link == p) { /* found it */
            return(*link = (*link)->next);
        }
    }
    /*NOTREACHED*/
}
```

## CHAPTER 11

Linked Lists of Anything

This chapter describes how to build reusable data structures. As an example, I'll use linked lists but the general idea can be applied to any type.

Everyone has written linked list structures. What they all have in common is some data in a structure with a "next" element that points to another structure of the same type. Here is an example:

```
struct foo {
    int an_int;
    struct foo *next;
};
```

Building lists is now just a matter of arranging a pointer or two. However, if you want to access, say, the fifth element on the list, or free the whole list, or add to the end instead of the beginning, you're going to write a function to do it rather than just in-line code.

It certainly would be nice to write such functions only once. One solution is to make every **struct** that could potentially be part of a linked list have **next** as the first element. This is not portable, but it works on some systems and is popular because of its convenience.

I'm going to describe routines that allow you to build linked lists of any type of data in a completely portable way. You'll never have to write a linked list function again. And you'll be able to apply this technique to other abstract data structures.

The trick is to separate the data from the structure. It is possible to describe a generic link as follows:

```
#include "proto.h"        /* define Generic */

struct link {
    struct link *next;
    Generic data;
};
```

Any data pointer can be cast to **Generic**. Thus we can assign addresses of our data to the **data** element of a link. Compare this with the traditional implementation I described earlier. In that, the link is inside the application's data structure. In this new approach, the situation is reversed—the application's data structure is inside the link. Now it is possible to write generic functions to manipulate the links.

Since the whole idea of this is to avoid ever writing linked list code again, I'm going to describe a linked list that will be better than the one I just proposed. For one thing, many algorithms require doubly-linked lists, so we will build that in at the start. A link will be defined as follows:

```
typedef struct Link {
     struct Link *next;
     struct Link *prev;
     Generic data;
} Link;
```

Another idea that will impact the definition is how the linked list function will be called. In order to add links to a list, we could say:

```
list = link_add(list,foo);
```

This would create a new link with **foo** stored as the data and append it to the list. This function returns the same list that was passed in as an argument. Why does the function return a known value? Unfortunately, we're forced into returning the list in order to handle the case of the empty list. When the list is empty, the first parameter will be **NULL**, and we really do need to be told the address of the first link.

A macro could cover this up. Alternatively, passing the address of the beginning of the list would allow it to be reassigned as well. I'm going to use yet another approach, shown to me by Steve Clark of the National Institute of Standards and Technology[1]. Steve solved the problem by defining a *list header*. This header exists even if the list is empty. It is defined as follows:

```
typedef struct {
     Link *head;
} Linked_list;
```

All this **struct** does is point to a list (or **NULL** if the list is empty). This solves the earlier problem. Another benefit is that it also allows multiple variables to point to the same list. Without a header of some kind, if the first link was deleted, all the other variables would no longer point to the list. Instead, they would be pointing to a freed link.

We can now write a function to add elements to the beginning of the list:

```
LISTadd_first(list,data)
Linked_list *list;
Generic data;
{
     Link *link = LINK_new();
     link->data = data;
     if (list->head == 0) {
```

---

1. I wrote **LISTget_nth** and **LISTfree**. Steve wrote all the other functions and macros appearing here.

```
            list->head = link;
            list->head->next = list->head->prev = list->head;
    } else {
            link->next = list->head;
            link->prev = list->head->prev;
            link->prev->next = link;
            list->head->prev = link;
    }
}
```

If the list only contains one element, the sole link's **next** and **prev** pointers point back to the link. The next time around, **next** and **prev** are easily adjusted.

LINK_new allocates a new **Link**. It can call **malloc**, or even better, use the fast allocator I describe later (p. 261 in Chapter 29). **LIST_new** is an analogous function to create a **Linked_list**. **LINK_destroy** and **LIST_destroy** are corresponding functions that free **Link**s and **Linked_list**s respectively.

It is possible to avoid the test for **list->head == 0** by creating the list with a dummy link. Below is the creation code and the revised addition function. Note that **LIST_new** allocates space for a new list header, but **LISTcreate** sets up all the pointers and is actually what the user calls.

```
Linked_list *
LISTcreate()
{
        Linked_list *list = LIST_new();
        list->head = LINK_new();
        list->head->next = list->head->prev = list->head;
        return(list);
}


Generic
LISTadd_first(list,data)
Linked_list *list;
Generic data;
{
        Link *link = LINK_new();
        link->data = data;
        (link->next = list->head->next)->prev = link;
        (list->head->next = link)->prev = list->head;
        return data;
}
```

In this version of **LISTadd_first**, the new link is added after the head, instead of replacing it. The actual code is smaller since no test is necessary for the 0 case. The corresponding code to remove an element (shown later) is similarly simpler.

Code to free the list is tricky. It skips over **head** and frees the remaining links in order, stopping before the last. If it didn't stop before the last, the increment part of the **for** would cause **head->next** to be accessed after being freed. This can cause a fault on some implementations. `head` is skipped the first time around for the same reason. We need to use its address in order to determine when we have gone through the whole list.

```
void
LISTfree(list)
Linked_list *list;
{
     Link *p, *q = list->head->next;

     for (p = q->next; p != list->head; q = p, p = p->next) {
         LINK_destroy(q);
     }
     if (q != list->head) LINK_destroy(q);
     LINK_destroy(list->head);
     LIST_destroy(list);
}
```

When using lists, it is very common to perform a function on each member of the list by iterating through them. Another of Steve's ideas was to write a macro to make this easier. For example, to print a linked list of strings, you could write:

```
LISTdo(string_list,s,char *)
     int i = 0;
     printf("string %d is %s\n",i++,s);
LISTod
```

`LISTdo` declares a variable named by the second parameter with the type of the third parameter. Statements between `LISTdo` and `LISTod` are executed with the variable equal to the data portion of each link. Here is the implementation of `LISTdo` and `LISTod`.

```
#define LISTdo(list,elt,type) {                              \
  struct Linked_list *LIST = (list);                         \
  type elt;                                                  \
  Link *LINK;                                                \
  for (LINK = LIST->head; (LINK = LINK->next) != LIST->head;) { \
      (elt) = (type)(LINK->data); {

#define LISTod }}}
```

The macros create a block in which to declare the user-requested variable (`s`, in the example). A `for` iterates through the list, assigning the data portion of each link to the variable.

The declarations bear explaining. `LIST` is a temporary declared to hold a pointer to the list. This prevents any repeated side-effects that evaluation of `list` itself may cause. A final brace at the end of `LISTdo` defines a new block, allowing, for example, the user to declare new variables. This convenience requires that the macro take pains not to collide with the user's variables. `LINK` and `LIST` were chosen with the presumption that anything beginning with these names is reserved to this linked list implementation.

It is often useful to have access to the links themselves on each iteration. The macro `LISTdo_links` provides this. It uses the same `LISTod` macro to terminate the body. (This requires an extra opening brace at the end of the `LISTdo_links` macro.)

```
#define LISTdo_links(list,link) {                      \
  Linked_list *LIST = (list);                          \
  Link *link;                                          \
  for ((link) = LIST->head;                            \
        ((link) = (link)->next) != LIST->head; ) {{
```

For example, if we wanted to replace each string with a different one, we could say:

```
LISTdo_links(string_list,link)
    free((char *)link->data);
    link->data = (char *)another_string;
LISTod
```

Notice that `LISTdo_links` requires you to take responsibility for using the correct types. Indeed, you can reassign `link->data` with an entirely different pointer type if you want. This can be extremely useful, although it makes debugging difficult!

In contrast, `LISTdo` does the typechecking for you—at least to an extent. It cannot know whether `list->data` really points to the type that you say it does, but `LISTdo` will tell you if you try to assign the result to a variable of a different pointer type.

If your lists contain data of a single type, you can create macros that customize all the list functions so that all list accesses are typechecked. For example, if you are creating a list of pointers to `struct foo`, you could say:

```
#define FOO_LISTadd_first(list,foo) \
         LISTadd_first(list,(Generic)(struct foo *)foo)
```

The compiler would then complain if you tried to add to `FOO_LISTadd_first` something that was not a `struct foo` pointer. The `Generic` cast silences Classic C-style `lint`s and is not otherwise necessary.

Steve defined a number of other useful functions, a few of which follow. For the most part, what they do is obvious from their name. `LISTget_nth` returns the *n*th element of a list (`n==0` refers to the first element). `LISTadd_after` and `LISTremove` both take a `Link *` argument. `LISTadd_after` adds a new link after the named link while `LISTremove` removes the named link. The implementation of `LISTremove` does not need access to the list header itself. However, for consistency, it is supplied. The comment `/*ARGSUSED*/` is used to tell `lint` to ignore the fact that the parameter is not used.

A Caveat

Standard C does not guarantee that function pointers can be stored in objects of type
`Generic`. I avoided this issue only by my earlier statement that the technique
described in this chapter works for any *data* pointers. It is possible to remedy this
by making `Link` contain a `union` of a `Generic` and a function pointer, along with
some slight coding changes. But the high price you pay is likely not worth it, since
some environments have function pointers that are significantly larger than data
pointers. In this one case, you are better off having separate linked-list functions.

```c
Generic
LISTadd_last(list,data)
Linked_list *list;
Generic data;
{
    Link *link = LINK_new();
    link->data = data;
    (link->prev = list->head->prev)->next = link;
    (list->head->prev = link)->next = list->head;
    return data;
}


Generic
LISTremove_first(list)
Linked_list *list;
{
    Generic data;
    Link *link = list->head->next;
    if (link == list->head) {
        fprintf(stderr,"empty list: can't remove element\n");
        return NULL;
    }
    data = link->data;
    (list->head->next = link->next)->prev = list->head;
    LINK_destroy(link);
    return data;
}


/*ARGSUSED*/
void
LISTremove(list,link)
Linked_list *list;
Link *link;
{
    Generic data;

    link->next->prev = link->prev;
    link->prev->next = link->next;
    data = link->data;
    LINK_destroy(link);
```

```
}

Generic
LISTget_nth(list,n)
Linked_list *list;
int n;               /* first is 0 */
{
     int count = 0;
     Link *link = list->head->next;

     for (;link != list->head;link = link->next) {
          if (n == count++) return(link->data);
     }
     fprintf(stderr,"list element %d does not exist\n",n);
     return NULL;
}

Generic
LISTadd_after(list,link,data)
Linked_list *list;
Link *link;
Generic data;
{
     Link *link2;

     if (link == 0) LISTadd_first(list, data);
     else {
          link2 = LINK_new();
          link2->data = data;
          (link2->next = link->next)->prev = link2;
          (link->next = link2)->prev = link;
     }
     return data;
}
```

12

The 1986 Obfuscated C Code Contest

The 1986 Obfuscated C Code winners are even better (or maybe I mean "worse") than 1985's! Thanks go to Larry Bassel who volunteered to be a judge for this and succeeding years.

Earlier, I described how obfuscated C was good for testing compilers and educating ourselves about the dark corners of the language. I suppose there are some people who will believe that.

In fact, obfuscated C has received a good deal of attention for legitimate reasons. Specifically, obfuscated C has become an accepted means of distributing commercial source code with little risk of having a customer modify the code and/or resell it. The immediate benefit to selling obfuscated code is that vendors do not have to produce machine or operating system-dependent versions for hundreds of different computers. Instead, they supply a single source to clients, who compile the software themselves on their own platforms.

This kind of obfuscation is invariably done by an automated program. Indeed, for many years Gimpel Software has been selling "C Shroud," which automatically obfuscates a program. The result of shrouding is very effective—it renames every variable, removes all symbol constants, and plays lots of other games with the source. The result is quite impenetrable. (Some people claim that simply using C is a sufficient obfuscation tool.) A public-domain obfuscator called `opqcp` (for "opaque C processor") can be retrieved from any archive of the Usenet newsgroup `comp.sources.unix`.

One use for even partially obfuscated code is to establish program authorship. When a software house tried to sue a programmer for stealing their ideas, the programmer was able to show that the software house had actually stolen the code originally. Only the programmer was able to explain the coding style, including why seemingly meaningless variables had been named the way they were.

Now that I've justified this chapter, let's get on with it. The envelope please …

Best Layout

Eric Marshall
System Development Corporation, a Burroughs Company
Paoli, Pennsylvania

```
                                                          extern int
                                                            errno
                                                            ;char
                                                             grrr
                                           ;main(             r,
  argv, argc )                int     argc                      ,
    r        ;               char *argv[];{int                 P( );
#define x   int i,           j,cc[4];printf("     choo choo\n"  ) ;
x  ;if    (P(  !             i,                )  |  cc[  !      j ]
&  P(j     )>2  ?           j              :     i  ){*  argv[i++ +!-i]
;              for    (i=          0;;    i++                    );
_exit(argv[argc- 2    / cc[1*argc]|-1<<4 ]     ) ;printf("%d",P(""));}}
   P  (    a  )   char a   ;  {    a ;   while(    a  >     " B  "
   /* -    by E         ricM   arsh           all-      */);     }
```

Analysis

While amusing to look at, this program does nothing but print choo choo, and even
that is not hard to find. The rest of it is just filler that does nothing except give the
author something to draw his picture with. (Check out the odd arguments to main!)

Worst Abuse of the C Preprocessor

Jim Hague
University of Kent at Canterbury

```
#define DIT          (
#define DAH          )
#define _DAH         ++
#define DITDAH       *
#define DAHDIT       for
#define DIT_DAH      malloc
#define DAH_DIT      gets
#define _DAHDIT      char
_DAHDIT _DAH_[]=
     "ETIANMSURWDKGOHVFaLaPJBXCYZQb54a3c2g16g7c8a90l?e'b.s;i,d:"
;main                DIT                 DAH{_DAHDIT
DITDAH               _DIT,DITDAH         DAH_,DITDAH DIT_,
DITDAH               _DIT_,DITDAH        DIT_DAH DIT
DAH,DITDAH           DAH_DIT DIT         DAH;DAHDIT
DIT _DIT=DIT_DAH     DIT 81              DAH,DIT_=_DIT
__DAH;_DIT==DAH_DIT  DIT _DIT            DAH;__DIT
DIT'\n'DAH DAH       DAHDIT DIT          DAH_=_DIT;DITDAH
```

```
DAH_;__DIT          DIT                 DITDAH
_DIT_?_DAH DIT      DITDAH              DIT_ DAH:'?'DAH,__DIT
DIT' 'DAH,DAH_ __DAHDAH DAHDIT          DIT
DITDAH              DIT_=2,_DIT_=_DAH_; DITDAH _DIT_&&DIT
DITDAH _DIT_!=DIT   DITDAH DAH_>='a'?   DITDAH
DAH_&223:DITDAH     DAH_ DAH DAH;       DIT
DITDAH              DIT_ DAH __DAH,_DIT___DAH DAH
DITDAH DIT_+=       DIT DITDAH _DIT_>='a'? DITDAH _DIT_-'a':0
DAH;}_DAH DIT DIT_  DAH{                __DIT DIT
DIT_>3?_DAH         DIT                 DIT_>>1 DAH:'\0'DAH;return
DIT_&1?'-':'.';}__DIT DIT              DIT_ DAH _DAHDIT
DIT_;{DIT void DAH write DIT            1,&DIT_,1 DAH;}
```

A classic self-documenting program, it should be obvious what this does although, perhaps, not how it works. As an example, if you feed it the string "obfuscate", it prints out:

```
--- -... ..-. ..- ... -.-. .- - .
```

Analysis

After deciphering the macros, I found this to be an obscure table-lookup function. Of course, the table is stored in the **ETIAN...** string at the top of the function.

The actual string is rather clever. The author took advantage of the binary appearance of Morse code. Specifically, he encoded each letter in the position dictated by using its Morse code equivalent as a binary number.

For example, the letter **r** appears as ".-." in code. Assigning "." the value 0 and "–" the value 1 generates the binary string 010. Prefixing each string with a 1 preserves leading zeros that would otherwise be lost upon conversion to a number. After conversion, 2 is subtracted to account for the bias of forcing a 1 on every value. In the case of **r**, the binary string 1010 equals 10. Subtracting 2 leaves 8, so the letter **r** is placed in the eighth position of the table. Here is the function from the unobfuscated code that performs the decoding:

```
decode(i)
{
    putchar (i > 3 ? func (i >> 1) : '\0');
    return i & 1 ? '-' : '.';
}
```

This also explains why the letters with shorter Morse code representations appear at the beginning of the table, and longer ones appear at the end.

Best One-Liner

Jan Stein <jan@math.chalmers.se>
Chalmers Computer Society
Gothenburg, Sweden

```
typedef char*z;O;o;_=33303285;main(b,Z)z Z;{b=(b>=0||(main(b+1,Z+
1),*Z=O%(o=(_%25))+'0',O/=o,_/=25))&&(b<1||(O=time(&b)%0250600,
main(~5,*(z*)Z),write(1,*(z*)Z,9)));}
```

This odd little program prints out the time as a six-digit string. Because of its cryptic formatting, it took me a while to even figure out *what* it was doing, never mind *how* it was doing it!

Analysis

The program recursively calls itself six times, each time calculating one digit to be printed. `argc` (here called `b`) is initially set to ~5 (i.e., –6 on a 2's-complement machine) and uses that as a counter, incrementing until 0 is reached. There are several different paths through the code, depending upon `b`.

The first time through, the function `time` is called to retrieve the number of seconds in the date. The magic 0250600 is exactly 60*60*24. Using this as a modulus results in the number of seconds into the current day (ignoring leap seconds).

The other interesting part is the following fragment.

```
_=33303285;
*Z=O%(o=(_%25))+'0',O/=o,_/=25;
```

Using 25 as a base, the author encoded just the right factors (3, 10, 6, 10, 6, and 10) to divide and modulo through the number of seconds. Iterating six times gives all the digits in the time. Each invocation of `main` offsets `z` by one position so that each new character is next to the previous one. When the last invocation returns, the entire string is printed out.

Most Adaptable Program

Jack Applin <neutron@hpfcls.fc.hp.com>
Hewlett-Packard
Ft. Collins, Colorado

```
cat =13 /*/ >/dev/null 2>&1; echo "Hello, world!"; exit
*
*  This program works under cc, f77, and /bin/sh.
*
*/; main() {
      write(
cat-~-cat
     /*,'(
*/
     ,"Hello, world!"
, cat); putchar(~-~-~-cat); } /*
    ,)')
      end
*/
```

As the program says, this can be interpreted as a C program, Fortran program, or shell script. This is achieved primarily by taking advantage of the different quoting and commenting conventions (and assuming a twos-complement machine).

After removing the comments, the C program looks like this:

```
cat =13

; main() {
        write(
cat-~-cat
    ,"Hello, world!"
, cat); putchar(~-~-~-cat); }
```

This writes "`Hello, world!`" to file descriptor 1 (standard output on a UNIX system). The final statement (`putchar`) writes a newline by very cleverly converting a 13 to a 10 (ASCII newline) by a series of alternating mathematical and bitwise conversions that subtract 1 with every `~-` pair.

The Fortran program is:

```
write(*,'("Hello, world!")')
end
```

By itself this isn't very interesting. It is just the Fortran version of the "Hello world" program. The amusing part is how we get here.

A `c` or `*` as the first character on a line marks the entire line as a comment. This allows about half the lines to be discarded (and also explains the strange formatting). Some characters that were necessary to the C program but unnecessary here are discarded by placing them in column six. Any character in column six is used to indicate that the rest of the line should be joined to the previous line. This character is discarded. (The actual rules are slightly more complex, but this is the idea.)

The shell script is simpler yet. Most of the script isn't even read because of the `exit` at the end of the first line. The semicolons separate the first line into three statements that are executed sequentially. When the third line is executed, the script terminates. What's left?

The first statement (`cat =13 /*/ >/dev/null 2>&1`) calls the `cat` program, which prints the contents of the named files. The chances of having a file named `=13` are unlikely, but the rest of the statement makes sure that any possible output and errors are never seen by redirecting them to the null device. Before stopping at the third statement, the second statement (`echo "Hello world!"`) calls the echo program to output:

```
Hello, world!
```

Most Useful Obfuscation

Walter Bright <bright@nazgul.UUCP>
Zortech
Seattle, Washington

```c
#include <stdio.h>
#define O1O printf
#define O1O putchar
#define O1O exit
#define O1O strlen
#define QLQ fopen
#define O1Q fgetc
#define O1Q abs
#define QOO for
typedef char 1OL;

1OL*QI[] = {"Use:\012\011dump file\012",
          "Unable to open file '\x25s'\012",  "\012","    ",""};

main(I,I1)
1OL*I1[];
{    FILE *L;
     unsigned 1O;
     int Q,OL[' '^'0'],11O = EOF,

     O=1,1=0,111=O+O+O+1,OQ=056;
     1OL*11L="%2x ";
     (I != 1<<1&&(O1O(QI[0]),O1O(1011-1010))),
     ((L = QLQ(I1[O],"r"))==0&&(O1O(QI[O],I1[O]),O1O(O)));
     1O = I-(O<<1<<O);
     while (L-1,1)
     {    QOO(Q = OL;((Q &~(0x1O-O))== 1);
               OL[Q++] = O1Q(L));
          if (OL[0]==11O) break;
          O1O("\0454x: ",1O);
          if (I == (1<<1))
          {    QOO(Q=O1O(QI[O<<O<<1]);Q<O1O(QI[0]);
               Q++)O1O((OL[Q]!=11O)?11L:QI[111],OL[Q]);/*"
               O1O(QI[1O])*/
               O1O(QI[111]);{}
          }
          QOO (Q=OL;Q<1<<1<<1<<1;Q+=Q<0100)
          {    (OL[Q]!=11O)? /* 0010 1010Q 000LQL */
               ((D(OL[Q])==0&&(*(OL+O1Q(Q-1))=OQ)),
               O1O(OL[Q])):
               O1O(1<<(1<<1<<1)<<1);
          }
          O1O(QI[01^10^9]);
          1O+=Q+O+1;}
```

```
    }
    D(l) { return l>=' '&&l<='\~';
}
```

Given a file, this program prints out a hex and ASCII dump. While not the most thrilling program, it makes up for it by being extremely useful. In fact, after I figured it out, I wrote a set of subroutines around it and spent an entire chapter describing it! The deobfuscation of the code is actually quite easy, so I'll omit that here and refer you to Chapter 19 (p. 157) for the whole story.

Now don't say you didn't get anything useful out of this contest!

Best Simple Task Performed in a Complex Way

Bruce Holloway
Digital Research
Monterey, California

```
#include <stdio.h>
#define e 3
#define g (e/e)
#define h ((g+e)/2)
#define f (e-g-h)
#define j (e*e-g)
#define k (j-h)
#define l(x) tab2[x]/h
#define m(n,a) ((n&(a))==(a))

long tab1[]={ 989L,5L,26L,0L,88319L,123L,0L,9367L };
int tab2[]={ 4,6,10,14,22,26,34,38,46,58,62,74,82,86 };

main(m1,s) char *s; {
    int a,b,c,d,o[k],n=(int)s;
    if(m1==1){ char b[2*j+f-g]; main(l(h+e)+h+e,b); printf(b); }
    else switch(m1-=h){
        case f:
            a=(b=(c=(d=g)<<g)<<g)<<g;
            return(m(n,a|c)|m(n,b)|m(n,a|d)|m(n,c|d));
        case h:
            for(a=f;a<j;++a)if(tab1[a]&&!(tab1[a]%((long)l(n))))
                                                    return(a);
        case g:
            if(n<h)return(g);
            if(n<j){n-=g;c='D';o[f]=h;o[g]=f;}
            else{c='\r'-'\b';n-=j-g;o[f]=o[g]=g;}
            if((b=n)>=e)for(b=g<<g;b<n;++b)o[b]=o[b-h]+o[b-g]+c;
            return(o[b-g]%n+k-h);
        default:
            if(m1-=e) main(m1-g+e+h,s+g); else *(s+g)=f;
```

```
            for(*s=a=f;a<e;)  *s=(*s<<e)|main(h+a++,(char *)m1);
    }
}
```

When run, this prints out "`hello world!`" However, it will never be used in a C textbook. It is just incredibly weird.

Analysis

The textual obfuscation is straightforward and easily cleaned up by hand. This exposes the real problem—the algorithm. In fact, there are several algorithms working simultaneously to generate the desired characters in the `hello` string—all quite obscure.

The program as a whole is structured in a few different paths of logic, the most mystifying appearing in a large `switch` (viewable even in the obfuscated form).

The program recurses a couple of dozen times (just to warm up, I suppose) before doing anything useful. It then proceeds to generate each character in the message by bringing together bits from three different algorithms.

The high- and low-order bits of each character are generated by divisibility testing, while the middle three bits come out of some specially handcrafted logic just for this sequence of letters. To give you an example, the high-order bits are arrived at with the following code:

```
case 2:
    for (a = 0; a < 8; ++a)
        if (tab1[a] && !(tab1[a] % tab2[n]))
            return (a);
```

Table 2 is a table of primes (despite the way it looks in the program) and table 1 is composed of numbers chosen so that when we're looking for, say, the third letter in the string, the first number that is divisible by the third prime will have as its index (i.e., where it was found in table 1) the very bits of the letter currently being generated.

Best Complex Task Done in a Complex Way

Lennart Augustsson <augustss@cs.chalmers.se>
Department of Computer Science
Chalmers University of Technology
Gothenburg, Sweden

```
typedef struct n{int a:3,
b:29;struct n*c;}t;t*
f();r(){}m(u)t*u;{t*w,*z;
z=u->c,q(z),u->b=z->b*10,
w=u->c=f(),w->a=1,w->c=z->
c;}t*k;g(u)t*u;{t*z,*v,*p,
*x;z=u->c,q(z),u->b=z->b,v
```

```
=z->c,z->a=2,x=z->c=f(),x
->a=3,x->b=2,p=x->c=f(),p
->c=f(),p->c->a=1,p->c->c=
v;}int i;h(u)t*u;{t*z,*v,*
w;int c,e;z=u->c,v=z->c,q(
v),c=u->b,e=v->b,u->b=z->b
,z->a=3,z->b=c+1,e+9>=c&&(
q(z),e=z->b,u->b+=e/c,w=f(
),w->b=e%c,w->c=z->c,u->c=
w);}int (*y[4])()={r,m,g,h};
char *sbrk();main(){t*e,*p,*o;
o=f(),o->c=o,o->b=1,e=f(),
e->a=2,p=e->c=f(),p->b=2,
p->c=o,q(e),e=e->c,(void)write
(1,"2.",2);for(;;e=e->c){q(e),
e->b=write(1,&e->b["0123456789"],
1);}}t*f(){return i||(i=1000,
k=(t*)sbrk(i*sizeof(t))),k+--i;
}q(p)t*p;{(*y[p->a])(p);}
```

This program arrived with the instruction: "Works best with an infinite amount of stack space." This is what the output looked like when I ran it:

```
2.7182818284590452353602874713526624977572470936999595749669
6762772407663035354759457138217852516642742746639193200305992
1817413596629043572900334295260595630738132328627943490763233
82988075319525101901157383418793070215408914993488416750927
< . . . and on and on, until some time later . . . >
7741185374234544243710753907774499206955170276183860626133138
4583000752044933826560297606737113200709328709127443747047230
696
Segmentation fault (core dumped)
```

Author's Analysis

"I started with a program written in a lazy functional language (LML). (Notation: "." is *infix cons* on lists.)

```
let rec ones = 1.ones
and  convert (d.x) = (d.convert (normalise 2 (0.mult x))
            where mult x = map (\y.y*10) x)
and  normalise c (d.e.x) = (if e+9<c
                then d.normalise (c+1) (e.x)
                else carry c (d.normalise (c+1) (e.x))
            where carry c (d.e.x) = d+e/c . e%c . x)
in let e = convert (2.ones)
in   e
```

"This was a rewrite of a Miranda (or maybe SASL) program written by David Turner. I don't think he invented the algorithm. The idea is that you can write e as 2.11111111 . . . if you imagine the base of the number changing with each digit (0.1

is in base 2, 0.01 is in base 3—i.e., a third of the previous digit—etc.). Then you do an ordinary base conversion to base 10, except that you have to change the base all the time. The only remaining problem is when to stop looking down the list of digits.

"Choosing a nontrivial algorithm was the first step of the obfuscation. The second step was to code this nicely in a non-imperative language. The third step was to do a faithful translation of this program into C. This is not entirely trivial, as the original program uses lazy lists heavily. But here it is:

```
#include <stdio.h>
/*
letrec  mul10 (a.b) = a*10 . mul10 b
and   ones = 1.ones
and   convert (d.x) = d.convert (normalise 2 (0.mul10 x))
and   normalise c (d.e.x) = (e+9<c => d.normalise (c+1) (e.x)
                               :  carry c (d.normalise (c+1) (e.x))
                      where carry c (d.e.x) = d+e/c . e%c . x)
in let e = convert (2.ones)
in    e
*/


struct node {
     enum { tcons, tap, tint, tfun } tag;
     union {
          struct {
               struct node *Uhd, *Utl;
#define hd U.uc.Uhd
#define tl U.uc.Utl
          } uc;
          struct {
               struct node *Ufun, *Uarg;
#define fun U.ua.Ufun
#define arg U.ua.Uarg
          } ua;
          struct {
               int Uint;
          } ui;
#define num U.ui.Uint
     struct {
          int (*Ufunc)();
#define func U.uf.Ufunc
     } uf;
     } U;
};

struct node *ones, *zero, *one, *two; struct node *fm10, *fmul10,
*fconvert, *fcarry, *fnormalise;

#define NEW() ((struct node *)malloc(sizeof (struct node)))
```

```
m10(u, av)
struct node *u, *av[];
{
      struct node *ct;

      eval(av[0]);
      ct = NEW(); ct->tag = tint;
      ct->num = 10*av[0]->num;
      *u = *ct;
}

/* mul10 (a.b) = a*10 . mul10 b */
mul10(u, av)
struct node *u, *av[];
{
      struct node *ct, *ht, *tt;

      eval(av[0]);
      ct = NEW(); ct->tag = tcons;
      ht = ct->hd = NEW(); ht->tag = tap;
      ht->fun = fm10;
      ht->arg = av[0]->hd;
      tt = ct->tl = NEW(); tt->tag = tap;
      tt->fun = fmul10;
      tt->arg = av[0]->tl;
      *u = *ct;
}

/*    convert (d.x) = d.convert (normalise 2 (0.mul10 x)) */
convert(u, av) struct node *u, *av[];
{
      struct node *ct, *tt, *p, *xt;

      eval(av[0]);
      ct = NEW(); ct->tag = tcons;
      ct->hd = av[0]->hd;
      tt = ct->tl = NEW(); tt->tag = tap;
      tt->fun = fconvert;
      xt = tt->arg = NEW(); xt->tag = tap;
      p = xt->fun = NEW(); p->tag = tap;
      p->fun = fnormalise;
      p->arg = two;
      p = xt->arg = NEW(); p->tag = tcons;
      p->hd = zero;
      p->tl = NEW(); p->tl->tag = tap;
      p->tl->fun = fmul10;
      p->tl->arg = av[0]->tl;
      *u = *ct;
}
```

```
/* carry c (d.e.x) = d+e/c . e%c . x */
carry(u, av) struct node *u, *av[];
{
    struct node *ct, *tt, *p;
    int c, e;

    eval(av[0]);
    eval(av[1]);
    eval(av[0]->hd);
    eval(av[0]->tl);
    eval(av[0]->tl->hd);
    ct = NEW(); ct->tag = tcons;
    p = ct->hd = NEW(); p->tag = tint;
    c = av[1]->num;
    e = av[0]->tl->hd->num;
    p->num = av[0]->hd->num + e/c;
    tt = ct->tl = NEW(); p->tag = tcons;
    p = tt->hd = NEW(); p->tag = tint;
    p->num = e%c;
    tt->tl = av[0]->tl->tl;
    *u = *ct;
}


/*    normalise c (d.e.x) = (e+9<c => d.normalise (c+1) (e.x)
                       :  carry c (d.normalise (c+1) (e.x)) */
normalise(u, av)
struct node *u, *av[];
{
    struct node *ct, *tt, *xt, *p;
    int c, e;

    eval(av[0]);
    eval(av[1]);
    eval(av[0]->tl);
    eval(av[0]->tl->hd);
    c = av[1]->num;
    e = av[0]->tl->hd->num;
    if (e+9<c) {
        ct = NEW(); ct->tag = tcons;
        ct->hd = av[0]->hd;
        tt = ct->tl = NEW(); tt->tag = tap;
        p = tt->fun = NEW(); p->tag = tap;
        p->fun = fnormalise;
        p->arg = NEW(); p->arg->tag = tint;
        p->arg->num = c+1;
        tt->tl = av[0]->tl;
    } else {
        ct = NEW(); ct->tag = tap;
        p = ct->fun = NEW(); p->tag = tap;
```

```
            p->fun = fcarry;
            p->arg = av[1];
            tt = ct->arg = NEW(); tt->tag = tcons;
            tt->hd = av[0]->hd;
            xt = tt->tl = NEW(); xt->tag = tap;
            p = xt->fun = NEW(); p->tag = tap;
            p->fun = fnormalise;
            p->arg = NEW(); p->arg->tag = tint;
            p->arg->num = c+1;
            xt->tl = av[0]->tl;
            eval(ct);
        }
        *u = *ct;
}

eval(p)
struct node *p;
{
        struct node *q, *av[2];
        int i;

        if (p->tag == tap) {
            for(i = 0, q = p; q->tag != tfun; q = q->fun)
                av[i++] = q->arg;
        (*q->func)(p, av);
        }
}

print(p)
struct node *p;
{
        for(; ; p = p->tl) {
            eval(p);
            eval(p->hd);
            printf("%d ", p->hd->num);
        }
}

main()
{
        struct node *e, *p;

        zero = NEW(); zero->tag = tint; zero->num = 0;
        one = NEW(); one->tag = tint; one->num = 1;
        two = NEW(); two->tag = tint; two->num = 2;
        ones = NEW(); ones->tag = tcons;
        ones->hd = one;
        ones->tl = ones;
        fm10 = NEW(); fm10->tag = tfun; fm10->func = m10;
        fmul10 = NEW(); fmul10->tag = tfun; fmul10->func = mul10;
```

```
fcarry = NEW(); fcarry->tag = tfun; fcarry->func = carry;
fnormalise = NEW(); fnormalise->tag = tfun;
     fnormalise->func = normalise;
fconvert = NEW(); fconvert->tag = tfun;
     fconvert->func = convert;
e = NEW(); e->tag = tap;
e->fun = fconvert;
p = e->arg = NEW(); p->tag = tcons;
p->hd = two;
p->tl = ones;
setbuf(stdout, NULL);
print(e);
}
```

"The expression to be evaluated is represented by nodes tagged by `tcons`, `tap`, `tint`, or `tfun` representing list nodes, application nodes, integer nodes, and function nodes. This is a standard technique in implementation of functional languages (and similar to LISP, etc.). Note that the C program does not use garbage collection, which it really should, but this is too complicated.

"The major change is a change of representation. Nodes are now represented by the function that should be applied plus two (optional) arguments: one integer and one complex thing (cons or suspension). This rewrite was possible because of the special structure of the functions used. Cons nodes are represented by having a function pointer of 0.

"The obfuscation continues by choosing special purpose data structures that work only for this particular program. Other obfuscations are:

- that only four different function pointers are ever used; code a function number in two bits, and use the rest for the integer;
- the non-obvious use of | | in `NEW`;
- the integer is only a single digit, and is used with a silly indexing.

"From here to the final result you just apply some simple changes:

- Change all identifiers to one letter.
- Use explicit numbers instead of `define`s.
- Replace `if` by `&&` or `| |`.
- Use "," instead of ";" wherever possible.
- Remove indentation and pack the code in an unpleasing way.
- Maybe more??? I forget."

Most Illegible Code

Michael Pawka <mikey@cisco.nosc.mil>
Naval Ocean Systems Center
San Diego, California

```
#include "stdio.h"
#define xyxx char
#define xyyxx putchar
#define xyyyxx while
#define xxyyyx int
#define xxxyyx main
#define xyxyxy if
#define xyyxyy '\n'
xyxx *xyx [] = {
"]I^x[I]k\\I^o[IZ~\\IZ~[I^|[I^l[I^j[I^}[I^n[I]m\\I]h",
"]IZx\\IZx[IZk\\IZk[IZo_IZ~\\IZ~[IZ|_IZl_IZj\\IZj]IZ}]IZn_IZm\\IZ
m_IZh",
"]IZx\\IZx[I^k[I\\o]IZ~\\IZ~\\I]|[IZl_I^j]IZ}]I^n[IZm\\IZm_IZh",
"]IZx\\IZx[IZk\\IZk[IZo_IZ~\\IZ~_IZ|[IZl_IZj\\IZj]IZ}]IZn_IZm\\IZ
m]IZh",
"]I^x[I]k\\IZo_I^~[I^|[I^l[IZj\\IZj]IZ}]I^n[I]m^IZh",'\0'};
/*xyyxyxyxxxyxxxyy*/xyxx *xyyx; xxyyyx xyyyx,xyyyyx,xyyyyyx=0x59,
xyyyyyyx=0x29,/*yxxyxyyyxxyyyxyy*/xxyx=0x68;xxxyyx(){xyyyyx=0;
xyyyxx(xyx[xyyyyx]){xyyx=xyx[xyyyyx++];/*xyyyxxyx*/ xyyyxx(*xyyx)
{xyyyx=*xyyx++-xyyyyyx;xyyyxx(xyyyx--)xyyxx(*xyyx-xyyyyyyx);/*x*/
xyxyxy(*xyyx==xxyx)xyyxx(xyyxyy);*xyyx++;}}}
/*xyxyxyyyyxxyxxxyyxyyyxyxxyyy*/
```

This program is rather self-describing. When run, it prints:

```
OOOOO  BBBB   FFFFF  U   U  SSSSS  CCCCC  AAAAA  TTTTT  EEEEE  DDDD   ????
O   O  B   B  F      U   U  S          C  A   A    T    E      D   D      ?
O   O  BBBBB  FFF    U   U   SSSS   C       AAAAA    T    EEEEE  D   D      ?
O   O  B   B  F      U   U       S  C      A   A    T    E      D   D  ?
OOOOO  BBBB   F      UUUUU  SSSSS  CCCCC  A   A    T    EEEEE  DDDD   ?
```

Author's Analysis

"First I thought it would be cute if the program printed the word "obfuscated" in block letters, but I wanted it to be a little more obfuscated than just **printf**, so I used the following technique. The data structure **lines** contains a description of each output line and is processed sequentially. Each pair of characters is interpreted as follows: the first character is the count of the number of times the next character should be printed.

"For example, the first entry prints four spaces followed by five o's. I actually used the technique years ago in a module for an OS where disk space and memory were precious. Most of the space saving was in the spaces.

"I further obscured the data by running it through a filter program I wrote to change the value of the text bytes. I came up with the offsets through several trials. Finally, I used #defines to make the program look as much like random noise as I could. Here is the program in non-obfuscated form:

```
/* program to print 'obfuscated' in block letters */
#include "stdio.h"

    char *lines [] = {
"4 5O2 4B3 5F2 1U3 1U2 5S2 5C2 5A2 5T2 5E2 4D3 4?",
"4 1O3 1O2 1B3 1B2 1F6 1U3 1U2 1S6 1C6 1A3 1A4 1T4 1E6 1D3 1D6 1?",
"4 1O3 1O2 5B2 3F4 1U3 1U3 4S2 1C6 5A4 1T4 5E2 1D3 1D6 1?",
"4 1O3 1O2 1B3 1B2 1F6 1U3 1U6 1S2 1C6 1A3 1A4 1T4 1E6 1D3 1D4 1?",
"4 5O2 4B3 1F6 5U2 5S2 5C2 1A3 1A4 1T4 5E2 4D5 1?",
'\0'};
    char *lp;
    int cnt,ix;

main()
{
    ix=0;
    while (lines[ix]) {
        lp=lines[ix++];
        while (*lp) {
            cnt = *lp++ - '0';
            while (cnt--)
                putchar(*lp);
            if (*lp == '?')
                putchar('\n');
            *lp++;
        }
    }
}
```

Most Well-Rounded Confusion (Grand Prize)

Larry Wall <lwall@netlabs.com>
Netlabs, Inc.
Los Altos, California

```
#define _c(C)_  (C)&('|'+3):c_()(C)>>('\n'-3)  __; /**/
#define C char*
#define keyboard ",,B3-u;.(&*5., /(b*(1\036!a%\031m,,,,\r\n"
#define main(o,oo)oo(o){
#define _ ;case
C
#define c_(cc)c cc=
#define C_(sand)_O(sand)witch
o=keyboard;
#define __ ;break;
```

```
C
ccc(
cc)
C
cc;
{
C
cccc=
cc;int
#ifndef lint
#define keyboard "dijs QH.soav Vdtnsaoh DmfpaksoQz;kkt oa, -dijs"
#endif
c;
main(;c_(=(*cc);*cc++)c,for);
#define _O(s)s
main(0xb+(c>>5),C_(s))
_'\v'
:__ _'\f':
main(c,C_(s));
_c(8098)_c(6055)_c(14779)_c(10682)
#define O_(O)_O(O)stem(ccc(
_c(15276)_c(11196)_c(15150)
#define _C ;return
_c(11070)_c(15663)_c(11583)
}
__
default
:c_(+)o[c&__LINE__-007];
main(c_(-)'-'-1,C_(s))_
0214
:_
0216
:c_(+)025 _
0207
:c_(-)4 _
0233
:c_(+)' '-1;
}}c_(&)'z'+5;
}_C cccc;
}main(,cc)
C
#define O write(1,
c="O";
O_(sy) keyboard));
main(;;,for);
read(0,
c,1);*
c_(&)'~'+1
;O ccc(
c),
```

```
'\0');
main(*c,
C_(s));_
4
:O_(sy)";kkt -oa, dijszdijs QQ"))_C
_
13
:O o+' ',
3
)
#undef main
__ _ 127:O"\b \b",3)__
default
:O
c,1)
__}}}main(){
cc();
}
```

The author of this program declined to provide any explanation for it, saying that it was unnecessary since the C compiler itself documents it. That sounds a little odd until you try compiling it:

```
cc confusing.c
confusing.c: 21: keyboard redefined
```

Actually running it drives home the point when it announces **Dvorak Keyboard Emulator**. And as you type, your qwerty keystrokes are translated to Dvorak!

Analysis

The bulk of this program does the translation of qwerty to Dvorak. Part of it is done through special-case logic, and part of it is done through a character-mapping table. For a twist, the table contains not the new Dvorak characters, but a number that when added to the old character produces the new character. (I'm simplifying slightly, but that is the general idea.)

Amusingly, the program uses the conversion function itself to initialize the terminal and print out a welcome message. In particular, the first thing the program does is:

```
system (ccc("dijs QH.soav Vdtnsaoh DmfpaksoQz;kkt oa, -dijs"));
```

ccc turns that odd string into:

```
echo "Dvorak Keyboard Emulator";stty raw -echo
```

which is then executed by **system**. The program then translates anything typed using the **ccc** function for each character. At the end of the program, a similar string is used to restore the terminal mode.

Note that the string (**dijs...**) is exactly the sequence of qwerty keystrokes you would have to press to produce the "echo "Dvorak ..."" message.

## CHAPTER 13

For a Good Time, Call . . .

This chapter presents a short but useful application: Setting your computer's clock to a national reference, the Naval Observatory in Washington, D.C.

Having a precisely set clock may not seem important, but it can be. It is often critical when systems are interconnected. For example, suppose you are using `make` to compile programs. Some files are stored on your local disk. Others are stored on a networked disk. If the network file server has a later time than your system, it is possible for someone to modify files on the network file server. `make` would then malfunction because the new file looks older than it really is.

Another example is when several systems are being backed up across a network. If the remote systems' dates are newer than the system that is controlling the backup, modified files will not get backed up. These problems and others like them can be extremely difficult to track down—better to prevent them from occurring in the first place. As systems are interconnected, working from the same date will be just as important as working with the same character set.

Most systems have a real-time clock implemented in hardware, which is very reliable. To the application programmer, it is useful in only one way—reading the current time of day. However, when the clock is incorrect, say if the battery has run down, it becomes necessary to manually reset the correct time.

This program will set the time for you. It calls up the Naval Observatory in Washington, D.C. The Naval Observatory keeps time for the military, and provides timestamps in ASCII from 1200 to 9600 baud to anyone that dials them up. After connecting to their system, the program requests the time. Once receiving it, the time is set locally.

Here is the `main` program to do it:

```
int main(argc,argv)
int argc;
char **argv;
{
    options(argc,argv);
    select_modem();
    setup_modem();
    dialup();
    login();
```

```
        gettime();
        settime();
        logout();
        cleanup();
        return 0;
}
```

I will go through each procedure in the order called from **main**, discussing the program and mentioning the particular dependencies, if any.

A number of operations in the program necessarily require some assumptions about the underlying operating system and hardware. The body of code is written for a UNIX-like operating system and a Hayes-style modem, although I've made most of the dependencies configurable. In the text, I'll describe any additional changes necessary for DOS.

options(argc,argv);

There are two important command-line options to process. If the user specifies "**-l**", the following field is taken as the name of the modem to be used (e.g., **COM1:**). Specifying "**-s**" will have the program actually set the system time. Without it, the program will go through the motions of dialing up the Naval Observatory and retrieving the time, but will not do anything with it.

The remaining options are helpful while getting the program running. "**-d**" kicks in some useful things for debugging. For instance, if you specify the modem to be the current terminal (so that you can play the part of the remote system), the speed is not changed. "**-v**" sets a verbose mode that causes every byte received from the modem to be echoed to the terminal.

getopt is used to do command-line argument processing. If you don't already have it, see p. 35 in Chapter 6.

select_modem();

Some systems have more than one modem; hence, we have to choose one. As printed, the constants are set for three modems named **/dev/tty4**, **/dev/tty5**, and **/dev/tty6**. If all you have is **COM1:** then change the **define**s to:

```
#define MODEM_FIRST 1
#define MODEMS      1
#define MODEM_MASK  "COM%d:"
```

setup_modem();

Once we have selected a modem, we must set the appropriate line characteristics. In particular, we want to turn off buffering, character translations, etc. As printed, the code does this for UNIX.

For MS-DOS, you should do the following:

```
setmode(fd,O_BINARY);                    /* raw mode */
sprintf(buffer,"MODE %s1200",modem);     /* 1200 baud */
system(buffer);
```

The Naval Observatory also requires even parity. While some systems can generate even parity automatically, mine doesn't, so I have taken the hard way out. **even** takes a character and returns it with even parity. **even** is called from **send**, which does all the actual output for the program.

dialup();

Now we are ready to dial up the Naval Observatory. This requires that the system handshake with the modem in order to send the phone number to the system and make sure it connects properly. As written, the program expects to talk to a Rixon R212A modem. It is trivial to convert to any other modem. For example, the first #define for a Hayes-compatible modem would be:

```
#define MODEM_WAKEUP       "AT\n"
```

The phone number for the Naval Observatory is defined as:

```
#define NAVO_PHONE        "12026531079"
```

You may need to modify this number, if you are, for example, using a WATS line or a PBX.

dialup is just one of a number of subroutines in this program that need to handshake with the remote computer. This means that the program will send out a string and wait for a particular response. For example, the first thing we have do is get an acknowledgment back from the modem that it is okay. Because this kind of "send/expect" pattern occurs many times in this program, I have written a subroutine called **waitfor**. **waitfor** takes two arguments. The first is a string to expect from the modem. The second argument is the number of seconds to wait. If that much time goes by and the expected string is not seen (or too many characters go by), **FALSE** is returned. **waitfor** stores whatever characters it saw in the global buffer **input**.

waitfor resembles one of the functions I covered earlier (see p. 63 in Chapter 9). I have supplied a solution that is portable to any version of UNIX. If your system does not implement timed-reads using **alarm**, you may have to resort to polling, as I discussed in the earlier chapter. This makes the code much simpler at the expense of burning CPU time while waiting for characters to arrive.

login();

This routine does some more handshaking but now with the Naval Observatory, rather than with the modem. The Naval Observatory lets everyone use their system; however you must supply a name, organization, and where you are calling from, separated by three slashes. I use:

```
#define IDENTITY "DONLIBES/SELF/HOMETOWN,USA\r"
```

Please change this string (if only to keep their statistics correct).

gettime();

Some more handshaking occurs here to get the time. The Naval Observatory actually can provide much more information than just the time. If you are interested in the phase of the moon, times of the tides, etc., this is the place to get it.

When the time is returned, it is printed out followed by a format description. After seeing the format description go by, we go to the previous line and pick up the date and time.

settime();

Now we can set the time. Unfortunately, all machines set dates (and store dates for that matter) in their own way. Rather than deal with internal system interfaces (such as DOS calls), it is easier to simply call **system**. The behavior of **system** is to execute the arguments as if they had been typed in to the command processor. For variety, I've written this to set time for DOS systems.

DOS requires that the day and month be supplied separately rather than as the day of the year given to us by the Observatory. I use the function **month_day** from *K&R1* (p. 104).

The Naval Observatory returns the time relative to Greenwich, England. Most systems keep Universal Time Coordinated (UTC, previously known as GMT) internally, converting it to the local time zone upon output. If your system keeps local time internally, you will have to add an offset to the time from the Observatory before using it. Also, be careful that you correct the day, month, and year if you and Greenwich are currently in different days.

logout(); cleanup();

All that is left to do is to log out of the Naval Observatory's computer and hang up the phone.

Source Code

```
#include <stdio.h>
#include <ctype.h>
#include "getopt.h" /* see p. 35 in Chapter 6 */

#define TRUE                    1
#define FALSE                   0
#define LINE_BUFFER_LENGTH      80
#define MULTILINE_BUFFER_LENGTH (80*24)
char input[MULTILINE_BUFFER_LENGTH]; /* input buffer */
```

```
/* constants for selecting a modem */
#define MODEM_FIRST                 4
#define MODEMS                      3
#define MODEM_MASK                  "/dev/tty%i"
/* constants for dialing a Rixon R212A modem */
#define MODEM_WAKEUP                "\r\r"
#define MODEM_PROMPT                "$ "
#define MODEM_PROMPT_TIMEOUT        20
#define MODEM_ONLINE                "7"
#define MODEM_ONLINE_TIMEOUT        45
#define MODEM_BUSY                  '5'
#define MODEM_NUMBER_PREFIX         "<k"
#define MODEM_NUMBER_SUFFIX         "\r>"
#define MODEM_SPEED                 B1200


/* constants for talking to the Naval Observatory */
#define NAVO_PHONE                  "2026531079"
#define NAVO_LOGIN_REQUEST          "PLS IDENTIFY"
#define NAVO_LOGIN_REQUEST_TIMEOUT 60
#define NAVO_REQUEST_TIME           "@TIM\r"
  /* first string sent out after actual time */
#define NAVO_TIME_INDICATOR         "YYYY"
#define NAVO_TIME_INDICATOR_TIMEOUT 10
#define NAVO_LOGOUT                 "@BYE\r"
#define NAVO_PROMPT                 "*\r\n"
#define NAVO_PROMPT_TIMEOUT         10
#define IDENTITY                    "DONLIBES/SELF/HOMETOW-
N,USA\r"


int timed_out;      /* true if read was interrupted by alarm */
int set_time = FALSE;    /* true if we are going to try and set
*/
                    /* system time */
int verbose = FALSE;/* true if conversation should be printed */
int debug = FALSE;  /* this implies verbose */

char modem[LINE_BUFFER_LENGTH] = "";/* name of modem in /dev */
FILE *mp = 0;       /* stream corresponding to modem */

void
options(argc,argv)
int argc;
char **argv;
{
    while (EOF != getopt (argc, argv, "dvsl:")) {
        switch (optopt) {
            case 'd':
                debug = TRUE;
                verbose = TRUE;
                printf ("debugging enabled\n");
```

```
                            break;
                    case 'v':
                            verbose = TRUE;
                            break;
                    case 'l': /* line */
                            strcpy (modem, optarg);
                            break;
                    case 's': /* set system time */
                            set_time = TRUE;
                            break;
                    default:
                            printf ("unknown option: %c (%x)\n", optopt,
                                                                 optopt);
                            printf ("usage: naval [-dvls]\n");
                            exit(0);
            }
    }
}


/* following two functions are BSD UNIX specific.  See article */
/* text for how to rewrite for other systems */
#include <sgtty.h>
struct sgttyb ttybuf;
struct sgttyb oldttybuf;         /* save original tty config here */

void
setup_modem()
{
    ioctl(fileno(mp),TIOCGETP,&oldttybuf);
    ttybuf = oldttybuf;
    ttybuf.sg_flags |= RAW;          /* raw */
    ttybuf.sg_flags &= ~ECHO;        /* no echo */
    /* for debugging purposes, use /dev/tty, but don't */
    /* change the speed! */
    if (strcmp("/dev/tty",modem)) {
        ttybuf.sg_ispeed = ttybuf.sg_ospeed = MODEM_SPEED;
    }
    ioctl(fileno(mp),TIOCSETP,&ttybuf);
}

void
cleanup()
{
    /* if we are using /dev/tty for testing, clean up */
    if (mp && !strcmp("/dev/tty",modem)) {
        ioctl(fileno(mp),TIOCSETP,&oldttybuf);
        fclose(mp);
    }
    exit(0);
}
```

```
void
select_modem()
{
     int i;

     if (strcmp(modem,"")) {          /* user has specified modem */
         if (NULL != (mp = fopen(modem,"rw"))) {
             printf("failed to open %s",modem);
             perror("open");
             cleanup();
         }
     } else {
         for (i=MODEM_FIRST;i<MODEM_FIRST+MODEMS;i++) {
             sprintf(modem,MODEM_MASK,i);
             if (debug) printf("trying %s\n",modem);
             if (NULL != (mp = fopen(modem,"rw"))) break;
         }
         if (mp == 0) {
             printf("no modems available\n");
             cleanup();
         }
     }
}

void
send(buf)
char *buf;
{
     int i, cc, length = strlen(buf);

     if (verbose) {
         fwrite(buf,1,length,stdout);
         fflush(stdout);
     }
     /* make even parity */
     for (i=0;i<length;i++) buf[i] = even(buf[i]);
     cc = fwrite(buf,1,length,mp);

     if (cc != length) printf("fwrite(,,%d) = %d?\n",length,cc);
}

void
dialup()
{
     send(MODEM_WAKEUP);

     if (!waitfor(MODEM_PROMPT,MODEM_PROMPT_TIMEOUT)) {
         printf("failed to establish connection with modem\n");
         printf("make sure one is connected to %s\n",modem);
```

```
            printf("If it is, try resetting it.\n");
            cleanup();
    }

    send(MODEM_NUMBER_PREFIX);
    send(NAVO_PHONE);
    send(MODEM_NUMBER_SUFFIX);

    printf("dialing Naval Observatory...\n");

    if (!waitfor(MODEM_ONLINE,MODEM_ONLINE_TIMEOUT)) {
        printf("failed to connect to Naval Observatory\n");
        printf("last message: %s\n",input);
        printf("reason: ");
        switch (*input & 0x7f) { /* strip off parity */
        case MODEM_BUSY:
            printf("busy.  Try again later.");
            break;
        default:
            printf("unexpected response <%c>\n",*input & 0x7f);
            break;
        }
        cleanup();
    }
}

void
login()
{
    if (!waitfor(NAVO_LOGIN_REQUEST,NAVO_LOGIN_REQUEST_TIMEOUT)){
        printf("did not get request for identification\n");
        printf("instead, got %s\n",input);
        cleanup();
    }
    send(IDENTITY);
}

int year, day, hour, minute, second, msec;

void
gettime()
{
    int i;

    if (!waitfor(NAVO_PROMPT,NAVO_PROMPT_TIMEOUT)) {
        printf("N.O. failed to prompt %s\n");
        printf("instead got %s\n",input);
        cleanup();
    }
    send(NAVO_REQUEST_TIME);
```

```c
        if (!waitfor(NAVO_TIME_INDICATOR,
                            NAVO_TIME_INDICATOR_TIMEOUT)) {
            printf("N.O. failed to respond with time\n");
            printf("instead got %s\n",input);
            cleanup();
        }

        /* back up to beginning of time indicator */
        for (i=strlen(input)-strlen(NAVO_TIME_INDICATOR);i>=0;i--) {
            if (0 == strcmp(NAVO_TIME_INDICATOR,input+i)) {
                i -= 2; /* skip crlf */
                break;
            }
        }
        /* back up to beginning of actual date and time */
        for (;i>=0;i--) if (input[i] == '\n') break;

        if (6 != (sscanf(&input[i],"%d %d %d %d %d %d",
                &year,&day,&hour,&minute,&second,&msec))) {
            printf("failed to find date in <%s>\n",&input[i]);
            cleanup();
        }
}

void
logout()
{
    send(NAVO_LOGOUT);
    sleep(10);
}

void
settime() {
    int month;
    char command[80];     /* long enough, I hope */

    month_day(year,day,&month,&day); /* from K&R - see text */
    if (set_time) {
        /* DOS specific */
        sprintf(command,"TIME %d:%d:%d.%d",
                hour,minute,second,msec/10);
        system(command);
        sprintf(command,"DATE %d-%d-%d",month,day,year);
        system(command);
    }
}

void
dump(s,n)
char *s;
```

```
int n;
{
     int i;

     for (i=0;i<n;i++,s++) {
          *s &= 0x7f;
          if (isprint(*s) || *s == ' ') putchar(*s);
          else if (*s == '\r') printf("<cr>");
          else if (*s == '\n') printf("<lf>");
          else printf("<%x>",*s);
     }
}


/* the following two functions are specific to UNIX systems */
/* which do not restart reads.  See p. 63 in Chapter 9 */
/* for other approaches. */
#include <signal.h>

/*ARGSUSED*/
void alarm_handler(sig)
int sig;
{
     timed_out = TRUE;
}


/* waitfor() watches the input stream for occurrences of s */
/* it will timeout after "period" seconds */
int
waitfor(s,period)
char *s;
int period;
{
     int bytes_read = 0;       /* number of bytes read since */
                               /* entering this routine */
     int slen = strlen(s);     /* length of string being */
                               /* searched for */

     signal(SIGALRM,alarm_handler);
     timed_out = FALSE;
     alarm(period);
     for (;;) {
          int cc;
          char *p, *start_searching = input;
          /* alarm can go off in code AFTER the read, in which */
          /* case we must check for it here */
          if (timed_out) return(FALSE);
          cc = fread(input+bytes_read,1,LINE_BUFFER_LENGTH,mp);
          /* if alarm went off, or some other signal occurred */
          /* or read failed, give up. */
          if (cc == 0) {
```

```
                alarm(0);
                return(FALSE);
        }

        if (verbose) fwrite(input+bytes_read,1,cc,stdout);
        for (p = start_searching;
                p <= (&input[bytes_read+cc])-slen; p++) {
            /* move over one character and try again */
            if (debug) {
                printf("searching for ");
                dump(s,slen);
                printf(" in ");
                dump(p,slen);
                printf("\r\n");
            }
            if (!strncmp(s,p,slen)) {
                alarm(0);
                return(TRUE);
            }
        }
        start_searching = (&input[bytes_read+cc]) - slen;
        bytes_read += cc;
        /* if we have filled up the buffer without finding */
        /* the string, it's probably hopeless. */
        if (bytes_read + LINE_BUFFER_LENGTH >
                MULTILINE_BUFFER_LENGTH) {
            alarm(0);
            return(FALSE);
        }
    }
}

int
even(c)          /* return given character with even parity */
int c;
{
    int i, pbit = 0;

    for (i=0;i<7;i++) {
        if ((c>>i)&1) pbit = !pbit;
    }

    c &= 0x7f;
    if (pbit) c |= 1<<7;
    return(c);
}

/* insert main() (from article text above) here */
```

## CHAPTER 14

Byte Ordering

```
/* unportable */
int c = 0;
fread(&c,1,1,stdin);
printf("%d\n",c);
```

Try the above code fragment on your favorite machine. The output may surprise you. Even worse, it may surprise you later. If you include such code in a program that is ported to other machines, you will eventually find that it fails to behave the same way on all the machines.

To save you some trouble, I ran it on an Intel 80286, DEC VAX, and Motorola 68010. (They were handy.) The input to the program was the character "a". The results were as follows:

```
80286:    97
VAX:      97
68010:    1627389952
```

No, the 68010 isn't broken—or wrong. The program is, however. **fread** is defined to take the address of a **char** but we passed it the address of an **int**. What's the big deal, you say—**int**s are at least as big as **char**s, right? Yes, however, integers are stored differently on different machines.

Specifically, the least significant byte (lsb) is stored at the same address as the integer on the 80x86 and VAX families. This is commonly referred to as *little-endian* addressing. The most significant byte (msb) is stored at the same address as the integer on the 680x0 family. This is commonly referred to as *big-endian* addressing. (The phrases refer to Jonathon Swift's *Gulliver's Travels*, in which the Brobdingnagians engaged in a frivolous dispute regarding "on which end an egg should be broken.") Another phrase describing the same problem is *byte sex*, emphasizing the arbitrary but real difference between them, but begging the question as to which is better.

What happened in our example, then, was that the 97 got poked into the least significant byte of an `int` on the VAX and 80286, while it got poked into the most significant byte on the 68K. Hence when we printed out the `int`, we found 97×256^3 on the 68K.

Looking at the following table, we see the results of the statement `c = 0x03020100` when `c` is declared as an `int` that lies at address 100 on the various machines.

address	100	101	102	103
little-endian	00	01	02	03
big-little-endian	02	03	00	01
big-endian	03	02	01	00

The "big-little-endian" is found on the PDP-11. On that machine, an `int` is only two bytes, little-endian style. To form a 4-byte integer, you must declare it as a `long`. The words (two-byte values) in the `long` are stored in big-endian order.

While the 68K order may seem strange and the PDP-11 positively bizarre, you should not discredit either of these schemes on the basis of one wrong piece of code. Unfortunately, I constantly hear people claim that one or another of these formats is "wrong" or "a mistake." This is just stubbornness. As long as it is done consistently, either approach is valid. (Indeed, many other machines work like the 68K, including the AT&T 3B2, the IBM 370, and the HP 9000.)

If you are interested in more extensive treatment of this problem, I recommend a USC/ISI memo by Danny Cohen [1] and an article in *Computer Language* by Mike Higgins [2]. These also discuss the issue of bit numbering within bytes, referred to by -endian terms as well.

Depending on what you are doing, being able to choose one of these forms can be of great advantage in the efficiency of program execution. However, once the CPU has been chosen or the architecture designed, there isn't much you can do but live with it. (Some machines are configurable, e.g., microprogrammable ones).

For example, consider integer arithmetic. The natural method is to represent integers as polynomials by powers of two and do the arithmetic starting with the lsb and working up in little-endian style. On the other hand, if you are sorting integers, it is more useful to be handed a pointer to the msb. Then you can compare bytes and work down in big-endian style.

These justifications are typical, but others I've heard about are based on (1) multiprecision integers, (2) strings, (3) human readability, (4) mathematical history, and (5) bit-numbering within bytes. About the only thing that is clear, apart from the better fit of big-endian to block-oriented operations and of little-endian to stream-oriented ones, is that this is a religious issue.

Most of the time I leave these matters to assembly-language programmers who need to be very conscious of bit and byte ordering. However, communications between different architectures requires that even C programmers be aware of these issues. For example, if you are communicating between a 68K and an 8086, sending integers is not as simple as just handing the other guy a couple of bytes.

Solutions

One solution is to have one or both of the programs recognize that they are communicating with a different endian processor and adapt to that. Another solution is to select one of big or little-endian or possibly even a different method and use it as a standard. I favor the latter solution, and fortunately, recent history provides us with a clear choice.

Both ISO and Department of Defense networking protocols use big-endian as a standard 16 or 32-bit *network integer* format. Don't worry if you are on a little-endian machine. The proper technique is to convert all your integers to network-standard integers before putting them on the network. Similarly, when receiving information from the network, you must convert from network-standard form to the local host form.

By encapsulating the conversion in functions or macros, it is possible to produce code portable to any-endian machines. If your machine stores integers in network-standard form already, you can supply identity macros with no loss of efficiency. For example, to send the number 17 across a network, you might use the following code fragment:

```
long int c = 17;

/* convert host to network-long */
netc = htonl(c);
/* fictional send routine */
send(netc);
```

`htonl` (host to network `long`) performs any byte swapping if necessary. `send` takes the network-standard information and actually delivers it to the recipient.

The opposite of `htonl` is `ntohl` (network to host `long`), which applies the opposite conversion. Analogous functions exist for `short`s, namely `htons` and `ntohs`. These functions first appeared in Berkeley UNIX and have since become very commonly used in C programming, although they are not part of Standard C.

byteorder.c

At the end of this chapter are implementations of all the conversion functions I shall describe. The code requires that the machine represent `long`s in 32 bits and `short`s in 16 bits, but assumes nothing else—you don't even have to declare whether your machine is big or little-endian! In order to do this, the program stores a `long`, and then looks at the first byte. Based on that, it can tell what type of machine you are on, and how to convert to/from network-standard form. It does this one time only, of course, and from then on remembers the earlier result.

To use the function, include header `byteorder.h`, shown here:

```
/* byteorder.h */
#ifndef BYTEORDER_H
#define BYTEORDER_H
#include "proto.h"   /* define PROTO */

#define ntohs(x)    (htons(x))
#define ntohl(x)    (htonl(x))

#define htons(x)    (htons_func?(*htons_func)(x):x))
#define htonl(x)    (htonl_func?(*htonl_func)(x):x))

short (*htons_func) PROTO((short));
long (*htonl_func) PROTO((long));
void byteorder_init PROTO((void));

#endif /* BYTEORDER_H */
```

Notice that `ntohl` and `ntohs` are defined in terms of their inverses. This is because the exact same bytes are swapped (if necessary) in either direction. Swap twice and you're back where you started!

`htons` and `htonl` are macros, too. They call functions that do the real work. In the case of `htonl`, any one of three different types of swaps can be required. There is also a fourth case—when no swap is required. Thus, the macro calls one of three possible functions, or none at all. `htons` works similarly, except that it either calls one function or nothing.

The functions are defined below. The macro definitions work only if the special function pointers are initialized. This is done by calling `byteorder_init` at the beginning of the program. `byteorder_init` uses a value that has different subvalues in all four byte positions. Based upon examination of the first byte, it is possible to tell what kind of swapping is necessary.

Whereas the code to swap a `short` is simpler than the code to swap a `long`, the declaration is more complex! When `short` is used as a formal argument, it is widened to `int` when prototypes are not used. In order to have Standard C pass a `short` without being widened, the function must be defined with a prototype. Without this, callers could pass a `short` while the function expected an `int`.

In order to make this work in Classic C, the prototypes must be removed. Unfortunately, the `PROTO` macro is not powerful enough to do this and so I resorted to writing the function header twice.

Encoding More Complex Objects

While two- and four-byte integers are easily addressed using a scheme such as the one I presented here, it is not unreasonable to want to transmit more complex objects such as `float`s, `struct`s, and even pointers. Is this possible?

Depending upon your goal, different solutions are available. In general, converting everything to a printable representation is a very safe technique. For example, `printf` and `scanf` can convert floating point numbers to a printable representation (which every machine can understand), and vice versa. The drawback is that these are slower than necessary, consume more space and bandwidth than necessary, and in the case of floating point values, can lose precision.

If efficiency is a must, I recommend the use of one of several ISO standards for Presentation-Level encoding. ISO 8825 is called *Basic Encoding Rules* and defines network representations for all basic types and complex types such as `struct`s. There are several versions of the *Rules* aimed at addressing the different trade-offs that this problem presents.

Shipping pointers around is a little tricky but can be done. Raw pointers are seldom useful in another address space, but if that is what you want, they can be converted to an integer or printable representation. More likely, you need to transmit something constructed with pointers, such as a linked list. One approach is to build a temporary network-transmittable image of it and send that. On the other end, a subroutine awaits to translate the image back into a C pointer form. It may sound a little odd at first, but this is actually a common technique in cooperating programs that run across a network!

References

[1]   Danny Cohen, *"On Holy Wars and a Plea for Peace,"* University of Southern California, Information Sciences Institute, California, April 1, 1980.

[2]   Mike Higgins, *Computer Language*, Vol. 3, No. 4, Miller Freeman Publications, San Francisco, California, April 1986.

Source Code—byteorder.c

```
#include <stdio.h>
#include "byteorder.h"

/*
 * there are 4 possibilities (that we care about):
 *                                            MSB     LSB
 * Order in memory                             3 2 1 0
 *
 * Order in memory if you stepped a char * ptr thru the long
 *    - noswap:                                3 2 1 0   68K, 370
 *    - byteswap: (swap bytes in short)        2 3 0 1   PDP-11
 *    - halfswap: (swap shorts in long)        1 0 3 2   ?
 *    - bothswap: (swapbyte && halfswap)       0 1 2 3   VAX, 8086
 */

static long test_value = 0x03020100;
```

```
long longbothswap PROTO((long));
long longbyteswap PROTO((long));
long longhalfswap PROTO((long));
short byteswap PROTO((short));

void
byteorder_init()
{
    char *cp = (char *) &test_value;
    switch (*cp) {
    case 03:
        htonl_func = 0;
        htons_func = 0;
        break;
    case 02:
        htonl_func = longbyteswap;
        htons_func = byteswap;
        break;
    case 01:
        htonl_func = longhalfswap;
        htons_func = 0;
        break;
    case 00:
        htonl_func = longbothswap;
        htons_func = byteswap;
        break;
    }
}


long
longbothswap(1)      /* swap bytes 3 with 0 and 2 with 1 */
long 1;
{
    register char  *sp, /* source pointer */
                   *dp; /* dest pointer in r */
    long r;

    sp = (char *) &1;
    dp = (char *) &r;

    *dp++ = sp[3];
    *dp++ = sp[2];
    *dp++ = sp[1];
    *dp   = sp[0];
    return r;
}

long
longbyteswap(1)      /* swap bytes 0 with 1 and 2 with 3 */
long 1;
```

```
{
    register char  *sp, /* source pointer */
                   *dp; /* dest pointer in r */
    long r;

    sp = (char *) &l;
    dp = (char *) &r;

    *dp++ = sp[1];
    *dp++ = sp[0];
    *dp++ = sp[3];
    *dp   = sp[2];
    return r;
}

long
longhalfswap(l)        /* swap bytes 0 with 2 and 1 with 3 */
long l;
{
    register char  *sp, /* source pointer */
                   *dp; /* dest pointer in r */
    long r;

    sp = (char *) &l;
    dp = (char *) &r;

    *dp++ = sp[2];
    *dp++ = sp[3];
    *dp++ = sp[0];
    *dp   = sp[1];
    return r;
}

#if __STDC__==1 || PROTOTYPES_EXIST
short byteswap(short s)  /* swap byte 0 with 1 */
#else
short byteswap(s)
short s;
#endif
{
    register char  *sp, /* source ptr */
                   *dp; /* dest ptr */
    short r;

    sp = (char *) &s;
    dp = (char *) &r;
    *dp++ = sp[1];
    *dp   = sp[0];
    return r;
}
```

## CHAPTER 15

Double Trouble

In many people's eyes, C doesn't score too highly as a language for numerical programming. Indeed, there are quite a number of pitfalls when using floating-point. I will discuss the common ones in this chapter. Perhaps you can avoid repeating the same mistakes that I've made.

C's approach to real numbers is not unlike its approach to everything else. You get access to the machine-dependent floating type, with very little help beyond that. Don't assume that C floating-point protects you from the reality of hardware. The following fragment shows a classic example:

```
float f = 0;
while (f != 1) f += 0.1;
```

How many times will the loop execute? No, not 10; it will usually be many more, and it may not stop at all. Briefly, the problem is that 0.1 is not directly representable in binary. A small error occurs on each addition that is enough so that the termination condition fails on the eleventh test.

Critics have suggested banning the use of == (and !=) with floating-point operands. Like the `goto`, if you find yourself using it, you are probably doing something wrong although there are occasions where it is appropriate.

The point is that use of == with floating-point operands is usually a mistake. Many floating-point operations truncate or round results. Some classes of numbers (viz. irrationals) cannot be stored precisely, no matter how many bits of the mantissa (digits after the decimal point) you have. Perhaps the only time that == should be used is when testing against 0 (to prevent division by zero for example) or other constants that appear at discontinuities or undefined domains in functions. IEEE floating-point attempts to make all these cases "work," but it opens a different can of worms that I'm not going to discuss here.

A particularly nasty problem is that a computed result in a register and the same value stored in memory and returned to a register may fail a comparison for equality. For example:

```
c = a/b;
if (c != a/b) printf("I'm shocked\n");
```

This occurs in machines that have guard bits. These are extra bits at the ends of registers that are used to increase precision in calculations. Guard bits can also be used to properly round values when they are stored in memory.

An amusing anecdote is related by Kernighan and Plauger [1]. They describe how a version of Fortran at their installation failed an equality test when one number was on an input punchcard and the other, identically typed and also a constant, was in a program. This was because different scanning routines were used in the I/O library compiled with the Fortran program and the I/O routines that were part of the compiler!

There are ways around these problems. One is symbolic programming, using arbitrary-precision subroutines.[1] An easier approach for C programmers, however, is simply to leave room for the error. This is often called *fuzz*. Using fuzz, we can rewrite `if (x == y)` as:

```
double fuzz = .5E-14;
if (fabs(a-b) <= (fuzz * fmax(fabs(a),fabs(b))))
```

Choosing the fuzz can be extremely critical, of course, as it depends on the operations and numbers involved. Some languages, such as APL, have a fuzz variable built into all comparisons. Other languages, such as Forth, take the opposite view. Floating-point support is not provided at all, in the belief that it is never necessary anyway. And in the rare case that it is, you are probably better off representing reals as numerators and denominators and keeping track by hand.

When writing operating systems or device drivers, this makes a lot of sense. But C is now used for many higher-level applications where floating-point numbers are a necessity. Indeed, C is valued for its use in portable programs, which may well need to evaluate floating-point expressions.

Mistakes in Cement

Apart from the understandable problems discussed above, history has left us with some curios in the C language with regard to reals. While it is possible to avoid some of them simply by using Standard C, truly portable code should avoid these areas entirely.

1(a). Automatic Promotion from Float to Double in Expressions

In Classic C, automatic promotion occurs in expressions. While this has the benefit of decreasing the size of math libraries, it is often a drawback. In particular, some applications do not require more precision, and would run much faster on some systems if all computations were performed as `float`s. Some C compilers allow the programmer to turn off this particular automatic promotion.

---

1. There are several good packages available from the C Users' Group. `pub/gnu/gmp-1.2.tar.Z` is a fine package, available from `prep.ai.mit.edu` via anonymous `ftp`.

This behavior is historical. The original implementation of C—on the PDP-11— was not able to find out whether the previous process had left the floating-point processor hardware in single- or double-precision mode. Since double-precision arithmetic was not much slower than single, it was decided that all arithmetic would be done in double-precision, and the kernel could assume that all processes ran in double-precision mode, making for very fast context switches. Furthermore, not much floating-point programming was anticipated on the machine.

In Standard C, this promotion may or may not occur. The implementation can promote, although it is not obliged to. It may do it depending on the context. Or it may always do it. Clearly, you should use a cast if the behavior is important to you. Note that it is necessary to cast only one operand. For example, the following forces both operands to be converted to `double`s before the addition.

```
float a, b;
... = a + (double)b;
```

Without the cast, the expression `a+b` is of type `float` in Standard C, even if it were represented internally by a `double`. One reason this is allowed is that a lot of hardware works this way. The floating-point processor can convert values into an internal format, sometimes of greater precision and range than any external format. This is converted back when the value is stored in addressable memory. If this behavior were not allowed, acceptable floating-point performance would not be possible in a Standard C compiler on a wide variety of hardware.

1(b). Automatic Promotion from Float to Double in Function Calls

In unprototyped functions (including Classic C), if you pass a `float` as an argument, it will automatically be converted to a `double`. Similarly, a `float` parameter will be compiled as a `double`, although it will be converted to `float` (and then converted back to `double`) before being used in an expression. Depending on the subtleties of these implicit conversions is probably a mistake, as some compilers do not follow them completely. Just don't specify `float`s as formal arguments.

If performance reasons require you to use `float` formals on some systems, make sure the documentation is obvious, since using such code in a Classic C environment may require some system-dependent option.

With a prototype containing `float` formals, the compiler has a choice. It may pass the argument as a `float` directly, or it may convert the value to a `double`, pass it as a `double`, and convert it back to `float` inside the function. (This latter option is what a Classic C compiler was always forced to do.)

2. Remainder (%) Doesn't Work for Floats or Doubles

This is an odd restriction, as division is allowed on floating-point numbers. An obvious implementation is as follows:

```
#define remainder(x,y)    (x - y*floor(x/y))
```

where `floor(x)` returns the largest integer not greater than `x`.

Although some machines produce a remainder as the result of a division, it is often not mathematically usable. This is unfortunate, since when using a quotient the likelihood of also using the remainder is quite high (and vice versa). It is conceivable but unlikely that a compiler could discern that you want both remainder and quotient even if the hardware was capable of computing them together.

Standard C provides the functions `div` and `ldiv`, which return quotients and remainders simultaneously. Unfortunately, they are only defined for `int`s and `long`s.

3(a). Floating-point Operations May be Reordered Automatically

In Classic C, parentheses do not play the same role in C that they do in Fortran. In particular, according to *K&R1* (p. 185):

> . . . the compiler considers itself free to compute subexpressions in the order it believes most efficient, . . . Expressions involving a commutative and associative operator (`*`, `+`, `&`, `^`) may be rearranged arbitrarily, even in the presence of parentheses; to force a particular order of evaluation an explicit temporary must be used.

Thus a C expression such as `(x+y)+z` may be computed by first adding together `x` and `y` or perhaps first adding `y` and `z` or perhaps first adding `x` and `z`!

The reason for this is that the compiler might already have the values of `x` and `z` (but not `y`) in registers. By following the order suggested by the parentheses, it might require an extra save and load of a register. More complex examples are even worse. This can be very important in a piece of code that is executed frequently.

However, it is easy to come up with examples where a particular evaluation order is critical. For example, on a 68020 (8-byte `double`s), if `x == 1E8`, `y == -1E8`, and `z == 1`, then adding `x` and `y` first gives the desired result of 1, while adding `x` and `z` first gives the result of 0.

If you really want `x + y` to be evaluated first, you must write:

```
temp = x + y;
...  = temp + z;
```

In Standard C, this is unnecessary. Parentheses do force a particular evaluation order (or more specifically, *as if* it were so ordered). And your code may run a bit slower. Such is progress.

A different problem caused by undesirable evaluation order is demonstrated when `x` and `z` are close to the largest number that can be stored in a `double`. If `y` is a very large negative number, you might be depending upon `x+y` to be computed first, while `x+z` might cause an overflow.

Overflows and underflows usually expose themselves quickly during initial testing, because the results are complete garbage. However, a more subtle error due to the same reordering behavior is the loss of significance. Again, the order of evaluation is very critical to the precision of the result; however, the results of this are less likely to be noticed during initial testing since the results may still be accurate in the most significant digits, but completely inadequate for some purposes.

This type of problem is specific only to floating-point calculations, since integral types cannot lose precision in computations except by overflow and underflow as noted above.

Mathematically speaking, reordering of expressions in this way is perfectly valid (since there is no concept of overflow or underflow in mathematics). It is only the realization of mathematics on a computer that has added these notions. Notably, Fortran gave many people the idea that parentheses indicate order of evaluation. Remember that this is only true in Fortran. Not in mathematics (where it doesn't matter), and not in C (where it does).

3(b). Overflows and Underflows Generally Cause Undefined Behavior

Overflows and underflows cause undefined behavior, except in special cases that I shall not discuss here. In some cases, the result is simply computation of an incorrect value. In others, a machine fault occurs (such as when dividing by 0).

The most important cases, in the context of this discussion, are those where the true mathematical result of an operation cannot be represented as a value of the expected result type. These are semantically valid, but implementationally flawed.

Overflow and underflow were never guaranteed to be reported, because of deficiencies in several platforms. For example, the Gould PowerNode could report floating-point exceptions only if it could also report integer exceptions. This placed an unacceptable penalty on unsigned integer arithmetic.

4. Exception Handling—Or Lack of It

Except for `SIGFPE` and `setjmp/longjmp`, both Classic C and Standard C provide little help for exception handling. Nonetheless, there are a few popular techniques. Unfortunately, no one technique is suitable for all hardware.

One technique is to reserve special values for overflows and division by zero, such as *NaN* (*Not a N*umber) or infinity. For example, once a NaN is produced, further operations involving it continue to produce a NaN. This allows algorithms to skip argument checking during each operation. Instead, if the final result is not a NaN, then the entire sequence of operations is known to have succeeded.

It may also be possible for the hardware to raise C-style signals upon a mathematical exception. Control can be redirected with the `setjmp/longjmp` machinery.

Other techniques exist and each have their advantages and disadvantages. Unfortunately, the only completely portable technique is to perform argument checking before each operation. This can be slow, but is nonetheless quite usable.

Conclusion

Working with `floats` and `doubles` is fraught with danger, not only from the realities of computer realizations of abstract concepts but also from historical quirks in the C language that we have all learned to live with. Standard C has made the language definition clearer but has not really solved any of the hard problems. Handling overflow, division by zero, and other exceptions are not defined by the language.

An understanding of some of the weak spots of C and its support (or lack of it) of real numbers is essential for doing numerical programming in C. Furthermore, a good course in numerical methods is essential in understanding how to reduce loss of significant digits, designing algorithms that produce meaningful results, etc. Sometimes it is fun to learn by experience, but this is one area where the difficulties are extremely subtle, and understanding them takes perseverance—and maybe, in difficult cases, the choice of another language!

For information on current work that addresses many of the shortcomings I've discussed here, see p. 397 in Chapter 40.

Further Readings

Donald Knuth, "Seminumerical Methods," Volume 2, *The Art of Computer Programming*, Addison-Wesley, 1981.

IEEE Standard for Binary Floating-Point Arithmetic, ANSI/IEEE Std 754-1985, IEEE, New York, 1985.

References

[1]   Brian Kernighan and P. J. Plauger, *The Elements of Programming Style, 1st ed.*, Prentice Hall, 1974, p. 95.

## CHAPTER 16

Varargs—Varying Arguments

Varargs is a technique that provides the ability to pass varying numbers and types of arguments to functions in a portable way.

Of course, C already lets you pass arbitrary parameters, in spite of how you have them declared. (It's not a bug, it's a feature!) However, doing it portably is difficult because bypassing the C parameter mechanism requires understanding and handling of each machine's architecture.

Some implementations push parameters on the stack going down. Some do it going up. Depending on the type of parameter, a different amount of space may be pushed. Some systems do not even use a stack, but instead pass all parameters through registers. And some machines use a combination of both stack and registers.

Because of all this, there is no standard way, for example, to figure out how many arguments have been passed. Popular conventions are to: (1) pass the number of arguments as the first argument, (2) terminate the argument list with a special value, like NULL, or (3) provide a way of indirectly deducing the number of arguments (e.g., count the '%'s in a `printf` format).

C's approach to parameter types is no different from the way it handles the number of parameters. Most compilers simply don't check that they match between caller and callee. No information is passed as to what types the calling subroutine used. If you don't use prototypes or `lint`, you are on your own.

There is no way to fix this detriment while retaining efficiency for the bulk of function calls that do not need this information.

Using Varargs

Varargs provides a portable means of writing functions that take varying arguments. It was originally designed by Andrew Koenig of Bell Laboratories, and can be found in almost every C implementation.

As you will see, the syntax of varargs is unusual. It uses macros to manipulate the real arguments to provide the effect of varying arguments. The macros hide some nonportable machinery, but the result is that macros are portable to use. Alas, there are some C implementations for which varargs cannot be correctly implemented.

Portable Printf

`printf` takes a variable number of arguments. Because of this, it is impossible to explicitly list all of the parameters. Historically, implementations of `printf` used nonportable mechanisms for reading the arguments, often doing it in assembler. However, it can be written portably in C. Alas, Standard C and Classic C provide different ways of doing this. Fortunately, they only affect the first few lines in each function. Below is a skeleton `printf`. The Standard C version is on the left. The Classic C version is on the right.

```
/* Standard C */                 /* Classic C */
#include <stdarg.h>              #include <varargs.h>

                                 /*VARARGS*/
int printf(char *fmt, ...)       int printf(va_alist)
                                 va_dcl     /* no semicolon! */
{                                {
    va_list arg;                     va_list arg;
    char t;                          char t, *fmt;

    va_start(arg,fmt);               va_start(arg);
                                     fmt = va_arg(arg,char *);

    /* remainder common to both C's */
    while ((t = *fmt++) != '\0') {
        if (t != '%') putchar(t);
        else switch (t = *fmt++) {
            case 'c': /* character */
                print_character(va_arg(arg,int));
                break;
            case 'd': /* integer */
                print_integer(va_arg(arg,int));
                break;
            case 's': /* string */
                print_string(va_arg(arg,char *));
                break;
            case 'f': /* float */
                print_float(va_arg(arg,double));
                break;
            . . .
    }
    va_end(arg);
    . . .
}
```

In Standard C, `stdarg.h` is a header file that defines macros necessary to pass varying arguments. The declaration begins with all the known fixed arguments, and "`...`" at the right-most position indicates the rest are varying. At least one fixed argument type must be declared.

`va_list arg` declares an object that will point into the argument list. We can step `arg` to the next argument in the list or move it back to the beginning of the list and start over. You can use any name—it doesn't have to be "`arg`." You can also declare multiple objects that can point to different places in the argument list.

To initialize `arg` to the first varying argument, use `va_start(arg,last)` where `last` is the last fixed parameter in the declaration. `va_end(arg)` is called at the end of processing the argument list whether or not you want to reread it with `va_start`.

To read the next argument, use `va_arg`. The first parameter is the name of the argument pointer. The second parameter should be the type of the expected object after the default argument widening rules have been applied. To read an `int`, use `va_arg(arg,int)`. To read a `float`, use `va_arg(arg,double)` because `float`s are promoted to `double`s in function calls.

In our `printf`, we can infer the type of each successive argument by scanning `fmt`.

Classic C is slightly different. It uses the header `varargs.h`. The function declaration uses the single argument `va_alist`. The declaration for `va_alist` is `va_dcl` (without a semicolon). If you already know some of the argument types, do not declare them. You must get them through the varargs macros. The only other difference is that `va_start` does not take a second parameter. The `/*VARARGS*/` comment preceding the function tells `lint` not to complain when it sees the function called with varying arguments.

A Related Problem—Dprintf

Given `printf`, suppose we would like to write a function that uses it underneath. I have in mind a function I call `dprintf`. `dprintf` takes all the same parameters as `printf` with one addition. This extra parameter is compared against a global `int`. If the parameter is larger than the global, `printf` is called, otherwise nothing happens.

This is especially useful for controlling diagnostics. If I want a lot of debugging information, I set `global_debug_level` to 10. Lower numbers print out less information. And if I don't want any debugging information, I set it to 0, so that none of the `dprintf`s output anything.

By passing the debug level as an argument to the program, I don't have to recompile the program in order to turn on any level of diagnostics.

Here was one of my attempts at it:

```
void dprintf(error_level,fmt,arg0,arg1,arg2,arg3,arg4)
int error_level;
char *fmt;
int arg0,arg1,arg2,arg3,arg4;
{
```

```
        if (global_error_level >= error_level)
            printf(fmt,arg0,arg1,arg2,arg3,arg4);
}
```

Actually, this was my second attempt. My first attempt never made it past the C compiler, because I could not figure out how to declare a single `args` variable. No matter how I declared it (`char`, `int`, `char *`, etc.) or passed it (`args`, `&args`, `*args`), `printf` never saw the second argument. What it did see was a lot of "stack junk." `dprintf` got the stack with a good list of arguments, but all that it could pass to `printf` was the address of my stack. It couldn't pass the stack itself!

My second version has the arguments specified explicitly. However, it still has problems. First of all, I have arbitrarily limited myself to five arguments. No matter what number I pick, there is always the potential of exceeding it. The second problem is that I have declared every argument as an `int`. This actually worked pretty well, because `char`s are always converted to `int`s, and pointers (the other thing that I print out a lot while debugging) fit into `int`s on my machine. Nonetheless, I could not print out `double`s because they didn't fit into `int`s, so I always got the wrong answer. I didn't want to declare all the arguments as `double`s either, because then the `int`s wouldn't be handled correctly.

One might think that varargs could be useful here, but it doesn't completely solve the problem. Varargs still requires that you determine the types of the arguments. I didn't want to do that. Rather, I just wanted to pass everything on to `printf` uninterpreted.

Vprintf and Friends

The solution is to use a set of routines that are defined to take varargs-style parameters as their arguments. These were also written by Koenig (who evidently did a lot of struggling with these same problems). `vprintf` is very similar to `printf`; both have a `char *` format as the first argument. However, instead of an optional list of untyped arguments like `printf`, `vprintf` has a second argument declared to be of type `va_list`.

Does this look familiar? Yes, it is the same `va_list` from the varargs package! Now we can correctly rewrite `dprintf` as follows:

```
/* Standard C */              /* Classic C */
                              /*VARARGS*/
void dprintf(int error_level, void dprintf(va_alist)
char *fmt,...)                va_dcl
{                             {
    va_list arg;                  va_list arg;
                                  int error_level;
                                  char *fmt;

    va_start(arg,fmt);            va_start(arg);
                                  error_level = va_arg(arg,int);
                                  fmt = va_arg(arg,char *);
```

```
        /* remainder common to both C's */
        if (global_error_level >= error_level)
            vprintf(fmt,arg);
        va_end(arg);
}
```

Just as with `printf`, there are two other varieties of `vprintf`. They are, naturally, `vsprintf` and `vfprintf`. (See p. 366 in Chapter 38 for an example that uses `vsprintf`.) They are declared as follows:

```
        char *vsprintf PROTO((char *s, char *fmt, ...));
        int vfprintf PROTO((FILE *stream, char *fmt, ...));
```

All of the `printf` family are defined by Standard C to return the number of characters output. Unfortunately, some Classic C compilers don't do this, so it is wise to avoid depending on it.

Writing Library Routines that Use Varargs

If you would like to implement a variable-argument function that will be part of a library, make sure you provide an interface that accepts a `va_list` as well as a list of varying arguments. In addition, consider a third interface that accepts an array of arguments. A function that accepts an array is useful when you know you need to call a function, but you won't know until runtime how many arguments to pass to it.

I find that it is easiest to make the array-style interface be the real routine. For example, here is code for a list-style function that takes a variable-length list of `char *` arguments.

```
/* Standard C */                        /* Classic C */
void va_foo(char *arg0,...)             void va_foo(va_alist)
                                        va_dcl
{                                       {
    va_list arg;                            va_list arg;
    va_start(arg,arg0);                     va_start(arg);

    for(i=1;;i++) {                         for (i=0;;i++) {
        arg = va_arg(arg,char *);           .
        if (!arg) break;                    .
    }                                       .
    va_end(arg);

    argv = (char **)malloc((i+1)*sizeof(char *));
    va_start(arg,arg0);                     va_start(arg);
    argv[0] = arg0;
    for (i=1;;i++) {                        for (i=0;;i++) {
        argv[i] = va_arg(arg,char *);       .
        if (!argv[i]) break;                .
    }
    i = array_foo(argv);
```

```
        free((Type)argv);
        va_end(arg);
}
```

`va_foo` gathers up all of its arguments, packages them in an array and calls `array_foo`. (Notice how the argument list is read twice.) After `array_foo` returns, `va_foo` frees the array before returning itself. `array_foo` can also be called by the user directly.

```
        void array_foo(argv)
        char **argv;
        {
                for (arg = argv;*argv;argv++) {
                        ...
                }
        }
```

Classic C versus Standard C

It is possible to use macros to hide some but not all of the differences between `stdarg.h` and `varargs.h`. For example, a macro by the name `VA_START` could reference `va_start` with the appropriate parameters depending on `__STDC__`.

Whereas many Standard C compilers support varargs in the name of backward compatibility, it takes only a little more work to support both `varargs.h` and `stdarg.h`. You should make the effort. If you find yourself on a platform that supports `varargs.h` but not `stdarg.h`, consider writing a `stdarg.h` header yourself (or vice versa). This may save you from the hassle of future software that depends on it.

You might even consider adding code for environments that are so old that they have no form of varargs. In this case, assume that all arguments are `int`-sized—the most likely size of any type. This can fail of course, but it's the best you can do under the circumstances.

Conclusion

Passing a varying number of arguments may seem distasteful at first, but this is probably because it was not originally possible to do portably. Nonetheless, it is a legacy of C. And done correctly, elegant functions like `printf` are possible.

Using varargs, it is possible to write portable code. The only pitfall you must be aware of is vararg's use of C's rules for promotion of formal parameters. Otherwise, varargs is a delight to use.

## CHAPTER 17

The 1987 Obfuscated C Code Contest

This chapter presents the 1987 Obfuscated C Code Contest winners. I must mention that each year, the contest becomes more and more difficult to win. The rules are constantly expanded to try and plug all the loopholes that entrants continually find to put something over on the judges. In 1987, however, guidelines were also issued for the first time—more information was supplied about style and how the programs are analyzed by the judges.

In particular, entries are examined for non-clarity and levels of confusion. Programs should be obscure to look at as well as in function. Odd algorithms are very important. Simply abusing #defines won't go as far as a more well-rounded program! Of course, programs can't excel in all areas, which is why different awards are given, but doing well in a few areas helps. Of course, the best is when the judges laugh or throw up. (Extra points awarded if you make lint abort.)

Although awards like "best abuse of the preprocessor" and "strangest source layout" are common from year to year, there are no set awards—they depend upon the submissions and the judges' moods. Whereas the judges claim strictness, they have tended toward leniency in their own guidelines for reasons unknown. In particular, a couple of winners have been quite similar to earlier winners, despite the judges' admonishments to not look at old winners for ideas. ("What was unique and novel last year might be old hat this year.") Very stern warnings about size have also been continually relaxed. When the contest began, program size was restricted to 512 characters. In 1986 and 1987, the limit was raised to 1024, and then raised again to 1536 in following years. Undoubtedly, the limits will rise again in the future.

In early years, entrants were encouraged to use code conforming to *K&R1*. Machine and operating system specific features (especially after the 1984 first place winner) were forbidden. Coming full circle, the judges now allow Standard C and permit use of a variety of extensions such as sockets and X windows. (Admittedly, it is a feat to squeeze any of these things into such short programs!)

And now the 1987 winners. Note that entries did not pass lint unless stated otherwise. Hmm!

Best Obfuscator of Programs

Paul Heckbert <ph@pixar.com>
Pixar
Richmond, California

```
#include <ctype.h>
#include <stdio.h>
#define _ define
#_ A putchar
#_ B return
#_ C index char*r,c[300001],*d=">=<=!===||&&->++-->><<",*i,*l,*j,
*m,*k,*n,*h,*y;e,u=1,v,w,f=1,p,s,x;main(a,b)char**b;{p=a>1?atoi(
b
[1]):79;r=c+read(0,j=l=i=c,300000);v=g( j,&m);for(k=m;v!=2;j=k,m=
n,v=w,k=m){w=g(k,&n);if(v==1&&m-j==1&&*j==35)e&&-
A(10),e=f=0;if(!f
&&v==3&&(char*)C(j,10)<m)A(10),e=0,f=1;else if(v>2&&(u||w)&&(f||u
)&&(1-i>1||*i!=61||n-k>1|||C("-*&",*k)))continue;else if(v==3)if(
f&&e+1+n-k>p&&e)A (10),e=0;else A(32),e++;else{if(f&&e+m-j>p&&e)A
(10),e=0;e+=m-j;k=j;while(k<m)A( *k++);}i=j;l=m;u=v;}e&&A(10);}g(
j,m)char*j,**m;{if(j>=r)B*m=j,2;s=isdigit(*j)|| *j==46&&isdigit(j
[1]);for(h=j;h<r;h++)if(!isalnum(*h)&&*h!=95&&(!s||*h!=46)&&(! s|
|h[-1]!=101&&h[-1]!=69|||C("+-",*h)))break;if(h>j)B*m=h,0;x=1;-
for
(h=j;h<r&&C( " \t\n",*h);h++);if(h>j)h--,x=3;if(*j==34||*j==39)
for(h=j+1;h<r&&*h!=*j;h++)if( *h==92)h++;for(y=d;*y&&strncmp(y,j,
2);y+=2);if(*y)h=j+1;if(!strncmp("/*",j,2)){ h=j+2;while(*++h!=42
||*++h!=47);x=4;}*m=h+1;B x;}
```

On some systems, this needs to be compiled with: `#define index strchr`. To compile on a 16-bit machine, change 300000's to 30000. It passes `lint`.

This program *folds* programs. That is, given a column number and C program, it will break lines at the given column. It correctly understands C, so that identifiers, strings, etc., are not broken up. For example, when run on itself and given the argument 40, it prints:

```
#include <ctype.h>
#include <stdio.h>
#define __ define
#__ A putchar
#__ B return
#__ C index
char*r,c[300001],*d=
">=<=!===||&&->++-->><<",*i,*l,*j,*m,*k,
*n,*h,*y;e,u=1,v,w,f=1,p,s,x;main(a,b)
char**b;{p=a>1?atoi(b[1]):79;r=c+read(0,
j=l=i=c,300000);v=g(j,&m);for(k=m;v!=2;j
=k,m=n,v=w,k=m){w=g(k,&n);if(v==1&&m-j==
```

```
1&&*j==35)e&&A(10),e=f=0;if(!f&&v==3&&(
char*)C(j,10)<m)A(10),e=0,f=1;else if(v>
2&&(u||w)&&(f||u)&&(1-i>1||*i!=61||n-k>1
|||!C("-*&",*k)))continue;else if(v==3)if
(f&&e+1+n-k>p&&e)A(10),e=0;else A(32),e
++;else{if(f&&e+m-j>p&&e)A(10),e=0;e+=m-
j;k=j;while(k<m)A(*k++);}i=j;l=m;u=v;}e
&&A(10);}g(j,m)char*j,**m;{if(j>=r)B*m=j
,2;s=isdigit(*j)||*j==46&&isdigit(j[1]);
for(h=j;h<r;h++)if(!isalnum(*h)&&*h!=95
&&(!s||*h!=46)&&(!s||h[-1]!=101&&h[-1]!=
69||!C("+-",*h)))break;if(h>j)B*m=h,0;x=
1;for(h=j;h<r&&C(" \t\n",*h);h++);if(h>j
)h--,x=3;if(*j==34||*j==39)for(h=j+1;h<r
&&*h!=*j;h++)if(*h==92)h++;for(y=d;*y&&
strncmp(y,j,2);y+=2);if(*y)h=j+1;if(!
strncmp("/*",j,2)){h=j+2;while(*++h!=42
||*++h!=47);x=4;}*m=h+1;B x;}
```

Analysis

This program consists of two functions. One is a scanner that successfully recognizes most of the tokens of the C language. For example, two-character operators are compared from a map that appears on the first long line in the original program. Most of the single-character operators are not recognized explicitly, but just assumed. While the program explicitly handles things like strings, comments, and floating-point numbers, it does not retain anything useful about them except for the length. Below is the comment scanning code.

```
if(!strncmp("/*",j,2)){ h=j+2;while(*++h!=42||*++h!=47);x=4;}
```

The length is returned to the second function, which takes care of output formatting. Very little is actually necessary to do this, since C is relatively free-format. For instance, # must be handled specially, so that it is always placed on a new line (unless we are already on a new line).

One other thing worth noting is that the entire program is read in at once by the statement:

```
r=c+read(0,j=l=i=c,300000)
```

where c is the pointer to the first character of the program, and r points to the end of it. This kind of logic avoids an extra loop, while giving up a little flexibility in handling larger programs. Alas, this is just one example of the kind of sacrifices that obfuscated programs have to make.

Most Useful Obfuscation

Larry Wall <lwall@netlabs.com>
Netlabs, Inc.
Los Altos, California

```
#define iv 4
#define v ;(void
#define XI(xi)int xi[iv*'V'];
#define L(c,l,i)c(){d(l);m(i);}
#include <stdio.h>
int*cc,c,i,ix='\t',exit(),X='\n'*'\d';XI(VI)XI(xi)extern(*vi[])(
)
,(*signal())();char*V,cm,D['x'],M='\n',I,*gets();L(MV,V,(c+='d',
i
x))m(x){v} signal(X/'I',vi[x]);}d(x)char*x;{v}write(i,x,i);}L(MC,
V,M+I)xv(){c>=i?m( c/M/M+M):(d(&M),m(cm));}L(mi,V+cm,M)L(md,V,M)
MM(){c=c*M%X;V-=cm;m(ix);} LXX(){gets(D)||(vi[iv])();c=atoi(D);
while(c>=X){c-=X;d("m");}V="ivxlcdm" +iv;m(ix);}LV(){c-=c;while((
i=cc[*D=getchar()])>-I)i?(c?(c<i&&l(-c-c, "%d"),l(i,"+%d")):l(i,
"(%d")):(c&&l(M,")"),l(*D,"%c")),c=i;c&&l(X,")"),l (-i,"%c");m(iv
-!(i&I));}L(ml,V,'\f')li(){m(cm+!isatty(i=I));}ii(){m(c=cm =++I)v
)pipe(VI);cc=xi+cm++;for(V="jWYmDEnX";*V;V++)xi[*V^''']=c,xi[*V++
]
=c,c*=M,xi[*V^' ']=xi[*V]=c>>I;cc[-I]-=ix v)close(*VI);cc[M]-=M;}
main(){ (*vi)();for(;v)write(VI[I],V,M));}l(xl,lx)char*lx;{v}
printf(lx,xl)v) fflush(stdout);}L(xx,V+I,(c-=X/cm,ix))int(*vi[])(
)={ii,li,LXX,LV,exit,l, d,l,d,xv,MM,md,MC,ml,MV,xx,xx,xx,xx,MV,mi
};
```

This might appear to be simply another self-documenting program, but it has a few
surprises. Running it on a UNIX system and piping the output into bc (the desk calculator) and back into itself results in the following:

```
% useful | bc | useful
x*x                            (I typed this)
c                              (system answered)
c^2                            (I typed this)
mmmmmmmmmmmm                   (system answered)
```

Analysis

It's hard to shower compliments on these programs, but this one is really deserving.
It has a nice mix of the usual obfuscations plus a couple of unusual twists.

The program is structured as a finite state automaton. Each new state has its own
function. Interestingly, functions are called by setting up a signal and then trigger-
ing it. (The author gives credit to Mark Biggar for this technique.)

The main loop looks something like this:

```
main() {
        (*vi) ();
        for (;; (void) write(fd,"junk",10);
}
```

The first call primes the pump. In particular, it opens a file descriptor (via `pipe`) and closes it (to make sure the value is definitely illegal to write). Then it proceeds to write to the file descriptor! What is written is irrelevant. (There aren't 10 characters in "`junk`" but so what?) A signal is triggered and the previously arranged function is called. For example, one function looks like this:

```
LXX () {
        gets (D) || (vi[4]) ();
        c = atoi (D);
        while (c >= X) {
                c -= X;
                d ("m");
        } V = "ivxlcdm"
                + 4;
        m (ix);
}
```

The first line attempts to read input. If none is found, it calls `vi[4]`, which points at `exit`. The `vi` array points to various functions (for more obscurity). In fact, the first line in `main` called the pump-priming function from `vi`.

In case you haven't figured out what this program is doing, it is converting arabic to roman numerals (at least, so far). The code in the middle of this function prints out the appropriate number of `m`'s, by looping while subtracting 1000 each time. This may not be obvious because `x` was initialized to 1000 by the statement:

```
X = '\n' * '\d';
```

As demonstrated above, the program actually behaves differently when its input is coming from a pipe. In particular, `li` calls `isatty` to see whether input is coming from a tty or not. It then arranges (again, via `signal`) to enter the arabic-to-roman or the roman-to-arabic states of the FSA. This allows the resulting program to work with the UNIX calculator as displayed earlier.

Here is the program with "correct" indenting:

```
#include <stdio.h>
int     *cc, c, i, ix = '\t', exit (), X = '\n' * '\d';
int     VI[4 * 'V'];
int     xi[4 * 'V'];
extern  (*vi[]) (), (*signal ()) ();
char    *V, cm, D['x'], M = '\n', I, *gets ();
MV () {
    d (V);
    m ((c += 'd', ix));
}

m (x) {
    ;
    (void) signal (X / 'I', vi[x]);
}
```

```
d (x) char    *x; {
     ;
     (void) write (i, x, i);
}

MC () {
     d (V);
     m (M + I);
}

xv () {
     c >= i ? m (c / M / M + M) : (d (&M), m (cm));
}

mi () {
     d (V + cm);
     m (M);
}

md () {
     d (V);
     m (M);
}

MM () {
     c = c * M % X;
     V -= cm;
     m (ix);
}

LXX () {
     gets (D) || (vi[4]) ();
     c = atoi (D);
     while (c >= X) {
          c -= X;
          d ("m");
     }
     V = "ivxlcdm" + 4;
     m (ix);
}

LV () {
     c -= c;
     while ((i = cc[*D = getchar ()]) > -I)
          i ? (c ? (c < i && 1 (-c - c,
                                   "%d"), 1 (i, "+%d")) : 1 (i,
"(%d")) : (c && 1 (M, ")"), 1 (*D, "%c")), c = i;
     c && 1 (X, ")"), 1
          (-i, "%c");
     m (4 - !(i & I));
```

```
}

ml () {
    d (V);
    m ('\f');
}

li () {
    m (cm + !isatty (i = I));
}

ii () {
    m (c = cm = ++I);
    (void) pipe (VI);
    cc = xi + cm++;
    for (V = "jWYmDEnX"; *V; V++)
        xi[*V ^ ' '] = c, xi[*V++]
            = c, c *= M, xi[*V ^ ' '] = xi[*V] = c >> I;
    cc[-I] -= ix;
    (void) close (*VI);
    cc[M] -= M;
}

main () {
    (*vi) ();
    for (;; (void) write (VI[I], V, M));
}

l (xl, lx)
char *lx;
{;
    (void) printf (lx, xl);
    (void) fflush (stdout);
}

xx () {
    d (V + I);
    m ((c -= X / cm, ix));
}

int (*vi[]) () = {
            ii, li, LXX, LV, exit, l,
            d, l, d, xv, MM, md, MC, ml, MV, xx, xx, xx, xx, MV,
mi
};
```

Best Layout

Merlyn LeRoy (Brian Westley) <merlyn@digibd.com>
DigiBoard, Inc.
St. Paul, Minnesota

```
                        char rahc
                          [ ]
                           =
                        "\n/"
                           ,
                        redivider
                          [ ]
                           =
                "Able was I ere I saw elbA"
                           ,
                           *
                     deliver,reviled
                           =
                          1+1
                           ,
                     niam ; main
                          ( )
                        {/*\}
                        \*/
                       int tni
                          =
                         0x0
                           ,
                    rahctup,putchar
                          ( )
                   ,LACEDx0 = 0xDECAL,
                       rof ; for
                     (;(int)(tni);)
                       (int)(tni)
                 = reviled ; deliver =
                       redivider
                           ;
for((int)(tni)++,++reviled;reviled**deliver;deliver++,++(int)(tni))rof
                           =
                     (int) -1- (tni)
                    ;reviled--;--deliver;
                      (tni)  =  (int)
                    - 0xDECAL + LACEDx0 -
                       rof ; for
        (reviled--,(int)--(tni);(int) (tni);(int)--(tni),--deliver)
                    rahctup = putchar
                    (reviled* *deliver)
                           ;
                    rahctup * putchar
                    ((char) * (rahc))
                           ;
                         /*\
                        {\*/}
```

The author's analysis of this "C inkblot" follows.

Author's Analysis

"I was inspired to write this when someone posted a self-reproducing C program that was also a palindrome. If I remember right, it used the obvious commenting trick of:

```
/*/ regular C code /*/ edoc C raluger /*/
```

or something similar. I decided to make a left-right symmetrical program. At first, I started doing:

```
#include <stdio.h>    /*\    <h.oidts> edulcni#
;a rahc               \*/              char a;
```

but this made the program trivial. I decided to get rid of as much comment cheating as I could (I only had to cheat for the opening and closing braces for `main`). It had to do something, so I made it print a string out backwards. The earlier versions had more palindrome variables, like `tot`, but I realized that I could cast the backwards versions of the type names as `(int)(tni)` instead, so I reduced the number of unused variables (only `niam` was unused). I also added a palindrome pair, `LACEDx0` and `0xDECAL`, a variable and a hex constant, even though I didn't need them. The algorithm is not too hard to figure out; it counts the string until it reaches the end, then counts back down, printing the string out backwards."

Best One-Liner

David Korn <ulysses!djk>
AT&T Bell Labs
Murray Hill, New Jersey

```
main(){printf(&unix["\021%six\012\0"],(unix)["have"]+"fun"-0x60);}
```

Analysis

It is hard to believe this program does anything, unless you are a fairly experienced UNIX programmer. The key is that `unix` is not explicitly defined. How is this possible?

This symbol is commonly **defined** to be 1 on UNIX systems. Even if you don't program on UNIX systems, you should be familiar with the common preprocessor macros, because many people take UNIX sources and compile them on non-UNIX machines without change. Armed with this knowledge, the program can be rewritten as:

```
main() {printf(&1["\021%six\012\0"],(1)["have"]+"fun"-0x60);}
```

The C language defines array indexing in terms of pointer operations. That is, `a[b]` is equivalent to `*(a+b)`. We use this to rewrite to the program again.

```
main() {printf(&*(1+"\021%six\012\0"],*(1+"have")+"fun-0x60);}
```

What is the meaning of `*(1+string)`? The compiler adds 1 to the address of the string to get the value of the second element of the string. The `&*` prefix is dropped (technically illegal, but not a surprising result of an aggressive optimizer) and the expressions returns the address of the new part of the string, so that the program could be thought of as:

```
main() {printf("%six\012\0",'a' + "fun" - 0x60);}
```

Let's rewrite `'a'` as its hex equivalent.

```
main() {printf("%six\012\0",0x61 + "fun" - 0x60);}
```

Because addition is commutative, the second expression can be simplified:

```
main() {printf("%six\012\0",1 + "fun");}
```

Again, interpreting the addition of 1 to a string, and making the explicit null character implicit in the first string, leaves the program like this:

```
main() {printf("%six\n","un");}
```

Running this program, finally, `printf` will replace the `%s` with `un` and the program will print `unix` (followed by a newline).

It is worth noting that the author is responsible for a shell of his own (`ksh` or "Korn shell") that has become very popular.

Best Abuse of the Rules

Mark Biggar <mab@wdl1.wdl.loral.com>
Loral Western Development Labs
San Jose, California

```
    P;
```

The instructions included with this program (for a UNIX C compiler) said to compile with the command:

```
cc -DC="R>0" -DI="if(T)O" -DO="c=write(1,&c,1);" -DP="main(){X}"
-DR="read(0,&c,1)" -DT="c!=015" -DW="while(C)I" -DX="char c;W"
markb.c
```

This ridiculous compile instruction drives the program through a series of transformations:

```
P;
```

```
main(){X};
```

```
main(){char c;W};
```

```
main(){char c;while(R>0)I};
```

```
main(){char c;while(read(0,&c,1)>0)I};

main(){char c;while(read(0,&c,1)>0)if(T)O};

main(){char c;while(read(0,&c,1)>0)if(c!=015)O};

main(){char c;while(read(0,&c,1)>0)if(c!=015)c=write(1,&c,1)};
```

I'll leave the interpretation of the final result to you. Note that you can make the program do anything you want by changing only the compile line—the height of flexibility! Also, this is a very efficient way to transfer source, though it does increase the size of `Makefiles`. (This winner caused the judges to put a limit on compile lines in following contests.)

It is worth noting that the semicolon at the end is actually illegal. Perhaps this is what threw off one vendor's `lint`, which got hung in an infinite loop over this entry!

Worst Style

Spencer Hines <spencer@zeus.ocs.com>
OnLine Computer Systems
Hyattsville, Maryland

```
#include <stdio.h>
char *malloc();
main(togo,toog)
int togo;
char *toog[];
{char *ogto,  tgoo[80];FILE *ogot; int    oogt=0,ootg,  otog=79,
ottg=1;if (    togo== ottg)  goto    gogo;  goto    goog;  ggot:
if (   fgets( tgoo,  otog,  ogot)) goto    gtgo;  goto    gott;
gtot:   exit();ogtg:++oogt;  goto    ogoo;  togg:  if (   ootg > 0)
goto    oggt;  goto    ggot;  ogog:  if (   !ogot) goto    gogo;
goto    ggto;  gtto:   printf("%d    goto    \'s\n",oogt); goto
gtot;  oggt:   if (    !memcmp(ogto,  "goto",4))   goto    otgg;
goto    gooo;  gogo:   exit( ottg); tggo:  ootg=   strlen(tgoo);
goto    tgog;  oogo:--ootg;  goto    togg;  gooo:  ++ogto;goto
oogo;  gott:   fclose(ogot); goto    gtto;  otgg:  ogto=   ogto +3;
goto    ogtg;  tgog:   ootg-=4;goto    togg;  gtgo:  ogto=   tgoo;
goto    tggo;  ogoo:   ootg-=3;goto    gooo;  goog:  ogot=   fopen(
toog[ ottg],  "r");  goto    ogog;  ggto:  ogto=   tgoo;  goto
ggot;}
```

This was yet another program whose subject matter I could predict. What it was going to do with it, on the other hand, I hadn't a clue.

This program takes `goto` statements to their logical conclusion. The layout and choice of names are classic. But what does the program do? It analyzes C programs and counts the number of gotos in them! Running this program on itself results in the following:

```
% style style.c
24 goto's
```

That is rather startling, but indenting the program made me a believer!

```
#include <stdio.h>
char *malloc();
main(togo, toog)
int togo;
char *toog[];
{
        char *ogto, tgoo[80];
        FILE *ogot;

        int oogt = 0, ootg, otog = 79, ottg = 1;
        if (togo == ottg) goto gogo;
        goto goog;
ggot:   if (fgets(tgoo, otog, ogot)) goto gtgo;
        goto gott;
gtot:   exit();
ogtg:   ++oogt;
        goto ogoo;
togg:   if (ootg > 0) goto oggt;
        goto ggot;
ogog:   if (!ogot) goto gogo;
        goto ggto;
gtto:   printf("%d    goto   \'s\n", oogt);
        goto gtot;
oggt:   if (!memcmp(ogto, "goto", 4)) goto otgg;
        goto gooo;
gogo:   exit(ottg);
tggo:   ootg = strlen(tgoo);
        goto tgog;
oogo:   --ootg;
        goto togg;
gooo:   ++ogto;
        goto oogo;
gott:   fclose(ogot);
        goto gtto;
otgg:   ogto = ogto + 3;
        goto ogtg;
tgog:   ootg -= 4;
        goto togg;
gtgo:   ogto = tgoo;
        goto tggo;
ogoo:   ootg -= 3;
        goto gooo;
goog:   ogot = fopen(toog[ottg], "r");
```

```
        goto ogog;
ggto:   ogto = tgoo;
        goto ggot;
}
```

Try removing all the `goto`s from the program. It's harder than it sounds, even for a simple program like this one. Toward the end, you may find it helpful to rewrite a dummy `while` and `for` loop using `goto`s. Then try to find things in this program that look like what you've produced.

Amusingly, assembler code for many RISC and microcoded machines essentially include a `goto` on each line. This is rarely seen by the user, and the hardware expects it so there is no real penalty, much as it might seem. I suspect *that* style of programming makes the author of this program feel right at home!

Most Well-Rounded Confusion (Grand Prize)

Roemer B. Lievaart <roemer@cs.vu.nl>
Vrije University—Informatica
Amsterdam, Netherlands

```
#define D define
#D Y return
#D R for
#D e while
#D I printf
#D l int
#D C y=v+111;H(x,v)*y+= *x
#D H(a,b)R(a=b+11;a<b+89;a++)
#D s(a)t=scanf("%d",&a)
l V[1100],u,r[]={-1,-11,-10,-9,1,11,10,9},h[]={11,18,81,88},ih[]=
{22,27,72,77},bz,lv=60,*x,*y,m,t;S(d,v,f,a,b)l*v;{l c=0,*n=v+100,
bw=d<u-1?a:-9000,w,z,i,zb,q=3-f;if(d>u){R(w=i=0;i<4;i++)w+=(m=v[h
[i]])==f?300:m==q?-300:(t=v[ih[i]])==f?-50:t==q?50:0;return w;}H(
z,0){if(GZ(v,z,f,100)){c++;w=-S(d+1,n,q,-b,-bw);if(w>bw){zb=z;bw=
w;if(w>=b||w>=8003)Y w;}}}if(!c){bz=0;C;Y-S(d+1,n,q,-b,-bw);}bz=
zb;Y d>=u-1?bw+(c<3):bw;}main(){R(;t<1100;t+=100)R(m=0;m<100;m++
)V[t+m]=m<11||m>88||(m+1)%10<2?3:0;V[44]=V[55]=1;V[45]=V[54]=2;I(
"Level:");s(u);e(lv>0){do{I("You:");s(m);}e(!GZ(V,m,2,0)&&m!=99);
if(m!=99)lv--;if(lv<15&&u<10)u+=2;I("Wait\n");I("Value:%d\n",S(0,
V,1,-9000,9000));I("move: %d\n",(lv-=GZ(V,bz,1,0),bz));}}GZ (v,z,
f,o)l*v;{l*j,q=3-f,g=0,i,h,*k=v+z;if(*k==0)R(i=7;i>=0;i--){j=k+(h
=r[i]);e(*j==q)j+=h;if(*j==f&&j-h!=k){if(!g){g=1;C;}e(j!=k)*((j-=
h)+o)=f;}}Y g;}
```

This program plays Othello. It can play at ten different skill levels, and is pretty good. It actually includes some rather sophisticated algorithms in the form of alpha-beta pruning, a sophisticated method of reducing the amount of searching in trees of possible moves. For a program under 1024 bytes (the limit under the rules), this is quite impressive. (Oh, and too bad about the formatting!)

The original program is now lost to history, alas, but was a perfectly readable Othello program that the author simply kept on mutilating until it fit the 1024 character limit.

The program prompts for input with "`You:`" and in response you are expected to enter moves by a two-digit number where one number represents the column and the another the row. If you get stuck, it is possible to pass by entering "`99`". Here is the beginning of a sample session:

```
Level:2
You:34
Wait
Value:-16
move:33
You:43
Wait
Value:-32
move:35
You:36
Wait
Value:16
move:64
You:65
Wait
Value:0
move:37
```

## CHAPTER 18

Win a Gold Medal in the Longjmp

`setjmp` and `longjmp` are functions for "unwinding the stack." I will explain what this is shortly. First, I will motivate it by an example.

Assume we have written an interactive program such as a shell or editor. Its basic structure is that of a command loop as follows:

```
while (1) {
    prompt_for_command();
    read_command();
    execute_command();
}
```

A typical problem arises when the user types in a command that begins running, taking a while to run. Suppose the user attempts to cancel the command, perhaps by pressing a key predefined to generate an interrupt.

Whenever an interrupt occurs, control is given to an interrupt handler. The interrupt handler can call the main program to reenter the loop, but because the interrupt handler hasn't actually returned, the stack is never cleaned up. Enough interrupts of this type will eventually cause a stack overflow.

Simply returning from the interrupt handler isn't a viable solution either, because control will return to the same computation that the user wanted to escape from.

The only realistic solution is to pop off stack frames until we get to the one for the main loop and then jump directly from the interrupt handler back into the top of the read/execute loop. (A *stack frame* or *activation record* is everything on the stack pertinent to one procedure call.) Popping stack frames like this is called *unwinding the stack.*

Setjmp and Longjmp

C provides a function called `longjmp`, which unwinds the stack. As its first argument, `longjmp` takes a location to jump to. The location is stored in a *jmp_buf* (defined in `<setjmp.h>`), which is set with `setjmp`. Just call `setjmp` at locations you may need to jump to, and call `longjmp` when you want to actually jump back. This is similar to `goto`s, where labels indicate where you can jump to, and executing the `goto` actually causes the jump to occur. Unlike `goto`, however, `longjmp` can jump out of procedure calls and unwind the stack as necessary. Also, `longjmp` can jump only to a location where you've already been.

When the jump occurs, the program behaves as if `setjmp` is returning again, but this time with the value of the second argument of `longjmp`. The following code shows our original loop using an interrupt routine that unwinds the stack. We ignore any value that `setjmp` returns.

```c
#include <setjmp.h>

jmp_buf restart;

set_interrupt_handler();
while (1) {
    setjmp(restart);
    prompt_for_command();
    read_command();
    execute_command();
}

interrupt_handler() {
    longjmp(restart,0);
}
```

`setjmp` returns 0 the first time it is called. When `longjmp` is called, `setjmp` returns again but with the value of the second argument passed to `longjmp`. This allows the program to figure out whether `setjmp` is returning from `longjmp` or not.

We saw an example of how this could be useful earlier (see p. 63 in Chapter 9). The problem was to read from a file and to time out if no bytes were available. Here I will show the simpler problem of just interrupting a `read`. The problem is that on some systems, `read`s that are interrupted may be restarted automatically. On some systems, interrupted `read`s are not restarted. With `setjmp` it is possible to handle both cases with the same code, as follows:

```c
#include <setjmp.h>

jmp_buf env;

int interruptible_read(fd,buffer,length)
int fd;
char *buffer;
int length;
{
    if (0 == setjmp(env))
        return(read(fd,buffer,maxlength));
    else return 0;
}

interrupt_handler() {
    longjmp(env,1);
```

```
    }
```

When we call `interruptible_read`, `setjmp` returns 0 and executes `read`. If `read` is interrupted, `interrupt_handler` is called and `longjmp` is executed, causing `setjmp` to return with the value 1. Because 0 != 1, `read` is not reexecuted and `interruptible_read` returns.

This is a paradigm for handling interrupts and other low-level errors in a variety of functions. You should get used to seeing this type of code, and immediately recognize what it is doing. It may be illustrative to refer back to Chapter 9 (p. 63) to see another example of how `setjmp` and `longjmp` are used to solve a similar problem. Neither of these problems are solvable without `setjmp` and `longjmp`.

How Do They Work?

How do `setjmp` and `longjmp` work? `setjmp` saves the PC (program location), stack pointer, and some of the other registers in `jmp_buf`. `longjmp` restores the registers.[1] After calling `longjmp`, the effect is that we appear to return from `setjmp`, completely ignoring all the stack frames that were set up between the `setjmp` and the `longjmp`.

If we have returned from the function that executed `setjmp`, then the saved environment is useless since an old frame beyond the current one is meaningless. You must be careful when setting up `jmp_bufs`, since it is unlikely that the system will catch this kind of error, and you can find yourself jumping into oblivion.

Fast Returns

`longjmp` works equally well popping one stack frame or popping ten stack frames. Because of this, it can be used as a fast return that exits many functions at once. While this is not a technique that makes code easy to follow, there are valid uses.

For example, a recursive-descent parser may use many stack frames just parsing a single expression. It is quite typical that a low-level routine can determine that the entire expression must be aborted. Rather than return with a failure and have each caller do the same thing, the routine detecting the problem simply calls `longjmp` to restart or abort the parse. By aborting with a `longjmp` rather than a `return`, there is no need to put error-checking code after each call. The code actually becomes more readable because most functions can now assume that every function they call always succeeds (if control returns).

Multitasking

It is actually possible to do a limited form of multitasking with `setjmp` and `longjmp`. Restating the restriction I just mentioned, you can't `longjmp` to a routine if it is not in the calling chain of the current function. Then how can you pass con-

---

1. The details of this discussion apply to register-based machines. Others are similar in concept but operate differently internally.

trol to multiple procedures that do not follow a strict hierarchical call sequence? Well, the restriction is simply there to avoid the possibility of jumping to a stack frame that is no longer valid due to its parent frames having been changed. But we can guarantee this doesn't happen by using separate stacks for each thread of control.

The idea is that you set up a number of tasks (top-level procedures). Each task allocates its own stack initially and starts using it immediately. Then, as each task wants to release the processor temporarily for other tasks to run, it puts itself on a queue of tasks to run, pulls off the next process to execute, saves the registers with `setjmp` and then calls `longjmp` with the environment of the next process. These functions can all be packaged up into one function called `schedule_next_task`. Here is the basic idea of such a function.

```
schedule_next_task() {
    task_insert(ready_queue,old_task);
    task_remove(ready_queue,new_task);
    if (0 == setjmp(old_task))
        longjmp(new_task,1);
    }
}
```

In the above code fragment, `old_task` and `new_task` represent places where one task is giving up control of the CPU, and another task is going to get control of the CPU (where it previously gave up control). `task_insert` puts the current task on a queue of tasks that are ready to execute. `task_remove` returns the highest priority task from those ready to execute. It also removes this task from the queue.

Now, with `setjmp`, we save the current task for later resumption, and resume the new task with `longjmp`. Where does the task resume? Of course, the new task resumes at the `setjmp`, so we must signify that we do not wish to execute the `longjmp` again by returning 1. Does this code look familiar? It should. It is exactly the same code that we used to write our `interruptible_read`!

What I have outlined here is a *non-preemptive* multitasking scheduler. Non-preemptive means that tasks must explicitly give up control of the CPU (in this case, by calling `schedule_next_task`). A *preemptive* scheduler will take the CPU away from the tasks whether or not they are done with it. It is not possible to do preemptive scheduling with `setjmp` and `longjmp`.

Writing a preemptive scheduler requires a little assembly coding (mainly to save and restore *all* the registers at task-switch time). If you would like to read more about it, I highly recommend the book on Xinu by Douglas Comer [1]. This unusually well-written text describes the complete implementation of an operating system written almost entirely in C. The book includes the necessary assembler for bringing the system up on a DEC LSI 11/2 (a microcomputer version of the PDP-11). It has been ported to several other microcomputers; you may want to try doing it yourself.

Warnings

As I mentioned earlier, `setjmp` actually works by saving most of the registers; however, it might not save *all* the registers. The reason is that some implementations use registers as temporaries that are never saved across procedure calls. For example, if our compiler always reserves two registers for temporary results, `setjmp` does not have to waste time saving those two at procedure calls. Because `setjmp` itself is a procedure, these two registers will not have useful values anyway at the time `setjmp` is called or returns. For the same reason, the condition codes of the CPU are not saved either.

This explains why we cannot do preemptive multitasking with `setjmp` and `longjmp` alone. If tasks are interrupted (by a clock interrupt, for example) at any point in the code, we may well be using the temporary registers and condition codes. Since `setjmp` doesn't save any of this information, we will not be able to restart the task later in the same state that we found it.

Understanding how `setjmp` works is helpful in using it correctly. It should be clear now that when you call `longjmp`, your variables that are stored in registers will contain the same values that they had when `setjmp` was called. On the other hand, your memory variables will not be changed, but will contain whatever value they had at the time `longjmp` was called. The only problem is—how do you determine whether a variable is stored in a register or memory?

Variables not local to the function containing the `setjmp` will be stored in memory (or act like it). There is no guarantee that variables declared as `register` will actually be in registers so don't depend on that. Standard C provides the `volatile` type qualifier that guarantees variables will not be changed after a `longjmp`. Without this, you must assume the worst possible case and write your code in such a way that you do not depend on having variable values revert after a `longjmp`.

Conclusion

We have seen how `setjmp` and `longjmp` are useful in dealing with low-level conditions such as interrupts and error-handling code. Used correctly, they are appropriate for certain problems that can be solved in no other way. However, like `goto`, they can be overused and abused. Indeed, they are worse than `goto`s in the sense that they make program control flow nonhierarchical. Please use them carefully and only when you cannot otherwise avoid it.

References

[1]   Douglas Comer, *Operating System Design: The Xinu Approach*, Prentice Hall, 1984.

Dump from the Hip

This chapter presents a useful debugging tool—a dump routine. While rather mundane in function, the implementation illustrates several things:

- It is possible to treat memory like a file (or "stream").
- It is possible to pass pointers to functions as parameters.
- It is possible to package code in such a way that it can be called from a program, a debugger, or run standalone.

As a program, `dump` is invoked as `dump filename`. The contents of the file are then listed in hex and ASCII side by side. Each line of 16 bytes is preceded by its hex offset from the beginning of the file. Here is the beginning of this chapter, run through dump.

```
% dump chapter
 0: 54 68 69 73 20 63 68 61 70 74 65 72 20 70 72 65    This chapter pre
10: 73 65 6e 74 73 20 61 20 75 73 65 66 75 6c 20 64    sents a useful d
20: 65 62 75 67 67 69 6e 67 20 74 6f 6f 6c 20 2d 20    ebugging tool -
30: 61 20 64 75 6d 70 20 72 6f 75 74 69 6e 65 2e 0a    a dump routine..
40: 57 68 69 6c 65 20 72 61 74 68 65 72 20 6d 75 6e    While rather mun
50: 64 61 6e 65 20 69 6e 20 66 75 6e 63 74 69 6f 6e    dane in function
60: 2c 20 74 68 65 20 69 6d 70 6c 65 6d 65 6e 74 61    , the implementa
```

`dump` may be called from a program as follows:

```
#include "dump.h"

dump(address,length,outfile)
```

`address` is the address of memory at which to start dumping. `length` is how many bytes should be dumped. `outfile` is the name of an output file, so that we can capture the results for study later.

Notice that the `dump` program doesn't take the same arguments as the `dump` subroutine. For example, the program doesn't require an output file because we can assume the standard output can be redirected, perhaps by a shell or a command processor. The other differences between the arguments should be obvious.

By using `#ifdef MAIN`, it is possible to generate both the standalone program and the dump subroutine from the same source. When **MAIN** is defined, **main** is created, otherwise `dump` is. Both `main` and `dump` call a function that does the real work of dumping, called `real_dump`.

Consider the problem of writing `real_dump`. The formatting part is simple enough, but where does the input come from? `getc` is the solution for reading in a file, but when `real_dump` is called from `dump`, it needs to get input directly from memory. We could pass the address and a length to `real_dump` but that wouldn't work for files.

One solution is to define two different dump routines, but that is somewhat annoying since so much of the code is the same. A cleaner solution is to pass an input routine to `real_dump`. Whenever it needs the next byte, `real_dump` simply calls the input routine. The input routine passed by `main` will return the next character from the file, while the input routine passed by `dump` will return the next character from memory.

Here is the input routine for `main`:

```
int file_reader() {
      return(getc(ifp));
}
```

The input routine for `dump` is only a little more complicated.

```
int mem_reader() {
      if (count++ >= length) return(EOF);
      else return(*address++);
}
```

Three global variables set by `dump` allow `mem_reader` to appear as if it is reading from a stream. In particular, when we have read `length` bytes, `EOF` is returned, otherwise we simply return the character at the next address.

`count` must also be global rather than declared `static int count = 0;`. Consider what happens inside of `mem_reader` when `dump` is called twice. The second time, `count` will not be reinitialized to 0. The solution is to make it global, and initialize it in the calling routine.

It is instructive to contrast the use of the global variables versus parameter passing. Each of the global variables could have been passed as a parameter, however this breaks the *stream* paradigm that we have used. There are few global variables here and they can all be declared `static`; however, if you are building a more complex application, you should reconsider this approach.

Notice that each of these routines returns an `int`, rather than a `char`. This is to allow passing `EOF` to terminate the input. This, again, follows the stream paradigm. Now we have enough to declare `real_dump`. It is declared:

```
real_dump(address,infunc,ofp)
char *address;
int (*infunc)();
FILE *ofp;
```

Here, `infunc` is declared as a "pointer to function returning `int`." Inside `real_dump`, the line where we use `infunc` looks like this:

```
... = (*infunc)();
```

The last argument of `real_dump`, `ofp`, is an output `FILE` pointer that is presumed to be opened by the caller, in this case either `main` or `dump`. `main` simply passes `stdout`, but `dump` requires some elaborate coding.

Unfortunately, some debuggers cannot create new string literals, making it impossible to interactively name an output file when calling `dump`. The problem is that the C compiler normally places literal strings in the initialized data space of a program. After linking, it may be impossible to increase this space. The debugger therefore is left with the choice of inserting the literal into another segment having different properties than the initialized data space, or not doing it at all. Debuggers that choose the latter prevent you from conveniently passing literal strings as arguments to procedure calls.

To avoid the problem, `dump` will prompt you to type in a filename if `outfile == 0`. Supplying a zero-length file name (`""`) will send the output to `stdout`.

To create `dump`, you need to create an object file that you can link to. Simply compile `dump.c` with no change. To compile `dump.c` and create a standalone program, define the macro, `MAIN`. If you compile `dump.c` with `TEST` defined, an executable will be produced with an empty `main` (just to satisfy the linker), the subroutine `dump`, and a variable, `foo`, to try dumping.

Source Code—dump.h

```
/* dump.h */
#ifndef DUMP_H
#define DUMP_H

#include "proto.h"   /* define PROTO */
void dump PROTO((char *,int,char *));

#endif /* DUMP_H */
```

Source Code—dump.c

```
/* dump.c - dump from file or memory */

#include <stdio.h>
#include <ctype.h>
#include "dump.h"

#define ROWLENGTH 16

#ifdef MAIN
static FILE *ifp;    /* shared by main and file_reader */
```

```
int
file_reader()
{
    return(getc(ifp));
}

int main(argc,argv)
int argc;
char **argv;
{
    if (argc == 1) ifp = stdin;
    else if (argc != 2) {
        printf("usage: dump file\n");
        exit(1);
    } else if (!(ifp = fopen(argv[1],"r"))) {
        perror(argv[1]);
        exit(1);
    }

    /* nonportable assumption that internal null ptr == 0 */
    /* if incorrect, only display will suffer slightly */
    real_dump((char *)0,file_reader,stdout);
    return 0;
}

#else

static int length;      /* shared by dump(), mem_reader() */
static char *address;   /* ditto */
static int count;       /* ditto */

int
mem_reader()
{
    if (count++ >= length) return(EOF);
    else return((int)*address++);
}

void
dump(address_parm,length_parm,outfile)
char *address_parm;
int length_parm;
char *outfile;
{
    char outfilebuffer[80];
    FILE *ofp;

    if (!outfile) {
        printf("output file (<cr> for stdout): ");
        gets(outfile = outfilebuffer);
```

```
        }

        if (*outfile) {
            if (!(ofp = fopen(outfile,"w"))) {
                perror(outfile);
                exit(1);
            }
        } else ofp = stdout;

        count = 0;
        length = length_parm;
        address = address_parm;

        real_dump(address,mem_reader,ofp);

        if (outfile && *outfile) fclose(ofp);
}

#endif

real_dump(address,infunc,ofp)
char *address;
int (*infunc)();
FILE *ofp;
{
        int i, row[ROWLENGTH];

        while (1) {
            for (i=0;i<ROWLENGTH;i++)
                row[i] = (*infunc)();
            if (row[0] == EOF) break;

            /* first print address */
            fprintf(ofp,"%lx: ",address);

            /* then print hex */
            for (i=0;i<ROWLENGTH;i++)
                fprintf(ofp,
                    (row[i] != EOF) ? "%02x ":"   ",
                    row[i]);

            /* lastly print characters */
            fprintf(ofp,"   ");
            for (i=0; i<ROWLENGTH; i++) {
                if (row[i] == EOF) break;
                if (isprint(row[i])) putc(row[i],ofp);
                else putc('.',ofp);
            }
            putc('\n',ofp);
            address += ROWLENGTH;
```

```
        }
}

#ifdef TEST
/* here is something to dump */
/* as well as containing a file to dump to */
char foo[] = {
'f', 'o', 'o', 0x0, 0x10, 'a', 'b', 0x18, 0xff, 0, 0x4
};

main()
{
}
#endif
```

Credits

Thanks to Walter Bright who provided the prototype for the dump code that appears here. While its origin is hard to recognize, that is his fault! For the original way this program appeared, see p. 92 in Chapter 12.

CHAPTER 20

Pointers to Functions

Chapter 19 (p. 157) showed a simple tool that was able to take input from either memory or a file. In order to do that cleanly, we used parameters that were pointers to functions. I am going to discuss this topic in more detail here.

First, I will point out a common mistake made in trying to pass functions as parameters. That is, functions cannot be passed, only *pointers to functions* can be. Thus, the following declaration will not work:

```
subr(fun)        /* WRONG */
int fun();       /* WRONG */
```

The declaration of `fun` says that it is a function returning an `int`, but we are not allowed to pass functions as parameters. (My compiler says "**warning: a function is passed as an argument.**") What we want instead is to pass a pointer to a function.

```
subr(fun)
int (* fun)();
```

`fun` is now declared as "pointer to function returning `int`." This is read *inside out*.

```
    (* fun)        "fun is a pointer"
    (* fun)()      "            to function"
int (* fun)()      "                    returning int"
```

This may be used in a prototype. However, prototypes should also include parameter declarations of the function pointer parameters. For example, if `subr`'s argument is a function that takes a pointer to a `double`, the complete prototype for `subr` (using the `PROTO` macro) would be:

```
int subr PROTO((int (*)(double *)));
```

It is not necessary to embed `PROTO` inside the declaration of `fun`. If you are using a non-prototyping compiler, the first `PROTO` will strip out everything immediately, anyway.

More complex function declarations are constructed in the same fashion. `cdecl` may also help. `cdecl` is a program that converts declarations from C to English and vice versa. A simple version can be found in *K&R2* (p. 123), and numerous versions can be found in public archives.

When calling `subr`, we supply it with a parameter simply by naming a function. The compiler arranges for the address of the function to be passed when it sees the function name. An `&` is not necessary.

To use the parameter while inside of `subr`, dereference `fun` using `*`, and then treat the result as a function. In other words, give it a set of parentheses with arguments. For example, to call the function (passed to `subr`) with arguments `17` and `"hello world"` we would write:

```
foo = (*fun)(17,"hello world");
```

Notice that the usage looks just like the declaration we made earlier.

Chapter 19 (p. 157) presented a program doing exactly what we just discussed. The function `real_dump` took a function parameter and was declared this way:

```
real_dump(address,infunc,ofp)
...
int (*infunc)();
```

This allowed us to read input from either a file or memory, depending entirely upon the function passed in `infunc`. `real_dump` called `(*infunc)()` each time it needed the next input character. In a multitasking system, `infunc` could also return input from a coroutine, that is, another process executing concurrently. Once again, `real_dump` would not need to be changed.

Sorting Anything

`qsort` is a function that encapsulates the essence of sorting—it can sort any type. This includes integers, floats, strings, and any set that you can define an ordering on (e.g., dates). You can find implementations in *K&R2* and Plauger's *The Standard C Library*.

The trick is that you, the caller, define the ordering on the type and pass a comparison function to `qsort`. Your ordering function will be called with arguments that are pointers to two of the data elements to be sorted. If the first is "larger" (in whatever sense you decide), your function should return 1. If it is "smaller," return –1. Otherwise it must be equal, so return 0.

To sort integers we can define `int_order` as:

```
int
int_order(x,y)
Generic x, y;
{
        return *(int *)x-*(int *)y;
}
```

To sort an array of `doubles` represented as strings, we could define `double_string_order` as:

```
int double_string_order(x,y)
Generic *x, *y;
{
    extern double atof();
    double dx = atof(*(char **)x);
    double dy = atof(*(char **)y);
    return(dx<dy?(dx==dy?0:-1):1);
}
```

Doing Anything to Anything!

As `qsort` demonstrates, it is possible to reuse higher-level code by calling the type-dependent subroutines whenever dealing with multiple types. This can be extended to just about any abstract data type.

Languages like C++ do this automatically. In C, it is possible to get similar benefits although it takes a little more work. A crude but effective scheme uses an array that encodes knowledge about all object types in your program. Here, `obj` is assigned some basic functions for dealing with a type FOO.

```
obj[TYPE_FOO].print   = foo_print;   /* printer */
obj[TYPE_FOO].new     = foo_new;     /* constructor */
obj[TYPE_FOO].cmp     = foo_cmp;     /* comparator */
obj[TYPE_FOO].destroy = foo_destroy; /* destructor */
obj[TYPE_FOO].copy    = foo_copy;    /* copier */
```

Types can be retrieved from the values themselves if they share a common object structure. Alternatively, they may be passed as an additional parameter.

Then the type-dependent functions can call upon the type-independent functions by retrieving the appropriate functions from the `obj` array. For example, here is a function that prints an object if its two arguments are the same. (Macros can make the indirection through `obj` much less noticeable.) `object` should either be a generic-style `typedef` or a `union` of all types.

```
void
print_if_equal(x,y,type)
object x, y;
object_type type;   /* type of x and y */
{
    if (obj[type].cmp(x,y) == 0) obj[type].print(x);
}
```

`print_if_equal` can be called upon any type for which the `obj` array has defined. Using techniques like this can greatly reduce the duplication of high-level code in your programs. More sophisticated solutions are provided directly by C++.

Condition Handlers

Another use of function pointers is with signal handlers or condition handlers. Condition handlers are functions called whenever some condition occurs.

For example, on many machines, division by 0 generates an arithmetic-exception signal. Rather than aborting the program, we may transfer control to an error recovery routine. At the very least, it can print out an error message. While we are debugging, the routine can trap back to the debugger.

The signal handler is set up as follows:

```
#include <signal.h>
#include "proto.h"

void sigfpe PROTO(int);  /* func to handle arithmetic errs
*/
main()
{
    signal(SIGFPE,sigfpe);
    .
    .
}
```

The first argument of `signal` designates the condition to catch. Some other signals are `SIGABRT` (abnormal termination), `SIGILL` (illegal instruction), `SIGINT` (interrupt from keyboard), `SIGSEGV` (memory access violation), and `SIGTERM` (normal termination). Many systems will also have extra operating system-dependent or machine-dependent signals.

The second argument to `signal` is the function to be executed upon receipt of the signal. It is also possible to pass predefined values in place of a user-declared function. `SIG_IGN` means that a given signal should be ignored and `SIG_DFL` means that the default behavior of a signal should be established.

Here is an example of how we might use signals in a real application. First, let us assume that `matrix_inverse` computes the inverse of a matrix. If the matrix is singular (i.e., has no inverse), a mathematical exception (such as division by 0) could take place, which will cause our signal handler to be called.

```
#include <setjmp.h>
#include <signal.h>

void sigfpe();

jmp_buf env;

main() {
    .
    .
    if (SIG_ERR == signal(SIGFPE,sigfpe))
        perror("signal")
```

```
        exit(-1);
    }
    if (0 == setjmp(env)) {
        printf("inverse = %f\n",matrix_inverse(mat));
    } else {
        printf("no inverse\n");
    }
    .
    .
    .
}
```

And here is the condition handler:

```
void sigfpe(sig)
int sig;
{
    longjmp(env,1);
}
```

The first call to `signal` registers the signal handler. If `signal` does not like its arguments, it returns `SIG_ERR`, which we duly check for. (Otherwise `signal` returns a pointer to whatever handler was last registered for the condition.)

Next, we save our context using `setjmp`. (For more on `setjmp`, see p. 151 in Chapter 18.) Initially, `setjmp` returns 0 so that we proceed to call `matrix_inverse`. If the matrix inverse is computed successfully, we continue after the `else` clause.

If `matrix_inverse` raises any sort of arithmetic condition, such as would happen for a singular matrix, a `SIGFPE` will occur, calling `sigfpe`. `sigfpe` executes `longjmp`, which returns to the `setjmp` and enters the `else` condition, printing "no inverse."

Declarations—Typedefs Help

Earlier I demonstrated how to read function declarations "inside out." A final suggestion is to use `typedef`s. For example, suppose we want to declare an "array of pointers to 17 functions." In this case, let us say they each take an `int` parameter and return an `int`. Now we can set up `typedef`s starting with the functions and working up.

```
typedef int FUNC PROTO((int));        FUNC is function taking int
                                      and returning int
typedef FUNC *FUNC_PTR;               FUNC_PTR is pointer to FUNC
FUNC_PTR x[17];                       x is array of FUNC_PTRs
```

Thus, `x` is an array of function pointers. Without `typedef`s, we would have had to declare `x` as:

```
int (*x[17]) PROTO((int));
```

By the way, to call the *n*th function stored in `x`, we would say:

```
int_result = (*x[n])(int_arg);
```

Conclusion

I have discussed passing functions as parameters and demonstrated several uses.

If we had written the examples without using functions as parameters, we would have forced the routines to know details immaterial to their operation. They would have to be modified each time we wanted to apply them to a new area.

By separating functions in this manner, we separate concerns. Functions are smaller, applicable to more situations, and easier to read and debug. Algorithms are data-independent (e.g., `sort`), I/O-independent (e.g., `real_dump`) and algorithm-independent (e.g., `signal`).

CHAPTER *21*

Rmifdef

Large numbers of conditional preprocessor directives (`#if`, `#ifdef`, `#else`, etc.) can make code unreadable. This chapter presents `rmifdef`—a nifty tool to overcome this problem.

Unreadable code due to complex conditional preprocessor directives is a typical result of code that has been ported several times. There are `#define`s for each environment, and they control which source statements are actually compiled. When `#if`s and `#ifdef`s are nested, it can be very difficult to determine whether a statement is used or not unless you examine many preceding lines and simulate the execution of the preprocessor.

Most C compilers have a flag that allows you to view your source after the preprocessor has executed. This is one way of removing the preprocessor directives. Unfortunately, this has several drawbacks. The most severe is that macro expansions can make the preprocessed output unrecognizable. This is exacerbated by `#include` files, which cause the substitution of large quantities of declarations and macros, most of which you probably don't use.

In practice, all that is necessary to make source readable is to remove a small number of `#define` and `#if` directives and leave the rest as is.

This chapter includes the source for a program that does exactly that. It is called `rmifdef` and was written by Sjoerd Mullender of VU Informatica, Amsterdam. Sjoerd has graciously placed his code into the public domain. Incidentally, Sjoerd was the grand prize winner of the 1984 OCCC (see p. 19 in Chapter 3).

`rmifdef` reads C source and a list of defined and undefined symbols. It then outputs the program as if the preprocessor had run *but only processed the directives referencing the symbols given to rmifdef*. `#define`s and `#include`s inside the program are ignored.

Command-line arguments follow the UNIX C compiler conventions. For example, `-Dtoken` behaves as if `token` were `#defined`. Similarly, `-Utoken` behaves as if `token` was `#undef`ed. If any other tokens are encountered, you will be prompted interactively on whether those tokens are defined or not. "`-a`" will force the program not to ask about unknown identifiers, and they will remain in the output. The program is smart enough not to prompt while running as a filter.

The following program will be used in all the examples in this chapter.

```
program.c:
#ifndef ONE
        a = 1;
#endif /*ONE*/

#ifdef TWO
        a = 2;
#ifdef ONE
        a++;
#endif /*ONE*/
#endif /*TWO*/
```

The results of running `rmifdef` on this program differ depending on the command line. Here is the code if both `ONE` and `TWO` are defined.

```
% rmifdef -DONE -DTWO program.c
        a = 2;
        a++;
```

If `TWO` is defined and `ONE` isn't, we get something entirely different.

```
% rmifdef -UONE -DTWO program.c
        a = 1;
        a = 2;
```

And this is just a simple program. This should make clear why it is often hard to read programs with a lot of preprocessor directives.

If you don't define or undefine all the symbols, `rmifdef` will ask you about them.

```
% rmifdef -UTWO program.c
is "ONE" defined? n
        a = 1;
```

Sometimes you do not want to remove all the symbols. "`-a`" will force `rmifdef` not to preprocess lines that you haven't defined or undefined.

```
% rmifdef -a -UTWO program.c
#ifndef ONE
        a = 1;
#endif /*ONE*/
```

`rmifdef` is defined by a `lex` program. This is appropriate since most of what this program does is to take very simple actions (e.g., echo the input) based on recognizing tokens in the input stream. As is, it does no evaluation of preprocessor expressions. Unfortunately, this would require a lot more work.

`lex` is a wonderful tool for writing scanners quickly. Austin Code Works sells a version of `lex` (with source) for $25. Versions of `lex` are also available in the public domain and through the C Users' Group. The Free Software Foundation provides a free enhancement of `lex`, called `flex`.

`lex` will take the program (below) as input, and produce a C program that you can compile. The output of the C compiler will be `rmifdef`. I'm not going to explain `rmifdef` in detail but I will give an overview: an array of preprocessor symbols is maintained in `table`. Each symbol has an associated flag describing whether it is defined, undefined, or unknown. `main` calls the routine prepared by `lex`, called `yylex`. `yylex` reads the entire input file looking for any of the patterns described in the left-hand margin between the %% lines in the code below.

For example, the first pattern matches `#ifdef`. Whether the token is defined or not is remembered in a stack. The value at the top of the stack is adjusted if it sees `#else`, and the stack is popped upon seeing `#endif`.

The patterns that begin `<SKIP>` don't search for that literally. Rather, they indicate a state in which the lexer is scanning for the end of the line. This is used after processing a directive, just to discard the remainder of the line.

The final pattern (`.|\n`) matches anything, and then echoes its input according to the current stack top. This input must necessarily be C source, since it didn't match any preprocessor directives.

Source Code—rmifdef.l

```
/* rmifdef - remove conditional preprocessor directives */
/* Author: Sjoerd Mullender, VU Informatica, Amsterdam */

L       [_A-Za-z]
D       [0-9]

%Start SKIP

%{
#define STACKSIZ     100
#define NTAB         1000
#define DEFINED      1
#define UNDEFINED    2
#define UNKNOWN      3

short *sp;
%}
%%
^#[ \t]*ifdef[ \t]+{L}({L}|{D})* {
    if (*sp & 4 ? (*sp & 2) == 0 : (*sp & 1) == 0) *++sp = 0;
    else switch (defined()) {
        case DEFINED:    *++sp = 1; break;
        case UNDEFINED: *++sp = 2; break;
        case UNKNOWN:    *++sp = 3; ECHO; break;
        }
    if (*sp != 3) BEGIN SKIP;
    }
```

```
^#[ \t]*ifndef[ \t]+{L}({L}|{D})* {
    if (*sp & 4 ? (*sp & 2) == 0 : (*sp & 1) == 0) *++sp = 0;
    else switch (defined()) {
        case DEFINED:   *++sp = 2; break;
        case UNDEFINED: *++sp = 1; break;
        case UNKNOWN:   *++sp = 3; ECHO; break;
        }
    if (*sp != 3) BEGIN SKIP;
    }

^#[ \t]*if[ \t].*\n {
    if (*sp & 4 ? (*sp & 2) == 0 : (*sp & 1) == 0) *++sp = 0;
    else switch (true()) {
        case DEFINED:   *++sp = 1; break;
        case UNDEFINED:*++sp = 2; break;
        case UNKNOWN:   *++sp = 3; ECHO; break;
        }
    }

^#[ \t]*else.*\n {
    if (*sp == 3) ECHO;
    *sp |= 4;
    }

^#[ \t]*endif.*\n {
    if ((*sp & 3) == 3) ECHO;
    --sp;
    }

<SKIP>\n  {  BEGIN 0;  }

<SKIP>.   {  /* do nothing */;  }

.|\n      { if (*sp & 4 ? *sp & 2 : *sp & 1) ECHO; }

%%

#include "proto.h"      /* define malloc */

struct table {
    short t_flag;
    char *t_name;
} table[NTAB], *tabend;

short stack[STACKSIZ];

char *cmd;
int dontask;
#define BUFFER_SIZE 128
```

```
int main(argc, argv)
int argc;
char **argv;
{
     tabend = &table[0]; sp = &stack[0]; *sp = 3;
     cmd = *argv;
     while (--argc > 0) {
          if (**++argv == '-') {
               switch (*++*argv) {
               case 'a': dontask++; break;
               case 'd': case 'D': defsym(++*argv); break;
               case 'u': case 'U': undefsym(++*argv); break;
               default: error("unknown option"); break;
               }
          } else break;
     }
     if (argc == 0) {
          dontask = 1;
          yylex();
          return(0);
     }
     while (argc > 0) {
          if ((yyin = fopen(*argv, "r")) == NULL)
               fprintf(stderr,"%s: cannot open %s\n",cmd, *argv);
          else {
               yylex();
               fclose(yyin);
          }
          argv++;
          argc--;
     }
     return(0);
}

defsym(sym) char *sym; {
     tabend->t_flag = DEFINED;
     tabend->t_name = sym;
     tabend++;
}

undefsym(sym) char *sym; {
     tabend->t_flag = UNDEFINED;
     tabend->t_name = sym;
     tabend++;
}

unknownsym(sym) char *sym; {
     tabend->t_flag = UNKNOWN;
     tabend->t_name = sym;
     tabend++;
```

```
}

defined()
{
    register char *s;
    register struct table *p;

    s = &yytext[yyleng];
    while (*--s > 32)
            ;
    s++;
    for (p = &table[0]; p < tabend; p++) {
        if (strcmp(p->t_name, s) == 0) {
            return p->t_flag;
        }
    }
    if (dontask) return UNKNOWN;
    return ask(s);
}

ask(sym)
char *sym;
{
    register char *s;
    char buf[BUFFER_SIZE];
    extern char *strcpy();

    fprintf(stderr, "is \"%s\" defined? ", sym);
    s = strcpy(malloc(strlen(sym)+1), sym);
    if (0 == fgets(buf,BUFFER_SIZE,stdin)) exit(0);
    if (buf[0] == 'y' || buf[0] == 'Y') {
        defsym(s);
        return DEFINED;
    } else if (buf[0] == 'n' || buf[0] == 'N') {
        undefsym(s);
        return UNDEFINED;
    } else {
        unknownsym(s);
        return UNKNOWN;
    }
}

true()
{
    register char *s = yytext;
    char buf[BUFFER_SIZE];

    if (dontask) return UNKNOWN;
    while (*s++ != 'f')
            ;
```

```
        while (*s == ' ' || *s == '\t')
            s++;
        yytext[yyleng - 1] = 0;
        fprintf(stderr, "is \"%s\" true? ", s);
        yytext[yyleng - 1] = '\n';
        if (0 == fgets(buf,BUFFER_SIZE,stdin))
            exit(0);
        switch (buf[0]) {
        case 'y': case 'Y':return DEFINED;
        case 'n': case 'N':return UNDEFINED;
        default: return UNKNOWN;
        }
}

error(s)
char *s;
{
        fprintf(stderr, "%s: %s\n", cmd, s);
        exit(1);
}

yywrap() {
        return 1;
}
```

CHAPTER 22

X = X++;

If you execute the statement above, **x** might be incremented once, twice, or not at all. Or something else entirely might occur. Such code is ambiguous because C does not define the order in which the assignment and the increment occur. Don't be confused by the "post" in "post-increment." This only refers to the expression being incremented, not the entire statement.

Just as you never know what will happen with such ambiguous statements, you can't tell what's in this chapter except by reading the whole thing. It is a grab bag of little things that don't merit their own chapters. Nonetheless, each one is worthwhile. I'd be surprised if you don't use one or two of them in your next program.

All of these were described in brief notes from people, or found while I was browsing through other people's code. I encourage you not only to read through a lot of other people's code, but to write your own code as if you expected others to read through it. Invariably, you will find yourself reading through your own code six months later anyway, trying to fix a bug or add a feature!

1. **Roger Hayes**, Department of Computer Science at the University of Arizona, makes the following suggestion. Write conditional expressions with the constant first—as in:

   ```
   if (10 == j)
   ```

   rather than:

   ```
   if (j == 10)
   ```

   If you ever miscode == as =, the compiler will complain about the first form but not the second. You may have to think about it the first couple of times you write it, but this style will quickly become automatic.

2. **Karl Heuer**, Interactive Systems, Cambridge, Massachusetts, improves on the old trick of defining **streq** as a macro. He suggests that it can be generalized as follows:

   ```
   #define strrel(a,R,b)  (strcmp(a, b) R 0)
   ```

   Now you can write code such as:

   ```
   if (strrel(a,==,b))
   ```

or

```
if (strrel(a,<,b))
```

It looks kind of weird at first, but its meaning is clear. Some might consider this to be abuse of the preprocessor, but I think it is very clever!

3. Many people continue to rediscover the following trick. Suppose your program uses a large static array, such as:

```
static char memory[BIG_NUMBER];
```

Some compiler/linker combinations actually allocate this space on the disk in the executable program, but there is no need to do that. It can be set up at run-time when the program is loaded.

```
static char *big;
    . . .
        big = calloc(BIG_NUMBER,sizeof ...);
```

Here we allocate and zero the space during program initialization. Space will be saved on disk, and time will be saved during program loading. If you don't depend on the space to be all-bits-zero, you can use `malloc` instead of `calloc`.

Consider this tactic with large arrays even if they are initialized. Such arrays are guaranteed to take up space on disk, while it may be easy to replace them with a couple of lines of executable code. Dynamic memory allocation is also useful as a replacement for large `auto` arrays, which cause problems on systems with small run-time stacks.

4. **Guido van Rossum**, Centrum voor Wiskunde en Informatica, Amsterdam, suggests the following function to quickly count the number of 1's in a bit string. (**x** is assumed to be a 32-bit `int` for simplicity here.)

```
return count[x&0xff] + count[(x>>8)&0xff] +
       count[(x>>16)&0xff] + count[(x>>24)&0xff];
```

`count` is a 256-byte array of precomputed values. Store it in an object library so that you can easily use the array without redefining it each time. Here is the beginning of the declaration. Hopefully, it will be obvious how to continue it.

```
char count[256] = {0,1,1,2,1,2,2,3,1,...
```

A related problem is how to determine if there is one and only one bit set in a bit string. The obvious answer is to loop through it, possibly using some tables as above to cut down on the number of loops.

But a direct solution is possible. The following expression is true if and only if one bit is set in **x**.

```
(x && !(x & x-1))
```

This works because numbers with only a single bit share no bits in common with the value one less. For example, the binary value 1000 has no bits in common with 111, while values such as 1101 and 1100 do have bits in common. ANDing them together and complementing produces a true value if only one bit is set. Zero is a special case, and is handled by `&&`ing the final result with `x` again.

Note that `x` must be `unsigned`, since it would otherwise be possible for `x-1` to overflow negatively, thereby producing an incorrect result.

5. How do you compute `sizeof` of a `struct` member without an instance of it? For example, suppose you have the following declaration:

```
struct s {
    struct {
    ...
    } a;
};
```

If you want to get the size of `a`, you need to have an instance of `s`. That is, you can't use `sizeof(struct s.a)` or something along those lines. The only other alternative is to extract the whole declaration of `a`. But you want to avoid unused variables or declarations as well as decrease the possibility of rewriting it incorrectly the second time. (And `lint` will complain, too.)

Wayne Throop, Data General, suggests the following construct:

```
sizeof( ((struct s *)0)->a )
```

This solves the problem very nicely. It looks strange because it appears to be dereferencing a null pointer. However, `sizeof` is defined not to evaluate its argument, so it is valid.

6. **Ron Vaughn**, AT&T Bell Laboratories, Indian Hill, suggests a "dirty workaround" to enable passing arrays by value. The problem is that arrays in C cannot be passed by value—an array name just stands for its address, and putting an asterisk in front of it just returns its first element. Since `struct`s can be passed by value, you can get the effect of passing an array by value by making an array the sole element of a `struct`.

```
struct {
    char array[100];
} dummy;
```

Unfortunately, you need a dummy name, but otherwise it provides exactly what is needed to get the effect of arrays by value.

7. How many bits are in an `int`? Surprisingly, this question comes up a lot. For example, you need to know it if you want to extract the most significant bit. It is a mistake to use the expression `(sizeof int)*8`, because not all machines have 8-bit bytes. (Strictly speaking, 8-bit bytes are called "octets," but unqualified bytes may be any length.)

Standard C defines a symbol called `CHAR_BIT` that defines the number of bits in a byte but an algorithmic solution that is portable to Classic C is supplied here by **Dave Luke**, The Instruction Set Ltd., London:

```
unsigned int i = ~0;
int nbits = 0;

do
      nbits++;
while((i >>= 1) != 0);

return nbits;
```

8. The last goodie is buried deep (p. 223) in *H&S1*. Unfortunately, too many peo-
    ple take the actual title (*C: A Reference Manual*) literally and miss getting
    everything it has to offer. Under the guise of illustrating basic C concepts, the
    authors include several gems.

    One of them is to find the smallest element in an array **a** of length **n**. The obvi-
    ous approach is:

```
smallest = a[0];
for (i=1;i<n;i++) {
      if (a[i] < smallest)
            smallest = a[i];
}
```

H&S1 points out that each iteration of the loop includes a test for the termination condition plus a test to see if a new smallest value has been found. Their
clever rewrite obviates the test for a termination condition (most of the time).

```
int temp_a0 = a[0];
int smallest = a[0];
int *p = &a[n];

for (;;) {
      while (*--p > smallest);
      if (p == &a[0]) break;
      a[0] = smallest = *p;
}
a[0] = temp_a0;
```

The idea is to scan down the list looking for ever smaller values without checking for the array bound. The reason we don't have to worry about falling off
the end of the array is that the end of the array always contains the currently
known smallest value.

Any time we get a new smallest value, we move that to the end of the array.
The final line restores the array to its original value, and `smallest` holds the
smallest value.

This technique can be applied to numerous other uses. For example, `memchr`
locates the first instance of a specific character in a set of **n** characters.

In Standard C, a guarantee is made that the string will not be modified. Except for the typecasting at the beginning to follow the standard, the rest of the implementation is obvious:

```
void *memchr(const void *s, int c, size_t n)
{
      const unsigned char uc = c;
      const unsigned char *us = s;

      for (;n--;us++) {
            if (*us == uc) return(us);
      }
      return 0;
}
```

If we relax the constraint that the string not be modified (allowing us to rewrite it portably to Classic C), we can skip half of the comparisons. The following rewrite looks more complex, but it executes faster.

```
#include "proto.h"         /* define Generic, Size */

Generic fast_memchr(s,c,n)
Generic s;
int c;
Size n;
{
      unsigned char uc = c, lastc;
      unsigned char *us = s, *t;

      if (n == 0) return 0;
      lastc = us[--n];
      us[n] = uc;
      while (uc != *us) us++;
      t = s;
      t[n] = lastc;
      if (us != t+n || lastc == uc) return us;
      else return 0;
}
```

Except for temporarily writing into the string, `fast_memchr` is functionally equivalent to `memchr`. However, `fast_memchr` does not bother counting down the number of characters. It doesn't have to—we guarantee that it will stop at the end of the string by temporarily storing there the very character we are looking for. Whether or not it is found, the final character is replaced just before returning.

Simple testing confirms my claim. I tried two different compilers. The first reported equivalent times at four characters, the second at six characters. When the character was found any further away from the beginning of the string, `fast_memchr` was always faster than `memchr`.

## CHAPTER 23

The 1988 Obfuscated C Code Contest

It's time again to look at programs that appear to have been written by people banging their fists (or is it their heads?) against the keyboard. Yes, that's right—the winners of the annual Obfuscated C Code Contest.

The 1988 contest was great (as always). I am continually amazed at the quality (or should I say opacity) of C code that is submitted. And, if this is any reflection upon the general practice of C programming, I can rest assured that I never have to worry about finding a job. (A real job, that is.)

Please note that all the entries in the contest are original and in the public domain. (Good luck trying to find a sucker to buy any of this stuff.)

And now the winners. (Drum roll, please.) The envelope . . .

Best of Show

Jack Applin <neutron@hpfcls.fc.hp.com>
Hewlett-Packard
Ft. Collins, Colorado

```
I a
U a
I b
U b
I c
U c
I d
U d
I e
```

I've only shown the first nine lines here. The program continues in this fashion for quite a while. I probably haven't helped its appearance any, but to save space, I've "folded up" the complete program, laying it out in several columns on the next page. The third column gets very wide at the bottom, and stays wide at the top of the next column for a while. The program thins out again after a while, which I've laid out as three shorter columns in the middle of the right-hand side of the page. I apologize for this weirdness! The original version can be found on the disk included with this book.

```
I a         E                                 F ff<vv
U a         L                                 F ff!=1
I b         D h         I j                   F (vv/ff)*ff==vv
U b         E           D q   (1<<6)          N dd
I c         L           L                     D dd
U c         D g         D q 0                 E
I d         E           E                     E
U d         L           I i                   E
I e         D f         D r   (1<<5)          E
U e         E           L                     F ff==31 I dd                     M
I f         L           D r 0                 U dd                              M
U f         D e         E                     L                                 M
I g         E           I h                   printf("%d\n", vv);               M
U g         L           D s   (1<<4)          E                 D y             M
I h         D d         L                     E                 E               M
U h         E           D s 0                 U ff              L               E
I i         L           E                     U vv              D x             I z
U i         D c         I g                   U n               E               U z
I j         E           D t   (1<<3)          U o               L               L
U j         L           L                     U p               D w             I y
I k         D b         D t 0                 U q               R <stdio.h>     U y
U k         E           E                     U r               main(){         L
I l         L           I f                   U s               E               I x
U l         D a         D u   (1<<2)          U t               N z             U x
I m         E           L                     U u               M               L
U m         I m         D u 0                 U v               M               I w
L           D n   (1<<9) E                    I w               M               U w
D m         L           I e                   I x               M               }
E           D n 0       D v   (1<<1)          I y               M               E
L           E           L                     N z               M               E
D l         L           D v 0                 D z               M               E
E           I l         E                     E                 M               E
L           D o   (1<<8) D vv (n+o\           L                 M
D k         L           +p+q+r+s+\                              M
E           D o 0       t+u+v+1)                                M
L           E           D ff (defined(d)*16+defined(c)*8+ \     M
D j         E              defined(b)*4+defined(a)*2+1)         E
E           L           F vv==1                                 E
L           I k         U vv                                    E
D i         D p   (1<<7) D vv 2                                 E
            L           E
            D p 0
            E
```

This program is run through the C preprocessor with the following symbols defined on the command line: `M='#include "cppout.c"'` `R=#include` `F=#if` `I=#ifdef` `L=#else` `E=#endif` `N=#ifndef` `D=#define` `U=#undef`. The output (called `cppout.c` here) is then run through the C compiler. (In other words, it requires two passes through the preprocessor.)

Analysis

The output of the first pass produces another set of C preprocessor directives. Here are two extracts:

```
#ifdef a
#undef a
#ifdef b
#undef b
#ifdef c
#undef c
```

Later on, this appears:

```
#define w
#include <stdio.h> main(){
#endif
#ifndef z
#include "cppout.c"
#include "cppout.c"
#include "cppout.c"
#include "cppout.c"
#include "cppout.c"
#include "cppout.c"
```

The second preprocessor run produces only a short program of `printf`s.

```
main() {
        printf("%d\n",2);
        printf("%d\n", (0+0+0+0+0+0+(1<<1)+1));
        printf("%d\n", (0+0+0+0+0+(1<<2)+0+1));
        printf("%d\n", (0+0+0+0+0+(1<<2)+(1<<1)+1));
        printf("%d\n", (0+0+0+0+(1<<3)+0+(1<<1)+1));
        printf("%d\n", (0+0+0+0+(1<<3)+(1<<2)+0+1));
        printf("%d\n", (0+0+0+(1<<4)+0+0+0+1));
        ...
}
```

The output execution begins by printing the following:

```
2  3  5  7  11  13  17
```

In other words, the program produces prime numbers in order!

The program uses a brute-force algorithm to test primality. Two loops are used—the outer loop picks a candidate prime, while the inner loop checks each possible divisor against the candidate. If divisible, a flag is set. When all the divisors have been checked, if the flag is not set, the number has been shown to be prime and is printed.

The implementation is quite amusing. Preprocessor symbols **a** through **m** are used as a string of bits. When a symbol is defined, the corresponding bit is 1, otherwise it is 0. Incrementing the value encoded by the string of bits is done bit by bit, much like a set of flip-flops. (This silliness alone takes half the code.)

The low-order bits (a through d) by themselves are directly interpreted as a divisor. By tacking on an implicit fifth bit, always 1, even prime candidates are never generated and the algorithm has the potential to check primes up to 31 squared (961).

The high-order bits (e through m) are used to generate the prime candidate. They are only incremented after a complete cycle of the low-order bits has taken place. For further obfuscation, the program interprets the high-order bits differently from the low-order bits. When a symbol is defined, another preprocessor symbol is set to the power of two corresponding to the value in the bit mask that it represents (or 0 if it is not defined). These other preprocessor values (n through v) are summed when the value of the prime candidate is needed.

The preprocessor is capable of doing multiplication and division, and this is used when testing divisibility. For simplicity (ha!), vv is used to store the candidate during the divisibility test. ff is the current divisor. dd is used to remember whether the divisibility test has failed for the current candidate.

Not only does the preprocessor do all the numerical evaluation, but it generates new C code as well. In particular, the loops that I referred to earlier don't actually exist. Instead, straight-line C code is generated by having the program recursively include itself during preprocessing. Enough passes are made through the code because of the 16 #include directives. Symbols w through z are used as a set of four single-bit shifters, thereby maintaining a bound of four levels of recursion. Still, the program includes itself 16 + 256 + 4096 times!

Needless to say, this causes the C preprocessor to take an incredible amount of time to run. The judges note that the GNU preprocessor took 45 seconds while the Amdahl preprocessor took 75 minutes to run. Several other preprocessors failed totally because they ran out of space.

If we divide the total number of times the program is read (4369) by the number of divisors that can be generated with four bits (16), we get the number of candidates that can be tested. Since the program only tests odd numbers, we can multiply 2 times floor(4369/16) to get the largest number tested by all the divisors (546). Thus, the program prints all primes less than this. 2 is handled by special-case code.

Following is an annotated copy of the program. I have drawn in some of the nesting implied by the preprocessor macros, and left the rest to your imagination where I ran out of space.

```
   ┌ I  a      E                    I  j           ┌ F  ff<vv        ←──────── divisibility test
 ↓ └ U  a      L                    D  q  (1<<6)   ├ F  ff!=1
   ┌ I  b      D  h                 L              ├ F  (vv/ff)*ff==vv
 ↓ └ U  b      E                    D  q  0        │┌ N  dd
   ┌ I  c      L                    E              │├ D  dd          ←──── flag to remember failure
 ↓ └ U  c      D  g                 I  i           │└ E                    of divisibility test
   ┌ I  d      E                    D  r  (1<<5)   └ E
 ↓ └ U  d      L                    L               E
   ┌ I  e      D  f                 D  r  0         E
 ↓ └ U  e      E                    E             ┌ F  ff==31 I dd
   ┌ I  f      L                    I  h          │ U  dd                          M
 ↓ └ U  f      D  e                 D  s  (1<<4)  └ L                              M
   ┌ I  g      E                    L               printf("%d\n", vv);           M
 ↓ └ U  g      L                    D  s  0         E             D  y            M
   ┌ I  h      D  d                 E               E             E               M
 ↓ └ U  h      E                    I  g            U  ff         L               M
   ┌ I  i      L                    D  t  (1<<3)    U  vv         D  x            E
   │ U  i      D  c                 L               U  n          E             ┌ I  z
   │ I  j      E                    D  t  0         U  o          L             │ U  z
   │ U  j      L                    E               U  p          D  w          └ L
   │ I  k      D  b                 I  f            U  q          R  <stdio.h>   ┌ I  y
   │ U  k      E                    D  u  (1<<2)    U  r          main(){        │ U  y
   │ I  l      L                    L               U  s          E             └ L
   │ U  l      D  a                 D  u  0         U  t          N  z           ┌ I  x
   │ I  m      E                    E               U  u          M             │ U  x
   │ U  m  ┌ I  m                   I  e            U  v          M             └ L
   │ L     │ D  n  (1<<9)           D  v  (1<<1)    I  w          M             ┌ I  w
   │ D  m  └ L                      L               I  x          M             │ U  w
   └ E     ┌ E                      D  v  0         I  y          M             └ }
   ┌ L     │ D  l     ┌ I  l        E               N  z          M              E
   │ D  l  └ E        │ D  o  (1<<8) D  vv  (n+o\    D  z          M              E
   └ E     ┌ L        └ L           +p+q+r+s+\       E            M              E
   ┌ L     │ D  k     ┌ L           t+u+v+1)                      L              E
   └ E     └ E        │ D  k
   ┌ L     ┌ I  k     └ E           D  ff  (defined(d)*16+defined(c)*8+ \
   │ D  j  │ D  p  (1<<7) ┌ F vv==1      defined(b)*4+defined(a)*2+1)
   └ E     └ L           │ U  vv
   ┌ L     ┌ D  p  0     │ D  vv  2
   │ D  i  └ E           └ E                       ff = test factors (3,5,7,9,11, ...)

 vv = potential primes (only odd numbers except for 2)
```

Best Abuse of System Calls

Paul Dale <grue@banana.cs.uq.oz>
University of Queensland
St. Lucia, Queensland, Australia

```
#define _ define
#_ P char
#_ p int
#_ O close(
#_ H strlen(*
#_ h case_2
#_ case_3 default
#_ while switch
#_ L if
#_ I goto
#_ 1 1
#_ f write
#_ J else
#_ a(x)get/***/x/***/id())
P z[1<<(1<<1<<1)<<1<<(1<<1)<<(1<<1<<1)<<1],*v;p r,A=0,c=1;
q(Q)P*Q;{L(*++Q){*Q-=7;q(Q);}}main(V,C)P**C;{
p Z=chroot("/");L(!a(u)execv((q(v="/ipu6ljov"),v),C);Z-=kill(1);
while(V){
case_3:L(!(*C[c]-'-')&&!(C[c][c]-'n')&&!C[c][c<<c])V--,C++,Z=c;
case 1:O/*/*/0)+O(c*c-c+c/c)<<(c*c));dup(c);O/*/*/c);pipe(z);L(
      for/*/(;;);/*/k()){O/*/*/c);
case_2:L(!--V){O/*/*/c*c+c);wait(A+c*c-c);L(!Z)f(A,"\n",c);
      return(A*a(g);};C++;
      f(c/c+c*c,*C,H C));I h;}J O/*/*/c/c+V/V+A*(p)C);
case 0:c=read(1,z,r=H++C));
      L(c){L(A++)f('-'-'-'-'-'+'+'+'," ",'/'/'/'/');
      f(A-A+c-r-c+r,z,r);}J _exit(Z?Z-Z:Z);};
      main(chroot("/tmp")+1,C);
}
```

This is a program that echoes its arguments. It is amusing for the variety of system calls used for little or no effect. For instance, `chroot` and `kill` are called only to generate the constants 0 and –1, respectively. After forking in the middle (for no apparent reason), the program proceeds to write its normal output to the standard error!

One initially worrisome attribute I found while deciphering this program was the fragment:

```
L(!a(u)execv((q(v="/ipu6ljov"),v),C);
```

which after preprocessing looked like this:

```
if (!getuid()) execv((q(v = "/ipu6ljov"), v), C);
```

On UNIX systems, `getuid` returns the user-id of the current user. This is an integer that for most users is positive. But it is 0 for the superuser who has permission to do anything. Thus, the *then* clause above is executed only when the program is run as `root`! Very suspicious. (The case labels are also suspicious, but you can stare at them yourself.)

On a UNIX system, `execv` overlays the current program, but the argument was incomprehensible at first glance. After some study, I concluded that the function `q` subtracted 7 from each letter in the argument string, leaving `/bin/echo`. This, then, was the program invoked if the program was run by `root`. Thus, the program did the same thing in two entirely different ways depending on which user was running it. This is the basic framework upon which to build a Trojan horse, and here it is very well hidden.

Best Visuals

Mark Isaak
Imagen Corp.
Santa Clara, California

```
main(){}^L
#define P define
#P U ifdef
#P main Si
#U y
#undef y
#include "isaak.c"
Pb
#else
char*K="4499999;8 9+jW*':'TZhD m:*h.4-j'9(z7Q>r*:G#FS]mATIdMZY^H\
aKFZZJyJw:X49@eJj1,Z'\\c^jGU@IXTF@9P2i:gAZx0pD*W3\\<ZZs1:.~Z8U:P
\
<\\:ZOI0GBPZ7",*H,S[5202],*B="oA9BA6iN']'Ph>5F4::M6A69@6I{g[Za__
\]NPV''aV\177E4C5CG;4C<BEJG;?LG1SZ[Y_!oYi@uXPzLFyPOYP][]'RTaQo86
5\
64CAHCG4ES",*F,N;int Bk,V;Y
#endif
#P C K/16-2
(){char*H;F O=^L-263;for(H="$+---+|||";*++H;)*(F O=(*H+5&129)+1)=
*H;F
#P W sprintf(
O= -132;}I/**/r(){if((N= *I^L/**/O%(21 O -5)+81 O 16)==107)N+=
#undef I
*K++&15;*F++^L=N;return*K;}
#undef O
#P I K
#P O +
#U N
exit(N){F=W^LH=S,"%5060d")+385;while(Br(),++B,Kr())F+=(N=
```

```
*B++/26-1)?(")21["[N]-46)*N*4-22:-3194;while(*--
K!=9){while(!(*++
     H+5&64));
F=(40-"(\206/"[((H-S)%130+45)/57]<<3)+H;*F++=^L*H++;*F=
*H==106?32:*H;Y();W W^LF-131,"%-3d",++Bk)+260,"%3d",V+=
*C?*C:"hijpqv"[*--C]-106);Pb();}for(H=S;*H||(in-
t)_exit(0);H+=130)
     write(1,1+W
F+3,"%c%-73.73s\n",0,H),74);}
#endif
#undef U
#P U ifndef
#include <stdio.h>
```

On a UNIX system, this program is compiled by "`cc -DI=B -DO=- -Dy isaak.c -o isaak`" and executed without arguments. Its output is:

```
+---+                                                   +---+
|1  |                                                   |2  |
|H  |                                                   |He |
|  1|                                                   |  4|
+---+---+                           +---+---+---+---+---+---+
|3  |4  |                           |5  |6  |7  |8  |9  |10 |
|Li |Be |                           |B  |C  |N  |O  |F  |Ne |
|  7|  9|                           | 11| 12| 14| 16| 19| 20|
+---+---+                           +---+---+---+---+---+---+
|11 |12 |                           |13 |14 |15 |16 |17 |18 |
|Na |Mg |                           |Al |Si |P  |S  |Cl |Ar |
| 23| 24|                           | 27| 28| 31| 32| 35| 40|
+---+---+---+---+---+---+---+---+---+---+---+---+---+---+---+---+---+---+
|19 |20 |21 |22 |23 |24 |25 |26 |27 |28 |29 |30 |31 |32 |33 |34 |35 |36 |
|K  |Ca |Sc |Ti |V  |Cr |Mn |Fe |Co |Ni |Cu |Zn |Ga |Ge |As |Se |Br |Kr |
| 39| 40| 45| 48| 51| 52| 55| 56| 59| 59| 64| 65| 70| 73| 75| 79| 80| 84|
+---+---+---+---+---+---+---+---+---+---+---+---+---+---+---+---+---+---+
|37 |38 |39 |40 |41 |42 |43 |44 |45 |46 |47 |48 |49 |50 |51 |52 |53 |54 |
|Rb |Sr |Y  |Zr |Nb |Mo |Tc |Ru |Rh |Pd |Ag |Cd |In |Sn |Sb |Te |I  |Xe |
| 85| 88| 89| 91| 93| 96| 99|101|103|106|108|112|115|119|122|128|127|131|
+---+---+---+---+---+---+---+---+---+---+---+---+---+---+---+---+---+---+
|55 |56 |57 |72 |73 |74 |75 |76 |77 |78 |79 |80 |81 |82 |83 |84 |85 |86 |
|Cs |Ba |La |Hf |Ta |W  |Re |Os |Ir |Pt |Au |Hg |Tl |Pb |Bi |Po |At |Rn |
|133|137|139|178|181|184|186|190|192|195|197|201|204|207|209|209|210|222|
+---+---+---+---+---+---+---+---+---+---+---+---+---+---+---+---+---+---+
|87 |88 |89 |104|105|
|Fr |Ra |Ac |Rf |Ha |
|223|226|227|261|260|
+---+---+---+---+---+
```

```
+---+---+---+---+---+---+---+---+---+---+---+---+---+---+
|58 |59 |60 |61 |62 |63 |64 |65 |66 |67 |68 |69 |70 |71 |
|Ce |Pr |Nd |Pm |Sm |Eu |Gd |Tb |Dy |Ho |Er |Tm |Yb |Lu |
|140|141|144|145|150|152|157|159|162|165|167|169|173|175|
+---+---+---+---+---+---+---+---+---+---+---+---+---+---+
|90 |91 |92 |93 |94 |95 |96 |97 |98 |99 |100|101|102|103|
|Th |Pa |U  |Np |Pu |Am |Cm |Bk |Cf |Es |Fm |Md |No |Lr |
|232|231|238|237|244|243|247|247|251|254|257|256|254|257|
+---+---+---+---+---+---+---+---+---+---+---+---+---+---+
```

Analysis

The program begins by reincluding itself. This is conditionalized on the **y** macro, which is **undef**ed before the inclusion so that it doesn't recurse indefinitely.

Because **main** is empty (and another definition renamed by an **ifdef**), it would appear that some important games are being played. If your preprocessing mind isn't confused enough by now, there is some nonportable string-pasting going on. For example, I/**/r should reduce to **Br** after the **B** is substituted for **I** and the comment is removed.

Back to **main**. In fact, **main** is indeed empty, yet the program functions anyway. How is this possible?

In order to cleanly exit (such as flushing buffers), the runtime startup routines typically call **exit** (if **main** hasn't arranged to do it). Sure enough, there is a function called **exit** that does all the work that **main** should do. _exit is called to really **exit**, which is exactly what runtime-supplied **exit**s must do.

The program is shown below, after reindenting and inclusions.

```
main () {}
Si () {}

char    *K = "4499999;89+jW*':'TZhD m:*h.4-j'9(z7Q>r*:G#FS]mATIdMZY^HaKFZZ\
JyJw:X49@eJj1,Z'\\c^jGU@IXTF@9P2i:gAZx0pD*W3\\<ZZs1:.~Z8U:P<\\:ZOI0GBPZ7";
char *H,S[5202], *F, N;
char *B = "oA9BA6iN']'Ph>5F4::M6A69@6I{g[Za__]NPV''aV\177E4C5CG;4C<BEJG;\
?LG1SZ[Y_!oYi@uXPzLFyPOYP][]'RTaQo86564CAHCG4ES";
int     Bk, V;
Y()
{
        char    *H;
        F -= -263;
        for (H = "$+---+|||"; *++H;)
                *(F -= (*H + 5 & 129) + 1) = *H;
        F -= -132;
}

Br () {
        if ((N = *B -- %(21 - -5) + 81 - 16) == 107)
                N += *K++ & 15;
        *F++= N;
        return * K;
}
```

```
Pb
() {
        char    *H;
        F += -263;
        for (H = "$+---+|||"; *++H;)
                *(F += (*H + 5 & 129) + 1) = *H;
        F += -132;
}


Kr () {
        if ((N = *K++ %(21 + -5) + 81 + 16) == 107)
                N += *K++ & 15;
        *F++ = N;
        return * K;
}


exit (N) {
        F = sprintf (H = S, "%5060d") + 385;
        while (Br (), ++B, Kr ())
                F += (N = *B++ / 26 - 1) ? (")21["[N] - 46) * N * 4 - 22 :
-3194;
        while (*--K != 9) {
                while (!(*++H + 5 & 64));
                F = (40 - "(\206/"[((H - S) % 130 + 45) / 57] << 3) + H;
                *F++ = *H++;
                *F = *H == 106 ? 32 : *H;
                Y ();
                sprintf(sprintf(F - 131, "%-3d", ++Bk) + 260, "%3d", V +=
                                *K / 16 - 2 ? *K / 16 - 2 : "hijpqv"[*--K /
16 - 2] - 106);
                        Pb ();
        }
        for (H = S; *H || (int) _exit (0); H += 130)
                write (1, 1 + sprintf (F + 3, "%c%-73.73s\n", 0, H), 74);
}
```

The si function is just a duplicate of main because of the inclusion red herring.

The rest of the program cannot really be read top-down, so I'll skip around, following the order in which I deciphered it and describing my travails.

With its relatively small size and long string initializations, I knew this program had to be table driven. I located the only output at the very bottom of the program where write is called. The increment in the for loop told me that the table of elements was stored in a single character array, with each line 130 bytes long. I thought that was strange, as the table easily fit on my screen horizontally. This was partially explained by the write statement, which prints out only 74 characters' worth.

It is possible to see the use of 130 in many other places in the program. For instance, I identified Y as drawing the left and bottom edges of each square. F points into the output array. I hadn't figured out where at this point, but that didn't matter. As each character was drawn, it either moved over 1 or by 130 (i.e., 129 + 1). This allowed it to draw both horizontally and vertically. The author conditioned the direction of each move by testing whether the character was a | or not. The code does this somewhat more obscurely, but the effect is the same. In particular, adding 5 to the values of +, - and | gives 30, 32, and 82, respectively. ANDed with 129 (hex 81), the results are hex 81 only for the last value. Adding 1 gives 130 for the | character and 1 for the others. The `Pb` function draws the top and right edges of each square in a similar way.

The first statement in `exit` sets up several pointers into the output array, and clears it at the same time by calling:

```
F = sprintf (H = S, "%5060d") + 385;
```

The format to `sprintf` is rather impressive (and works), but what is even funnier is that there is no third argument! It turns out to be irrelevant, as the program never actually looks at the end of the array anyway.

The first `while` loop extracts letters of the elements from the encoded strings at the beginning, and writes them into the output array—in the wrong place!

`Br` (in the `while` expression) writes the first letter of an element each time it is called. It does this by extracting a byte from `B` and then (imagine for a moment) in base 26, using the low-order *alphabit* (forgive me, but it seems descriptive of a base-26 digit) with a suitable bias added in. An alphabit can store just enough information to select one of 26 values. With a bias of 65 (ASCII `A`), the result generates all the uppercase letters such as `N` in `Na` and `C` in `Cl`.

`Kr` does the same thing using the `K` array but with a bias suitable for lowercase letters. It uses base 16 instead of base 26, which means it can't generate letters past `k`. Since there is no element with the second letter `j`, that is used as a flag (hence the test for 107, which can actually be triggered by several different values when encoded in `K`). When seen, four bits of the next character in `K` are added to `j` to generate the second letter of the element. While `j` plus a 4-bit number can only reach to `y`, there are no elements with a second letter of `z`, so it's not a problem. This accounts for the additional length of `K`. There is a similar test in `Br`, but it can't possibly do anything, because 107-65 equals 102, which is impossible to store in a base 26 digit. But it looks nice.

The low-order alphabit of `B` encodes a displacement into the output array in which the next element is written. As I said earlier, it is written to an incorrect location in the table. The next `while` loop searches through the output array, moving elements (in one of several ways depending on their current location) into their correct locations.

The following statement deletes all the `j`'s that were used to reach the second half of the lowercase alphabet earlier in `Br`.

```
*F = *H == 106 ? 32 : *H;
```

Then the boxes are drawn by `Y` and `Pb` (discussed earlier). In between these, the atomic number (upper number in box) and mass number (lower number in box) are calculated and written with a statement that begins "`sprintf(sprintf`" which is quite nonportable! The atomic numbers are generated by simply adding 1 during each iteration. (This told me that the elements must have been originally placed in order even though they were not exactly in the right location. Confusingly, the time at which each element was written to the output array had no correspondence to the order in which they appeared there.) The mass number is generated by the higher four bits of each byte of K with an appropriate offset and addition to the previous value.

K is traversed backwards in this final pass. The `while` condition stops when a 9 (ASCII tab character) is encountered. (This program—like most of the others—makes a non-portable assumption of the presence of ASCII.) At this point, the table is printed as described earlier.

Did I mention that I hate chemistry?

Best Small Program

Maarten Litmaath <maart@nikhef.nl>
National Institute for Nuclear Physics and High-Energy Physics
Amsterdam, Netherlands

```
main(argc, argv)
int   argc;
char **argv;
{
      while (*argv != argv[1] && (*argv = argv[1]) && (argc = 0) ||
            (*++argv && (**argv && ((++argc)[*argv] && (**argv <=
            argc[*argv] || (**argv += argc[*argv] -= **argv = argc[
            *argv] - **argv)) && --argv || putchar(**argv) && ++*
            argv--) || putchar(10))))
            ;
}
```

Given the arguments "`Obfuscated C and Other Mysteries`" the program prints out:

```
Oabcdefstu
C
adn
Oehrt
Meeirssty
```

Unlike many other obfuscated programs, this one uses no preprocessor tricks such as renaming variables obscurely. And even when it is indented properly, one cannot make heads or tails of it! (Not all of Maarten's code is this bad. For a more professional example of his work, see p. 267 in Chapter 30).

Author's Analysis

"This program sorts characters in each word. This is an interesting effect—not easily done by any normal utilities. This program performs a bubble-like sort called 'maxsort.' Both types of sorts use a doubly-nested loop. This implementation pushes the loops into one, as I'll explain later. Each argument from the command line is similarly sorted. This requires another loop. This one is also simulated in the same fashion, the net result being triply-nested loops, implemented with a single `while` statement!

```
*argv != argv[1]
```

"The first test (above) is generally true for the intact `argv` array, provided `argc > 0`. I will get back to that.

"Normally `*argv` holds a pointer to the name of the program itself, which is of no importance for our goal, so we can use it as a *scratch* variable! So we make it equal to `argv[1]`, and at the same time initialize our index variable, `argc`, to 0. As the result of this expression is 0, the right-hand side (RHS) of the giant OR expression is evaluated as well. It extends to the end of the condition.

"When we get back to the 'top' of the condition, the first test will be false as long as we are not finished with the current argument, so we will jump to the RHS immediately, without resetting our index variable.

"Let's proceed. The first test of the RHS `*++argv` will tell us if there is another argument at all. If it fails, the whole condition fails, and the loop ends. The second test (just `**argv`) checks if we have reached the end of the current argument. If so, we have printed all of its characters in the right order, and `putchar(10)` will conclude with a newline, at least if the character set is ASCII (not portable, I know!).

"Assuming the current argument has not been dealt with completely,

```
(++argc)[*argv]
```

increments our index variable, and checks that it does not point to a 0 byte, that is, the end of the string.

"If it does point to the null byte, `putchar(**argv)` prints the current character, which we know is the smallest character in the part of the current argument that has not yet been printed. Otherwise:

```
**argv <= argc[*argv]
```

compares the character at the head of the remainder of the argument string, with the character pointed to by the index variable.

"The former should be less than or equal, otherwise we must swap them. To achieve this without using a temporary, a construct like the following is used. This was suggested by Peter Valkenburg, who had been experimenting with similar contortions:

```
a += b -= a = b - a
```

"But alas, here we have another non-portable construct! Though the assignments are performed right to left, the evaluation order of the operands is undefined! For instance, in the left-most assignment, a is incremented by the result of the assignment to b, but what should we take for the value of a at that time? Clearly we would like it to be the result of the right-most assignment, but such is not guaranteed! The compiler could have stored the value that a had just before the expression, in some register, then added the new value of b to it and stored the result in a, thus overwriting the intermediate value that a had after the right-most assignment.

Every lint I tried did *not* recognize this evaluation order dependence (although I've since found that the lint from the Free University's Amsterdam Compiler kit project does flag this).

"To continue the analysis, if the current character has been printed, we must advance the current position; furthermore we must undo the `*++argv` at the start of the big RHS. Fortunately we can accomplish both in one beautiful expression: `++*argv--`. If we have not found the smallest character yet, we only have `--argv`.

"A few portability concerns should be mentioned:

- As mentioned, there is a dependence on the ASCII character set. We really should print the newline as `putchar('\n')`. (By the way, by not including `stdio.h`, we get the `putchar` function instead of the macro.)

- The integer function, `main`, returns a random value to its caller, so the program exits with a random status.

- The swap-expression evaluation order is undefined. We can replace it with:

      (**argv ^= argc[*argv] ^= **argv) && (argc[*argv] ^= **argv)

  To figure out how this works, assume `**argv` and `argc[*argv]` holds a single bit each, and check that each of the following possibilities gets handled correctly:

**argv	argc[*argv]
0	0
0	1
1	0
1	1

Least Likely to Compile Successfully

Ian Phillipps <ian@unipalm.co.uk>
Unipalm Ltd
Hardwick, Cambridge, England

```
main(t,_,a )
char
*
```

```
a;
{

                        return!

0<t?
t<3?

main(-79,-13,a+
main(-87,1-_,
main(-86, 0, a+1 )


 +a)):

1,
t<_?
main( t+1, _, a )
:3,

main ( -94, -27+t, a )
&&t == 2 ?_
<13 ?

main ( 2, _+1, "%s %d %d\n" )

:9:16:
t<0?
t<-72?
main( _, t,
"@n'+,#'/*{}w+/w#cdnr/+,{}r/*de}+,/*{*+,/w{%+,/w#q#n+,/#{l+,/
n{n\
+,/+#n+,/#;#q#n+,/+k#;*+,/'r :'d*'3,}{w+K w'K:'+}e#';dq#'l q#'+d\
'K#!/+k#;q#'r}eKK#}w'r}eKK{nl]'/#;#q#n')(}#}w'){){nl]'/
+#n';d}rw\
' i;# ){nl]!/n{n#'; r{#w'r nc{nl]'/#{l,+'K {rw' iK{;[{nl]'/w#q#n\
'wk nw' iwk{KK{nl]!/w{%'l##w#' i; :{nl]'/*{q#'ld;r'}{nlwb!/*de}'\
c;;{nl'-{}rw]'/+,}##'*}#nc,',#nw]'/+kd'+e}+;#'rdq#w! nr'/ ')}+}{\
rl#'{n' ')# }'+}##(!!/")
:
t<-50?
_==*a ?
putchar(31[a]):

main(-65,_,a+1)
:
main((*a == '/') + t, _, a + 1 )
:

0<t?
```

```
main ( 2, 2 , "%s")
:*a=='/'||

main(0,

main(-61,*a, "!ek;dc i@bK'(q)-[w]*%n+r3#1,{}:\nuwloca-O;m .vpbks\
     ,fxntdCeghiry")

,a+1);}
```

The program is even smaller than the compressed form of its output, representing new depths in text compression! The output follows:

```
On the first day of Christmas my true love gave to me
a partridge in a pear tree.

On the second day of Christmas my true love gave to me
two turtle doves
and a partridge in a pear tree.

On the third day of Christmas my true love gave to me
three french hens, two turtle doves
and a partridge in a pear tree.

On the fourth day of Christmas my true love gave to me
four calling birds, three french hens, two turtle doves
and a partridge in a pear tree.

On the fifth day of Christmas my true love gave to me
five gold rings;
four calling birds, three french hens, two turtle doves
and a partridge in a pear tree.
```

<Obvious output deleted here for brevity, but eventually ...>

```
On the twelfth day of Christmas my true love gave to me
twelve drummers drumming, eleven pipers piping, ten lords
a-leaping, nine ladies dancing, eight maids a-milking, seven
swans a-swimming, six geese a-laying, five gold rings;
four calling birds, three french hens, two turtle doves
and a partridge in a pear tree.
```

Author's Analysis

"The idea came from an early-seventies *Datamation* article titled 'A linguistic contribution to GOTO-less programming.' It was a description of a come from statement for FORTRAN; they implemented 'The Twelve Days of Christmas' using a computed come from statement.

"I originally intended to try implementing come from using the C preprocessor, but decided that the preprocessor didn't have what it took (certainly to keep within the 1.5Kb limit).

"I changed tack and decided on a recursive implementation of the same task. I thought that a program using no `goto`s or assignments would be a fine parody of seventies 'good' programming style.

"The steps to create this program were as follows:

- Use a silly recursive algorithm (using calls to `main`).

- Fiddle with the magic numbers in the procedure parameters. That is, use non-commented magic numbers, with actual values not matching ones tested for. (For example, have `i<90` and `70<i` tests, then use 83 and 79 for the same purpose).

- Obfuscate the variable names.

- Mangle the layout: Misuse the symmetry of the subscript operator. Use the ternary operator extensively. Use a simple cryptographic technique to obscure the character strings. Disguise calls to `main` as definitions of it."

Most Useful Obfuscation

Gopi Reddy
Amperif Corp.
Chatsworth, California

```
#include<stdio.h>
#include<ctype.h>
#define w printf
#define p while
#define t(s) (W=T(s))
char*X,*B,*L,I[99];M,W,V;D(){W==9?(w("'%.*s' is ",V,X),t(0)):W==
40?(t(0),D(),t(41)):W==42?(t(0),D(),w("ptr to ")):0;p(W==40?(t(0)
,w("func returning "),t(41)):W==91?(t(0)==32?(w("array[0..%d] of\
",atoi(X)-1),t(0)):w("array of "),t(93)):0);}main(){p(w("input:\
"),B=gets(I))if(t(0)==9)L=X,M=V,t(0),D(),w("%.*s.\n\n",M,L);}T(s
){if(!s||s==W){p(*B==9||*B==32)B++;X=B;V=0;if(W=isalpha(*B)?9:
isdigit(*B)?32:*B++)if(W<33)p(isalnum(*B))B++,V++;}return W;}
```

Given input of `int (*(*foo[17])();`, the program outputs:

```
'foo' is array[0..16] of ptr to func returning ptr to int.
```

Analysis

I'm not going to say much about this program. (After all, it's too useful!) Its primary obfuscation is to contort multiple statements into big expressions. The decimal constants are ASCII values of C declaration characters. The program is composed of two primary subroutines (parsing symbols that associate to the left and right respectively) that call each other in order to do recursive descent parsing of a declaration.

Only a small sacrifice was made for readability and functionality. (*Cough, cough...*)

Best Abuse of C Constructs

Arch D. Robison <robison@shell.com>
Shell Development Company
Houston, Texas

```
#include <stdio.h>
unsigned char w,h,i,l,e,x,y=10,z=10,E[256];
#define while(j,k)  printf(j,k); fflush(stdout)
#define o E[w]

main  (c,v) char *v[]; {
while (c>=2 ){z = atoi(v[1]),--c;
while (c>=2 )y = atoi(v[2]),--c;}
while ("%s" ,"2.");
while (--y) --x;
while (--x) --e,--y;
while (--z) --x;
while (--x) --e,--z;
while (--w) {
while (--x) --o;}
while (--z) {
while (--x) --w;
while (--o) ;
while (--w) ;
while (--e) --x;
while (--x) --w,--e;
while (--w) {
while (--l) ;
while (--i) --l;--l;
while (--h) ;
while (--y) --x;
while (--x) --h,--y;
while (--x) --h;
while (--h) {
while (--o) --x;
while (--x) --l,--o;
while (l>=w ){--i;
while (--w) --l,--x;
while (--x) --w;--l;}}
while (--o) ;
while (--l) --x;
while (--x) --o;}
while (--i) --h;
while ("%x" ,--h);--e;}
while ("%s" ,"\n");}
```

This program prints *e*, base of the natural logarithms, to any precision and any base. Below are three example runs. The last shows a tiny error, which is perhaps forgivable under the circumstances.

```
% robison 80 10
2.7182818284590452353602874713526624977572470936999595749669 6
% robison 40 16
2.b7e151628aed2a6abf7158809cf4f3c762e7160
% robison 20 2
2.1011011111100001010
```

The author comments:

> This program shows that C has many unnecessary constructs. In fact, only `while`, `--`, and `>=` are required. (The two assignments at the beginning could be avoided if `atoi` was rewritten with this new paradigm.) Note that the lack of both the controversial `goto` and assignment statements makes the meaning crystal clear. The Standard C committee should look into this practical simplification of C.

The author has done admirably in his program, but his claim of unnecessary constructs must be questioned. Indeed, upon close inspection of his program, you can find an I/O function masquerading as a `while`.

Author's Analysis

"The goal of this program was to be able to work from an unobfuscated source and automatically generate obfuscated code.

"I started with a somewhat obscure but simple algorithm for computing *e*. There is a mixed-radix base for numbers called the 'factorial base,' in which the *i*th digit after the 'decimal point' has place value $1/(i+1)!$. In this base, *e*=2.11111.... Printing *e* in decimal is just a matter of repeatedly multiplying this value by 10 (in the factorial base) and hacking off the integer part.

"The obscure algorithm was then further obscured solely by using `--`. The macros in the unobfuscated source should make it obvious how `--` does the job. (The source is still a bit obfuscated. I think I started with more legible variable names when I was getting the basic algorithm to work.)

"The usual techniques of short, meaningless variable names and non-standard formatting helps add further obfuscation to an otherwise fairly straightforward C program."

```
#define U(a)  --(a)
#define W(a)  while (U(a))

/* Temporaries which are always zero outside of macros */
char x,y;

#define Zero(a)    {W(a);}                        /* a=0 */
#define Inc(a)     {W(x)U(a);}                     /* a++ */
#define Copy(b,a)  {W(b); W(a)U(x); W(x)U(b),U(a);}  /* a=b */
```

```
#define Swap(a,b)   {W(a)U(y); W(b)U(x); W(y)U(b); W(x)U(a);}
#define Add(b,a)    {W(a)U(x); W(x)U(b)U(a);}                 /* b+=a */

char e[1024];

main (argc,argv)
   char *argv[];
   {
      char i,j,k,l,c,d;
      char MAXN = atoi(argv[1]);
      printf ("2.");
      j = atoi(argv[2]);
      Copy(i,MAXN);
      W (i) {Zero(e[i]); Inc(e[i]);}
      W (j) {
         Zero(e[1]);
         Zero(c);
         Copy(k,MAXN);
         while (--k) {
            d=c;
            c=0;
            l=11;
            while (--l) {
               d += e[k];
               if (d >= k) {c++; d-=k;}
            }
            e[k]=d;
         }
         printf ("%d",c);
      }
      printf ("\n");
   }
```

Best Abuse of the Rules

Diomidis Spinellis <dds@doc.ic.ac.uk>
Imperial College of Science, Technology and Medicine
University of London
London, England

```
#include "/dev/tty"
```

To compile this program, type:

```
cc spin.c
```

While it is compiling, try typing some arbitrary C code followed by an EOF ('^D').
The following is a good example:

```
main() {
        printf("Hello world\n");
}
```

Analysis

The author points out that this program can do just about anything and is limited only by the imagination of the person supplying the data. That's because this program makes light of the fact that an included file can be generated during compilation, in this case right from the keyboard! Legend has it that people have actually done this for quick solutions that required little thought and were not worth saving. In fact, many C compilers will not read source files from the terminal, so this provides a way around that "problem."

Naturally, this program forced the judges to add yet another rule preventing entries that cannot be compiled without need of human intervention.

Best Layout

Merlyn LeRoy (Brian Westley) <merlyn@digibd.com>
Digiboard Inc.
St. Paul, Minnesota

```
#define _ -F<00||--F-OO--;
int F=00,OO=00;main(){F_OO();printf("%1.3f\n",4.*-F/OO/OO);}F_OO()
{
                    _-_-_-_
                 _-_-_-_-_-_-_
              _-_-_-_-_-_-_-_-_-_
           _-_-_-_-_-_-_-_-_-_-_-_
          _-_-_-_-_-_-_-_-_-_-_-_-_
         _-_-_-_-_-_-_-_-_-_-_-_-_-_
        _-_-_-_-_-_-_-_-_-_-_-_-_-_-_
       _-_-_-_-_-_-_-_-_-_-_-_-_-_-_-_
       _-_-_-_-_-_-_-_-_-_-_-_-_-_-_-_
       _-_-_-_-_-_-_-_-_-_-_-_-_-_-_-_
        _-_-_-_-_-_-_-_-_-_-_-_-_-_-_
         _-_-_-_-_-_-_-_-_-_-_-_-_-_
          _-_-_-_-_-_-_-_-_-_-_-_-_
           _-_-_-_-_-_-_-_-_-_-_-_
              _-_-_-_-_-_-_-_-_
                 _-_-_-_-_-_
                    _-_-_-_
}
```

Author's Analysis

"This entry came out of a bizarre macro I wrote which would call C functions with a variable number of arguments plus a count of the number of actual arguments as the first parameter. Here is that program (slightly improved):

```
static int z = 0;
#define max(a,b,c,d) \
        z=0,m(4+z,- -a-z+z,- -b-z+z,- -c-z+z,- -d-z+z)

int m(count,a,b,c,d)
int count,a,b,c,d;
{
        printf("%d %d %d %d %d\n",count,a,b,c,d);
}

main() {
        max(1,2);
        max(1,2,3);
        max(1,2,3,4);
}
```

"This is totally non-portable—it depends on order of evaluation and what happens when an argument in a macro is omitted. It depends on the variable **z** being decremented when an argument is missing, so the count passed as the first argument is 4—the number of missing arguments! Notice the danger in doing `max(i,j,-k)` . . .

"Anyway, somehow I thought of a `#define`:

```
#define x -a
```

which would act differently as **x** versus **-x** (**-x** expands to **--a**, which decrements **a**). This is not portable, but is fun. I realized that a circle made up like this:

```
    x-x
   x-x-x-x
  x-x-x-x-x-x
  x-x-x-x-x-x
   x-x-x-x
    x-x
```

would decrement **a** once for each occurrence of **x** not preceded by a hyphen—i.e., the diameter. All I needed now was something to decrement once for each occurrence of **x** and I'd have the area, and I could compute π. This is essentially what my program does. The number of **x**'s is critical since I can only have an integer number for the area and diameter; $\frac{4 \times 201}{16^2}$ was the best I could do with small integer values. It is 3.140625, which when rounded for printing is 3.141. Changing **x** to _ made it look weirder, so I did that. I knew this entry would win!"

## CHAPTER 24

Speeding Up Strcpy

`strcpy`—we use it all the time, and take it for granted; we assume that it not only works, but that it is optimally fast. The C idiom for string copying is so simply stated, it is hard to see at first how it could possibly be improved.

```
while (*dest++ = *src++) ;
```

Wrapping this with formal parameters and arranging for the return value gives us a complete `strcpy`.

```
char *strcpy(dest,src)
char *dest, *src;
{
    char *s = dest;
        while (*dest++ = *src++) ;
        return(s);
}
```

Surprisingly, this is not necessarily the fastest implementation of `strcpy` for most machines and most compilers. For example, some machines have a `strcpy`-like machine instruction. This obviously makes things much easier. For now, however, I will discuss reality for the rest of us.

A dramatic improvement can be made by having the compiler put the `while` loop variables in registers. This can be done by modifying the parameter declaration so that it reads:

```
strcpy(dest,src)
register char *dest, *src;
```

Many compilers pass arguments on the stack and cannot obey this request directly. However, some compilers simulate it as if the code was written as follows:

```
strcpy(dest2,src2)
char *dest2, *src2;
{
    register char *dest = dest2;
    register char *src = src2;
```

Other compilers are not so smart. It may seem obvious how to optimize when looking at a simple subroutine like `strcpy`, but subroutines with many variables cannot be optimally compiled. Thus, it is generally not worth using `register` declarations on formal parameters unless you are coding for a particular compiler.

Notice that `strcpy` returns its first argument. It has never been clear to me why this is, as returning the end of the string is much more useful. For example, if you are going to append strings to a new string you have created, you will need to know where to start from. The only way to get this information is with `strlen`. `strlen` has to walk across every character in the string, which is exactly what `strcpy` does. What is the point of returning something that we obviously had to know to call the function in the first place? Let's write a new function called `endstrcpy`.[1]

```
/* strcpy, but return end of dest */
char *endstrcpy(dest,src)
char *dest, *src;
{
      while (*dest++ = *src++) ;
      return(dest-1);
}
```

Having a pointer to the end of a string is very useful. For example, we can calculate the length of the string by subtracting the beginning from the end. We can also reverse this operation if we have the length and want to calculate the end of the string. Sometimes we may already know the length of a string without having to call `strlen` or another string routine. In that case, we can do string copying even faster.

Many machines have single machine instructions that can copy a given number of bytes. These are available through the C library function called `memcpy`. Some Classic C systems called this `bcopy`.

`memcpy` is likely to be faster than `strcpy`, so if you already have the length or a pointer to the end of a string, you should call `memcpy` instead of `strcpy`. Both `memcpy` and `strcpy` are defined only on non-overlapping strings. For instance, using the `strcpy` we defined earlier, the result of the following code leaves `s` with the string `"model"`.

```
char s[80] = "/model";
/* strip leading slash */
strcpy(s,s+1);
```

Attempting to add space into the string is a bad idea.

```
strcpy(s+1,s);
```

`s` will be filled with slashes, and `strcpy` will attempt to fill all remaining memory with slashes. The problem is that `strcpy` copies each character over the next one that it is about to use. It will never see the terminating null, because it will have already written over it with a slash.

---

1. Standard C reserves all names beginning with "str" for future standardization.

Reversing `strcpy` so that it copies rear to front fixes the latter problem but then breaks `strcpy(s,s+1)`. Reverse copying is also slower since we have to find the end of the string. One solution is to compare the pointers to each other. If the source is greater than the destination, `strcpy` runs from the front of the string to the rear; otherwise it runs from the rear to the front. Let's call this `lapstrcpy`.

```
/* strcpy that handles overlap */
char *lapstrcpy(dest,src)
char *dest, *src;
{
    return(src>dest?
        forward_strcpy(dest,src):
        backward_strcpy(dest,src));
}
```

Alas, this is not portable. For example, on segmented architectures, segment-relative addresses cannot be meaningfully compared. Because segments may overlap, you could conceivably find that a lower address is not lower in reality. Fortunately, Standard C defines the `memmove` function, which is guaranteed to copy objects even if they overlap. This is the only portable solution.

A lot of string processing is done by ad hoc code because the string routines in the libraries don't quite match the programmer's requirements. My comment about returning string ends rather than string beginnings is one such example. Another is not requiring `strcpy` to behave "correctly" when dealing with overlapping strings. This is an unfortunate fact of life, spelled out by Standard C.

Making Strcpy Fast on a RISC

Complex machine architectures demonstrate the problems of producing optimal code. For example, the VAX has a single instruction that can do copies of arbitrary-length blocks, and another that can locate the ends of null-terminated strings. Using these, it becomes very easy to write an efficient `strcpy` (as well as `strlen`, `strcat`, and others). The first instruction finds the end of the string, and the second uses it to do the copy. That's two machine instructions!

In the case of the VAX, this worked fine. However, when a new machine was introduced, the MicroVAX II, it turned out that the engineers couldn't fit all the old VAX microcode into the microcode space of the MicroVAX. The obvious solution was to emulate the instructions in software. This worked fine except that `strcpy` now executed much more slowly than the original test-and-branch loop! The reason was that the optimized (two-instruction) version traversed the source string twice, while the unoptimized (C `while` loop) version traversed it only once.

This demonstrates a general problem of complex architectures, often referred to as *CISC* (for Complex Instruction Set Computers). They cause problems for compiler writers trying to create optimal compilers and libraries. Implementors generally have to learn large sets of complex instructions and gain a much deeper level of understanding about how they execute. For example, instruction timings vary depending on context because of caching and pipelines. While some of these factors affect RISC machines as well, all RISC instructions take one cycle (well, almost all do), making choices of instructions much simpler. The result is that the time you spend optimizing a compiler for a RISC machine will be less than for a CISC machine.

When the next version of your RISC machine appears, programmers won't have to spend time rewriting the optimizer to account for new instruction timings. The VAX—a CISC machine—presents exactly this problem because there are so many models. One approach is to make the code straightforward, and avoid the specialized instructions that are slow or aren't implemented on some machines.

By analogy, you can use the same reasoning for per-compiler optimization. Since your C code may run on many different compilers, operating systems, and machines, it is often better to write straightforward code that maximizes portability. Super- optimizing code is difficult. Are you sure it is better to code it this way on an 80286? 80386? 68000? VAX? SPARC? Cray? Let the compiler do the optimization.

Having said this, I'll now discuss some source code optimizations that have demonstrated value.

Loop Unrolling

The following was first expressed by Tom Duff, Bell Laboratories, and is known as *Duff's Device*. (I've taken the liberty of adapting it to do a copy operation—it was originally designed just to write to a single I/O register.)

```
switch (n&7) {
    do {
            *dest++ = *src++;
    case 7: *dest++ = *src++;
    case 6: *dest++ = *src++;
    case 5: *dest++ = *src++;
    case 4: *dest++ = *src++;
    case 3: *dest++ = *src++;
    case 2: *dest++ = *src++;
    case 1: *dest++ = *src++;
    case 0: ;
    } while (0 <= n-=8);
}
```

My compiler said "`warning:  loop not entered through top`" but compiled it correctly. Besides demonstrating what bizarreness is allowable with `switch`, this piece of code implements an optimization known as *loop unrolling*. The idea is that code you expect to loop many times can be sped up by not checking the termination condition each time through the loop. In this implementation, we check once every eight assignments. We handle the remainders separately.

For example, if `n` is 10, the switch branches to case 2. Case 2 falls into case 1, thereby executing two assignments (notice the missing `break`s) and the `while` returns us to the top of the loop to execute the remaining eight assignments with no intervening tests.

This would make the heart of a very fast `memcpy` (although its real intent is just to express the concept of loop unrolling in C). Notice that it is not dependent on the data types. You can copy by `char`, `int`, `long` or even `struct`—whatever you decide. However, there are trade-offs. For example, while larger types can store as quickly as smaller types, larger types often require alignment or you pay a speed penalty. Excessive unrolling can also cause your instruction cache to overflow and behave worse than if you had just used a simple loop. Compilers can do loop unrolling automatically, but only if they are assured of a payoff. This is difficult to determine in C programs, where so many miscellaneous functions call `memcpy`. You might like to create a second version of `memcpy`, which has this optimization in it. Which one you would call depends on the situation.[2]

Tom adds:

> Many people have said that the worst feature of C is that switches don't break automatically before each case label. This code forms some sort of argument in that debate, but I'm not sure whether it's for or against.

In case you are wondering whether Duff's device is legal in Standard C, rest assured that it is. The committee specifically considered it and called it strictly conforming.

A Real Fast Strcpy

Why did I bring up loop unrolling? Partly to demonstrate it, but also to improve `strcpy`. `strcpy` can use loop unrolling, although it is a little trickier than `memcpy`. The actual assignment is easy—the hard part is the termination condition.

Suppose we are copying four bytes at a time. We want to stop if any of the four bytes are null. The obvious test is:

```
(*x == 0) || (*(x+1) == 0) || (*(x+2) == 0) || (*(x+3) == 0)
```

Unfortunately, implementation of this expression is more expensive than the simple test we were hoping to avoid. Fortunately, there is a way to detect null bytes in a multibyte constant with only a few machine instructions. The following macro does the job.

```
#define has_null_byte(x) \
        (((x) - 0x01010101) & ~(x) & 0x80808080)
```

This particular version is written for four-byte `unsigned`s on a 2's complement machine. The basic idea is that the subtraction propagates bits up to the most sig-

---

2. According to Donald Knuth, "Premature optimization is the source of all error."

nificant bit in each byte by successive carries. If you want to really understand this, try running an example by hand, watching how the bits move.

Here is a rewrite of `strcpy` using this macro.

```
#define has_null_byte(x) (((x) - magic1) & ~(x) & magic2)

char *real_fast_strcpy(dest,src)
char *dest, *src;
{
        register long *d = (long *)dest;
        register long *s = (long *)src;
        register long magic1 = 0x01010101;
        register long magic2 = 0x80808080;
        register char *dc, *sc;
        /* copy four bytes at a time */
        while (!has_null_byte(*s)) {
                *d++ = *s++;
        }
        /* prepare to copy remaining chars */
        dc = (char *)d;
        sc = (char *)s;
        while (*dc++ = *sc++) ;
        return(dest);
}
```

`real_fast_strcpy` copies four bytes at a time, once each block is determined to be null-free. If there is a null, it just reverts back to the old behavior. Since this only happens close to the end of a string, there isn't much penalty for this.

By declaring `d` and `s` as `long` (four bytes on my machine), I am able to have the compiler provide the fastest way of copying. This will turn out to be a single instruction on most machines.

Historically, compilers implemented `register` on a first come–first served basis (although Standard C makes no such guarantees.) Thus, the `register` declarations are carefully ordered. `s` and `d` are going to be accessed the most frequently, so they come first. I modified the macro so the magic numbers are stored in registers. Only if the compiler has any registers left over will the old-style `strcpy` get the benefit of using them.

As I remarked earlier, heavily optimized code like this starts to sacrifice portability. In this case, I assume I know how `long`s are stored, assigned, and mathematically manipulated and I assume that `long`s can be accessed on arbitrary byte boundaries. I also hope that I'm going to get several registers for this to pay off. The worst aspect of all is that I have to guarantee that none of my strings are butted up against the end of my address space, and if one is, that it is aligned on a longword boundary. While such an occurrence is extremely unlikely, the algorithm will cause an address fault when `has_null_byte` attempts to look at several nonexistent bytes at the end of the string.

Sprintf

One final note. While `sprintf` may seem like overkill for a lot of simple string manipulations, it is defined to return the total number of characters written (not including the terminating null character). Adding this (plus 1) to the beginning of the string gives you the end of the string. This avoids exactly the problem I was complaining about earlier with `strcpy` and friends. If you are writing code where clarity is more important than performance, don't bother with the low-level functions—use `sprintf` for everything! Alas, it is not common among Classic C compilers, so do this only if you can guarantee that your code will be compiled only by Standard C compilers.

## CHAPTER 25

Register

The `register` keyword is used to indicate to the compiler that a variable should be stored in a register if possible. The idea is that the programmer is telling the compiler that a variable is frequently used, and that placing it in a register will speed up the program.

This sounds pretty intuitive, and the idea really is. But there are nonintuitive points to be aware of and that is what this chapter is all about. For example, it is a common belief that good compilers obviate the need for `register` declarations. This simply isn't true, as I will explain later. To get the best performance from your code, you must be prepared to use `register`.

`register` declarations are used during code generation. At that time, the compiler decides what machine instructions will be used to execute your program. The `register` keyword requests that the variable be stored in a machine register. However, this may not always be possible. One obvious reason is that the machine may not even use registers. For example, stack-oriented machines such as the Pyramid don't have registers.

Compilers are free to ignore `register`. Naturally, the Pyramid's C compiler does exactly that.

However, even register-oriented machines can ignore `register` in a declaration. For example, suppose you have a machine with eight registers and you declare nine `register` variables. Obviously, the compiler is not going to be able to satisfy your request—right? Not necessarily, as we will see.

In fact, most compilers will not allow the user to dictate the allocation of all the registers of the machine. For example, one register is typically reserved for the stack pointer and another for the frame pointer (or activation record). A couple are generally reserved for temporary computations. If you need to allocate and manipulate the registers more efficiently than the compiler, you are going to have to resort to assembler.

Well then, how many can we declare with any assurance? If your code is going to be ported to other architectures, the guaranteed answer is zero. Otherwise, you should look for the answer only in your particular compiler's manual. This is precisely what is stated by Standard C.

If the documentation doesn't specify—and this is not uncommon—experiment with different types of code and examine the assembler output to see how many are manipulated directly as registers.

A simple program to do this may not always be possible. Some compilers perform *live range analysis*. This technique moves values out of registers when they are no longer being accessed even though they are still in the current scope.

```
register int i, j;
/* no use of j in loop */
for (i=0;...;i++) {
    ...
}
/* no further use of i */
for (j=0;...;j++) {
    ...
}
```

For example, some compilers can create code that uses only one register for controlling both loops instead of two. Since uses of i and j don't overlap, it is easy to share the register.

This is a particularly easy case, since i and j could actually share the same storage whether or not they were kept in registers or not. That is, if we literally substituted "i" for "j" throughout the function, it would still work correctly. This is often not possible, even when register sharing is.

```
for (i=0;...;i++)
for (j=0;...;j++)
for (;...;i++)
```

In this piece of code, we see that i is used throughout, but the compiler can save it before entering the middle loop and restore it afterward. This again allows i and j to use the same register with a small amount of overhead. Of course, you will have to experiment to see whether your compiler can do this.

Good compilers can do it automatically (without the `register` declaration), but there are certainly compilers that do not do this. In any case, complicated expressions are even more unlikely to be handled optimally. It is to your benefit to declare as `register` all the variables that are heavily used.

The most obvious problem is that compilers have no way to tell how many times loops are going to be executed. Bounded loops like the ones above are easy, but analysis is generally impossible for unbounded loops like the following:

```
while (1) {
    if (expr) break;
    ...
}
```

In the face of these, the compiler cannot justify saving and restoring registers when there is no guarantee that it will save time during execution. To combat this, people have proposed language extensions to indicate primary flow of control, such as which branch of an `if` is more likely to be taken. However, these have not been adopted into the mainstream of C.

The only solution is to make judicious use of `register` yourself. Don't hold out for optimizing compilers to produce optimal code—that's not what they do. They just produce better code. You still have a responsibility to help the compiler generate the best code possible. A general rule of thumb is that if a variable is accessed more than four times, you should consider declaring it `register`. Time your code with and without `register` declarations to see how *four* feels on your system.

Some people advocate using only one or two `register` declarations in a function, but I believe you should use *as many* `register` *declarations as necessary*. Even if your current compiler uses only the first two of them, you will get improvement in your code, since you are telling the compiler what is heavily used rather than having it guess. On the other hand, some compilers give up registers that would otherwise be used for compiler optimization. Thus, there is a trade-off between which can optimize better, the programmer or the compiler. Use blocks to delimit the lifetime of register variables and help tell the compiler that variables overlap. For example, the original example could be rewritten as:

```
{
    register int i;
    for (i=0;...;i++) {
    ...
}
{
    register int j;
    for (j=0;...;j++) {
    ...
}
```

Although Standard C makes no guarantees, historically, compilers wanted to see `register` declarations in decreasing order of importance (and in separate statements to avoid the vagaries of a compiler parsing `register a, b, c;` from right to left). When the compiler allocates registers to variables, it will often follow your order of declarations. If it runs out of registers before getting to the end of your list, you may have `register` variables that are not stored in registers.

In Chapter 24 (p. 209), I presented a function (`real_fast_strcpy`) that declared six `register` variables. This is more than most compilers will allow you to allocate, but they were arranged in descending importance. The ones at the end were used in loops that would loop only a few times, while the ones in the beginning were used in loops that would usually execute many times.

Addressing Register Variables

Do not use `register` on variables whose address you intend to take. For example, consider the following code fragment:

```
int *i;
register j;

i = &j;
```

Some Classic C compilers allowed such code. While the compiler executed the code, you would not get the speedup you expected. The problem is that most machines do not have addressable registers. If a compiler saw such a code fragment, it could do one of two things:

1. ignore `register`, or

2. generate extra instructions to move the value between register and memory whenever necessary.

Needless to say, implementors almost always took the first option. Standard C outlaws these constructs outright. Fortunately, the optimization precluded by this is considered to be extremely rare.

Register Parameters

The previous chapter went into some detail on the use of `register` on function parameters. I suggested that you skip using `register` when declaring function parameters if this was to be portable code, because many compilers will ignore them. The best way to get the same effect is to declare new variables as `register` inside the body of the function and then assign them values from the parameters. You will not lose any speed, even if the compiler does correctly handle `register` parameters.

Standard C function prototypes ignore the use of `register` entirely. So, for example, the following two declarations for `strcpy` are equivalent:

```
char *strcpy(char *dest, const char *src);
char *strcpy(register char *dest, register const char *src);
```

These lines are not the function definitions, just declarations. Use of `register` is noted in function definitions. The rationale is that function prototypes are used to check that parameter types match, but `register` does not change the parameter type. If anything, this helps separate specification from implementation.

By the way, in case it isn't obvious, you cannot use `register` on variables declared `extern` or `static`. Since all variables declared outside of any function are implicitly `extern`, this means you can use `register` only inside of a function.

Register Types

If you say `register foo`, `foo` is declared to be of type `int`; you can also create `register` pointers. `register` can be applied to other types, although such use is generally not portable to all types in Classic C.

Most compilers will generate code for `register short` and `register char` because these will fit in an `int`. However, keep in mind that the natural word size of a machine is an `int`. Registers are generally `int`-sized. Using `register` `char`s, for example, usually causes the compiler to simulate small registers by performing some of the computations in registers and some in memory. For example, a series of additions may normally cause overflow in memory, but not when done by `int` register computations. In order to preserve semantics, the compiler may generate extra instructions. It is better for the programmer to be aware of this and write the code using `int register` than to expect the compiler to work around the problem.

Larger `register` declarations such as `struct`s may not see any improvement, either because they are too large for a register, or the compiler writer chose to ignore the use of `register` on anything but `int`s. This is not uncommon.

`register` floating-point declarations are more likely to be used because many machines have floating-point registers. However, you run the risk that your code may someday run on a machine that has no floating-point registers, and your request for registers will bump into your requests for `int` registers.

Setjmp and Longjmp

In Chapter 18 (p. 151), I discussed `setjmp` and `longjmp` in detail, and made two important points. I'll repeat them both here, and add a third.

1. `longjmp` restores only variables stored in registers, but no others, when the saved environment is restored.

2. There is no guarantee that the variables declared as `register` will have their values saved by `setjmp`, because there is no guarantee that the compiler will actually put your variables in a register (remember, `register` is only a hint to the compiler).

3. Standard C guarantees even less (and more). It says that all local variables, whether `register` or not, have indeterminate values after `longjmp`, unless declared volatile.

Saving Space

A `register` declaration can occasionally cause unexpectedly good speedups. Why? Some compilers generate shorter instructions or instruction sequences for accessing registers. This can decrease your code size. This is not impressive overall, but if it happens to occur in a loop that might otherwise not fit in the machine's instruction cache, the payoff can be substantial.

Conclusion

Most people think that the good thing about `register` is that if it is misused, it will be ignored. This simply isn't true. At best, misuse of `register` can cause your program to execute more slowly than without it. At worst, `register` can cause great confusion due to subtle interactions with `setjmp` and `longjmp`.

On the other hand, `register` declarations are great when used correctly. By allowing you to give hints to the compiler during code generation, you can get better performance than would be possible even from the best optimizing compilers without `register` declarations.

CHAPTER 26

Portability

Portability is one of the best things about C. It is also one of the most difficult things to achieve in a C program. It should be obvious, but I'll say it anyway: programs are not portable just because they are written in C. Even Standard C doesn't guarantee portability (although it can help).

It is extremely depressing to receive source to a C program and get errors running the program—or worse, while compiling it. C programs are supposed to be portable, right?

Automatic portability of C programs is one of those myths, like the portability of UNIX source or DOS executables. I probably don't need to explain what portability is. Every reader of this book has probably run into it—perhaps even trying to execute some of the code I have printed here. It is surprising how large a percentage of public-domain code cannot readily be compiled because the authors gave little thought to portability. I see many of the same problems in code published in books and magazines.

This chapter discusses portability, gives some guidelines, presents some examples and makes some suggestions. I cannot possibly make an exhaustive treatise—after all, there are entire books written on the subject—but I will discuss the most important and common aspects, and I'll recommend some of those books!

Much of what constitutes *portable programming practice* is common to the tenets of *good programming practice*. For example, you should always check return codes. Unfortunately, code can be very difficult to read when conditions surround every statement. If the code is going to appear as a standalone example in a piece of text, and the error codes are not relevant, that *must be noted*. Only then is it acceptable for the error-checking to be omitted. However, the production code should have the error-checking.

In the same fashion, nonportable code may be presented but *only if it is so noted*. I have often presented code that works on a subset of machines but have always tried to identify it as such. If you do similarly in production code, make sure your comments explain any potential problems. To do otherwise would be cruel, as well as poor economics.

You should always make an effort to produce portable code. Only if you absolutely must sacrifice efficiency or functionality should you write nonportable code. And then, you should try and provide a hook so that the programmer who inherits the job of porting your code to a different machine doesn't have to completely rewrite it.

Your code *will* be ported to other machines[1]. Unless you live on a desert island (in which case you won't have this book), it is inevitable. Face the music. From another viewpoint, *you* will use code from another environment eventually. To believe otherwise means that you will be stuck using the same machine you are currently on for the rest of your life. In the computer field, this is not reality.

Why Is Portable Code So Important?

One of the things that C has become famous for is making it possible to write portable system code. For example, 99 percent of all UNIX system software is written in C. This is one of the reasons it is much easier to port UNIX programs than, say, CP/M programs, 99 percent of which were written in 8080 and Z80 assembler. Many UNIX programs, for example, run under DOS with almost no change.

DOS programs imply an x86 architecture, and one might think that its corresponding assembler language would be portable. To a certain degree this is true; however, few people write x86 assembler. Although assembler programs can be faster than C programs, the speed improvements simply aren't worth all the drawbacks. If you don't need the utmost in speed, there is almost no reason why you can't code in C. By writing in C, you increase the likelihood that your programs can be easily moved to other operating systems or machine architectures.

Portability is not always easy to achieve and there are degrees to which different people believe differently. Many people aren't concerned in the least. Should you be? Is the price too high to pay? Alas, there is no simple answer. The reason is because portability has disadvantages as well as advantages.

The primary advantage is that code is easier to port (this is by definition). Portable code usually has the additional benefit that it is better written. Almost always, more thought will have gone in to low-level code writing (as opposed to design) in order to achieve portability.

However, producing portable code *the first time* can be more expensive, especially if you are not going to port right away.[2] Another drawback is that portable code can be unreadable or unwieldy (although more often, it is nonportable code that is unreadable and unwieldy). Lastly, portable code often sacrifices environment-dependent hacks that are more efficient than slower, portable techniques.

There are other issues, but elaborating them hardly affects the conclusion. The fact is, if there is any likelihood code will be ported, it is worth the immediate expense to make it portable in the first place. This covers the majority of C code.

---

1. According to Stephen Friedl, "If you strive to write portable code when it doesn't matter, you'll have a much easier time of it when someday it *does* matter."
2. According to Rex Jaeschke, "The real world: no time to do it right, but always time to do it over."

What's Left?

What am I willing to code nonportably? Parts of a C compiler are inherently nonportable, such as the code generator, function entry and exit, and certain run-time functions like `setjmp`. System boot code, drivers that cannot afford the overhead of C function calls, such as the clock driver, and other time-critical code are examples of software that usually have to be written in assembler.

Finally, if you are optimizing code, you may find one or two hot spots that allow large speedups with just one or two lines of assembler. However, cavalier abuse of this can be a drawback rather than an advantage. In Chapter 24 (p. 207), I discussed how `strcpy` was sped up by rewriting it in assembler for the VAX. While this worked for the first VAX model, the resulting code was actually slower than the portable C version on some later VAX models.

Before giving up on C, try rethinking the algorithm. If an algorithm can be improved, this will buy more speed than rewriting it in assembler. For example, you can optimize your bubble sort till the end of time, but even the most simplistic C implementation of Quicksort will be able to beat an assembler-coded bubble sort.

What Does Portability Mean?

There are portability issues at many different levels. Here are some broad groupings.

Machine and Language Data and Instruction Formats

Byte ordering is an excellent example of this. Byte ordering is inconsistent from one architecture to another. Programs should never depend on byte ordering. (See p. 117 in Chapter 14 for more detail on this subject.)

There are many other problems that crop up at this level, such as code that assumes a particular character set, or assumes one of `signed` or `unsigned char`s. Your programs should not depend on any of these characteristics.

`lint` will catch most of these problems. There is no excuse for not using `lint` or an analogous tool. Don't assume `lint` is no longer useful because of Standard C. (Gimpel Software sells an inexpensive and amazingly good `lint`.)

Low Level Operations

Null pointer dereferencing is a good example of nonportability. On some VAX C implementations, a null pointer can be dereferenced (and the result is usually 0). It may seem strange but a lot of sloppy code has actually been written that inadvertently depends on this. Most machines do not allow users to dereference location 0. On unmapped systems, it is usually reserved for interrupt vectors, and on mapped systems, it often simply isn't available for process data. Such references can produce address faults.

Another example of nonportable low-level operations is accessing memory in ways that violate alignment constraints. For example, a 68000 does not allow word access beginning on odd-byte boundaries.

C Language Syntax and Semantics

Standard C has been of great help in codifying acceptable programming practices. For example, the standard says that whether identifiers with external linkage are distinguishable beyond six initial characters is implementation-defined. This rule is provided for very archaic linkers that you should pray you will never have to deal with. Along these lines, there are hundreds of things now identified as "implementation-defined," "undefined," or whatever. It is your responsibility to be aware of these.

In reality, it is sometimes necessary to violate some element of the standard. And common practice violates many elements of the standard. If—no, make that *when* you violate the standard, please document your violations or assumptions, so that others can easily detect whether and where your code is going to break.

Operating System Environment

Differing environments can cause many problems to C programs. For example, DOS, UNIX, and VMS all have different restrictions on filenames. If possible, code to the least common denominator (DOS in this case). Unfortunately, directory paths have no correspondingly easy solution.

Another problem is system calls that are not portable from one operating system to another. A generally useful guideline is to avoid all system calls and instead use standard library functions. Unless speed is a problem, library calls are typically higher-level and easier to use, anyway. (Alas, libraries corresponding to developing or specialized areas such as window systems and networks can make it exceedingly difficult to even find a common set of "standard" library calls.)

Some General Guidelines

- `lint` is particularly helpful with low-level coding. It specifically looks for portability problems that can be detected at the syntactic level and is very comprehensive. There is no reason why you shouldn't have `lint` (or an equivalent) in your toolbox. A Standard C compiler is not necessarily a replacement for `lint`.

- Reduce the use of magic numbers as much as possible. Generally, the only numbers that should appear in-line in your code are 0, 1, 2, and -1. The rest should be specified as manifest constants in `#define`s.

- Avoid going behind the C compiler's back. This means not assuming detailed knowledge of structure layout or byte ordering, and avoiding excessive casting when you really should be using a `union`.

- If you can't find documentation on how something behaves, don't run experiments to find out. It's probably not well-defined and it may behave differently in another environment.

- Avoid questionable practices, even if they aren't behind the compiler's back. Never assume that `char` is `signed`. Never assume you can dereference a null pointer. Be careful when declaring variables to be `int`. `int` is a convenience for the architecture and provides few guarantees about how big or small it will be. The same goes for `short` and `long`.

- Be sure that function arguments match parameter types. For example, if a routine expects a `long`, make sure it gets one. Never pass 0's without casting when they are going to be used as anything other than `int`s.

- Try porting your software to several different architectures (and memory models). This is an amazingly useful and sometimes painful way to learn about the real world.[3]

- Isolate nonportable code in separate files, or through preprocessor directives such as `#if` and `#ifdef` (if the differences are small).

- Document the standards your work relies on. Document (loudly) the places where you knowingly violate those standards or depend on undefined or implementation-defined results. Look for portable alternatives.

Books on Portability

This chapter is only the tip of the iceberg in the area of portability. Porting expertise can only be gained through close reading of many manuals, years of experience trying to actually move software from one environment to another, and occasional visits to the psychiatrist after finding out that your favorite coding practice is nonportable and you've got to change hundreds of programs.

I can recommend several books that you might like to read for further information on writing portable code. An excellent book for writing portable C is *Portability and the C Language* [1]. It recommends practices when writing for Standard C, or for writing to both Standard C and Classic C. Another fine book is *Portable C Software* [2], which provides comparisons between various implementations and provides high-level discussion offering lots of advice on what approaches to take to solve various problems. While not strictly a book on portability, *C Traps and Pitfalls* [3] is a delightful book describing the most common things that can go wrong. It is good for both beginning as well as experienced programmers.

I have already mentioned *H&S* (*C: A Reference Manual*). This book is not really a text on portability, but because it is so comprehensive in scope, the authors continually mention how many compilers diverge from each other. Many examples of how to code portably are presented.

---

3. According to Henry Spencer, "If you haven't ported your software, it's not portable."

Portable C and UNIX System Programming [4] is not as comprehensive about the C language as *C: A Reference Manual*, but is oriented more toward information about libraries and environments. The book covers the differences between calls in System V, Berkeley, XENIX, and several other UNIX variants.

The Standard C Library is an excellent reference for its namesake. This book provides a complete implementation of the C library. While not entirely portable, it spells out exactly the degree of portability in each part. The book continually stresses the fine line between efficiency and portability.

Last but not least, you should also have the C standard itself (plus the Rationale). While others may provide interpretations, this is the final authority for C.

Conclusion

Portability is not guaranteed just by writing in C. You must make a deliberate effort to create portable code, but the results are almost always worth it. Portable code can be moved to other environments with practically no cost, while nonportable code can require complete rewriting, and substantial redesign at worst.

Keep in mind some of the guidelines I have suggested as you write your next program. There is no reason to write nonportable code if you don't have to. The next programmer to receive your code will thank you. And don't forget to use `lint`!

References

Books mentioned in this chapter that do not appear here are listed in Chapter 40 beginning on p. 400.

[1]   Rex Jaeschke, *Portability and the C Language*, Profession Press, 1989.

[2]   Mark Horton, *Portable C Software*, Prentice Hall, 1990.

[3]   Andrew Koenig, *C Traps and Pitfalls*, Addison-Wesley, 1989.

[4]   J. E. Lapin, *Portable C and UNIX System Programming*, Prentice Hall, 1987.

## CHAPTER 27

Threads

This chapter discusses *threads*, a word you may have seen in OS/2 advertisements and wondered about. Threads are not something new, but few people know about them. They are a very elegant and powerful concept available in many multiprocessing systems. I will introduce them by telling you about a program I recently wrote.

The program would detect when my console was idle for several minutes. It would then paint images on the screen one at a time. At the rate of one per second, this was a very effective way of telling someone that my console was turned on, without letting the screen burn in, or using up very much CPU time.

My first cut at writing this program was something like the following:

```
int maxpictures = 0;

main() {
    /* read in all the pictures */
    dir = opendir(PICTURE_DIRECTORY);
    while (read_next_picture()) ;

    /* now display them, one per second */
    /* until user presses a key */
    while (TRUE) {
        if (key_pressed()) exit(0);
        draw_picture(pictures[random(maxpictures)]);
        sleep(1);
    }
}

int  /* returns FALSE if no more pictures to read */
read_next_picture() {
    picture = readdir(dir);
    if (NULL == picture) return(FALSE);
    pictures[maxpictures] = read_picture(picture);
    maxpictures++;
    return(TRUE);
}
```

You can imagine what all of the routines did by their names.

This program worked nicely for a while. But, all of a sudden, one day it stopped working. At least, it *seemed* like it had stopped working. When I ran it, it just sat there; the screen didn't change.

After a little investigation, I discovered that the program was actually still running correctly. The program just wasn't making it to the display part of the program as quickly as it used to. It seems that someone had received a supply of several hundred pictures from another site, and added them to our local picture directory. The directory had only had 20 pictures in it the week before. Originally, the program took about five seconds to load the 20 pictures in and begin displaying them. But now, it took much longer—about five minutes to even begin displaying the first picture.

At first I was a little annoyed with the person who added all the pictures. But I realized that my anger was misdirected. After all, it was inevitable that more pictures would be added. Indeed, I and my colleagues were guilty of doing that, albeit at a much slower rate. However, the real culprit was the program itself. I resolved to rewrite the program so it would run much more quickly.

Unfortunately, I found there was little I could do to speed up the picture-reading routine or the loop that read the pictures in. So, what I did instead was to rewrite the main routine as follows:

```
dir = opendir(PICTURE_DIRECTORY);
read_next_picture();
read_next_picture();
read_next_picture();

while (TRUE) {
    if (key_pressed()) exit(0);
    read_next_picture();
    draw_picture(pictures[random(maxpictures)]);
    sleep(1);
}
```

read_next_picture would read in the next picture and update `maxpictures`. I called it several times before the loop, just so the program wouldn't always have to start with the same picture.

Notice that `maxpictures` was shared by the two routines. The routines were also sharing control, although as I've sketched it here, `read_next_picture` was clearly subservient to `main`. Ideally, I would have liked `read_next_picture` to run at the same time that the drawing routine was running.

Both of my solutions shared control rather crudely. Because of that, the program was prohibited from reading faster than one picture per second even if it were possible. And if it took longer than a second to read a picture, the screen updating would have slowed down correspondingly. Similarly, the keyboard was being checked only at the same interval.

We could rewrite this program in several ways. For example, after each picture has been read, we could have **main** check whether one second of time has passed (or is likely to before the next picture is read) and if so, display a new picture. And although a second doesn't seem that long a period to wait to get control back to the user, we would really like to check for keystrokes more frequently. In fact, the way the program is written, we are going to be waiting one second plus however much time it takes to read in a picture, which is actually close to another second on my system. So another possibility is to read in parts of a picture, intermittently checking for keystrokes.

This is a rather trivial application, and yet making it work intuitively is hard. The suggestions I have made all sound incredibly kludgy. The problem is that we only have one *thread of control* yet inherently have tasks that should be performed concurrently. In a single-threaded program like the two above, only one function can be in execution at a time.

Rewritten Using Threads

With a system like OS/2, which supports multiple threads, our original program becomes much simpler. First we create individual functions to perform the unrelated tasks.

```
read_all_pictures() {
     dir = opendir(PICTURE_DIRECTORY);
     while (read_next_picture()) ;
}

display_all_pictures()
{
     while (TRUE) {
          draw_picture(pictures[random(maxpictures)]);
          sleep(1);
     }
}

listen() {
     getchar();
     exit(0);         /* terminate process */
}
```

The only obvious remaining problem is to get them all running at the same time. To do that, we write **main** as follows:

```
main()
{
     createthread(read_all_pictures);
     createthread(display_all_pictures);
     createthread(listen);
}
```

`createthread` takes a pointer to a function and calls it. Then without waiting for it to return, `createthread` itself returns! It's as if there were one program before the function call and two after. In reality, there are indeed two programs—they share the same address space and code, but with separate stacks. In the above example, we can share `maxpictures` between the two programs just by using the same name.

Here, the program has been separated into threads. The first thread reads in the pictures. The second one displays them. The third one waits for a keystroke to terminate the program.

Notice how simple the subroutines are. The thread that reads in pictures is just a loop. It doesn't wait for anyone else. As soon as it finishes reading one picture, it can begin reading the next. The second thread is just as simple. It chooses a new picture, displays it, and goes to sleep for one second.

The third thread is amazingly trivial now. It just uses `getchar` to wait for a character to be pressed. No interrupts, signal handlers, or I/O kludges need to be dealt with (which I passed over in my first solution). And it works better than before. The program will terminate as soon as a key is pressed, rather than waiting up to a second. `exit` is defined to terminate the process—this includes all the threads.

All programs start out single-threaded. The thread is whatever is defined by `main`. In this case, `main` created three new threads. For an instant, then, there were four threads running, but then `main` terminated. The `main` thread terminates just like any other thread—it goes away and leaves the remaining threads in a process in execution. In a similar way, the picture-reading thread will go away after it has read all the pictures.

In my second non-threaded attempt at the program, `read_next_picture` continued to be called even after all the pictures had been read. Clearly, the threaded solution is much cleaner, more efficient, and simpler to understand and code.

More Details about Threads

Don't confuse threads with processes. A process may have one thread or many. But each process has a different address space, while all the threads in a single process share the same address space. Some people refer to threads as *lightweight processes* or *tasks*.

Threads are not defined simply by subroutines. For example, it is possible to have two threads executing the same subroutine. What really defines a thread is a set of register values (including a program location). As threads are given a chance to run, the system saves the registers of one thread and restores the registers of another. However, the process's address-map registers are not changed.

The register values of a thread include a stack pointer. Each thread has its own stack. When the system restores the register values from a new thread, the stack pointer is changed to point to the new thread's stack.

If this makes you think of `setjmp` and `longjmp`, you have the right idea. `setjmp` and `longjmp` save and restore the registers in the same way. The only difference is that they have to be called explicitly by the user. When the operating system supports threads, it automatically saves and restores the registers as threads are given or relieved of control. Another difference is that `setjmp` does not save all the registers, as I discussed earlier (see p. 151 in Chapter 18).

Threads in the Real World

Threads are not just a creation of OS/2. Many other systems support them, such as Mach, Xinu, Ada and PolyForth. It is also possible to layer threads on top of any multiprocessing system (such as UNIX). Threads are conceptually handled strictly as multitasking between parts of one process, so there is no inherent reason why the operating system has to know about them.

However, some implementations of threads have mixed the ideas of processes and threads a little, leading to some confusion. For example, OS/2 schedules threads, not processes. Thus, a process may get more of a slice of the processor by breaking the task into many threads.

It will take you a little while to become comfortable with multithreaded processes. In general, you should avoid them unless it is absolutely clear (as in the example above) that they are necessary. One of the drawbacks of threads is that they can be very difficult to program correctly and debug.

Drawbacks of Threads

Any programs that update shared data structures have to use some sort of interlocking in order to maintain integrity. For example, if two threads are incrementing the same variable, one thread could be temporarily suspended after loading the variable and before incrementing it. Meanwhile, the second thread could load and increment the variable. Then the first thread resumes adding 1 to the *old* value and saving it. The final value reflects only the operations performed by the first thread, and this error is thus referred to as the *lost update problem*.

Another problem is illustrated in my example. The careful reader will notice that it is possible for `display_all_pictures` to attempt to display a picture before any have been read in! Try correcting the program so this can't happen.

When *processes* manipulate shared resources, they go through the operating system. The operating system protects processes against lost updates. However, threads aren't protected against each other, and the thread programmer must take responsibility for this. Any system providing threads also provides a way of synchronizing thread control, such as monitors or semaphores. There are many books on the subject of concurrent programming. One I particularly like is *Structured Concurrent Programming with Operating Systems Applications* [1].

More on Thread Calls

All I've shown so far is how to create threads with `createthread`. I have actually simplified things a bit. For example, OS/2 calls this function `DosCreateThread` and requires a second argument that is a block of storage to use for stack space. The priority of the thread is the same as the priority of the calling thread.

Xinu, on the other hand, does things slightly differently. The Xinu `create` call creates a suspended thread. Then you call `resume` to start it running. Xinu also has slightly different parameters. For example, its second argument is the size of the stack rather than the address of the stack. Additional arguments include priority and optional arguments to be passed to the thread when it starts running.

I find Xinu threads to be slightly more elegant and orthogonal than OS/2 threads, although the differences really are quite minimal. *The Programmer's Essential OS/2 Handbook* [2] does a nice job describing all the OS/2 thread calls along with other calls related to asynchronous processing.

There are only a couple of other thread functions. Threads can implicitly terminate by `return`, or they can be explicitly killed. A thread can also be suspended or resumed.

There are also functions to manipulate thread priorities. Typically, one function will get the priority of a thread, and another will set it. It is easy to think of a reason why you would want to prioritize threads. For example, a multi-threaded editor might have a thread reading and echoing keystrokes, another maintaining a window of files in the current directory, and a third doing garbage collection for other threads. The keyboard and screen-updating threads would have highest priority, the thread maintaining the list of files intermediate priority, and the garbage collection the lowest priority, effectively running only when nothing else in the program is (or can be) running.

Processes do not exist in DOS, so it is not surprising that threads don't either. I mentioned earlier that any multiprocessing system can support threads. UNIX, for example, has no thread calls built into the operating system, but it is possible to write your own.

I recently wanted to use threads on UNIX, so I ported Xinu to it. Xinu is about 900 lines of C plus six lines of assembler. The assembly language was needed to save and restore the registers. No changes were necessary to the C compiler and only minor changes were necessary to support multiple-thread access to the standard libraries. If you are interested in this, you can read *Multiple Programs in One UNIX Process* [3]. Xinu itself is described in the *Operating System Design: The Xinu Approach* [4]. This is a wonderfully written book—a real gem in the field of operating systems.

Conclusion

When used appropriately, threads can dramatically simplify programs that would otherwise be arcane or ugly. On the other hand, threads have drawbacks and pitfalls of their own, such as requiring the programmer to deal with synchronizing access to shared data structures.

I encourage you to become as familiar with threads as you are with processes. I guarantee you will find them handy. Threads are an important tool in the repertoire of an applications programmer on a multitasking system.

References

[1] R.C. Holt, E.D. Lazowska, G.S. Graham, M.A. Scott, *Structured Concurrent Programming with Operating Systems Applications*, Addison-Wesley, 1978.

[2] David Cortesi, *The Programmer's Essential OS/2 Handbook*, M&T Books, 1990.

[3] Don Libes, "Multiple Programs in One UNIX Process," *;login:*, USENIX Association, Berkeley, California, July/August, 1987.

[4] Douglas Comer, *Operating System Design, The Xinu Approach*, Prentice Hall, 1984.

## CHAPTER 28

The 1989 Obfuscated C Code Contest

If Gary Larson wrote C code, what do you suppose it might look like? I can only imagine that it would be as bizarre as his cartoons.

Fortunately for us, Gary doesn't write C. (And he is probably relieved that I don't draw cartoons.) Nonetheless, there are people who have taken a *Far Side*–view of what C programming is all about. Their efforts grace this chapter.

Without further ado, then, here are the winners of the 1989 Obfuscated C Code Contest. (*Drum roll.*) The envelope, please . . .

Best Self-Modifying Program

Jay Vosburgh
Sequent Computer Systems, Inc.
Beaverton, Oregon

```
                 <first line intentionally left blank!>
#include <stdio.h>
#define QQ        1
#define TT              1
#define cc main(c,v) int c; char **v;{char tt[12],qq[7];\
    int q=0,o=1,l=1,m=1;struct {int c;} f;
#define ouroboros qq[6]='\0';tt[11]='\0';if(QQ==atoi(v[1])+1)\
    {(void)fprintf(stderr,"%s factorial = %d\n",v[1], TT);\
    exit(1);}o=c+f
#define x ;while(EOF!=(o=getchar())){if(l && q=='Q' && o=='Q')\{l
    =0;(void)getchar();(void)fread(qq,6,1,stdin);(void)printf(\
    "Q %6d",atoi(qq)+1);}else if(m && q=='T' && o=='T'){m=0;(\
    void)fread(tt,11,1,stdin);(void)printf("T %9d\n",atoi(tt)*\
    QQ);}else{q=o;(void)putchar(o);}}exit(0);}
cc ouroboros.c -o x
#define zxc ;{/*
cat ouroboros.c | x $1 > x1
if [ $? -ne 0 ]; then
exit
fi
mv x1 ouroboros.c
chmod +x ouroboros.c
```

```
exec ouroboros.c $1
exit
*/
```

This ghastly program actually causes its own compilation. That is, the program, called `ouroborus.c`, can be interpreted as a script of commands to compile itself, as well as a C program.

First, the program is given to the UNIX shell (`/bin/sh`). The C program is hidden by preprocessor directives that are ignored because of the hash mark at the beginning—a comment to the shell.

The program is compiled. Then the source is piped to itself. This produces a new "improved" version as the standard output, here called `x1`. If the final return code from the previous version was 0, we replace the old source with the new source and then invoke the shell on that! This starts the whole mess over again! To reinvoke the shell, the script uses `exec` (a small concession to efficiency), which overlays the current invocation of the shell with the next, using the exact same arguments.

Now let us look at the C code. First notice that almost all of the shell commands are cleverly hidden from the compiler by the following line `#define zxc ;{/*` which opens a comment containing the rest of the shell script. Only one shell command remains—the `cc ouroboros.c -o x`. If you look at the `#define`s, sure enough, there are replacements for `cc`, `ouroboros` and `x` (`o` is a real variable)!

After substitution (and a lot of reformatting) the program (shown below) looks a little different. Notice that I have done all the macro preprocessing except for `QQ` and `TT`. Why? To show that before substitution is performed on them, the program massages those lines (and only those lines). 1 is added to `QQ`, and the current `TT` (the one actually supplied by the C preprocessor) is multiplied by `QQ`. Hence, each time through, the program computes the next factorial, beginning with 1.

When `QQ` finally reaches the original user input (passed as an argument to the shell script and finally turning up in `argv`), the program changes the return code, signalling the shell script to stop rerunning and recompiling the code. Oh, and the rest of the program? It just echos its input.

A variety of other types of obfuscation are liberally sprinkled throughout the code. For example, it is amusing to examine the formatting of the `TT` and `QQ` lines. The author did not use `scanf`, but instead called `fread` and then `atoi` since he knew exactly where the numbers were in their lines. This explains the odd placement on the `#define` lines, as well as the size of the declarations in the arrays `tt` and `qq`.

Incidentally, the first line is blank in order to stop the "clever" behavior of the C-shell (`csh`), which tries to guess whether a file is a `csh` or `sh` script. Without going into a gory explanation, the `#include` line would cause the C-shell to guess incorrectly.

In summary, this program computes a factorial by modifying itself, compiling and running the new executable. The new executable repeats the process. To compute

X!, the program is recompiled X+1 times. Now who wanted to know why factorial isn't built into the language?!

```c
#include <stdio.h>
#define QQ       1
#define TT          1

main(c,v)
int c;
char **v;
{
    char tt[12],qq[7];
    int q=0,o=1,l=1,m=1;
    struct {int c;} f;
    qq[6]='\0';tt[11]='\0';
    if(QQ==atoi(v[1])+1){
        (void)fprintf(stderr,"%s factorial = %d\n",v[1], TT);
        exit(1);
    }
    o=c+f -o ;
    while(EOF!=(o=getchar())) {
        if(l && q=='Q' && o=='Q'){
            l=0;
            (void)getchar();
            (void)fread(qq,6,1,stdin);
            (void)printf("Q %6d",atoi(qq)+1);
        } else if(m && q=='T' && o=='T'){
            m=0;
            (void)fread(tt,11,1,stdin);
            (void)printf("T %9d\n",atoi(tt)*QQ);
        } else {
            q=o;
            (void)putchar(o);
        }
    }
    exit(0);
}
```

Strangest Abuse of the Rules

Jari Arkko <jar@hutcs.cs.hut.fi>
Oy L M Ericsson Ab
Jorvas, Finland

This is yet another "Hello world" program, but with a twist. It is not meant to be run, but produces the output when compiled! Here is the program:

```c
char*_="Hello world.\n";
```

The trick is in compiling it. For example, on a UNIX system, it should be compiled as `cc -c -o /dev/tty ja.c`. This forces the object code to be sent to the terminal. `Hello world` will be part of that. You may see some extra characters printed as well—namely, the symbol table! Just ignore it.

Thanks to this program, the judges added a rule requiring entries to actually compile and run. I think this is fair, since the author claims his program to be the shortest program to print out `Hello world`.

Most Algorithms in One Program

Merlyn LeRoy (Brian Westley) <merlyn@digibd.com>
Digiboard, Inc.
St. Paul, Minnesota

```
/**//*/};)/**/main(/*///**/tang      ,gnat/**//*/,ABBA~,0-0(avnz;)0-0,tang,raeN
,ABBA(niam&&)))2-]--tang-[kri         - =raeN(&&0<)/*clerk*/,noon,raeN){(!tang&&
noon!=-1&&(gnat&2)&&((raeN&&(          getchar(noon+0)))||(1-raeN&&(trgpune(noon
)))))||tang&&znva(/*///**/tang        ,tang,tang/**|**//*/(((||)))0(enupgrt=raeN
(&&tang!(|||)))0(rahcteg=raeN(        &&1==tang((&&1-^)gnat=raeN(;;;)tang,gnat
,ABBA,0(avnz;)gnat:46+]552&)191+gnat([kri?0>]652%)191+gnat([kri=gnat
(&&)1-^gnat(&&)1& ABBA(!;)raeN,tang,gnat,ABBA(avnz&&0>ABBA{)raeN
,/**/);}znva(/*///**/tang,gnat,ABBA/**//*/(niam;}1-,78-,611-,321
-,321-,001-,64-,43-,801-,001-,301-,321-,511-,53-,54,44,34,24
,14,04,93,83,73,63,53,43,33,85,75,65,55,45,35,25,15,05,94,84
,74,64,0,0,0,0,0,0,/**/){ABBA='N'==65;(ABBA&&(gnat=trgpune
(0)))||(!ABBA&&(gnat=getchar(0-0)));(--tang&1)&&(gnat='n'<=
gnat&&gnat<='z'||'a'<=gnat&&gnat<='m'||'N'<=gnat&&gnat<='Z'
||'A'<=gnat&&gnat<='M'?(((gnat&/*//**/31/**//*/,21,11,01,9,8
,7,6,5,4,3,2,1,62,52,42,/**/)+12)%26)+(gnat&/*//**/32/**//*/,
22,12,02,91,81,71,61,51,41{=]652[kri};)/*pry*/)+65:gnat);main
(/*//**\**/tang^tang/**//*/,/*        */,~/*//*-*/tang,gnat,ABBA-
0/**//*/(niam&&ABBA|||))))tang(        rahcteg&&1-1=<enrA(|||)tang(
enupgrt&&1==enrA((&&)2&gnat(&&         )1-^tang(&&ABBA!(;)85- =tang
(&&)'a\'=gnat(&&)1-==gnat(&&)4         ==ABBA(&&tang!;)))))0(enupgrt=
gnat(&&)tang!((|||))0(rahcteg         =gnat(&&tang((&&ABBA;;)1-'A'=!
'Z'=tang(&&ABBA{)enrA/***/);gnat       ^-1&&znva(tang+1,gnat,1+gnat);
main(ABBA&2/*//*\\**/,tang,gnat        ,ABBA/**//*/(avnz/**/);}/*//**/
```

This is a filter. If it is run with no arguments, it copies `stdin` to `stdout`. With one argument, it rot13s (Caesar substitution) `stdin` to `stdout`. With two arguments, it reverses `stdin` to `stdout`. With three arguments, it does both. It requires the ASCII character set with all characters being in 0..255 and `EOF` must be −1. It assumes 2's-complement arithmetic.

The source code will run if rot13ed and/or reversed, using a different algorithm for each version, hereafter referred to as `ver0` (original), `ver1` (rot13), `ver2` (reversed), and `ver3` (rot13 and reversed).

The body of the code of `ver0` and `ver1` is a large lumpy K (for Kernighan); the code of `ver2` and `ver3` is a flat-topped and lumpier R (for Ritchie). Judicious use of spaces and tabs helped here. It barely fits on an 80x24 screen. Squint at it. Note that the code must start with a blank line, or the reversed version will lack a terminating newline. When compiling these versions, define `trgpune` in the compile line. For example:

```
cc -Dtrgpune=putchar ver3.c -o ver3
```

Author's Analysis

"I've seen a lot of simple C code that implements rot13. I thought it should be possible to write a program that worked after being rot13ed, since only a-zA-Z are affected. I realized soon into it that I couldn't use `if`, `while`, etc., since the names turn into what looks like function calls. I could just as well do:

```
(i>2)&&(j=3);
```

instead of:

```
if (i>2) j=3;
```

"`ver0` and `ver1` use a range check and a calculation to do `rot13`, while `ver2` and `ver3` use table lookup. All versions contain `main` and its rot13 function, `znva`. `ver0`/`ver1` [`ver2`/`ver3`] are (of course) syntactically identical, since the syntax is in the nonalphabetic characters. However, since one program starts at `main` while its rot13 counterpart starts at `znva`, `znva` calls `main` (`znva` is also used for output).

"All versions use recursion to work. If the program is not reversing its output, it prints out the (possibly rot13ed) character before recursing, otherwise it prints it out afterward (or doesn't recurse at all when `EOF` is reached). Since most of this code is identical, it is put into `znva` and called with a first parameter of 0 as a flag (as `main`, its first argument (`argc`) must be at least 1).

"Here is the code with all the comments stripped out and rearranged.

```
main(tang,gnat,noon,raeN)
{
    (!tang && noon != -1 && (gnat&2) &&
      ((raeN && (getchar(noon+0)))||(1-raeN && (putchar(noon)))))
        || tang && znva(tang,tang,tang);
}

znva(tang,gnat,ABBA)
{
    ABBA='N'==65;
    (ABBA && (gnat=putchar(0)))
     || (!ABBA && (gnat=getchar(0-0)));
    (--tang & 1) &&
     (gnat='n'<=gnat&&gnat<='z'||'a'<=gnat&&gnat<='m'
     ||'N'<=gnat&&gnat<='Z'||'A'<=gnat&&gnat<='M'?
     (((gnat&31)+12)%26)+(gnat&32)+65:gnat);
```

```
    main(tang^tang,~tang,gnat,ABBA-0);
    gnat^-1 && znva(tang+1,gnat,1+gnat);
    main(ABBA & 2,tang,gnat,ABBA);
}
```

"All I care about at this point is `argc` being 1, 2, 3, or 4, for normal printout, rot13, reverse, or both, respectively. In this example, `main` is testing the first argument for zero or non-zero. If the argument is non-zero, it simply calls `znva` (`main` in rot13). `znva` re-calls `main` with a zero as the first argument. This makes the code start in the second function whether the code is rot13ed or not.

"`znva` determines whether it is running as rot13 or not by checking `'N'==65` (false now, true when it's rot13ed into `'A'==65`). Then it calls the 'right' `getchar` via the `-Dtrgpune=putchar` compiler switch. `trgpune` is the rot13 of `getchar`, so `getchar` and `putchar` are exchanged in the rot13 counterpart. It is easy to see that this is unavoidable. I must have a `#define` for a library function, otherwise I would have an unidentified `extern` for the rot13 version. If I then define this function, it won't link in the library version for the original code since my definition will supersede the library function. Hence, the compiler option gives me `putchar`, and allows me to use `getchar`. I pass a dummy argument to `getchar` to eliminate "`variable number of args`" from `lint` (unless it checks against the library). Otherwise, all versions `lint` reasonably (except for `main`, which returns a random value and has a constant in a conditional context when I check for the rot13 version, but this is all it complains about).

"The original `argc` is decremented to make it 0, 1, 2, and 3, and is tested by `tang&1` (which means rot13) and `tang&2` (which means reverse). If rot13 is true, the character is rotated in the big range-check statement.

"Then `main` is called with 0 as the first argument. When this happens, `main` prints out the first character *only if it isn't* reversing output, until −1 (`EOF`) is reached. Then `znva` calls itself recursively if `EOF` hasn't been reached to do the next character. However, if output *is* being reversed, the first call to `main` does nothing, `znva` calls itself recursively to `EOF`, and then the call to `main` *after* the recursive call to `znva` prints out the characters (which come out reversed). When it prints out text backwards, it has to call itself recursively to a depth equal to the total count of characters.

"Then I added the reversed code and the secret `Hello, world!` (which you can get by taking the original code, rot13ing and reversing it, compiling and running *that*, telling it to rot13 and reverse the input, and giving it null input). I kept the code unscrambled at this point; when I combined them, I could use comment cheating to interlace the code where it overlaps (13 in one code becomes 31 in another).

"Normally (!), a reversible C program is done thus:

```
/**/ forward code /*/ edoc drawkcab /**/
```

"If your compiler nests comments (which is shouldn't), it will get this wrong. However, I have made some bits of the code palindromic (or different, but reversible), so it is more like:

```
/**/forward/*//**/ palindromic /**//*/drawkcab/**/
```

"The code can therefore be interlaced. There are eight such palindromic bits. You can find them within the `/*//**/` `/**//*/` pairs. The reversed code is similar, but it uses some slightly different techniques:

```
main(NOON,gnat,tang,Near)
{
  NOON && (tang='M'!='N'-1);
  NOON && ((tang&&(gnat=putchar(0)))||((!tang)&&(gnat=
                                              getchar(0))));
  !tang && (NOON==4) && (gnat==-1) && (gnat='\n') && (tang=-58);
  (!NOON && (tang^-1) && (gnat&2) &&
    ((Near==1 && getchar(tang))||(Near<=1-1 && putchar(tang))))
      ||NOON && znva(0-NOON,gnat,tang,tang^tang);
}
vex[256]={14,15,16,17,18,19,20,21,22,23,24,25,26,
1,2,3,4,5,6,7,8,9,10,11,12,13,0,0,0,0,0,0,46,47,48,49,50,51,52,5
3, 54,55,56,57,58,33,34,35,36,37,38,39,40,41,42,43,44,45,-35,-
115, -123,-103,-100,-108,-34,-46,-100,-123,-123,-116,-87,-1};

znva(NOON,gnat,tang,Arne)
{
  NOON>0 && main(NOON,gnat,tang,Arne);
  !(NOON&1) && (gnat^-1) &&
    (gnat=vex[(gnat+191)%256]>0?vex[(gnat+191)&255]+64:gnat);
  main(0,NOON,gnat,tang);
  (Arne=gnat)^-1 &&
    ((tang==1&&(Arne=putchar(0)))||(!tang&&(Arne=getchar(0)))
      ||((tang,tang,tang)<0 && (Arne=-vex[-tang--]-2))) &&
        znva(NOON,Arne,tang,0-0);
  main(0-0,~NOON,gnat,tang);
}
```

"Again, `main` is called with zero versus non-zero. This time, since `main` gets the first character, it checks for `argc==4` (rot13 version). If the first character is EOF, it is changed to a newline and the special variable `tang` is set to point to the encoded `Hello, world!` The same 'recurse to reverse' trick is used, and this time characters are rot13ed by table lookup in `vex`. When the next character is gotten, if `tang` is nonzero, the next character of `Hello, world!` is used instead.

"The variable names are worth noting. `irk` and `vex` are rot13 pairs and synonyms. `Near` and `Arne` are rot13 pairs and are anagrams. `NOON` and `ABBA` are rot13 pairs and palindromes. `tang` and `gnat` are rot13 and palindrome pairs!

"I also did the K and R trick because I thought too many C entries were just uninteresting monolithic blocks; I tried my initials first, but that wouldn't work. K and R was an obvious and easy choice.

Here is the ver2—the R—and remember to squint!"

```
/**//*/};)/**/znva(/*//**/ABBA,tang,gnat,/**\\*//*/2&ABBA(niam
 ;)tang+1,tang,1+gnat(avnz&&1-^tang;)/***/Arne){ABBA&&(gnat='Z'
!='A'-1);;ABBA&&((gnat&&(tang=        getchar(0)))||((!gnat)&&(tang
=trgpune(0))));!gnat&&(ABBA==      4)&&(tang==-1)&&(tang='\a')&&(
gnat= -58);(!ABBA&&(gnat^-1)     &&(tang&2)&&((Arne==1&&trgpune
(gnat))||(Arne<=1-1&&getchar       (gnat))))||ABBA&&main(/*//**/0
-ABBA,tang,gnat/*-*//*/~,/*     */,/*//**/gnat^gnat/**\**//*/(
niam;)tang:56+)/*yrp*/);}irk[256]={14,15,16,17,18,19,20,21,22
,/*//**/23/**//*/&tang(+)62%)21+)/**/,24,25,26,1,2,3,4,5,6,7,
8,9,10,11,12,/*//**/13/**//*/&tang(((?'M'=<tang&&tang=<'A'||
'Z'=<tang&&tang=<'N'||'m'=<tang&&tang=<'a'||'z'=<tang&&tang
=<'n'=tang(&&)1&gnat--(;)))0-0(rahcteg=tang(&&ABBA!(|||)))0(
enupgrt=tang(&&ABBA(;56=='N'=ABBA{)/**/,0,0,0,0,0,0,46,47,
48,49,50,51,52,53,54,55,56,57,58,33,34,35,36,37,38,39,40,41,
42,43,44,45,-35,-115,-123,-103,-100,-108,-34,-46,-100,-123,-
123,-116,-87,-1};main(/*//**/ABBA,tang,gnat/**//*/(avnz};)/**/,
Near){ABBA>0&&znva(ABBA,tang,gnat,Near);!(ABBA &1)&&(tang^-1)&&(
tang=irk[(tang+191)%256]>0?irk[(tang+191)&255]+64:tang);znva(0,ABBA,
tang,gnat);;;(Near=tang)^-1&&((gnat==1&&  (Near=getchar(0)))||(!gnat&&(
Near=trgpune(0)))||((/*//**|**/gnat,gnat,    gnat/**//*/(avnz&&gnat||)))))
noon(enupgrt(&&Near-1(|||))0+noon(rahcteg   (&&Near((&&)2&tang(&&1-=!noon
&&gnat!({)Near,noon,/*krelc*/)<0&&(Near= -  irk[-gnat--]-2)))&&main(ABBA,
Near,gnat,0-0);znva(0-0,~ABBA,/*//**/tang,   gnat/**//*/(niam/**/);}/*//**/
```

Best of Show

Jari Arkko <jar@hutcs.cs.hut.fi>
Oy L M Ericsson Ab
Jorvas, Finland

Ora Lassila
Esko Nuutila
Laboratory of Information Processing Science
Helsinki University of Technology
Espoo, Finland

```
#define d define
#d a include
#a <stdio.h>
#a <string.h>
#a <ctype.h>
#d p char*
#d P ,(p)
#d T(E) !strcmp(E,"()")
#d U return
#d W while
#d X sbrk(199)
```

```
#d z atof
#d e isspace
#d D A(_)
#d E S(C(_))
#d B(y) p y(_)p _;{
#d G(y,V) B(y)p i;U sprintf(i=X,"%lf",z(E)V z(S(C(D)))),i;}

        p sbrk(),*S(),*j(),*O,*H;K,Y,M=14;double
        z();Q(_)p _;{int V=0;W(e(*_))_++;H=_;W(V|!(e
       (*H)|*H=='')'||(*H=='('&&H-_)))V+=(*H=='(')-(*H==
       ')'),H++;U H-_;}B(C)U _++,Y=Q(_),_=strncpy(X,_,Y),_[
   Y]=0,_;}B(A)_++,_+=Q(_);W(e(*_))_++;U O=X,*O='(',strcpy(
   O+1,_),O;}B(Z)U _;}B(c)U C(E);}B(q)U A(E);}B(t)p i=E;U H=S(C
(D)),sprintf(O=X,T(H                      )?"(%s)":"(%s %s",i,H+1)

        ,O;}B(F)U S(C(A(T(E)?D:_))));}L(i,s)p

i,*s;{U isdigit(*i)             ?             z(i)!=z(s):strcmp(i,s);}
  B(b)U L(E,S(C(D)))?"()":"t";}B(R)U E;}B(o)U z(E)<z(S(C(D)))?
   "t":"()";}G(f,+)G(g,-)G(h,*)p r[4][2]={"function"    P R,
    "quote"P C,"lambda"P Z,"defun"P j};B(j)U r[M][1]=D,*
     r[M++]=C(_);}p not[99][2]={"if"P F,"equal"P b,"<"
      P o,"+"P f,"-"P g,"*"P h,"car"P c,"cdr"P q,
       "cons"P t,"t","t"};B(S)int Li,s;p u;if(
        isdigit(*_)|T(_))U _;for(Y=M;Y--;)
         if(!strcmp(_,*r[Y]))U r[Y][1]
        ;u=E,_=D;if(*u-'(')U(*((p(*)())u)
        )(_);s=Li=M;W(!T(_))r[M][1]=E,*r[M++]
      ="",_=D;O=C(u);W(!T(O))*r[Li++]=C(O),O=A(O);U O=S
   (C(A(u))),M=s,O;}main(){H=O=X,Y=0;W(Y|!e(K=getchar()))K==
  EOF?exit(0):0,Y+=(K=='(')-(K==')'),*H++=K;*H=0,puts(S(O))
                             ,
           main();{printf("XLISP 4.0\n");}}
```

This program implements a LISP interpreter. In only 1465 bytes, it includes all the essential elements of LISP such as recursion, lists, `lambda`, `defun`, `car`, `cons` and (of course) some bugs. For example, `(cons (quote (a b)) (quote c d))` correctly yielded `((a b) c d)`, whereas the simpler `(cons (quote a) (quote ()))` caused the program to blow up. (This would be stated as `(cons 'a ())` in real LISP, but still should have worked.)

A more complicated (but successful) example implemented a factorial function:
```
(defun ! (n) (if (equal n 0) 1 (* n (! (- n 1)))))) (! 6)
720.000000
```

A couple of oddities are evident, such as using `if` instead of `cond`, but this is forgivable because everything else can still be implemented. The authors warn that there is no error checking, so for example, a misspelled function name can cause the program to blow up. Oh well.

Authors' Analysis

"The program implements a LISP interpreter using techniques that are quite unusual. Before we go into the details of these techniques, I would like to explain the general strategy that was employed in the creation of the program. The decision to write this program was made after I had invented the basic mechanism on which it *might* be possible to write it in such a small amount of code. Traditional LISP implementations use `cons` cells as the main data structure. Lists are pointer chains of these cells. The disadvantage of this type of implementation is that it would probably consume more than 1.5K of source to handle all the necessary management of these `cons` cells. An alternate representation of the lists would be to represent them simply as their printed forms, in C's strings. All list operations, including the ones in the interpreter, would therefore have to be made using string representations of the lists. These operations must count parentheses and skip whitespace. For instance, to take the `cdr` of a list we would have to skip one parenthesis, skip an arbitrary amount of characters until a whitespace would be found in the same parenthesis level, and finally copy the rest of the list to a newly allocated memory location.

"After the invention of the basic principle, we made some experiments and then selected the features we would support in the program. Only then began the actual implementation of the final program. We analyzed what was required to implement the required features. However, we did not accept conventional implementation techniques for any of those before careful inspection of other—possibly shorter—alternatives. In many cases, we were able to write algorithms that worked in our program but could not be extended or modified to support even minor new features. In fact, the basic principles of the interpreter were derived from our small set of requirements, and to change the requirements would mean the whole program would have to be rewritten. This way we were able to take the concept of unmaintainable software to its final form. An example of the effects of the simplification that we did in the implementation is the basic principle of the list representation. This works fine (if inefficiently) while data structures need not be changed. If they have to be changed, well, the basic principle has to be abandoned as we are unable, for example, to grow the length of a string.

"Specific obfuscations include trying to write things shorter at all costs. For example,

```
if (x) { a(); b(); }
```

can be written with fewer tokens as:

```
if (x) a(),b()
```

"We used lots of macros for common subexpressions, and transformed (by software) the program with long identifiers to a program with only one-character identifiers. It turned out that [_a-zA-Z] was ample name space; there were even some unused symbols left. After removing all unnecessary whitespace, we added some decoy code, e.g., the `printf` at the end of the program. It looks like it is the first statement in `main`, but it is really the next statement after a recursive call to `main`.

"The recursion was placed in the program earlier because

```
main() { foo(); main();}
```

is shorter than

```
main() { while (1) foo(); }
```

"We wanted some part of the program to spell "`obfuscated lisp`", so we searched for a sequence of 14 different symbols, and then made (through software) transformation of symbol names to get the text we wanted. Note that the text actually performs important tasks in the program. We cannot tell what, because even we had lost a grip on the program after all the transformations.

"Here are some fragments of the unobfuscated program. This should give you the general idea:

```
#define nullp(x) !strcmp(x,"()")

int skipp(s)
char* s;
{
    char* n;
    int p = 0;
    while (isspace(*s)) s++;
    n = s;
    while (p!=0 || !(isspace(*n) || *n==')' || (*n=='('&&n!=s))) {
      p += (*n == '(');
      p -= (*n == ')');
      n++;
    }
    return n-s;
}

char* car(s)
char* s;
{
    while (isspace(*s)) s++;
    s++;
    itemp = skipp(s);
    s = strncpy(sbrk(itemp+1),s,itemp);
    s[itemp] = '\0';
    return(s);
}

char* lt(args)          /* Less Than */
char* args;
{
    double a1;
    double a2;
```

```
    sscanf(eval(car(args)),"%lf",&a1);
    sscanf(eval(car(cdr(args))),"%lf",&a2);
    return a1<a2 ? "T" : "()";
}

char* ti(args)        /* times */
char* args;
{
    double a1;
    double a2;
    sscanf(eval(car(args)),"%lf",&a1);
    sscanf(eval(car(cdr(args))),"%lf",&a2);
    sprintf(temp = sbrk(99),"%lf",a1*a2);
    return temp;
}

int context_counter = 7;

char* context[99][2] =
{"DEFUN",(char*)defun,
 "IF",(char*)iff,
 "<",(char*)lt,
 "+",(char*)pl,
 "-",(char*)mi,
 "*",(char*)ti,
 "T","T",
 0,0
};

char* defun(args)
char* args;
{
    context[context_counter][1] = cdr(args);
    return context[context_counter++][0] = car(args);
}

char* fncall(fnexpr,fargs,aargs)
char *fnexpr,*fargs,*aargs;
{
    if (nullp(fargs))
      return(eval(fnexpr));
    context[context_counter][0] = car(fargs);
    context[context_counter][1] = eval(car(aargs));
    context_counter++;
    temp = fncall(fnexpr,cdr(fargs),cdr(aargs));
    context_counter--;
    return temp;
}

char* eval(e)
```

```
char* e;
{
    char* fndef;

    if (isdigit(*e) || *e == '(' && e[1] == ')') return(e);
    for (itemp = context_counter; itemp--;)
      if (!strcmp(e,context[itemp][0]))
       return context[itemp][1];
    fndef = eval(car(e));
    e = cdr(e);
    if (*fndef - '(') {
     return (*(   (char*(*)())fndef   ))(e);
    }
    return fncall(car(cdr(fndef)),car(fndef),e);
}

main()
{
    for(;;) {
     temp = sbrk(200);
     temp2 = temp;
     itemp = 0;

     while (itemp != 0 | !isspace(ctemp = getchar())) {
         itemp += (ctemp == '(');
         itemp -= (ctemp == ')');
         if (islower(ctemp)) ctemp = toupper(ctemp);
         *temp2++ = ctemp;
     }
     *temp2 = '\0';
     printf("%s\n",eval(temp));
    }
}
```

"By the way, in case you're wondering, the program is meant to resemble a wine glass. *Hölkynkölkyn!* (That's "Cheers!" in Finnish!)

Most Humorous Output

Oskar von der Luehe
Institut fuer Astronomie, ETH
Zürich, Switzerland

```
#include <string.h>
typedef char ape
#define D define
#D EA register
#D EP unsigned
#D A 1
#D AP (A<<A)
```

```
#D P (A<<AP)
#D AE ((P<<P)<<A)
#D PE (((A<<P)<<P)<<P)
#D E ((EP)A>>A)
#D APE {EA EP ape ea=AE;while(ea--) e[ea]=E;}
;ape a[PE+A],ap,*ae,p[P+A],e[AE];
main(){ape pe,*ep=a;srand((EP)time((long)E));
while((((*(ep++)=getchar())!=-A)&&((ep-a)<PE));
*(ae= --ep)=E;for(ap=E;ap<=P;){APE;if(pe=PA())
{putchar(pe);if(ap<P){p[ap]=pe;ap++;}else{
ep=p+A;while(*ep) *(ep-A)= *(ep++); *(ep-A)=pe;}}else break;}}
PA(){EA ape pe,*ep=a,pa,Ap=E;for(ep=a;ep<ae-P;ep++)
if(!strncmp(ep,p,ap)){e[*(ep+ap)]++;Ap++;}if(!Ap)return(Ap);
pa=rand()%Ap+A;pe=~E,Ap=!Ap;while((Ap+=e[++pe])<pa);return(pe);}
```

This program implements an "Eddington ape." The "apeness" should be obvious both from the variable names and output. The results are different each time, but here is an example of the output given the first two paragraphs of this chapter (with P equal to 4):

> Fortunately for us, Gary Larson wrote C code. And he is all about. I can only imagine that I don't write C. Their efforts grace this cartoon.

Author's Analysis

"The program calculates the statistics of characters that immediately follow a given string (correlator string) of a certain length (defined by P). A character is randomly chosen, weighted by its probability to occur after the correlator string. That character is printed to the standard output and placed at the end of the correlator string, whose first character is discarded. Meaningful words are therefore usually preserved, but the effect on sentences can be dramatically random.

"You might want to vary the definition of P between 2 and 10 and observe the result."

Most Complex Algorithm

Paul E. Black <paul@cirrus.com>
Cirrus Logic, Inc.
Milpitas, California

```
#include <stdio.h>
#define f int
#define v (void)printf(
#define x ),exit(1);
#define y ){if(n)c=z(n,u),u=n,n=c;o[i]=n?'0'+(1&*n):'0';}
#define z(a,b) (f*)(~1&*a^(f)b)
#define k(1) if(!(1=(f*)malloc(sizeof(1))))v 23+m x if(1&(f)1)v\
                                                   39+m x*1=
```

```
r(p,q,d)f*p,*q;{char o[81];f*n=p,i=39,*c,*u=d?q:z(-
p,q);o[40]='0'+(1&*p);
for(;i>=0;i--y u=d?z(p,q):q;n=p;for(i=41;i<79;i++y
o[i++]='\r';o[i++]=0;
v o);(void)fflush(stdout);sleep(1);}
main(a,c)char**c;{char*u,*malloc(),*m=
"Usage: black [string]\n\0No more memory\n\0Unusable memory\
     alignment\n\0jt,s@m@ (beleY%XX&Yz {z&z}i|R(|)*((.)i)hi\
     niFiGJ%FG.JJgJ: ;;&;z {z&z}-RS/ROiOV OP+PsaPh+ijainnjm\
     amfmfAlnnnnphppopv%vvgv.aABiB1/BVP11/1.%..&.OhrR-WV V1\
     #1VP1CcC0R\n\n'CVP0\n!\n\n'\nEaEEnEamat!akckk'kwaww'wz\
     ,zzozEit +",
*n=m;f*q,*p=0,*g,b=3,d;
if(a>2)v m x n=a>1?c[1]:n;
/*v"\t\t\t\t\tV\n");*/
k(q)0;u=n;a=~1&'j';
while(a!='x'){
     /*r(q,p,b);*/
     for(;;u+=3){
          u= *u?u:n;
          if((~1&*u)==a&&(1&*q)<<1==(2&u[2]))break;
     }
     a=~1&u[1];
     d=(8&u[2])>>3;
     if(16&u[2])putchar(u[3]);
     if(4&u[2])*q|=1;else*q&=~1;
     if(b==d)g=p;else{
          g=z(q,p);
          if(!g){k(g)(f)q;*q^=(f)g;}
     }
     p=q;q=g;b=1-d;
}
/*r(q,p,b);v"\n");*/exit(0);
}
```

Author's Analysis

"I knew from experience that 'embedded systems' are much harder to understand than other programs. For example, if one codes a pseudo-machine or language, then gets the actual work done in *that*, it is very hard to understand. Tracing execution (by hand or with a debugger) only gives the same 'inner interpreter' (or whatever) being executed over and over with slightly different data. This greatly obscures whatever is happening. Without guidance, it is impossible to judge whether some routine is performing a critical function which you should be looking at or is merely doing some peripheral housekeeping.

"With that in mind, I chose to implement a commonly discussed but rarely used paradigm: the Turing machine. The Turing machine is a general model of computation to compute any function. The Turing machine also has the characteristic that programs are structure-free, use lots of weak instructions to get anything done, and yet are quite compact. Ideal for the contest!

"The first step was to write the Turing interpreter in nicely structured C so I could get it to work. (How embarrassing it would be to have one's program published to the whole world and have it contain a bug!) For once, I didn't have to make trade-offs, and chose obscure but efficient data structures, and lots of pointers—always a good source of obfuscation. In particular, I decided that the fundamental data structure would be two pointers XORed together in one location. I could do this as long as I always had a copy of one of the values elsewhere. I also assumed that the two low-order bits of pointers are information-free (always 0), so I could store the tape value in the same word!

"After that was running, I developed the Turing program (using several sheets of paper with comments and notes). Even then I found I needed a trace routine to visualize what was going on. I included it (named r) in the entry for 'ease of use' but it is commented out for obscurity!

"I chose a coding scheme which had the potential of leaving some tantalizing strings to distract the reader. However, I wasn't able to do much with it.

"The actual Turing program that this program includes is a Fibonacci number generator. It has a further twist to confuse people in that it has more Turing code to convert the output from base 1 to base 2 (binary). Otherwise, I thought it might be too easy to understand. But just in case, I squashed the final code as much as I could, such as by renaming functions and variables meaninglessly. This renaming was done by a program I wrote that we use to send source code outside the company.

"Indeed, a similar embedded interpreter was used to write a production LISP in C, so you might say that much of this program was taken from real life.

"The original C code follows. For lack of space, the printing code is omitted."

```
#include <stdio.h>

extern char *malloc();

#define ADV(current, previous) ((int *)((~1)&*current ^ (int)previous))
#define GET(current) (1&*current)

main(argc, argv)
int argc;
char **argv;
{
    char *m = "Usage: black [string]\n\0No more memory\n\0Unusable mem-
ory alignment\n\0jt,s@m@ (beleY%XX&Yz {z&z}i|R(|)*((.)i)hiniFiGJ%F-
G.JJgJ: ;;&;z {z&z}-RS/ROiOV
OP+PsaPh+ijainnjmamfmfAlnnnnphppopv%vvgv.aABiB1/BVP11/1.%..&.OhrR-WV
V1#1VP1CcC0R\n\n'CVP0\n!\n\n'\nEaEEnEamat!akckk'kwaww'wz,zzozEit +";
    char    *program, *progptr;
    int     *scanHead, *previous, *next;
```

```
int     prevDir; /* direction to move to return to prev cell */
int     state, symbolScanned, direction;

if (argc > 2) {
  (void)printf(m);
  exit(1);
}

program = m;
if (argc > 1) {
  program = argv[1];
}
```

/* Simulate a turing machine using m as the program.

It begins (conceptually) with a tape of all zeros. (A header can be added to any program to write initial data and position the scanner, so this is no loss in generality.)

The tape is represented as a doubly linked list of pointers. The forward and backward link are XOR'd together and stored in one pointer. If we always keep one of the links on hand, we can recover the other link at any time. The state of the tape is stored in the low-order bit of the pointer. Since we will always allocate an even number of bytes, the low order bit carries no information. Memory representing tape is allocated as the corresponding tape position is first scanned. The doubly linked list is "rooted" at the scanHead.

The Turing machine is (1) change to the next state, (2) find the next instruction (given the state and the character under the scanHead), (3) write the tape symbol from the instruction, (4) print a character if indicated, (5) move the scanHead, and (6) print trace information (via displayTape) if indicated. The cycle is then repeated. The machine begins with a "next state" of 'j' to find the first instruction. */

```
    /* show the position of the scan head */
    (void)printf("\t\t\t\t\tV\n");

    /* create the first square of tape */
    if (!(scanHead = (int *)malloc(sizeof(scanHead)))) {
      (void)printf(m+23);
      exit(1);
    }
    *scanHead = 0;
    if (1&(int)scanHead) {
      /* low order bit is not 0; program won't run */
      (void)printf(m+39);
      exit(1);
    }
    prevDir = 3; /* we didn't come from any direction */
    previous = 0;

    /* set the starting state */
    state = 'j';
```

```
/* start scanning at the beginning of the program */
progptr = program;

/* interpret the Turing machine until state is 0 (halt) */
while (state != 'x') {
  /* get the symbol from the tape square under the scan head */
  symbolScanned = GET(scanHead) << 1;

  /* find state/symbol in program string */
  for (;; progptr += 3) {
      if (! *progptr) {
        /* end of program found, start scanning again */
        progptr = program;
      }

      if ((~1&*progptr) == state && symbolScanned ==(2&progptr[2])){
        break;
      }
  }
  direction = (8&progptr[2]) >> 3;
  if (16&progptr[2]) {
      /* print next character */
      putc(progptr[3], stderr); /* flushes only if \n included */
      /*(void)fflush(stdout);*/
  }

  /* write the symbol to the tape square under the scan head */
  if (4&progptr[2]) {
      *scanHead |= 1;
  } else {
      *scanHead &= ~1;
  }

  /* move the scan head to the direction indicated */
  if (prevDir == direction) {
      /* go back where we just came from */
      next = previous;
  } else {
      /* continue in the same direction */
      next = ADV(scanHead, previous);

      if (!next) {
        /* SKIMP allocate another tape sector and update */
        if (!(next = (int *)malloc(sizeof(scanHead)))) {
            (void)printf(m+23);
            exit(1);
        }
        /* check that low bit is still 0 */
        if (1&(int)next) {
            /* low order bit is not 0; program won't run */
            (void)printf(m+39);
            exit(1);
        }
```

```
            /* add the links */
             *next = (int)scanHead;
             *scanHead ^= (int)next;
            }
     }
     previous = scanHead; /* remember where we were */
     scanHead = next; /* "move" the head */
     /* This should never happen */
     if (scanHead == NULL) {
         (void)printf("Ran off end of tape!\n");
         exit(1);
     }
     prevDir = 1 - direction; /* prevDir opposite of this one */

     /* after scanHead moved, but before we change state */
/*   displayTape(state, scanHead, previous, prevDir);*/

     state = ~1&progptr[1]; /* get next state */
   }

   displayTape(state, scanHead, previous, prevDir);
   (void)printf("\n");
   exit(0);
}
```

Best Minimal Use of C

Arch D. Robison <robison@shell.com>
Shell Development Company
Houston, Texas

```
typedef struct A*B,*(*C)();struct A{C(*d)();B e;}*v(),*b;C
                                                  n[256];
# include <stdio.h>
#define a (d->e)
#define o (B)printf
#define X(_){return _;}
#define Y(_,A)B _(d,e)B d,e;X(A)
#define Z(P)C P(f,g,h,i)C f,g,h,i;X(P)
#define c(_)(b=(B)malloc(sizeof(*b)),b->d=_,b->e=d,b)
#define _(D,E,F,G,H)B D();Y(D/**/f,E)Y(D/**/g,F)Y(D/**/h,G)Y(D\
     /**/i,H)Y(D,(*(*d->d)(D/**/f,D/**/g,D/**/h,D/**/i))(d,e))
Z(f)
Z(g)
Z(h)
Z(i)
_(j,d,d,j a,j a)
_(k,d,c(h),c(h),c(h))
_(l,c(i),d,c(i),c(i))
_(m,c(g),c(f),l(m a),k(m a))
_(p,d,l(m(d)),k(p a),l(m a))
```

```
_(q,l(p(d)),m(d),l a,k(q a))
_(r,m(d),k(mf a),l(r a),k a)
_(s,d,e,o("0",s a),o("1",s a))
_(t,d,p(e),k(t(a,e)),v(k(t(a,e)),e))
_(u,k(e),l(r(e)),k(v(a,e)),l(v(a,e)))
_(v,e,r(e),u(e,a),u(q(e),a))
_(w,o("0"),d,s(d),s(d))
_(x,(*n[getchar()])(d),o("-1"),w(p(d,o("-"))),xh(d))
_(y,xf(mg()),v(d,p(yf())),v(d,yf()),t(d,yf()))
_(z,xf(yf()),(*(*j(d)->d)(w,x))(d),xf(k(d)),xf(l(d)))
main(){
n['(']=zf;n['x']=yi;n['-']=yg;
n['+']=yh;n['0']=zh;n['1']=zi;
n[' ']=xf;n[')']=n['\n']=kf;
o("\n",zg(yf()));}
```

The award for this program refers to the small subset of C constructs that the program uses. The author calls this C-- and goes on to say that

> The C-- language improves the C language by removing superfluous and confusing features: arithmetic, logical operations, shifts, relationals, address-of, and flow control. In fact, the only expressions retained are function calls, indirection, array assignments, the comma operator, and sizeof. Despite these restrictions, the C-- program does arithmetic on arbitrarily large binary numbers.

> To obtain a C-- reference, simply rip out the irrelevant pages from your *K&R* C manual. To obtain a C-- compiler, simply rip out the irrelevant bytes from your C compiler.

Curiously, the program is sorted by lines in ASCII order. Perfect for when you just happen to transfer it to a punched card deck, and then drop it.

This program is a subset of an APL interpreter. Functions are limited to unary minus and dyadic x,+,–. Numerals must be binary. Parentheses may be used for grouping. For example, `101x111-100` evaluates to `1111`. (APL groups from right to left.) The author notes that "Extending it to the full APL language should be trivial."

Author's Analysis

"This program is similar in spirit to my other one [see p. 200 in Chapter 23] in that it takes a particular programming paradigm to a minimalist extreme. However, this one uses the functional paradigm by trying to do everything with function calls. (I wanted to write a third entry in the 'logic paradigm' of Prolog, but could never quite figure how to do it elegantly and abusively in C.)

"With this function, I achieved my goal of working from unobfuscated source, and automatically generating obfuscated C, by using `sed` scripts to change variable names. Amusingly, running it backwards (through the preprocessor) probably hinders understanding it.

"In the program, binary numbers are represented as lists of functions. The first element in the list is the least significant bit. Except for the last element in the list, each bit must be `zero` or the empty string. The last element must be `plus` or `minus`. A `plus` represents an infinite string of zeros. A `minus` represents an infinite string of 1's, i.e., the number is the 2's-complement representation of a negative number. For example, 0 is represented by `plus`, 1 is `one plus`, 2 is `one zero plus` and 3 is `one one plus`; –4 is `zero zero minus`.

"The function for each bit takes four arguments and returns one of the arguments. For example, the function for `plus` returns the first argument, and the function for `one` returns the fourth argument. This is obfuscated by defining five functions at a time with the macro `ANY(prefix,a,b,c,d)`.

"The first four parameters are named `prefixplus`, `prefixminus`, `prefixzero`, and `prefixone`, and have expressions `a`, `b`, `c`, and `d` as their respective bodies. The fifth function defined takes two arguments, `a1` and `a2`, looks at the leading bit of `a1`, and applies the corresponding function (from the first four) to `a1` and `a2`.

"The original program does some non-portable token pasting which I've ANSI-fied here in this slightly deobfuscated version."

```
typedef struct A*STRING,*(*FUNCTION)();

struct A{FUNCTION(*bit)();STRING rest;} *add(), *global;

#define RETURN(_){return _;}
#define SELECT(P) FUNCTION P(plus,minus,zero,one)FUNCTION
plus,minus,zero,one;RETURN(P)

SELECT(plus)    /* Represents an infinite string of zeros */
SELECT(minus)   /* Represents an infinite string of ones  */
SELECT(zero)    /* Represents a zero bit   */
SELECT(one)     /* Represents a one bit    */

FUNCTION Read[256];
# include <stdio.h>

#define display (STRING)printf

#define ANY(D,E,F,G,H)STRING D();\
    DEF(D##plus,E)\
    DEF(D##minus,F)\
    DEF(D##zero,G)\
    DEF(D##one,H)  \
    DEF(D,(*(*a1->bit)(D##plus,D##minus,D##zero,D##one))(a1,a2))

#define DEF(_,A)STRING _(a1,a2)STRING a1,a2;RETURN(A)
#define integer(_)(global=(STRING)malloc(sizeof(*global)),
                   global->bit=_,global->rest=a1,global)
```

```
/* Function "sign" returns the sign bit element of a1 by recur-
sively searching for the last bit in a1.  The logic is:

    switch(first element of a1) {
        case "plus":  return a1;
        case "minus": return a1;
        case "zero":  return sign(a1->rest); // Move down list
        case "one":   return sign(a1->rest); // Move down list
    }*/

ANY(sign,a1,a1,sign(a1->rest),sign(a1->rest))

/* Func "twice" returns twice the value of a1; i.e. append a zero.
Note, does not append a zero to an infinite string of zeros.*/
ANY(twice,a1,integer(zero),integer(zero),integer(zero))

/* Like twice, only appends a one instead of a zero. */
ANY(append,integer(one),a1,integer(one),integer(one))

/* Return one's-complement of a1. */
ANY(onescomp,integer(minus),integer(plus),append(onescomp(a1->
            rest)),twice(onescomp(a1->rest)))

/* Return two's-complement of a1. */
ANY(twoscomp,a1,append(onescomp(a1)),twice(twoscomp(a1->rest
            )),append(onescomp(a1->rest)))

/* Return (a1+1). */
ANY(incr,append(twoscomp(a1)),onescomp(a1),append(a1->rest),twice
            (incr(a1->rest)))

/* Return (a1-1) */
ANY(decr,onescomp(a1),twice(onescompplus(a1->rest)),append(decr(
            a1->rest)),twice(a1->rest))

/* Function "mul" returns (a1*a2).  The logic is:
    switch(first element of a1) {
        case "plus":  return a1;  // 0*a2 = 0
        case "minus": return twoscomp(a2);    // -1*a2 = -a2
        case "zero":  return twice(mul(a1->rest,a2));
                                // 2*x*a2=x*2*a2
 *      case "one":   return add(twice(mul(a1->rest,a2)),a2);
                                // (2*x+1)*a2 = x*2*a2+a2
 *      }
 */
ANY(mul,a1,twoscomp(a2),twice(mul(a1->rest,a2)),add(twice(mul(a1
            ->rest,a2)),a2))

/* Carry-propagation for function "add".  Returns (a1+2*a2).*/
```

```
ANY(aux,twice(a2),append(decr(a2)),twice(add(a1->rest,a2)),ap-
pend
                (add(a1->rest,a2)))

/* Return (a1+a2).*/
ANY(add,a2,decr(a2),aux(a2,a1->rest),aux(incr(a2),a1->rest))

/* Print number in raw format.  Negative numbers printed in two's-
complement form, with a leading "n" */
ANY(out,a1,display("n"),display("0",out(a1->rest)),display("1",
                out(a1->rest)))

/* Print number that is presumed to be positive.*/
ANY(positive,display("0"),a1,out(a1),out(a1))

/* Print negative number by printing a "-" and then printing the
two's-complement of the value.  The "plus" position (2nd argument
to ANY) is never used for printing.  Since it's unused, we use the
position to define a function for input.  The position defines a
function called "negativeplus". */
ANY(negative,(*Read[getchar()])(a1),display("-1"),positive(
twoscomp(a1,display("-"))),negativezero(a1))

/* The next two functions define pieces of the parser.  They re-
ally have nothing to do with the purpose of macro ANY.  Macro ANY
was just a convenient way  to tersely define many functions. */
ANY(oper,negativeplus(onescompminus()),add(a1,twoscomp(operplus(
))),add(a1,operplus()),mul(a1,operplus()))

ANY(input,negativeplus(operplus()),(*(*sign(a1)->bit)(posi-
tive,negative))(a1),negativeplus(twice(a1)),negativeplus(append(
a1)))

main(){
    Read['(']=inputplus;
    Read['x']=operone;
    Read['-']=operminus;
    Read['+']=operzero;
    Read['0']=inputzero;
    Read['1']=inputone;
    Read[' ']=negativeplus;
    Read[')']=Read['\n']=twiceplus;
    display("\n",inputminus(operplus()));
}
```

Best Game

John Tromp <tromp@cwi.nl>
Centrum voor Wiskunde en Informatica (Inst. for Math. and CS)
Amsterdam, Netherlands

Freek Wiedijk <freek@fwi.uva.nl>
University of Amsterdam
Amsterdam, Netherlands

```
long h[4];t(){h[3]-=h[3]/3000;setitimer(0,h,0);}c,d,l,v[]={(int)t
,0,2},w,s,I,K=0,i=276,j,k,q[276],Q[276],*n=q,*m,x=17,f[]={7,-13,-
12,1,8,-11,-12,-1,9,-1,1,12,3,-13,-12,-1,12,-1,11,1,15,-1,13,1,18
,-1,1,2,0,-12,-1,11,1,-12,1,13,10,-12,1,12,11,-12,-1,1,2,-12,-1,
12,13,-12,12,13,14,-11,-1,1,4,-13,-12,12,16,-11,-12,12,17,-13,1,-
1,5,-12,12,11,6,-12,12,24};u(){for(i=11;++i<264;)if((k=q[i])-Q[i]
){Q[i]=k;if(i-++I||i%12<1)printf("\033[%d;%dH",(I=i)/12,i%12*2+28
);printf("\033[%dm  "+(K-k?0:5),k);K=k;}Q[263]=c=getchar();}G(b){
for(i=4;i--;)if(q[i?b+ n[i]:b])return 0;return 1;}g(b){for(i=4;i-
-;q[i?x+n[i]:x]=b);}main(C,V,a)char* *V,*a;{h[3]=1000000/(l=C>1?
atoi(V[1]):2);for(a=C>2?V[2]:"jkl pq";i;i--)*n++=i< 25||i%12<2?7:
0;srand(getpid());system("stty cbreak -echo stop u");sigvec(14,v,
0);t();puts("\033[H\033[J");for(n=f+rand()%7*4;;g(7),u(),g(0)){if
(c<0){if(G(x+ 12))x+=12;else{g(7);++w;for(j=0;j<252;j=12*(j/12+1)
)for(;q[++j];)if(j%12==10){for(;j%12;q[j--]=0);u();for(;--j;q[j+
12]=q[j]);u();}n=f+rand()%7*4;G(x=17)||(c =a[5]);}}if(c==*a)G(--x
)||++x;if(c==a[1])n=f+4**(m=n),G(x)||(n=m);if(c==a[2])G(++x)||--x
;if(c==a[3])for(;G(x+12);++w)x+=12;if(c==a[4]||c==a[5]){s=
sigblock(8192);printf("\033[H\033[J\033[0m%d\n",w);if(c==a[5])
break;for(j=264;j--;Q[j]= 0);while(getchar()-a[4]);puts(
"\033[H\033[J\033[7m");sigsetmask(s);}}d=popen("stty -cbreak echo
stop \023;cat - HI|sort -rn|head -20>/tmp/$$;mv /tmp/$$ HI;cat H\
I","w");fprintf(d,"%4d on level %1d by %s\n",w,l,getlogin());
pclose(d);}
```

While some might claim that the formatting of this program is as beautiful as the previous winner, the judges chose to create a new category for this implementation of Tetris, a popular Russian computer game. It requires a VT100 emulator. This version runs on a BSD UNIX system, but the author (obviously concerned about portability) also submitted an entry for System V UNIX.

The program takes two arguments. The first is a number defining how many sets of blocks are to be dropped each second. The second defines the key mappings to control the blocks. The default key mapping is "jkl pq", which defines j (left), k (rotate), l (right), p (pause), q (quit), and space (drop).

When asked for an explanation, the authors actually said it was too simple. John, in particular, said he would much prefer to explain a maze program he would rather have won with. Unfortunately, such a program had won in an earlier competition. Fortunately for John, I was unable to get an explanation of the maze program, so I agreed to let John explain his own maze program in place of the original one (see p. 55 in Chapter 8).

As a fair trade, I agreed to let this one go unexplained. Give it a shot yourself. If you are not on a UNIX system, you'll have to translate the calls to popen and system. These are used to set up the terminal driver appropriately and maintain the high-score file. Look closely at the cursor movement code, which necessarily exposes the row and column information. This should get you on your way to understanding the structure of how the playing board is maintained.

Best One-Liner

David Van Brackle <vanb@cs.ucf.edu>
IST
Orlando, Florida

```
main(Q,O)char**O;{if(--Q){main(Q,O);O[Q][0]^=0X80;for(O[0][0]=0;O
[++O[0][0]]!=0;)if(O[O[0][0]][0]>0)puts(O[O[0][0]]);puts("------\
----");main(Q,O);}}
```

The above program was originally one line, but I have split it up so that it would fit here. Given arguments of Obfuscated C Mysteries, the program prints:

```
C
Mysteries
----------
Mysteries
----------
Obfuscated
Mysteries
----------
Obfuscated
----------
----------
C
----------
Obfuscated
C
----------
```

Author's Analysis

"I wanted to write an OCCC entry which used recursive calls to main to perform a rather clever task, all on one line without using any variables except the command-line parameters. The following algorithm is one of which I have always been fond, and it seemed to fit the bill:

Let Element be an array of strings which represent elements of a set.

Let NumberOfElements be an integer representing the number of elements.

Let InOut be an array of 0's or 1's representing a subset (InOut[i]==0 if Element[i] is not in the subset, InOut[i]==1 if Element[i] is in the subset.)

Initialize InOut to all 1's.

"Now consider the following recursive routine:

```
void AllProperSubsets( int i )
{
   int j;
   if( i>0 ) AllProperSubsets( i-1 );
   InOut[i] = !InOut[i];
   for( j=0; j<NumberOfElements; j++ )
      if( InOut[j] ) puts( Element[j] );
   puts( "----------" );
   if( i>0 ) AllProperSubsets( i-1 );
}
```

"When called as `AllProperSubsets(NumberOfElements)`, it generates all proper subsets. Note its similarity to the standard recursive solution to the Towers of Hanoi problem:

```
void Hanoi( int disk, int from, int to )
{
   int other = 6 - from - to;
   if( disk>1 ) Hanoi( disk-1, from, other );
   printf( "Move disk %d from peg %d to peg %d.", disk, from, to );
   if( disk>1 ) Hanoi( disk-1, other, to );
}
```

"The steps to obfuscation are as follows: When calling `main` recursively, `argc` takes the place of `i`, and `argv` takes the place of `Element`. Since `argv[0]` is the name of the program rather than an actual parameter, all the 0's in the template must be replaced with 1's. With a little wrangling, and allowing an extra, unnecessary recursive call:

```
main( argc, argv )
int argc;
char **argv;
{
   int j;

   if( --argc )
   {
      main( argc, argv );
      InOut[argc] = !InOut[argc];
      for( j=1; j<NumberOfElements; j++ )
       if( InOut[j] ) puts( argv[j] );
      puts( "----------" );
      main( argc, argv );
   }
}
```

"Now, there are three variables used here which need to be dealt with: `NumberOfElements`, `InOut`, and `j`. `NumberOfElements` can be eliminated with the knowledge that if there are n parameters, then `argv[n]==0`. `InOut` can be eliminated as well. By making the nonportable (but popular) assumption that `char`s are signed, I can use the eighth bit as a flag, tested as a sign bit, while storing ASCII characters easily in the remaining seven bits. Thus the high bit of the first character of every parameter can be used as the `InOut` array:

```
main( argc, argv )
int argc;
char **argv;
{
  int j;

  if( --argc )
  {
    main( argc, argv );
    argv[argc][0] ^= 0x80;
    for( j=0; argv[++j]; ) if( argv[j][0]>0 ) puts( argv[j] );
    puts( "----------" );
    main( argc, argv );
  }
}
```

"There is no way around the need for a loop counter. However, remember that the first element of `argv` is the program name, which is not used as an element of the set. Thus, the first character provides the `char` variable needed for a loop counter. Replacing `j` with `argv[0][0]` yields:

```
main( argc, argv )
int argc;
char **argv;
{
  if( --argc )
  {
    main( argc, argv );
    argv[argc][0] ^= 0x80;
    for( argv[0][0]=0; argv[++argv[0][0]]; )
      if( argv[argv[0][0]][0]>0 ) puts( argv[argv[0][0]] );
    puts( "----------" );
    main( argc, argv );
  }
}
```

"The remaining obfuscation is owed to variable naming. Since there are lots of 0's already, `o` and `Q` are perfect for more visual confusion. Renaming `argv` and `argc` and removing remaining whitespace leaves the final product."

Best Layout

Roemer B. Lievaart <roemer@cs.vu.nl>
Vrije University (Free University)
Amsterdam, Netherlands

```
                                                                  char
                                                      _3141592654[3141
           ],__3141[3141];_314159[31415],_3141[31415];main(){register char*
       _3_141,*_3_1415, *_3__1415; register int _314,_31415,__31415,*_31,
       _3_14159,__3_1415;*_3141592654=__31415=2,_3141592654[0][_3141592654
       -1]=1[__3141]=5;__3_1415=1;do{_3_14159=_314=0,__31415++;for( _31415
       =0;_31415<(3,14-4)*__31415;_31415++)_31415[_3141]=_314159[_31415]= -
       1;_3141[*_314159=_3_14159]=_314;_3_141=_3141592654+__3_1415;_3_1415=
       __3_1415    +_3141;for            (_31415 = 3141-
                __3_1415  ;             _31415;_31415--
                ,_3_141 ++,              _3_1415++){_314
                +=_314<<2 ;             _314<<=1;_314+=
                *_3_1415;_31            =_314159+_314;
                if(!(*_31+1)            )* _31 =_314 /
                __31415,_314            [_3141]=_314 %
                __31415 ;* (            _3__1415=_3_141
                )+= *_3_1415            = *_31;while(*
                _3__1415 >=             31415/3141 ) *
                _3__1415+= -            10,(*--_3__1415
                )++;_314=_314           [_3141]; if ( !
                _3_14159 && *           _3_1415)_3_14159
                =1,__3_1415 =           3141-_31415;}if(
                _314+(__31415           >>1)>=__31415 )
                while ( ++ *            _3_141==3141/314
                )* 3_141--=0            ;}while(_3_14159
                ) ; { char *           __3_14= "3.1415";
                write((3,1),           (--*__3_14,__3_14
                ),(_3_14159            ++,++_3_14159))+
                3.1415926; }           for ( _31415 = 1;
                _31415<3141-           1;_31415++)write(
                31415% 314-(           3,14),_3141592654[
                _31415    ] +          "0123456789","314"
                [ 3]+1)-_314;          puts((*_3141592654=0
                ,_3141592654))         ;_314= *"3.141592";}
```

This program prints out the first 3141 digits of—no, not π but *e*, the base of the natural logarithms. So much for self-documenting code! It is worth spending a little time examining the variable names and array sizes in this program. The actual source itself is a rendition of the well-known Taylor expansion.

It is interesting to note that at the time, the author was a computer science graduate student like most of the other entrants in the OCCC. However, shortly after writing this program, Roemer gave up his computer science studies because he was no longer motivated to follow the theoretical courses of the curriculum. Nowadays he attends the Film Academy.

Perhaps you should think it over carefully before entering this contest.

## CHAPTER 29

Faster than Malloc

This chapter presents a storage allocator that is faster than `malloc`—any `malloc`, no matter how it is implemented. `malloc` is inherently slow because it is general purpose. Because it is general purpose, it necessarily sacrifices speed and space for flexibility. Often this results in a programmer using `malloc` in circumstances where a more specialized allocator would be sufficient.

A common example appears in compilers and interpreters while building a symbol table. Typically, each symbol table entry is a fixed size. An entry is usually small—say 16 bytes—providing space for a name and a couple of bytes for type and other attributes.

Using `malloc` for hundreds of 16-byte chunks is quite wasteful. At a minimum, `malloc` requires a length to be stored with each chunk. If the length is four bytes (say, on a 32-bit machine), this is a 20 percent overhead in space alone. Fancier implementations have much more overhead. On top of this, `malloc` has a lot of general-purpose code to support searching and coalescing arbitrary-size blocks. This code is potentially executed on every call to `malloc` and `free`.

A good introduction into the world of `malloc` is available in *K&R2* (p. 186). The implementation presented actually requires eight bytes of overhead for each allocated block. It is very similar to the `malloc` found in many real C libraries.

Quite often a much simpler memory allocation scheme will suffice, with a large decrease in space and time overhead. I present here the simplest allocator that still provides sufficient flexibility for the majority of programs that I write. I suspect it will for you as well.

The key idea is to assume many allocations are of sizes known beforehand. Then we can manage different pools of storage for each size very efficiently. In particular, we don't need a length stored with each block because we know the length is the same for each pool. We don't need to search for blocks of a given size, nor do we need to coalesce blocks when they are freed. And because there is no need to coalesce, there is need to keep the freelist sorted.

All that's left is to build a simple linked list of fixed-size blocks and maintain it. First, let me demonstrate how it is used.

Suppose I want to allocate a bunch of symbol table entries. I will call each a `struct st`. The following code declares a handle to the pool of symbol table entries. `freelist_head` is defined in `mem.h` below.

```
#include "mem.h"
struct freelist_head st_freelist;
```

Now initialize the storage:

```
memory_init(&st_freelist,sizeof(struct st),1000,0);
```

The first parameter is a pointer to the pool. The second is the size of each entry. Notice that we have used `sizeof` so that later we can change the size of `st` without changing any of this memory allocation code later. The third parameter is the number of blocks to pre-allocate. The closer this number is to the actual number of blocks you will use, the faster this code will run. The last parameter is the number of blocks to allocate by when you run out of the pre-allocated set. If you specify 0, as I did (above), the program will print out a message and stop after using up the initial allocation.

To actually allocate and deallocate `st`'s, you can now use `new` and `delete` (defined below). However, to make things easier, it helps to define two macros as follows.

```
#define new_st()          (struct st *)new(&st_freelist)
#define delete_st(x)      delete(&st_freelist,\
                           (Generic)(struct st *)x)
```

You will now be able to allocate and free `st`s very easily.

```
struct st *x = new_st();
delete_st(x);
```

If you are familiar with C++, you will undoubtedly notice the similarity to the C++ style of object allocation. Each object type has its own allocator. Not only does it look better, but it allows better typechecking. For example, if I had declared `x` as a pointer to something besides a `struct st` above, the C compiler would have warned of a pointer mismatch. With `malloc`, you will blindly fall into a hole. The casts in `delete_st` are not necessary, but will cause `lint` to complain if necessary or otherwise be silent.

This interface is generic—you can allocate other types as well. For example, if you want to allocate `foos` also, just declare a freelist for it, make the one-line `new`, and `delete` macros and call `memory_init`. Then you can say `new_foo()` to get a new `foo`.

Now that I've defined the interface, all that is left is to write the code for the functions that maintain the freelists.

Each freelist consists of a header describing the freelist, and a linked list of the blocks to be allocated. The actual code is straightforward. `create_freelist` requests enough memory from the system for the user's initial request of blocks.

Then, it runs through the memory chopping it up into little blocks and putting them all onto a linked list.

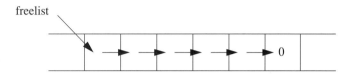

We temporarily borrow the first few bytes of each block to build the linked list. This is possible because when each block is linked into the freelist, the block is not in use. When the block is given to the user, we stop using the memory and depend on the user to remember it. (This is just like `malloc`, in this respect.) Notice how declaring `freelist` as a `union` (see below) makes this easy.

Eventually the memory becomes fragmented and the blocks in the linked list are no longer contiguous, but that is irrelevant since the functions only manipulate the first block in the list. The result is that they continue running the same way—very fast. The only drawback to this approach is that the same chunk of memory can never be reused for a different object. This is only a problem if you are allocating a large number of one type of object, then releasing many of them and allocating a large number of a different type of object.

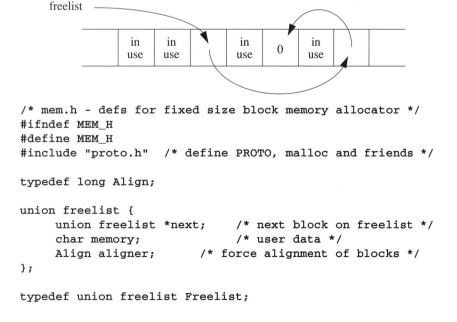

```
/* mem.h - defs for fixed size block memory allocator */
#ifndef MEM_H
#define MEM_H
#include "proto.h"   /* define PROTO, malloc and friends */

typedef long Align;

union freelist {
    union freelist *next;    /* next block on freelist */
    char memory;             /* user data */
    Align aligner;         /* force alignment of blocks */
};

typedef union freelist Freelist;
```

```
struct freelist_head {
    Size size;      /* size of single elt incl next ptr */
    Size bytes;     /* if we run out, alloc mem by */
                    /* this many bytes */
    Freelist *freelist;
};

Generic new PROTO((struct freelist_head *));
void memory_init PROTO((struct freelist_head *,Size,int,
                                              int));
void delete PROTO((struct freelist_head *, Generic));
#endif /* MEM_H */
```

The `union` also includes an element called `aligner`. This element isn't referenced, but its presence forces each block to be aligned on a worst-case boundary. This provides for machines that require objects to be stored on certain minimum boundaries. Here we have used `long` although some machines require `int` or `double`.

The remaining functions become trivial. `memory_init` sets up the freelist header and then calls `create_freelist`. `new` unlinks the first block in the freelist and hands it to the user. `delete` receives a block from the user and links it back into the freelist. The only complication is that `new` can run out of blocks. When this happens, we allocate another large chunk of memory from the system, divvy it up as before using `create_freelist`, and continue.

While the code shown below uses `malloc`, it is also possible to call other allocation functions. For example, on a UNIX system, you can call `sbrk` (with a slight change to account for `sbrk` returning -1 on failure). While unportable, bypassing `malloc` will speed things up even further. I have never personally seen problems with using `malloc` and `sbrk` in the same program. People have told me, though, that some `malloc` implementations assume `sbrk` is not called by the user, so it is safest to leave the code using `malloc`, as I've written it.

Whether you use `malloc` or `sbrk`, this code will execute faster than calling those directly, simply because they are so much more expensive to call. I've used these functions in many packages and consistently see a decrease in speed and space of 10 to 15 percent.

You can substitute any allocator that is compatible with `sbrk` and `malloc`, and this code will work fine.

Source Code—mem.c

```
/* mem.c - subroutines to allocate fixed-size blocks */

#include <stdio.h>
#include "mem.h"
```

```
/* chop up big block into linked list of small blocks */
static Freelist *           /* return 0 for failure */
create_freelist(flh,bytes)
struct freelist_head *flh;    /* freelist head */
Size bytes;                   /* new memory size */
{
     Freelist *current = (Freelist *)malloc(bytes);
     if (0 == current) return(0);
     flh->freelist = current;
     while ((char *)current + flh->size <
               ((char *)flh->freelist + bytes)) {
          current->next = (Freelist *)
               (&current->memory + flh->size);
          current = current->next;
     }
     current->next = NULL;
     return(current);
}


void
memory_init(flh,size,alloc1,alloc2)
struct freelist_head *flh;    /* freelist head */
Size size;     /* size of a single element */
int alloc1;    /* number to allocate initially */
int alloc2;    /* number to allocate if we run out */ {
     /* make block large enough to hold linked list ptr */
     flh->size = (size >
          sizeof(Freelist *)?size:sizeof(Freelist *));
     /* set up for future allocations */
     flh->bytes = flh->size * alloc2;

     if (0 == create_freelist(flh,flh->size*alloc1)) {
          fprintf(stderr,"memory_init: out of space");
          exit(1);
     }
}


Generic new(flh)
struct freelist_head *flh;
{
     Generic obj;
     if (flh->freelist == NULL && (flh->bytes == 0 ||
         0 == create_freelist(flh,flh->bytes))) {
          fprintf(stderr,"new: out of space");
          return(0);
     }
     obj = &flh->freelist->memory;

     flh->freelist = flh->freelist->next;
```

```
        return(obj);
}

void
delete(flh,link)
struct freelist_head *flh;
Generic link;
{
        Freelist *flink = link;

        flink->next = flh->freelist;
        flh->freelist = flink;
}
```

## CHAPTER 30

Updating Environment Variables

This chapter presents two functions to manipulate environment variables from within C. Most operating system user interfaces support environment variables. Such variables let you control certain aspects of your environment flexibly and easily. For example, the variable EDITOR is commonly used to hold the name of your preferred editor. If you set EDITOR to emacs, the next time your application needs you to edit something, it will run emacs for you. UNIX, DOS, OS/2, VMS, and other systems support such a mechanism, although the details differ.

The function getenv returns the value of an environment variable. It is declared:

```
char *getenv(const char *name);
```

If the value of name cannot be found, NULL is returned. So you can say:

```
if (NULL == (e = getenv("EDITOR")))
    e = DEFAULT_EDITOR;
printf("EDITOR = %s\n",e);
```

The C standard says that "the method for altering the environment list is implementation-defined." In *The C Users Journal* (*CUJ*), February 1989, Ken Pugh noted that "problems . . . with putenv are complicated to get around, so much so that the ANSI committee decided to standardize only getenv and not putenv."

Ken was referring to a function supplied with Microsoft C and some other implementations that alters an environment variable. However, putenv only updates the *copy* in the local process. As Ken discussed, getting around this is very difficult. For example, Scott Ladd described a method to modify the master environment for DOS in *CUJ*, July 1989. However, it isn't portable and it is likely to change in new releases of the operating system. Furthermore, it is very restrictive in the kinds of changes that can be made. I recommend that you not try to communicate with other processes in this way. Environment variables were never meant to do this. They are designed to be inherited and that's all.

Nonetheless, changing the environment variables for processes that will properly inherit your own environment is a useful task. I wrote just such a subroutine, but later found a public-domain version that is in common use. It was written by Maarten Litmaath of Vrije Universiteit, Amsterdam, and was released in Usenet's comp.sources, Volume 6, Issue 56. Maarten's routines are well designed and his code is quite elegant. Though the task (maintaining an array of pointers) sounds trivial, Maarten covers all of the hard cases and makes good judgments on various trade-offs. His code is a pleasure to read. (Well, not all of it—Maarten was also a winner of the OCCC! See p. 194 in Chapter 23.)

Maarten assumes environment variables are presented by the host environment as an array of strings in the `extern` variable `environ`. Each string in `environ` looks like "`var=val`" where `var` is a variable name and `val` is the value of that variable. The string is null-terminated. The last entry in the environment array is `NULL`, marking the end of the array.

Maarten defines two routines, called `setenv` and `unsetenv`. (He avoided reusing the name `putenv` so as to distinguish it from the version common to Microsoft and other environments.) The second routine removes a variable from the environment. `setenv` is defined as:

```
char *setenv(char *var, char *value);
```

`setenv` returns a pointer to the new "`var=value`" string if the call was successful. It can fail if the number of environment variables exceeds `MAX_ENV` (defined in listing 1), or if the system is unable to allocate space for the new environment variable. To indicate failure, `setenv` returns `NULL`. If `value` is a null pointer, `var` is assigned the empty string. For example:

```
setenv("EDITOR","emacs");
setenv("SHELL","command.com");
```

To remove variables from the environment, Maarten provides a separate function, declared as:

```
int unsetenv(char *var);
```

`unsetenv` returns 0 for success, or –1 for failure. The function can fail for lack of memory or if the initial number of environment variables exceeds `MAX_ENV`. If `var` is a null pointer, the complete environment is unset. This is extremely useful when creating a child process in which you don't want any variables around that you haven't specifically created.

Here are two examples:

```
unsetenv("SHELL");
unsetenv((char *)0);
```

To automatically declare both of these functions, include `setenv.h`:

```
/* setenv.h */
#ifndef SETENV_H
#define SETENV_H

#include "proto.h"   /* define PROTO, malloc and friends */
#define   MAX_ENV   256
```

```
extern char      **environ;
extern char      *setenv PROTO((char *var,char *value));
extern int       unsetenv PROTO((char *var));
int              _envc;

#endif /* !SETENV_H */
```

The remaining listings should be combined to form one file, called `setenv.c`.

Analysis

This analysis will just describe the highlights of the code of `setenv.c`, as well as anything unusual. Naturally, the very first line falls into one of these categories! The first line in `setenv.c` (see below) declares a character string, not referenced anywhere else in the program. The sole function of this is a quick way of identifying which release of `setenv` is being used. Because it is a static variable, it will remain in the program even after being compiled (unlike a C comment). The "`@(#)`" is used by the `what` utility to recognize that this string is an identifier of SCCS (a popular source code control system).

```
static char id[] = "@(#)setenv.c 2.1 89/02/22 \
                    Maarten Litmaath";
/* setenv.c - Sorted environment package. */

#include  <stdio.h>
#include  "setenv.h"

static char      *envbuf[MAX_ENV] = { 0 };
static int       initialized = 0;
int              _envc = 0;
```

The first initialization declares `envbuf`. This will be the array of string pointers used as the new environment. Why is a new array declared? Because the system gives us no way of finding out whether the old environment array has any more space in it. `envbuf` is initialized to an empty array. This will be useful later on.

`initialized` is a flag used to remember whether some initialization code has been executed. It is marked `static` so it cannot be seen outside this module. On the other hand, `_envc` is not `static` and will be seen by any module that has included `setenv.h`. `_envc` is the number of environment variables.

`initenv` (see below) is an initialization routine called by the other functions. The first thing it does is to copy the old environment to our new array. As each string is copied, space is `malloc`'d for it. Why? Further updating is easily done by freeing the old entry, and creating a new string with `malloc`. Although this is more expensive than testing to see whether there is sufficient space, it makes the code much simpler. Besides, this code isn't going to be executed so often that it has to be time-efficient.

```
static int
initenv()
{
     register char    **p = environ, **env = envbuf;
     extern char      *strcpy();
     static int       error = 0;

     if (error == -1) return -1;

     if (p)
          while (*p && p < environ + MAX_ENV)
               if (!(*env = malloc(strlen(*p)+1)))
                    return error = -1;
               else
                    (void) strcpy(*env++, *p++);

     if (p >= environ + MAX_ENV - 1)
          return error = -1;

     *env = 0;
     _envc = env - envbuf;
     qsort((char *)envbuf,_envc,sizeof *envbuf,i_strcmp);
     environ = envbuf;
     initialized = 1;
     return 0;
}
```

If any of the `malloc`'s fail, `error` is set to -1. This `static` variable is used as a reminder that we have failed to initialize the `setenv` package properly and forces all future calls to fail.

Once copied, `_envc` is set, and the array is sorted. By keeping the array sorted, it will be faster to update or delete variables. Finally, the new environment is assigned to `environ`. This will cause the old environment to become unreferenceable garbage in the process, but this is a very minimal price to pay. Avoiding this would only be possible if the number and size of the environment variables never grew, which is unlikely. Plus the code would be substantially more complicated. Note that the environment is not guaranteed to be dynamically allocated, so it is a mistake to try and `free` it.

`i_strcmp` (see below) is a utility routine to do string comparisons. The usual `strcmp` won't work here because of the double indirection used to store environment strings. Internally, it cleverly avoids a real call to `strcmp`. This optimization is probably unwarranted here but is certainly worth studying.

```
static int i_strcmp(p, q)      /* indirect strcmp */
char **p, **q;
{
     register char *s1 = *p, *s2 = *q;
```

```
        while (*s1 == *s2++)
            if (!*s1++) return 0;
        return *s1 - *--s2;
    }
```

envsearch (see below) is another utility routine that will search the environment array for any specified entry. The parameter **var** holds the name of the variable we are looking for. Since its length is of use to both the **envsearch** and the calling routine, it is computed by the caller and then passed in, just for convenience. The third parameter is a reference to the environment entry corresponding to the variable. Why is the triple reference necessary? ***pos** refers to the string itself. ****pos** is the address of the string. But we may need to dispose of that string and attach a new string (via **malloc**) in its place. Thus, we use *****pos**, which is the address of an element of **environ**.

```
        static int envsearch(var, n, pos)
        register char   *var;
        register int    n;
        char            ***pos;
        {
            register char   **env,
                            **first = envbuf,
                            **last = envbuf + _envc;
            register int    m;
            extern int      strncmp();

            while (first < last) {
                env = first + ((last - first)/2);
                if ((m = strncmp(*env, var, n)) < 0) {
                    first = env + 1;
                    continue;
                }
                if (m > 0) {
                    last = env;
                    continue;
                }
                if ((m = (*env)[n] - '=') == 0) {
                    *pos = env;
                    return 0;
                }
                if (m < 0) {
                    first = env + 1;
                    continue;
                }
                last = env;
            }
            *pos = last;
            return 1;
        }
```

The rest of this routine does a binary search. Some extra effort is required because
an exact string match cannot be done, since one string has an extra "`=value`" on the
end of it. If the string matches, `*pos` is set to that entry and 0 is returned. If not,
`*pos` is set to the entry where it *should go* and 1 is returned.

Now it is straightforward to read `setenv` (see below). After doing some housekeeping, it calls `envsearch` to find the correct position in `environ`. The old entry
is freed, and the new entry is installed in its place. If there is no old entry, and space
has to be made, the entries are shifted down. The author cleverly declares two `reg-
ister` variables to do it, right in place, providing for very fast copying.

```
char *setenv(var, value)
char *var, *value;
{
        char **env, *buf;
        int  n;

        if (!initialized && initenv() == -1) return NULL;
        if (!value) value = "";
        n = strlen(var);

        if (!(buf = malloc(n + strlen(value) + 2)))
                return NULL;

        (void) sprintf(buf, "%s=%s", var, value);

        if (envsearch(var, n, &env) == 0) {
                free(*env);             /* unsetenv old value */
                *env = buf;             /* setenv new value */
        } else if (_envc == MAX_ENV)
                        return NULL;
        else {                          /* *env > var */
                register char  **p, **q;

                p = envbuf + _envc++;
                q = p++;
                while (q > env)
                        *--p = *--q;    /* shift down */
                *env = buf;             /* insert new var */
        }
        return buf;
}
```

In `unsetenv` (see below), the opposite is done. In particular, if the variable is
found, the entry is freed and the remaining entries are shifted down to close up the
gap. If `var` is a null pointer (meaning *destroy the entire environment*), every element in `environ` is freed. However, if `initenv` has not been called, we just set
`environ` to `envbuf`, effectively zeroing the environment (and creating the same
garbage as did `initenv`, described earlier).

```
int
unsetenv(var)
char *var;
{
    register char  **p, **q;
    char           **env;

    if (!var)
        if (!initialized) {
            initialized = 1;
            environ = envbuf;
            return 0;
        } else {
            for (p = envbuf; *p; ) free(*p++);
            *envbuf = 0;
            _envc = 0;
            return 0;
        }

    if (!initialized && initenv() == -1) return -1;

    if (envsearch(var, strlen(var), &env) == 1) return 0;
    free(*env);         /* unsetenv var */

    p = env++;
    q = env;
    while (*p++ = *q++) /* shift up rest of environment */
        ;
    --_envc;
    return 0;
}
```

Conclusion

This is a well-written set of subroutines. It covers all the bases, and selects reasonable trade-offs in the face of hard decisions. When Maarten first made his code available, he went into some detail about how `setenv` was better than `putenv`. He was concerned with the user view. In particular, he noted that `putenv` took only one argument, a string of the form `"var=val"`. He then went on to claim that:

```
setenv(var,value)
```

is both easier and more natural than `putenv(string)`. Compare

```
setenv("HOME",home)
```

with

```
char buf[HOMESIZE];
strcpy(buf,"HOME=");
strcat(buf,home);
putenv(buf);
```

It is worth pointing out that Microsoft's `putenv` (as of version 5) does not make a copy of its argument. This can lead to disaster if you change or free it later. The advantage is that this releases the `putenv` package from any allocation responsibility, leaving it to the user. This could be desirable under certain circumstances.

Maarten's code originally included several comments. My discussion included all the material in these comments, therefore I trimmed the comments from the code. (I just didn't want you to get the wrong idea about his seeming lack of comments.) I made a few other modifications to the code to clean things up, and I take responsibility for any errors that remain.

## CHAPTER 31

Life with Static Buffers

The `static` keyword is used to express two concepts that are only loosely related—scoping and memory allocation. This chapter will concentrate on the latter—a seemingly intuitive concept, yet one that has led many to disaster. I will describe some of those disasters for you.

`static` variables are allocated space once in the lifetime of a program. Every appearance of the same name in a source file is associated with the same block of storage. This differs from `auto`s, which are allocated space each time their enclosing block is entered. That explanation sounds simple, yet in complex programs, `static` variables often have surprising interactions.

For instance, `getpwnam` is a UNIX function that fetches user information from the UNIX password file. `getpwnam` takes a user name as an argument, fetches the associated user information into a `static` buffer, and then returns a pointer to it. The fact that it uses a `static` buffer is clearly noted in the manual.

Oops!

Less than a month after the Internet worm had struck [1], someone took advantage of the implementation of `getpwnam` and exploited it to break into a machine on the MILNET. I'll explain the security flaw here since it was not described in detail, and it seems particularly relevant to the subject.

The program that (ab)used `getpwnam` was `ftp`, an Internet utility for file transfer. The `ftp` utility is actually composed of a pair of programs. One of the programs runs locally (the "client"), and the other runs on a remote machine (the "server").

Normally, the local `ftp` process acts on behalf of the server and prompts for a username followed by password. The client then passes this information to the server. In the server, there are separate functions to retrieve the username and to retrieve the password—something like this:

```
/* read username and lookup info */
getuser() {
    gets(user);
    if (0 == (pwent = getpwnam(user))) {
        ... complain about illegal user ...
        ... exit
```

```
        }

    /* read and test password */
    getpass() {
        gets(password);
        if (strcmp(user,"anonymous") == 0 ||
            strcmp(encrypt(password),pwent->pwd) == 0) ...
```

This is fine *if* getpass always follows getuser immediately. But an astute hacker noticed that not only was it possible to execute other code between the two, but that additional code could fiddle with the static buffer *already in use*!

Here is a typical sequence that compromised security:

(1)   cracker% ftp -n hostname
        <no username or password prompting occurs>
(3)   ftp> quote user anonymous
        331 Guest login ok, send ident as password.
(5)   ftp> quote cwd ~root
        530 Please login with USER and PASS.
(7)   ftp> quote pass foobar
        230 Guest login ok, access restrictions apply.
        ftp>

Line 1 invokes ftp locally. The client (local) ftp will contact the named site "hostname," which will start the server (remote) ftp process. The -n option turns off automatic prompting for a username and password. Line 3 uses the quote command to send an arbitrary command, in this case user. Without quote, user would have been recognized by the local ftp program, which would have followed up by asking for the password. Line 5 is an improper command (in terms of the protocol), which is rejected, but only after it is parsed. In doing the parsing, the "~" activates code to do (you guessed it) getpwnam("root").

Line 7 goes through the formalities of accepting a password to complete the login sequence, but then *ignores* the password mismatch because it remembers that anonymous is logging in. (ftp is designed so that a password is not required for the reserved username anonymous.)

Finally, the login is completed using the information in the static buffer. But the buffer was overwritten when "~root" was parsed. So the user ends up logged in with root's permissions. This means the user can read and write any file in the system. Oops!

Several fixes are possible, but the obvious one is to have getpass save the entire static buffer instead of just the pointer to it.

Making the Best of a Bad "Feature"

Being aware of functions that use static buffers is extremely important, as this example illustrates. Now that Standard C is a reality, we can find several functions in it that do indeed use `static` buffers. For example, `asctime` returns a pointer to a `static` string.

Both `getpwnam` and `asctime` are characteristic of functions that generate arbitrarily large amounts of data on behalf of their caller. This presents a general problem of deciding how to allocate space.

If the caller passes space into the function, the caller has to guess at a large enough size, usually resulting in a large amount being wasted. And there is always the potential that it will not be large enough.

On the other hand, the caller can depend on the utility function itself to take care of the allocation. The obvious way to allocate space non-statically is to use `malloc`, but this can fail, it is slow, and it may be overkill.

More sophisticated schemes allow the function to communicate back to the function the size of the buffer required. For example, a function parameter can supply a way for the caller to pass memory down using whatever scheme is desired. This kind of solution generally takes more time and coding, but can occasionally simplify the programmer's workload.

A Good Compromise

A compromise that works well in many cases avoids `malloc` and `free` entirely. I'll illustrate it with a simplified version of `asctime`, called `date_print`. `date_print` returns a printable copy of the month, day, and year. `Date` is a `typedef` for an internal date format, and is otherwise irrelevant to the discussion.

```
#define MAXDATEPRINTS 2         /* make this at least 2 */
typedef ... Date;               /* internal form of date */

char *
date_print(i)
Date i;    /* internal date form */
{
     static printable_date date[MAXDATEPRINTS];
     static inuse = 0;

     /* use next buffer */
     inuse = (inuse+1)%MAXDATEPRINTS;

     /* actually do the work and convert date */
     /* into a printable representation */
     .....
     memcpy(date[inuse],....);
     return(date[inuse]); }
```

Now `date_print`, which ostensibly uses a static buffer, can actually be called twice without worrying about clobbering intermediate results. For example, suppose we were reading dates (into `unknown_date`) while expecting a particular one (stored in `expected_date`). We could say:

```
printf("uh oh: expected date <%s> \
              but found <%s> in input\n",
    date_print(expected_date),
    date_print(unknown_date));
```

If you try the same thing with `asctime`, you will find that it contradicts itself and prints the same date twice. (Try it, you'll see.)

Caching with Static Buffers

Using our previous example, let us observe that it is expensive to actually perform the conversion from internal to external form. There may not be anything we can do to reduce the actual conversion time, but we might be able to skip the step entirely. In particular, if we can remember the result of having done it before, we can reuse the result. This is the heart of caching (pronounced "cashing").

In the following rewrite, results are cached. Also, several steps have been taken to speed up the code. For example, we have replaced all the array indexing with pointer operations. We have also replaced the slow but general modulus function with a very fast check using the arithmetic equality-test operation.

```
#define MAXDATEPRINTS 10

typedef ... Date;    /* some internal form */

date_print2(date)
Date date;              /* internal date form */
{
     static struct datecache {
          Date internal;
          printable_date external;
     } dates[MAXDATEPRINTS];

     static struct datecache *d_last_used = dates;
#define next_date(x) \
          ((x==&dates[MAXDATEPRINTS-1])?dates:x+1)

     /* last one used is highly likely */
     struct datecache *d = d_last_used;

     do {
          if (d->internal == date) {
               d_last_used = d;
               return(d->external);
          }
          d = next_date(d);
     } while (d != d_last_used);

     /* we have moved all the way around the buffer */
     /* and didn't find it in cache */
     /* get next buffer */
```

```
        d_last_used = next_date(d);

        /* actually do the work and convert date */
        /* into a printable representation */
        .....
        memcpy(d_last_used->external,....);
        return(d_last_used->external); }
```

The idea of **date_print2** is to search through a cache for the result before computing it. The cache is implemented as a **struct** of internal-to-external pairs. Naturally, the cache must be **static**. I have omitted any initialization of the cache but it should be obvious where it goes.

The logic is to compare the given date with each one in the cache. If we find it, we are done and can return the old copy immediately.

Some subtle points to notice are that we don't always search the cache from the beginning. While we search sequentially, we begin with the element that we matched (or computed) the last time. If no match is found, our new computation is stored in the element following the element we matched the previous time.

Computing cache positions and search strategies can often be improved in data-dependent ways (which isn't very relevant to C programming). Nonetheless, reexamining the most-recently computed result is a very reasonable thing to do, without knowing anything about the distribution of dates we are likely to see.

Improved Caching

To motivate a new caching algorithm, I'll point out some shortcomings in my last algorithm. For simplicity, I will represent the item to be cached as integers.

Assume our cache holds three elements and is initialized with 5, 6, and 7. The pointer to the last element cached is at the 5. (An arrow will indicate this.) What happens when it is called six times with the sequence 1 2 1 3 1 2?

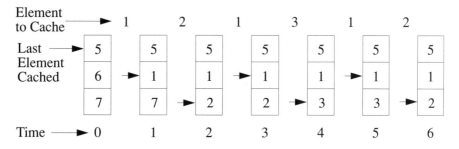

After caching the 3, we lose the results of caching the 2. When the 2 is cached again, we will lose the results of caching the 3. The problem is that caching the 1 loses the information that either of the 2 or the 3 is more recent than the 5.

FIFO Caching

By adding a second pointer, it is possible to avoid such poor behavior. Remember that one pointer is used to save the object that was last cached. The new pointer points to the oldest object in the cache, the idea being that it is less likely to be used than a newer object. If you make this change, the algorithm will fill the cache with 1 2 3 in the example above, and behave better on many other inputs.

This algorithm is called *FIFO* (First In, First Out) caching. Unfortunately, it performs poorly on more complex cases. The problem is that a frequently referenced element can be deleted from the cache just because it is old. For example, on input 1 2 1 3 1 4, the 1 will be lost while caching the 4 even though it is obvious that 1 is being referenced very often!

Clock Caching

A relatively simple addition to FIFO will allow us to improve its behavior dramatically. The idea is to keep a count of the number of times each element has been referenced in the recent past. By consulting this count, we can avoid tossing out objects that are frequently referenced.

If you think about the concept of "recent past," you may realize that this can be very tricky to do for an arbitrary history. Fortunately, simulations show that very little history is necessary for surprisingly good performance. Indeed, our algorithm will perform well with only a single bit per entry. With the extra "history" bit (called `inuse`), the date cache is declared this way:

```
static struct datecache {
    Date internal;
    printable_date external;
    unsigned inuse : 1;        /* new */
} dates[MAXDATEPRINTS];
```

This bit is used as follows. When an element is referenced (but not when it is initially stored), the bit is set. To find a new place in the cache to store an element, we search consecutively from where we last stopped searching. Upon encountering an element with `inuse` set, it is reset. If `inuse` is not set, we stop searching and use this location in the cache.

Here is an implementation of `date_print` to make this clear:

```
date_print3(date)
Date date;       /* internal date form */
{
    static struct datecache {
        Date internal;
        printable_date external;
        unsigned inuse : 1;
    } dates[MAXDATEPRINTS];
```

```
static struct datecache *d_last_used = dates;
static struct datecache *d_last_stored = dates;

/* last one used is highly likely */
struct datecache *d = d_last_used;

do {
    if (d->internal == date) {
        d_last_used = d;
        d->inuse = TRUE;
        return(d->external);
    }
    d = next_date(d);
} while (d != d_last_used);

/* we have moved all the way around the buffer */
/* and didn't find it in cache */
/* find a new buffer */
d = next_date(d_last_stored);
do {
    if (d->inuse) d->inuse = FALSE;
    else break;
} while (d != d_last_stored);

/* either found one not in use, or all in use */
d->inuse = FALSE; /* nec. if all are in use */
d_last_used = d;
d_last_stored = d;

/* actually do the work and convert date */
/* into a printable representation */
.....
memcpy(d_last_used->external,....);
return(d_last_used->external);
}
```

To denote the similarities to FIFO, this algorithm is called *FINUFO* (First In Not Used, First Out). It is used quite frequently in paging caches (where it is commonly called *Clock*) and on-chip memory caches (where it is commonly called *Look Aside* caching).

Clock has the nice property that it performs very well with a minimal cost in CPU cycles and extra memory. When used for on-chip memory caches, the algorithm is implemented in dedicated caching hardware. However, in both cases, all that is necessary for memory support is a single-bit for each entry (supported in hardware)—an exceedingly inexpensive overhead. While the software implementation I have shown here uses an entire `int`, you can invariably find an unused bit to steal from one of the other members of the cache.

Incidentally, the name "Clock" is suggested by the idea of two pointers moving around a "ring" of cache entries, much like the face of an analog clock.

Reentrancy Made Painful

A general problem when using `static` variables is that such code is not naturally reentrant. Indeed, the caching routines that I've just described are not reentrant. What does that mean?

Reentrance refers to calling a routine that is already executing. Recursion is a controlled form of reentrance, where a routine specifically calls itself. However, in recursion the programmer knows in advance what will happen to shared data structures. This does not hold for generalized reentrancy.

Generalized reentrancy means that the routine may be called at any point of the same routine's execution. There are several situations in which this can come about, apart from recursion:

- Interrupt handlers—these can occur at any time. For example, completion of I/O can cause asynchronous interrupts in unrelated code.

- Multitasking, threads, and lightweight processes—intentional program structuring in this manner allows functions to interrupt each other asynchronously.

Both of these require the programmer to deal with reentrancy problems. One big problem is handling `static` variables. Since `static` variables are shared by any invocation of the same procedure, it is possible for two threads to attempt to update the same data at the same time, or for one to read the data while it is in the middle of being written by a second task.

A good example is `malloc`. Any implementation of `malloc` necessarily uses `static` variables to remember what it has already done. For example, it may use a pointer to access a ring of free buffers.

Now imagine you have called such a `malloc`. It has located a piece of memory and is about to unlink it from the ring of free buffers. But it is interrupted by an interrupt handler. Now suppose that the interrupt handler needs some space to save some data, so it calls `malloc`. `malloc` does its thing and returns the first free space it finds—the very same one it was just about to return! Uh oh.

After the second `malloc` returns, the interrupted one gets control back and, having made up its mind earlier, returns the same chunk of memory. Oops!

There are ways to protect against this kind of confusion, but there isn't room for an entire computer science course here. I will just leave you with the sturdy rule that all you should do in an interrupt handler are simple assignments to "atomic" variables, such as

```
interrupted = TRUE;
```

or

```
interrupt_reason = OUTPUT_COMPLETE;
```

These flags should be checked outside any interrupt handler and acted upon there, where consistency can be assured.

This implies that you should avoid function calls in an interrupt handler. Even `printf` is dangerous, because `printf` can call `malloc` or attempt to modify internal I/O structures. You should not even do complex in-line code like addition, because even the statement `count += 1;` can end up with the wrong result if interrupted by the same statement in another interrupt handler. Of course, if you can guarantee that interrupt handlers sharing a common variable cannot interrupt each other, you can ignore this latter suggestion.

There are ways to guard against being interrupted, such as semaphores, but then you have to worry about deadlock and a host of other problems. See p. 335 in Chapter 35 and p. 351 in Chapter 37 for examples of this. Of course, semaphores and other synchronization mechanisms are not part of Standard C and are not portable.

Conclusion

This concludes my discussion of "fun things to do with static variables and horrible things to avoid." Along the way, we learned about caches and saw that it is possible to build a good one with only a little effort. If you are interested in learning more about caching, I highly recommend the paper *"Working Sets Past and Present"* [2], or *Sorting and Searching, The Art of Computer Programming* [3] as a general text on search/storage algorithms.

Try adding some `static` caches to your own code. You may be surprised at how many things lend themselves to this type of efficiency speedup. You can also try examining your own code for pitfalls from `asctime`, `getpwnam` and any other subroutines you use that return pointers to `static` buffers. (It's simply amazing how quickly this stuff propagates through well-bred code.)

References

[1]   Eugene Spafford, "The Internet Worm: Crisis and Aftermath," *Communications of the ACM*, 32(6), June 1989, pp. 678–687.

[2]   Peter Denning, "Working Sets Past and Present," *Computer Surveys* 6(4), December 1984.

[3]   Donald Knuth, *Sorting and Searching, The Art of Computer Programming, Vol. 3*, Addison Wesley, 1973.

## CHAPTER 32

Using Yacc or Lex Twice in One Program

In Chapter 31 (p. 275), I described various pitfalls you could fall into when using `static` variables. In this chapter, I will describe how to avoid a common pitfall by *using* `static` variables (and a couple of other techniques).

The question I am going to answer is the following: What do you do when computer-generated code uses names that conflict with others already in use? A simple answer is that you change the names in your code. Ah, but what if the computer-generated code conflicts with other computer-generated code?

The best example is one that comes up often when using the traditional UNIX implementations of `yacc` and `lex`. Both of these are programs that take a specification (not written in C) and produce C code. This code is then fed to the C compiler.

Fixing Yacc

`yacc` takes a file describing a grammar and actions. As output, `yacc` produces a file called `y.tab.c`. Much of it is specific to `yacc` and doesn't change based on the user input. Here is the beginning of a `y.tab.c` file:

```
#define yyclearin yychar = -1
#define yyerrok yyerrflag = 0
extern int yychar;
extern short yyerrflag;
#ifndef YYMAXDEPTH
#define YYMAXDEPTH 150
#endif
#ifndef YYSTYPE
#define YYSTYPE int
#endif
YYSTYPE yylval, yyval;
# define YYERRCODE 256

short yyexca[] ={
     -1, 1,
      0, -1,
     -2, 0,
};
```

Now don't expect this fragment to be understandable. We are going to examine it with other goals in mind. If you have been paying attention to the subject of this chapter, what should leap out at you immediately is that none of the variables are static. Instead, `yacc` attempts to avoid conflicts with user-provided variables by prefacing its own with the string `yy`.

This is fine if you are building a C compiler. All you have to do is avoid using variables beginning with `yy`. However, if you want to use *two* `yacc`-built parsers in one program, you will run into problems. Since both parsers are going to declare variables with the same names, there are going to be collisions.

I hear you asking "Two parsers in one program?" Sure. Here's an example. Suppose I am writing a database system. It could use an SQL parser for user queries. But it might also need to parse database schemas to support different databases. Both of these will need complex parsers and each will be entirely distinct, requiring a different `yacc` grammar. `yacc` is so flexible in other ways, it is surprising that the original designer did not foresee this problem!

Going back to our example, we will now fix the problem. There are several steps we have to take.

The `#defines` can be ignored because they are just local to the `.c` source file. We could rename all the global `yy` variables with a unique prefix, but there is no point in them being global anyway. Besides, making them `static` just requires the addition of one line for each, rather than globally searching and replacing each variable.

A good way to do this is to make a file called `yacc.hdr` (see below) containing all the `yacc` globals appropriately declared. Prefix this file to the `yacc` output file.

```
/* yacc.hdr - definitions to make yacc globals local */
static YYSTYPE yyv[];
static int yychar;
static int yynerrs;
static short yyerrflag;
static short yyact[];
static short yychk[];
static short yydef[];
static short yyexca[];
static short yypact[];
static short yypgo[];
static short yyr1[];
static short yyr2[];
/* end of yacc.hdr */
```

The remaining global symbols that start with `yy` are necessarily shared with the user. For example, `yyparse` is the function that the user calls to run the parser. Obviously this can't be made static or you wouldn't be able to call it. The alternative is to rename it. For my SQL example, we can rename `yyparse` to `sql_parse`. Following this convention, rename all the remaining variables in the same way.

There is one more thing to fix. yacc uses a typedef called YYSTYPE. This type-def defines the structure of a value returned by a yacc rule. Because this can be changed by the user, we need to change that too. It can be done in the same way.

Finally, we change the name of the yacc output file. yacc does not provide a direct way to do this (such as a command-line option) so it must be handled separately. Renaming it in the same way as the variables is reasonable. All of this can be isolated into a Makefile. The following Makefile fragment produces all the steps that I have discussed here:

```
.y.c:
    yacc -d $(YFLAGS) $*.y
    cat yacc.hdr > $*.yacc.c
    grep -v "^#.*line" y.tab.c |\
        sed -e 's/YYSTYPE/$*_STYPE/'\
            -e 's/yylex/$*_lex/'\
            -e 's/yylval/$*_lval/'\
            -e 's/yyparse/$*_parse/'\
            >> $*.yacc.c
        sed -e 's/YYSTYPE/$*_STYPE/'\
            -e 's/yylval/$*_lval/'\
            y.tab.h > $*.yacc.h
    rm y.tab.c y.tab.h
```

A couple of lines bear explanation. The first line informs make that the following actions are to be performed whenever it has to convert yacc specification (which always ends in .y) to a real parser (which always ends in .c).

The actions begin by running yacc to generate the normal y.tab.c. Next, a new file is created that begins with our static declarations. If it isn't obvious, I'm assuming the existence of several UNIX-like tools (although there are implementations of them for most other environments). For example, grep is a command that prints out lines matching the pattern. -v reverses the action, in this case removing all the debugging lines left by the C preprocessor. It is not that we don't want them. But with the addition of the static declarations, the line number information will be completely wrong. (Fixing them is left as an exercise for the reader).

The output of grep is piped into sed, the stream editor. sed performs the necessary substitutions to make the yy variables begin with whatever has been used to preface the yacc specification file. I already mentioned YYSTYPE and yyparse earlier. The remaining variables are yylex and yylval. yylex is called by the parser for each new token. lex is often used to generate this. yylval is the last value returned from a parse. Both YYSTYPE and yylval also appear in the y.tab.h output and must be renamed there as well.

New names for the variables and files are chosen based on the original user input filename. If the input is called sql.y, then the output file will be called sql.yacc.c and the parser will be invoked as sql_parse.

`y.tab.h` is an auxiliary file that is useful for interfacing with a scanner such as `lex`. The following lines perform similar transformations on that, leaving it in a file called (in this case) `sql.yacc.h`. Lastly, the `yacc` temporaries are deleted.

Fixing Lex

Although `lex` wasn't written by the same person that wrote `yacc`, its author nonetheless made the same mistake. You cannot use `lex` twice in a single program. Let's solve the problem again!

Below is a fragment of some `lex` output. As with `yacc`, most of this is the same from one `lex` output to another.

```
int yyleng;
extern char yytext[];
int yymorfg;
extern char *yysptr, yysbuf[];
int yytchar;
FILE *yyin = {stdin}, *yyout = {stdout};
extern int yylineno;
struct yysvf {
        struct yywork *yystoff;
        struct yysvf *yyother;
        int *yystops;};
struct yysvf *yyestate;
extern struct yysvf yysvec[], *yybgin;
#define YYNEWLINE 10
yylex(){
int nstr; extern int yyprevious;
```

It should be evident that `lex` has the very same problem as `yacc`. While `lex` promises that its external names all begin with `yy` or `YY`, this isn't sufficient to protect it from itself, only from the user.

Let's fix this in the same way we did for `yacc`. First make a file (see below) called `lex.hdr` containing all the `lex` globals but redeclared `static`. Prepend this file to each `lex` output file.

```
/* start of lex.hdr - defns to make lex globals local */
static int yyback();
static struct yysvf *yybgin;
static struct yywork yycrank[];
static yysvf *yyestate;
static char yyextra[];
static int *yyfnd;
static FILE *yyin;
static int yyinput();
static int yyleng;
static int yylineno;
static int yylook();
static yysvf **ylsp;
```

```
static yysvf *yylstate[];
static char yymatch[];
static int yymorfg;
static yysvf **yyolsp;
static FILE *yyout;
static int yyoutput();
static int yyprevious;
static char yysbuf[];
static char *yysptr;
static struct yysvf yysvec[];
static int yytchar;
static yywork *yytop;
static int yyunput();
static int yyvstop[];
/* end of lex.hdr */
```

The remaining global symbols that start with **yy** are necessarily shared with the user. For example, **yylex** is the function that the user calls to run the lex scanner. As in the **yacc** solution, we will rename **yylex** to **XXXX_lex** where **XXXX** is the base name of the file. Following this convention, rename all the remaining variables.

All of this can be isolated into the **Makefile**. The **Makefile** fragment below produces these additional steps for **lex**.

```
.l.c:
    lex $(LFLAGS) $*.l
    cat lex.hdr > $*.lex.c
    grep -v "^#.*line" lex.yy.c |\
        sed -e 's/yylex/$*_lex/'\
        -e 's/yytext/$*_text/'\
        -e 's/yywrap/$*_wrap/'\
        >> $*.lex.c
    rm lex.yy.c
```

As with **yacc**, new names for the variables and files are chosen based on the original user input filename. If the input is called **sql.l**, then the output file will be called **sql.lex.c** and the **lex** scanner will be invoked as **sql_lex**.

Alternatives

Now that I have gone to all this trouble, I will point out that the **lex** and **yacc** available from the Free Software Foundation (FSF), called **flex** and **bison**, respectively, do not have the problem that the original versions do. **flex** and **bison** can be used any number of times in the same program.

Nonetheless, the FSF code is not an option for some people, partly because of the copyright restrictions, and partly because **flex** and **bison** are not completely compatible with their predecessors. In any case, you may be quite happy with the solution I have sketched out in this chapter.

Another solution to this problem should be considered. For example, it may be possible to combine the `yacc` grammars to create a single parser. If you are limited by memory, this can greatly reduce various functions and tables that will be duplicated by my approach.

On the other hand, this can make the grammar much more complex, especially if there is any overlap in the specifications. In addition, debugging can be much more complicated because you have to test for interactions between the two (or more) grammars. Finally, the product of a more complex specification will undoubtedly run more slowly than choosing and then calling one of several parsers.

Conclusion

I have shown how to use `static` variables to solve the common problem of having to create programs that use multiple instances of `yacc` or `lex`. You can take these techniques and generalize them to fix other code generated from poorly designed programs. Finally, let this serve as a reminder: when writing programs that generate source code, allow for the possibility that such code might be used multiple times in a single program.

## CHAPTER 33

Tcl—Tool Command Language

This chapter discusses a set of subroutines that are helpful in building tools that require languages of their own. As an example, this can be useful for interpreting *startup* files.

You are probably already familiar with many tools that have startup files. For example, the UNIX C-shell reads a file called `.cshrc` upon startup. The DOS command interpreter reads a file called `COMMAND.COM`. (Sometimes these are called *initialization*, *configuration*, or *rc* files.) Similarly, many other tools use startup files that are executed at run-time. A few are truly general purpose, such as those used by shells or `emacs`. Most, unfortunately, are quite simplistic. Typically, you can set options and do some other magic things, but that's about it.

Many programs would benefit from a more flexible scheme. The reason few programs do is that evaluating a high-level language startup script requires a lot of code. This code may not be used by most people. And the people who do use it may not use all of it.

Is it overkill for a tool to have a powerful startup file? Many people might be tempted to automatically answer "yes." The problem is that we usually phrase the design as "For this new tool I am writing today, what minimal subset of language capabilities are necessary?"

Indeed, few people use more than a fraction of the programming capabilities provided by such tools. But this power is what makes these tools so much more attractive than their predecessors. Of course, no one wants to dump lots of unused code into a small project. But experience with highly configurable programs, such as editors and shells, suggests that highly configurable utilities provide answers to questions that their designers never imagined.

Tcl

At the University of California at Berkeley, John Ousterhout has addressed the problems of which I speak. John has developed a subroutine library that interprets language elements for tools. Reading a startup script is a natural application of it.

The subroutine library is called *Tcl*. Tcl stands for *Tool Command Language* and is a small interpreted system that is procedural in nature and command-oriented. The language resembles a mixture of C and the shell, although elements are derived from other languages. For example, the following Tcl fragment swaps two variable values.

```
if {$a < $b} {
      set tmp $a
      set a $b
      set b $tmp
}
```

`set` and `if` are built-in keywords. Tcl has about 30 other keywords that do a reasonable choice of language and string operations. Conversion to numerics is automatic, much like Snobol.

Tcl also allows users to declare new procedures and variables. The following command defines a recursive factorial procedure.

```
proc fac x {
            if {$x == 1} {return 1}
            return [expr {$x * [fac [expr $x-1]]}]
      }
```

The syntax and semantics are sufficiently close to C and the shell, so I am not going to go into detail about the user's view of Tcl; however, it is completely defined by Ousterhout [1]. Instead, I will focus on the programmer's view.

Tcl—Designed to be Embedded

The nice thing about Tcl from a C programmer's standpoint is that Tcl is designed to be embedded inside applications. Tcl supports this in three ways.

You Can Add New Commands to the Language

For example, if you are writing a program to communicate with a remote system, you might want to add a "dial" command. It could take a phone number argument and dial a remote system.

You can also delete or replace existing commands.

You Can Control Evaluation of Commands

A startup script is just one way of executing commands. This is completely under control of the programmer. Another way might be to take them from the command-line and feed them to the interpreter. Or you can synthesize commands dynamically. You decide.

You Can Read and Write the User's Environment

For example, if the user has the command "`set timeout 30`" in the script for your communications program, you can use that value in the `dial` procedure to timeout after 30 seconds without an acknowledgment.

You can also set values that the user can access. For example, your communications program might wish to save any results from the remote system in a variable.

The user could then reference this variable to use the results when deciding on the next action.

Tcl does all these things on a per-interpreter basis. Yes, you can actually have multiple interpreter instances, each with a different command set. (Perhaps the author of Tcl stumbled upon the same problems I described in Chapter 32?)

An Example

Let's take a look at how Tcl is actually embedded. First you must define your new application-dependent commands. For example, following the idea of writing a communications program, we might want to add a *send* and *expect* command to help us do automatic dialing.

```
cmdSend(clientData,interp,argc,argv)
char *clientData;
int argc;
char **argv;
{
        fprintf(modem,argv[1]);
}
```

All commands take four parameters. The first is a pointer to anything you want a particular command invocation to have access to. The second is a pointer to the current interpreter. This is necessary if you want to refer to variables. In that case, you need to access them from the right interpreter instance. The remaining two arguments resemble the `argc` and `argv` used by a C `main`. In fact, you can even call `getopt` to process them if you expect flag-style arguments!

`cmdSend` is very simple. It just sends the first argument on to the modem. A corresponding `cmdExpect` would be a lot more complicated. A simple version might just be a loop that reads from the modem, testing input against the user-supplied argument. Thus, to dial a Hayes modem, the user startup script might look like this:

```
send ATZ\r
expect OK
send ATD12016442332\r
expect CONNECTED
send \r\r
expect login:
send don\r
expect password:
send swordfish\r
```

A more sophisticated `expect` command would offer a way to timeout or check for multiple strings to match. You could test for what was returned and take different actions on different inputs.

Notice that the user doesn't actually call commands by their C function names. A mapping of commands names to functions is defined within the interpreter. Assuming that the cmdSend and cmdExpect functions are defined, an interpreter is defined as follows:

```
interp = Tcl_CreateInterp();

Tcl_CreateCommand(interp,"send",
    cmdSend,(ClientData)0,deleteProc);
Tcl_CreateCommand(interp,"expect",
    cmdExpect,(ClientData)0,deleteProc);
```

The arguments to Tcl_CreateCommand are straightforward. The first one defines the interpreter instance to add the command to. This creates the ability to support multiple interpreters with different command sets. The second argument is the name of the command as the user will invoke it. The third argument is a pointer to the function you define, which is called whenever the interpreter encounters your command. As I said earlier, ClientData is a pointer that allows your function to be passed an arbitrary object when your function is called later. One use for this is to differentiate between two commands that are implemented by the same procedure. The remaining argument is a procedure to be invoked before your command is deleted. (This is useful only if you want to remap command names.)

After these three calls, the interpreter is ready for use. Feeding commands to it from the startup file is a reasonable thing to do. Assuming the startup file was opened as standard input, the following code will evaluate all the commands:

```
while (EOF != (fgets(stdin,buf,BUFSIZ))) {
    Tcl_Eval(interp,buf);
}
```

Tcl_Eval does all the work of breaking arguments into the argc/argv style, calling the right command to execute, and handling errors. (The return value of Tcl_Eval should actually be checked for errors, but that is not the point here.)

After this, we can process anything else that needs to be done in the main procedure. That's the whole thing! Now you should be able to see that processing startup files is just one way of using Tcl. It is actually much more flexible than that.

Other Tcl Interfaces

You can actually execute Tcl commands directly from within C. You can also read and write user variables. For example, you could call the Tcl set command by the name cmdSet. cmdSet receives its arguments in exactly the same way as cmdSend. Thus, you have easy access to every variable that the user changes, and you can set variables that the user will read.

Actual Experience

I recently used Tcl in a very large program, and am extremely pleased with it. Tcl made the program much more useful than it ever would have been. It isn't that I didn't have the skill. I just wasn't about to write a flexible language for the tool that I was writing.

But since Tcl was already written, I could just drop it in, with zero cost to me. This is much like using `getopt` to perform argument parsing. If `getopt` wasn't around, most of my programs would have almost no options. But since it is so easy, I don't think twice about whether I should have command-line options or not. Similarly, I realize now that I will use Tcl again and again. It has become yet another tool in my workbench.

Like `getopt`, Tcl doesn't do everything. But it does make 90 percent of the interesting cases very easy. If all utilities used Tcl, everything would be a lot more flexible and easy to use.

The program that I recently built using Tcl is interesting in its own right. It is called *expect* and is used to control interactive dialogues. It is similar to what I suggested above with the `send`/`expect` commands, however it is not restricted to just communication tasks. While some programs (e.g., Kermit, Procomm) provide some of the capabilities of `expect`, they are oriented toward communications and aren't nearly as flexible in terms of controlling alternatives. `expect` is described further beginning on p. 343 in Chapter 36.

`expect` relies very heavily on Tcl. Tcl does all the work of deciding how to flow through the script. What's left is setting up the connections and then pattern matching to guide the script. All in all, it feels like Tcl does half of the work.

In my program, Tcl requires 110K. It seems like a lot at first, but is reasonable considering what it does. In systems where libraries can be shared, concurrent programs that use Tcl could be cheaper than individual programs using their own interpreters, no matter how skeletal these ad hoc interpreters are.

Conclusion

I found Tcl extremely easy to use. It is well thought out and highly adaptable. Just about any program you write can benefit from it. Unless you write the most trivial applications, Tcl will be helpful and can avoid messy entanglements with `lex` and `yacc`.

I've tried to give you a feeling for the flavor of Tcl, but you are best served by getting a copy immediately. Unlike most tricks that you may think of using a year later, Tcl is immediately useful. The day I discovered Tcl was the day I began using it. You will, too.

Source Code

The disk accompanying this book includes the source and documentation for Tcl under UNIX. As this book goes to press, Tcl is being ported to DOS. Ports to other platforms will undoubtedly occur as more people hear of Tcl.

A Usenet newsgroup exists for discussion of the language and its application. The newsgroup is called "`comp.lang.tcl`" and is a good place to ask questions about the language.

John Ousterhout may be contacted at the Computer Science Division, Electrical Engineering and Computer Sciences, University of California at Berkeley, Berkeley, CA 94720. His electronic mail address is `ouster@sprite.berkeley.edu`.

Tcl is in the public domain.

References

[1]   John Ousterhout, "Tcl—An Embeddable Command Language," *Proceedings of the Winter 1990 USENIX Conference*, Washington, D.C., January 22–26, 1990.

[2]   Don Libes, "Expect: Curing Those Fits of Uncontrollable Interaction," *Proceedings of the Summer 1990 USENIX Conference*, Anaheim, California, June 11–15, 1990.

## CHAPTER 34

The 1990 Obfuscated C Code Contest

This chapter contains the winners of the 1990 Obfuscated C Code Contest. (And if you've read and understood all the other winners in the earlier chapters, I'll eat my hat!)

If you would like to enter the next contest, find the latest rules (they change every year) that describe exactly how entries should be formatted and when they will be accepted. Typically, entries are accepted during one month in the spring. The winners are announced at the summer USENIX Conference, posted to the `comp.-lang.c` newsgroup on Usenet, and published in *The C Users Journal*.

If you keep missing the announcements for the contest, contact the judges at `judges@toad.com`. Rules and other contest material may also be `ftp`'d or `uucp`'d from the directory `/pub/ioccc` on `ftp.uu.net`.

And now the winners. It should also be noted that all the compilers used to test this year's winners bombed out on at least one entry. Hmm . . . .

Best Utility

Byron Rakitzis <byron@archone.tamu.edu>
Texas A&M University
College Station, Texas

Sean Dorward <sean@att.research.com>
Princeton University
Princeton, New Jersey

```
#define D ,close(

char            *c,q              [512          ],m[             256
],*v[           99], **u,        *i[3];int      f[2],p;main       (){for
  (m[m          [60]=   m[62      ]=32   ]=m[*    m=124    [m]=    9]=6;
    e(-8)       ,gets   (1+(     c=q)    )||     exit     (0);    r(0,0)
      )for(     ;*++    c;);    }r(t,    o){     *i=i     [2]=    0;for
        (u=v    +98            ;m[*--c]        ^9;m [*c]        &32   ?i[*c
          &2]=            *u,u-             v^98             &&++u:
```

```
3        )if(!m[*c]){for(*++c=0;!m[*--c];);
*        --u= ++c;}u-v^98?strcmp(*u,"cd")?*c?pipe(f),o=f[
1        ]:
4        ,(p=fork())?e(p),o?r(o,0)D o)D*f):
1        ,wait(0):(o?dup2(*f,0)D*f)D o):*i?
5        D 0),e(open(*i,0)):
9        ,t?dup2(t,1)D t):i[
2        ]?
6        D 1),e(creat(i[2],438)):
5        ,e(execvp(*u,u))):e(chdir(u[1])*2):
3        ;}e(x){x<0?write(2,"?\n$ "-x/4,2),x+1||exit(1):
5        ;}
```

Analysis

As I mentioned earlier, the inspiration for the contest was the UNIX shell. This program implements a primitive UNIX shell smaller (550 characters) and even more obfuscated than the original Bourne shell.

The formatting is highly creative, but micro-obfuscation abounds. For example, the same statement is used to print errors and the prompt. Input lines are parsed backwards. And the heart of the program, which performs all **exec**s, **open**s, etc., is one statement.

Rakitzis says that he gained experience for writing this when he wrote his implementation of Duff's **rc** shell. This is truly in the spirit of the contest! Incidentally, the authors claim that they wrote this entry in 12 hours (8 P.M. to 8 A.M.).

This entry was also of great help to me when I was giving a class on C to a group of physicists (some of them brilliant but not very smart). Anyway, there was this one guy in the front row who kept pestering me about where the line numbers were, and whether you could use them because his editor worked in those terms, and so on. For some reason I couldn't convince him that line numbers were not a part of the C source, so finally I pulled out this program (on a transparency—yes, I'm always prepared). He was instantly enlightened.

The unobfuscated source follows:

```
char *c,        /* character rover */
     q[512],    /* input buffer */
     m[256],    /* meta array for syntax characters */
     *v[99],    /* arg list */
     **u,       /* arg list rover */
     *i[3];     /* redirection pointers */

int  f[2],      /* pipe fd's */
     p;         /* pid */

main() {
     m[m['<'] = m['>'] = ' '] = m[m['\0'] = m['|'] = '\t'] = 6;

     while(1) {
```

```
        e(-8);                  /* print a prompt (!?) */
        if (!gets(1+(c=q)))  /* note q[0] == 0 always */
            exit(0);
        while (*++c)            /* walk to end of string */
            ;
        r(0,0);
    }
}

r(t,o) {
    i[0] = i[2] = 0;     /* reset redirections */
    u = v + 98;          /* reset arglist */

    while (m[*--c] != '\t') {/* while not '\0' or '|' */
        if (!m[*c]) {           /* a nonmeta? */
            *++c = '\0';   /* null terminate the argument */
            while(!m[*--c])
                ;               /* back to the beginning of word */
            *--u = ++c;    /* save word on argument list */
        }
        if (m[*c] & 32) {   /* ascii hack. '<' or '>'? */
            i[*c&2] = *u;  /* take last argument as a redir */
            if (u - v != 98)
                ++u;
        }
    }

    if (u - v == 98)
        return; /* no args? just return */

    if (strcmp(*u,"cd") == 0) {
        e(chdir(u[1]) * 2); /* *2 so we don't exit but do */
                             /* print err */
        return;
    }

    if (*c) { /* really, if *c != '\0' i.e., if *c == '|' */
        pipe(f);
        o = f[1];
    }

    if (p = fork()) { /* if pid is nonzero */
        e(p);
        if (o) {
            r(o,0); /* recurse to do pipe */
            close(o);
            close(*f);
        }
        wait(0);
    } else {
```

```
            if (o) {
                dup2(*f,0);
                close(*f);
                close(o);
            }
            if (*i) { /* < redirection? */
                close(0);
                e(open(*i,0));
            }
            if (t) { /* pipe? */
                dup2(t,1);
                close(t);
            }
            if (i[2]) { /* > redirection? */
                close(1);
                e(creat(i[2], 438));
            }
            e(execvp(*u,u)); /* exec! */
        }
}


e(x) {
    if (x >= 0)
        return;

    /* super hack with pointers and offsets */
    write(2,"?\n$ "-x/4,2);
    if (x == -1)
        exit(1);
}
```

Best Small Program

Doron Osovlanski
CADTECH—CAD/CAM Systems Ltd.
Givat–Shmuel, Israel

Baruch Nissenbaum <baruch@taunivm.tau.ac.il>
Tel-Aviv University
Tel-Aviv, Israel

```
v,i,j,k,l,s,a[99];
main()
{
    for(scanf("%d",&s);*a-s;v=a[j*=v]-a[i],k=i<s,j+=(v=j<s&&(!k
    &&!!printf(2+"\n\n%c"-(!l<<!j),"  #Q"[l^v?(l^j)&1:2])&&++l||a
    [i]<s&&v&&v-i+j&&v+i-j))&&!(l%=s),v||(i==j?a[i+=k]=0:++a[i])
    >=s*k&&++a[--i])
        ;
}
```

This program solves the problem of putting queens on a chessboard in such a way that they cannot capture one another in a single move. Not only does it solve the 8-queens problems, but it works for any number from 4 to 99.

The authors note that they use "no preprocessor statements and no ifs, breaks, cases, functions, gotos, structures . . . . In short, it contains no C language that might confuse the innocent reader." The authors also claim that they have lost the original unobfuscated source, which I suppose is all in the spirit of obfuscation. Here is a reconstructed version:

```
/*   q0.c  -  solve the N-queen problem, N<99

There can be exactly one queen per column.
a[i]  is the row of the queen in column i.

A solution is built by building the vector a[] incrementally
and backtracking if a bad partial solution has been found.

The vector a[] is printed on success

Variables
All variables are static, thus initialized to 0.
a[]   the (partial) result vector
i,j   counters
c     number of solution
s     size of board */

int i,j,c,s,a[99];       /* all static vars are initialized to 0 */

main()
{
    scanf("%d",&s);                      /* read size of board */

    for( i=0; i>=0; ) {
        /* test solution so far */
        for( j=0; j<i; j++ )
            if(a[j]==a[i] || a[j]-a[i]==i-j || a[i]-a[j]==i-j)
                break;
        if( i!=j )                       /* try next solusion */
            a[i]++;
        else if( i==s-1 ) {              /* a valid solution found */
            printf("\n %d: ",++c);       /* print solution number */
            for(j=0; j<s; j++)           /* print row of queen */
                printf("%d ",a[j]);
            a[i]++;                      /* try next solution */
        }
        if( a[i]>=s ) {
            i--;                         /* backtrack */
            if(i>=0)
```

```
                a[i]++;
        }
        else if( i==j && i!=s )
            a[++i] = 0;                    /* go forward */
    }
    putchar('\n');
}
```

Best Layout

Merlyn LeRoy (Brian Westley) <merlyn@digibd.com>
DigiBoard, Inc.
St. Paul, Minnesota

```
char*lie;
        double time, me= !0XFACE,
        not; int rested,    get, out;
        main(ly, die) char ly, **die ;{
            signed char lotte,

dear; (char)lotte--;
        for(get= !me;; not){
        1 -  out & out ;lie;[
        char lotte, my= dear,
        **let= !!me *!not+ ++die;
            (char*)(lie=

"The gloves are OFF this time, I detest you, snot\n\0sed GEEK!");
        do {not= *lie++ & 0xF00L* !me;
        #define love (char*)lie -
        love 1s *!(not= atoi(let
        [get -me?
            (char)lotte-

(char)lotte: my- *love -
        'I'  -  *love -  'U' -
        'I'  -  (long)  - 4 - 'U' ])- !!
        (time =out=  'a'));} while( my - dear
        && 'I'-11  -get-  'a'); break;}}
            (char)*lie++;

(char)*lie++, (char)*lie++; hell:0, (char)*lie;
        get *out* (short)ly   -0-'R'-  get- 'a'^rested;
        do {auto*eroticism,
        that; puts(*( out
            - 'c'
-('P'-'S') +die+ -2 ));}while(!"you're at it");

for (*((char*)&lotte)^=
        (char)lotte; (love ly) [(char)++lotte+
        !!0xBABE];){ if ('I' -lie[ 2 +(char)lotte]){ 'I'-11 ***die; }
        else{ if ('I' * get *out* ('I'-11 **die[ 2 ])) *((char*)&lotte) -=
        '4' - ('I'-11); not; for(get=!
```

```
get; !out; (char)*lie  &  0xD0- !not) return!!
        (char)lotte;}

(char)lotte;
        do{ not* putchar(lie [out
        *!not* !!me +(char)lotte]);
        not; for(;!'a';);}while(
            love (char*)lie);{

register this; switch( (char)lie
        [(char)lotte] -1s *!out) {
        char*les, get= 0xFF, my; case' ':
        *((char*)&lotte) += 15; !not +(char)*lie*'s';
        this +1s+ not; default: 0xF +(char*)lie;}}}
        get - !out;
        if (not--)
        goto hell;

            exit( (char)lotte);}
```

While this program may look like C code, it is really a set of love letters. Strangely enough, when compiled and run, it produces several verses of `loves me, loves me not`, as if someone were picking at a daisy. Nonetheless, the program is of interest only for its poetic value. It is full of useless C constructs, and `lint` complains loudly about much of it, at one point saying:

```
warning: eroticism unused in function main
```

Author's Analysis

"This took the longest to write [of five winners]. I started it around 1988 and worked on it on and off. I knew I wanted it to read like a conversation, and use C puns like `char*lie`, and, given the nature of the conversation, do `she loves me, she loves me not` depending on the argument passed. It was just a lot of jockeying variables; much of the code does nothing useful, it only sets up later useful code. `not` is assigned the number of steps in `not = atoi(let)` and `if (not--) goto hell` is the main loop. The string printed out is delimited by spaces and hidden as:

```
"The gLOVES are off this tiME, I detest you, sNOT\n\0sed GEEK!"
    ^loves                 ^me,                ^not, newline,
                                                and null terminator
```

"The name of the program is printed out in `puts(out)`, so you get:

```
program
loves me,
program
loves me, not
```

"It's pretty much just a mishmash."

Best Language Tool

Diomidis Spinellis <dds@doc.ic.ac.uk>
Imperial College of Science, Technology and Medicine
University of London
London, England

```
#define O(b,f,u,s,c,a)b(){int o=f();switch(*p++){X u:_ o s b();X\
 c:_ o a b();default:p--;_ o;}}
#define t(e,d,_,C)X e:f=fopen(B+d,_);C;fclose(f)
#define U(y,z)while(p=Q(s,y))*p++=z,*p=' '
#define N for(i=0;i<11*R;i++)m[i]&&
#define I "%d %s\n",i,m[i]
#define X ;break;case
#define _ return
#define R 999 typedef char*A;int*C,E[R],L[R],M[R],P[R],l,i,j;char
B[R],F[2];A m[12*R],malloc (),p,q,x,y,z,s,d,f,fopen();A Q(s,o)A s
,o;{for(x=s;*x;x++){for(y=x,z=o;*z&&*y== *z;y++)z++;if(z>o&&!*z)_
x;}_ 0;}main(){m[11*R]="E";while(puts("Ok"),gets(B) )switch(*B){X
'R':C=E;l=1;for(i=0;i<R;P[i++]=0);while(1){while(!(s=m[l]))l++;if
(!Q(s,"\""))){U("<>",'#');U("<=",'$');U(">=",'!');}d=B;while(*F=*s
){*s--='"'&&j ++;if(j&1||!Q(" \t",F))*d++=*s;s++;}*d--=j=0;if(B[1]
!='=')switch(*B){X'E':l=-1 X'R':B[2]!='M'&&(l=*--C)X'I':B[1]=='N'
?gets(p=B),P[*d]=S():(*(q=Q(B,"TH"))=0,p=B+2,S()&&(p=q+4,l=S()-1)
)X'P':B[5]=='"'?*d=0,puts(B+6):(p=B+5,printf("%d\n",S()))X'G':p=B
+4,B[2]=='S'&&(*C++=l,p++),l=S()-1 X'F':*(q=Q(B,"TO"))=0;p=B+5;P[
i=B[3]]=S();p=q+2;M[i]=S();L[i]=l X'N':++P[*d]<=M[*d]&&(l=L[*d]);
}else p=B+2,P[ *B]=S();l++;}X'L':N printf(I)X'N':N free(m[i]),m[i
]=0 X'B':_ 0 t('S',5,"w",N fprintf(f,I))t('O',4,"r",while(fgets(B
,R,f))(*Q(B,"\n")=0,G())))X 0:default:G() ;}_ 0;}G(){l=atoi(B);m[l
]&&free(m[l]);(p=Q(B," "))?strcpy(m[l]=malloc(strlen(p )),p+1):(m
[l]=0,0);}O(S,J,'=',==,'#',!=)O(J,K,'<',<,'>',>)O(K,V,'$',<=,'!',
>=)O(V,W,'+',+,'-',-)O(W,Y,'*',*,'/',/)Y(){int o;_*p=='-'?p++,-Y(
):*p>='0'&&*p<= '9'?strtol(p,&p,0):*p=='('?p++,o=S(),p++,o:P[*p++
];}
```

This program implements a BASIC interpreter—in exactly 1536 bytes and (as the author notes) "nicely formatted to fit on a 80*25 screen." It supports variable names from A to Z, and FOR, GOSUB, GOTO, NEXT, IF/THEN, RETURN and other constructs. It also implements RUN, LIST, NEW, OLD, SAVE, and BYE. Naturally, to show the program really functions, the author included the well-known Lunar Lander game (which must be at least 20 years old)! Needless to say, it works.

The author notes that "No error checking is performed. The message 'core dumped' signifies a syntax or semantic error."

Here is the original program (slightly trimmed and massaged for display). I don't think any explanation is necessary. (But see his 1991 winner in Chapter 39 (p. 377) for more information.)

```
#define recfunc(b,f,u,s,c,a)b(){int o=f();switch(*p++){X u:_ o s
b();X c:_ o a b();default:p--;_ o;}}
#define filefunc(e,d,_,C)X e:f=fopen(buff+d,_);C;fclose(f)
#define U(y,z)while(p=Q(s,y))*p++=z,*p=' '
#define foralllines for(i=0;i<11*R;i++)m[i]&&
#define I "%d %s\n",i,m[i]
#define X ;break;case
#define _ return
#define R 999

#define Case ;break;case                           /* DEBUG */
#define replace(y,z)while(p=strstr(s,y))*p++=z,*p=' '/* DEBUG */

typedef char * charp;

int
*stackp, stack[R],      /* Stack for GOSUB */
line[R], lim[R], var[R], /* Line for next, limits and vars */
l,i, inquote;           /* General purpose vars */

char buff[R],           /* General purpose line buffer */
two[2];                 /* For strchr using strstr */

charp
m[12*R], malloc(),      /* Line memory */
p, q,
x, y, z,                /* Used by strstr */
s, d,                   /* Used for removing whitespace */
f, fopen();             /* Files */

main()
{
    m[11*R] = "E";
    while(puts("Ok"),gets(buff))
        switch (*buff) {
/*RUN*/ Case'R':
            stackp = stack;
            l = 1;
            for (i = 0; i < R; var[i++] = 0)
                ;

            while (l) {
                while (!(s = m[l]))
                    l++;

                if (!strstr(s,"\"")) {
                    replace("<>", '#');
                    replace("<=", '$');
                    replace(">=", '!');
                }
```

```
                        /* Remove whitespace */
                        d = buff;
                        while (*two = *s) {
                              *s == '"' && inquote++;
                              if (inquote & 1 || !strstr(" \t",two))
                                    *d++ = *s;
                              s++;
                        }
                        *d-- = inquote = 0;
                        /* d points to last char */

                        if (buff[1] != '=')
                              switch(*buff) {
                              Case'E': /* END */
                                    l=-1
                              Case'R':
/*REM*/                               buff[2] != 'M' &&
/*RETURN*/                            (l = *--stackp)
                              Case'I':
/*INPUT*/                             buff[1] == 'N' ?
                                          gets(p = buff),
                                          var[*d] = cmp0()
                                    : (   /* IF */
                                          *(q = strstr(buff, "TH")) = 0,
                                          p = buff + 2, cmp0() && (p = q
+ 4, l = cmp0() - 1)
                                    )
/*PRINT*/                     Case'P':
/*string*/                            buff[5] == '"' ?
                                          *d=0,
                                          puts(buff + 6)
/*expression*/                      : (
                                          p = buff + 5,
                                          printf("%d\n", cmp0())
                                    )
                              Case'G':
/*GOTO*/                              p = buff + 4,
/*GOSUB*/                             buff[2] == 'S' && (
                                          *stackp++ = l,
                                          p++
                                    ),
                                    l = cmp0() - 1
/*FOR*/                       Case'F':
                                    *(q = strstr(buff, "TO")) = 0;
                                    p = buff + 5;
                                    var[i = buff[3]] = cmp0();
                                    p = q + 2;
                                    lim[i] = cmp0();
                                    line[i] = 1
/*NEXT*/                      Case'N':
```

```
                                  ++var[*d]  <=lim[*d]&&(l=line[*d]);
                        }
                    else /* V = expr */
                        p = buff + 2,
                        var[*buff] = cmp0();
                    l++;
                }
/*LIST*/  Case'L':
                foralllines
                    printf(I)
/*NEW*/   Case'N':
                foralllines
                    free(m[i]), m[i] = 0
/*BYE*/   Case'B':
                return 0
/*SAVE*/  filefunc('S',5,"w",
                foralllines
                    fprintf(f, I)
          )
/*OLD*/   filefunc('O',4,"r",
                while(fgets(buff, R, f)) (
                    *strstr(buff,"\n") = 0,
                    enterline()
                )
          )
                /* FALLTHROUGH */
          Case 0:
          default:
                enterline();
            }
        return 0;
}

enterline()
{
    l = atoi(buff);
    m[l] && free(m[l]);
    (p = strstr(buff, " ")) ?
        strcpy(m[l] = malloc(strlen(p)), p + 1)
    : (
        m[l] = 0,0
    );
}

recfunc(cmp0,cmp1,'=',==,'#',!=)
recfunc(cmp1,cmp2,'<',<,'>',>)
recfunc(cmp2,add,'$',<=,'!',>=)
recfunc(add,mul,'+',+,'-',-)
recfunc(mul,basic,'*',*,'/',/)
```

```
basic()
{
    int o;

    return *p == '-' ?
            p++, -basic()
        : *p >= '0' && *p <= '9' ?
            strtol(p, &p, 0)
        : *p == '(' ?
            p++,
            o = cmp0(),
            p++,          /* assert(*p == ')') */
            o
        :
            var[*p++];/* assert(isupper(*p)) */
}
```

Best Game

Chris Mills <cmills@wyse.com>
Wyse Technology
San Jose, California

```
#include<stdio.h>
#include<time.h>
#define S(q)B(*e=0),q,p);
#define W(w)if((w)<22)v= -v;else v-=10;else
#define F for(r=d;r<d+N;
#define H(v,g)v=h(v,*g++= *r++),*g=0;
#define B(n)b(1,n),(V)printf(1
V
exit();char*g,c[M],d[N],q[N],p[N],*e,*r=d+N,l[M],*t="??",*k,*m="\
DEATHISDSev2oinpohae3ttsluuln4a?uibfe 5l\0rtlfrb6 ?a?el:e7$!n\0?\
e t8%ccp\0.%s9deelc.s T.@?-t.\t<J /\0=a\nP=Q Sex \01 KW Sin a$\0\
ane-lay% ge#-slediefuk ar  r$via-:o ?+}:r? n \0:) ee%lone 1-esy6\
66!-~v\n.!^''~@#\0\np~====:=q";b(o,n)char*o;{for(k=n+m;*o++=*k;k+=
9);}int
y=M*2,v,x,s,f,j,o;u(s){B(s));if(!gets(l))exit(0);return(o=
*l)=='y'||o=='Y'||o!='n'&&o!='N'&&u(s);}h(v,m){for(k=c;*k!='J';)
if(m==*k++)break;m=k-c;if(v<0)W(v=m-v)
if(m==1)W(v+=11)
v+=m;return
v;}main(w,z)char**z;{b(c,2)*X;for(--w&&(y=atoi(l[z]));y>1;){if(r-
d>N*3/4){B(8));F++r)*r=c[(r-d)%13];F)w=
*(g=d+rand()%N),*g=
*r,*r++=w;r=d;}for(;;){B(3),y);if(!gets(l)||(w=atoi(l))<1)exit(0)
;if(w&1||w>M||w>y)B(1),y<M?y:M);else
break;}y-=w,s=f=j=x=v=0,g=q,e=p;H(x,g)H(x,g)H(v,e)H(v,e)*t=
*q;S(t)*q=='A'&&y>=w/2&&u(5)&&(y+=(3*(h(0,l[q])==10)-1)*w/
2);if(x==-21)goto
```

```
_;if(v==-21){y+=w/2;goto
_;}while(x>-17&&x<17)H(x,g)while((v==20||*p==-1[e])&&y>=w&&u(6)){
y-=w;++s;for(g=e++;2[g]=
*g,g!=p;)--g;*g++=
*e;*g=' ';i:v=h(h(0,*p),*e++=
*r++);S(t)if(*p=='A'&&-1[e]!=
*p)goto
_;}if(f=y>=w&&u(7))y-=w,H(v,e)while(!f&&v<22&&u(4)){H(v,e)if(v<22
)S(t)}_:x<0&&(x=
-x);v<0&&(v=
-v);if(v<22)if(v==x)j+=w*++f;else
if(x>21||v>x)j+=w*2*++f;if(s--){*e++=' ';*e++=
*p;*e=0;for(e=p;*e=2[e];)e++;goto
i;}y+=j;S(q)};}
```

In order to compile it, supply the following:

```
#define M /* max bet allowed */
#define N /* number of decks used */
#define X /* how to seed the rand() generator */
#define V /* void or int */
```

This program plays blackjack and understands all the rules and has no bound on the number of splits.

There are a number of peculiar elements to this program, but the one I had most fun figuring out is what the program does with the long string (hey, the only string!) declared at the beginning of the program. The key to decoding it is finding the function b:

```
b(o,n)char*o;{for(k=n+m;*o++=*k;k+=9);}
```

This function is used to fetch all the strings to be printed. Given a number, it treats it as an index into the string, m. It then takes every ninth letter from there until it finds a 0, which terminates the string. Thus, the reason the string in the original program starts with all capital letters is that all the messages themselves start with capital letters. For example, starting with element 0, the following string is extracted:

```
Dealer: %s\tPlayer: %s\n\0
```

Most Unusual Data Structure

Peter Ruczynski <pjr@pyra.co.uk>
Pyramid Technology Ltd.
Farnborough, Hants, England

```
#include <stdio.h>
#define A(a) G a();
#define B(a) G (*a)();
#define C(a,b) G a() { printf(b); return X; }
typedef struct F G;A(a)A(b)A(c)A(d)A(e)A(f)A(g)A(h)A(i)A(j)A(k)A(
l)A(m)A(n)A(o)A(p)A(q)A(r)A(s)A(t)A(u)A(v)A(w)A(x)A(y)A(z)A(S)A(N
```

```
)void Q();struct F{B(a)B(b)B(c)B(d)B(e)B(f)B(g)B(h)B(i)B(j)B(k)B(
l)B(m)B(n)B(o)B(p)B(q)B(r)B(s)B(t)B(u)B(v)B(w)B(x)B(y)B(z)B(S)B(N
)void(*Q)();}X={a,b,c,d,e,f,g,h,i,j,k,l,m,n,o,p,q,r,s,t,u,v,w,x,y
,z,S,N,Q};C(a,"z")C(b,"y")C(c,"x")C(d,"w")C(e,"v")C(f,"u")C(g,"t"
)C(h,"s")C(i,"r")C(j,"q")C(k,"p")C(l,"o")C(m,"n")C(n,"m")C(o,"l")
C(p,"k")C(q,"j")C(r,"i")C(s,"h")C(t,"g")C(u,"f")C(v,"e")C(w,"d")C
(x,"c")C(y,"b")C(z,"a")C(S," ")C(N,"\n")  void Q(){}main(){X=g().s
().v().S().j().f().r().x().p().S().y().i().l().d().m().S().u().l(
).c().S().q().f().n().k().v().w().S().l().e().v().i().S().g().s()
.v().S().o().z().a().b().S().w().l().t().N();}
```

This program simply prints out a string. Did I say "simply"? Well, your compiler might be unable to compile this, but such limitations shouldn't bother you if you understand that functions can return **structs** by value. The last line is the most amusing, with its extraordinarily long list of alternating **struct** element selections and function calls.

Author's Analysis

"I had this brainstorm one day and suddenly thought "I wonder if it's possible to write a line of C code that looks like `a().b().c()....`" It just rolled from there. I thought, what do I need to do to get this line of code? I needed:

- a function that returns a structure (this gives me the dot),
- a structure that contains a pointer to a function (the `()`s), and
- to be able to repeat this *ad infinitum* with preferably quite a few function names.

"I then sat down and had a few headaches whilst inventing the structure definition. The remaining obfuscations, such as the `#define`s, are there primarily to reduce the size of the final program.

"While I've never used this technique in a program, I suspect programs such as `cfront` (the C++ preprocessor) might very well, although perhaps not to the extent I did.

"Here is the development of the program. The first clever bit is that **struct f** uses itself in its definition, which effectively gives the unlimited recursion capability. This is quite common in linked lists of structures; the difference here is the combination of structure and pointer to function.

```
struct f
{
        struct f (*h)();
        struct f (*e)();
        struct f (*N)();
};

struct f h();
struct f e();
struct f N();
```

```
struct f x = { h, e, N };

struct f h()
{
    printf("h");
    return x;
}

struct f e()
{
    printf("e");
    return x;
}

struct f N()
{
    printf("\n");
    return x;
}

main()
{
    h().e().N();
}
```

"After finding that this worked, I just had to write the classic C program in what is perhaps the most convoluted manner possible (except for windows programming!) so I added a few more character-printing functions as well as the following:

```
struct f hello()
{
    h().e().l().l().o();
}

struct f world()
{
    w().o().r().l().d();
}
```

and main became:

```
hello().S().world().N();
```

where S prints a space and N prints a newline.

"About this time I started to think about the OCCC, which naturally demanded something a little more esoteric. I decided to print the phrase "the quick brown fox jumped over the lazy dog," which contains all the letters of the alphabet.[1] The

---

1. Or so I thought at the time, it ought to be 'jumps' rather than 'jumped'; as the code stands 's' is unused. I mentioned that there was a redundant bit of code in the submission in the accompanying hints file, but no one has ever mentioned finding it!

functions doing it are disguised by juxtaposing all the letters so **a** became **z**, **b** became **y**, etc., in the print functions. I also then started looking at how I could shrink the size of the source.

"This is perhaps where the code really started to become obfuscated in the true sense of the word.

"I added the line:

```
typedef struct f g;
```

and an evil grin came over my face as I realized the potential. A few judicious joining of lines and some movement to separate the **typedef** from the **struct** soon had the code looking like this:

```
typedef struct f g;

g h(); g e(); g N();

struct f { g (*h)(); g (*e)(); g (*N)(); } x = { h, e, N };

g h() { printf("h"); return x; }
g e() { printf("e"); return x; }
g N() { printf("\n"); return x; }

main() { h().e().N(); }
```

"Then a few carefully chosen **#define**s added the finishing touches:

```
#define A(a) g a();
#define B(a) g (*a)();
#define C(a,b) g a() {printf(b);return x;}

typedef struct f g;

A(h)A(e)A(N);

struct f{B(h)B(e)B(N)}x={h,e,N};

C(h,"h")C(e,"e")C(N,"\n")

        main(){h().e().N();}
```

"The actual competition entry was then easy to put together! I added a **void** function **Q** just to confuse matters (although I honestly cannot remember why!). **stdio.h** had to go in to make it compile reasonably cleanly as well as to assign the return value from the string of functions in **main** to a variable. It worked fine on the Pyramid under both universes (AT&T and BSD) but broke the C compiler on my PC (stack overflow), so at that point I decided it was done!"

Worst Abuse of C by a Committee

Larry Jones <scjones@sdrc.com>
SDRC
Milford, Ohio

```
char*a??(??)=??<
"??=include<stdio.h>",
"??=include<stdlib.h>",
"??=define o stdout",
"??=define b break;case",
"??=define s(p)fputs(p,o);",
"??=define c(p)fputc(p,o);",
"void t(p,f)char*p;??<f&&c('??/"')",
"for(;;p++)??<switch(*p)??<case 0:f&&",
"s(??/"??/??/??/",??/")c('??/??/n')return;case",
"'??=':s(??/"???/??/?=??/")b'??<':s(??/"???/??/?<??/")",
"b'??>':s(??/"???/??/?>??/")b'??(':s(??/"???/??/?(??/")b'??)'",
":s(??/"???/??/?)??/")b'??/??/??/??/':f&&s(??/"???/??/?/??/")",
"s(??/"???/??/?/??/")b'??/??/n':if(f)s(??/"???/??/?/n??/")",
"else case'??/"':if(f)s(??/"???/??/?/??/??/??/"??/")",
"else default:c(*p)??>??>??>main()??<char**p",
";t(??/"char*a??(??)=??<??/",0);for(p=a;*p",
";p++)t(*p,1);t(??/"0??>;??/",0);for(p=a",
";*p;p++)t(*p,0);exit(!ferror(o)&&",
"!fclose(o)?EXIT_SUCCESS",
":EXIT_FAILURE);",
"/*NOTREACHED*/",
"??>",
0??>;
??=include<stdio.h>
??=include<stdlib.h>
??=define o stdout
??=define b break;case
??=define s(p)fputs(p,o);
??=define c(p)fputc(p,o);
void t(p,f)char*p;??<f&&c('"')
for(;;p++)??<switch(*p)??<case 0:f&&
s("??/",")c('??/n')return;case
'??=':s("???/?=")b'??<':s("???/?<")
b'??>':s("???/?>")b'??(':s("???/?(")b'??)'
:s("???/?)")b'??/??/':f&&s("???/?/")
s("???/?/")b'??/n':if(f)s("???/?/n")
else case'"':if(f)s("???/?/??/"")
else default:c(*p)??>??>??>main()??<char**p
;t("char*a??(??)=??<",0);for(p=a;*p
;p++)t(*p,1);t("0??>;",0);for(p=a
;*p;p++)t(*p,0);exit(!ferror(o)&&
!fclose(o)?EXIT_SUCCESS
:EXIT_FAILURE);
```

```
/*NOTREACHED*/
??>
```

This program shows us how wonderful the new Standard C really is. To remind you of this, when run it produces itself as output. The author introduces it as follows:

> Since this year's contest is dedicated to Standard C, here is a strictly conforming entry. In accordance with the Standard definition of a strictly conforming program, it does not produce output dependent on any unspecified, undefined, or implementation-defined behavior, and it does not exceed any of the minimum implementation limits. It adheres to all of the syntactic and semantic constraints of the standard, #includes the relevant headers for the functions it uses, and uses the EXIT_SUCCESS and EXIT_FAILURE macros to return a correct success/fail status to the invoking program. It also uses trigraphs for characters which are not in the Invariant Code Set of ISO 646:1983, so it will be portable to machines with deficient (from C's standpoint) character sets. In short, it should be very widely portable. As an extra added attraction, all of the lines are under 72 characters long, which would allow for sequence numbers to be punched in columns 73–80.

I hope you enjoyed that. However, the really funny part is that the author *was* a longtime member of the ANSI committee, and thus can be held responsible for this wonderful new style of coding that we will all now adopt. Right?

Author's Analysis

"The genesis of my entry was actually another net contest: Karl Heuer's Portable Self-Replicating C Code Contest. The rules were:

1. The output of the program must be its own source code.

2. It may not be safely assumed that the source code resides in an openable file at runtime.

3. The program must be written in Strictly Conforming ANSI C.

4. The program must return a proper exit status, indicating whether or not its output calls succeeded.

5. The source must use only the ISO 646 character set, using trigraphs as needed.

6. No source line may exceed 72 characters.

7. There will be two winners: the first correct program to arrive at my site, and the shortest (measured in source characters, including newlines). No prizes will be awarded.

"This challenge piqued my intellectual curiosity. The traditional self-replicating C program:

```
char*f="char*f=%c%s%c;main(){printf(f,34,f,34,10);}%c";
main(){printf(f,34,f,34,10);}
```

is non-portable since it depends on ASCII. A popular alternative solution is to just open the source file and print it, but that is also non-portable since it requires a system-dependent filename. Just trying to write a strictly portable (in the ANSI sense) self-replicating program was a very good intellectual challenge. Whenever Karl received an entry which did not meet one of the rules, it was returned with an explanation of the problem, giving the author a chance to correct it and resubmit it. Even so, only two entries were received by the deadline (which was about four or six weeks after the start of the contest). I won for the first correct program[2] (presented here with the trigraphs replaced with their ASCII equivalents):

```
static const char *foo[] = {
"#include <stdio.h>\n",
"#include <stdlib.h>\n",
"\n",
"void out(q, f)\n",
"    const char *q;\n",
"    int f;\n",
"    {\n",
"    for (;; q++) {\n",
"        switch (*q) {\n",
"        case 0:\n",
"            if (f) fputs(\"\\\",\\n\\\"\", stdout);\n",
"            return;\n",
"        case '#':\n",
"            fputs(\"?\\?=\", stdout);\n",
"            break;\n",
"        case '{':\n",
"            fputs(\"?\\?<\", stdout);\n",
"            break;\n",
"        case '}':\n",
"            fputs(\"?\\?>\", stdout);\n",
"            break;\n",
"        case '[':\n",
"            fputs(\"?\\?(\", stdout);\n",
"            break;\n",
"        case ']':\n",
"            fputs(\"?\\?)\", stdout);\n",
"            break;\n",
"        case '\\\\':\n",
"            if (f) fputs(\"?\\?/\", stdout);\n",
"            fputs(\"?\\?/\", stdout);\n",
"            break;\n",
"        case '\\n':\n",
"            if (f) fputs(\"?\\?/n\", stdout);\n",
"            else putchar(*q);\n",
"            break;\n",
"        case '\"':\n",
"            if (f) fputs(\"?\\?/\\\"\", stdout);\n",
```

---

2. Diomidis Spinellis won the award for shortest program at 499 characters.

```
"            else putchar(*q);\n",
"            break;\n",
"        default:\n",
"            putchar(*q);\n",
"            }\n",
"        }\n",
"    }\n",
"\n",
"main()\n",
"    {\n",
"    const char **p;\n",
"\n",
"    out(\"static const char *foo[] = {\\n\", 0);\n",
"    out(\"\\\"\", 0);\n",
"    for (p = foo; **p; p++) out(*p, 1);\n",
"    out(\"\\\"};\\n\", 0);\n",
"    for (p = foo; **p; p++) out(*p, 0);\n",
"    exit(ferror(stdout) ? EXIT_FAILURE : EXIT_SUCCESS);\n",
"    }\n",
""};
#include <stdio.h>
#include <stdlib.h>

void out(q, f)
    const char *q;
    int f;
    {
    for (;; q++) {
        switch (*q) {
        case 0:
            if (f) fputs("\",\n\"", stdout);
            return;
        case '#':
            fputs("?\?=", stdout);
            break;
        case '{':
            fputs("?\?<", stdout);
            break;
        case '}':
            fputs("?\?>", stdout);
            break;
        case '[':
            fputs("?\?(", stdout);
            break;
        case ']':
            fputs("?\?)", stdout);
            break;
        case '\\':
            if (f) fputs("?\?/", stdout);
            fputs("?\?/", stdout);
```

```
                break;
        case '\n':
                if (f) fputs("?\?/n", stdout);
                else putchar(*q);
                break;
        case '"':
                if (f) fputs("?\?/\"", stdout);
                else putchar(*q);
                break;
        default:
                putchar(*q);
                }
        }
    }

main()
    {
    const char **p;

    out("static const char *foo[] = {\n", 0);
    out("\"", 0);
    for (p = foo; **p; p++) out(*p, 1);
    out("\"};\n", 0);
    for (p = foo; **p; p++) out(*p, 0);
    exit(ferror(stdout) ? EXIT_FAILURE : EXIT_SUCCESS);
    }
```

"The algorithm is visible in this state: out simply goes through the string q writing out each character. Plain characters are simply written directly, characters which need to be represented by trigraphs are written as trigraphs, and characters which need to be escaped or otherwise handled specially in strings are treated differently if the f flag is set. The main program simply calls out to write the string preamble, writes out the string array once in string context, closes the string definition, writes the string array again in non-string context, and then exits with the appropriate status.

"When encoded using trigraphs, the completed entry was horrendous enough that I felt it was a natural for the OCCC. All it needed was a few preprocessor macros to shorten it to an acceptable size (and introduce some more obfuscation in the process) and a few tricks using more obscure operators instead of the more obvious ones (e.g., using && instead of if). The final touch was rearranging the line breaks to make individual statements harder to recognize and to get an interesting sideways mountain range look to the code.

"Lest anyone get the wrong idea, X3J11 intended trigraphs to be used to transmit programs in a maximally portable form—they (we) never intended for anyone to actually have to read or write them. This program is an excellent example of why not. Amusingly, it was not necessary to write in trigraph form since once I had the readable form working, I added the code to produce trigraphs and then simply ran the program to create the trigraphified version! Thus, the program actually provided some of its own obfuscation!"

Strangest Abuse of the Rules

Stig Hemmer <lise.unit.no>
Norwegian Institute of Technology
Trondheim–NTH, Norway

```
c
```

When run, the program shown above (if you missed it, look again) says whether your C compiler allows nested comments! The compilation instruction (for the Korn shell) is given below.

```
echo alias c cc -E -o o.c shst.c -"\'´Dc=main(){printf("\"N%sest\
ed comments allowed.\\n\",'/*/*/0*/**/'1?\"\":\"o n\"");}'\'´;cc\
     -o c o.c' source shst.c"|csh
```

Author's Analysis

"This is not only a C obfuscation, but a shell obfuscation, too. The same one-character file is used both as a C source file and as a shell script.

"I was reading the rules when it struck me that 160 characters was *very* long for a compilation command. (And indeed, none of the other winning entries used nearly that much.) The program included double quote marks(") which I had to quote past the shell, so I had two levels of quoting. I decided that adding more levels of quoting was as good an obfuscation as any. Today I regret not adding any backquotes to the collection, but done is done.

"I can't say that I've ever used any of these techniques in a real program. I'm very fluent in shell quoting, but I don't really use it all that much. The only example of triple quoting I can recall created an alias that did an **rsh** (remote shell) command that should have a quoted space."

Most Transmittable

James Woods <jaw@riacs.edu>
Research Institute for Advanced Computer Science
NASA Ames Research Center
Moffett Field, California

Karl Fox <karl@morningstar.com>
Morning Star Technologies
Columbus, Ohio

Paul Eggert <eggert@twinsun.com>
Twin Sun Inc.
El Segundo, California

```
#define C char
#define F X,perror("oops"),1
#define G getchar()
#define I ;if(
#define P putchar
#define Q 256
#define W ;while(
#define X return 0
#include<stdio.h>
long M,N,c,f,m,o,r,s,w;y(l){o^=1;m+=l+1;f=f*2+l+(f>>31&1);}int
O,S,e,i,k,n,q,t[69001];b(g){k=4 W g<k)y(P((C)(w>>--
k*8)&255));w=0;}C D[Q*Q],h
[Q*Q];main(g,V)C**V;{I**V-97)X,a()W G-10)W(g=G)+1&&g-'x')if(g-
10){I
4<k)b(0)I g>32&g<'v')w=w*85+g-33,++k;else{I
g-'z'|k)F;w=0;k=5;}}W G-78)I scanf("%ld%lx E%lx S%lx R%lx
",&M,&N,&c,&s,&r)-5)F I M){b(g=3-(M-1&3))W g--)y(0);}I(M-N|c-o|s-
m|r-f)&4294967295)F;X;}long g(){C*p I m<f&n<k&&(m=(1L<<++n)-
1)||O>=S){O=0;S=fread(D,1,n,stdin)*8 I S<8)X-1;S-=n-1;}p=D+O/
8;q=O&7;O+=n;X,(1<<8-q)-1&*p>>q|m&((15<n+q)*p[2]*Q|p[1]& 255))<<8-
q;}a(){C*p=D+Q;G;G;k=G;e=k>>7&1;k&=31 I k>16)F;w=Q W w--
)t[w]=0,h[w]=w;n=8;f=Q+e;i=o=w=g()I o<0)X,1;P(i)W(w=g())+1){I
w==Q&e){W w--)t[w]=0;m=n=8;f=Q I(w=g())<0)X;}c=w I w>=f)*p++=i,-
w=o W w>=Q)*p++=h[w],w=t[w];P(i=h[w])W p>D+Q)P(*--p)I(w=-
f)<1L<<k)t[w]=o,h[f++]=i;o=c;}X;}
```

Analysis

This wonderful program solves the problem of receiving code requiring a program to unpack it that you don't have. To bundle up software into what the authors call a *sharkive*, all you do is compress your code (using the `compress` utility), run it through `atob` (which encodes eight bits into seven), and append this program to the front of it. When received, separate this program from the front, compile it, and run it on the back end of what you've received!

Amusingly, this program's function actually depends on it being as short as possible, since it is being transmitted with your other code each time, and the goal, of course, is to reduce transmission time!

Although the program was originally conceived of as an obfuscated beast, the final version is not so much obfuscated as simply "well-compacted." In fact, at one point the authors renamed the variables to make them clearer!

The program uses standard compaction tricks but is otherwise based on the BSD implementations of `compress` and `atob`. The authors courteously supplied the following secret decoding chart.

shark	atob	compress
a		decompress
b	decode	

c	oeor	incode
e		block_compress
f	Crot	free_ent
g		getcode
h		htab
i		finchar
k	bcount	maxbits
m	Csum	maxcode
n		n_bits
o	Ceor	oldcode
q		r_off
r	orot	
s	osum	
t		codetab
w	word	code
y	byteout	
main	main	
C	char	char
D		buf
F	perror("shark bite: resend"); return 1;	
G	getchar()	getchar()
H		(code=getcode())
I	;if(	;if(
K		[HSIZE]
M	n1	
N	n1	
O		offset
P	putchar	putchar
Q		256
S		size
U		*bp
X	return 0	return 0
X,<v>	return <v>	return <v>
X-1		return -1
V	argv	
W	;while(	;while(
Y	%lx	
Z		for (code=255; code>=0; code--) \
		tab_prefixof(code)=0

Best Abuse of the C Preprocessor

David Goodenough <wet!pallio!dg>
Newton, Massachusetts

```
#include <stdio.h>
#define d define
#d b12(x) 12 x
#d a13(x) x 13
#d a16(x) x 16
```

```
#d a32(x) x 32
#d acb(x) x]
#d acc(x) x}
#d aco(x) x:
#d bco(x) :x
#d acp(x) x)
#d bef(x) EOF x
#d aeq(x) x=
#d afo(x) x for
#d age(x) x fgetc
#d asi(x) x stdin
#d aso(x) x stdout
#d bgt(x) >x
#d ai(x) x i
#d aj(x) x j
#d al(x) x l
#d ami(x) x-
#d bne(x) !=x
#d aob(x) x[
#d aop(x) x(
#d apl(x) x+
#d bpu(x) fputc x
#d bqm(x) ?x
#d aqm(x) x?
#d aqu(x) x'
#d ase(x) x;
#d awh(x) x while
#d axo(x) x^
#d a0(x) x 0
#d b13(x) 13 x
#d b16(x) 16 x
#d b19(x) 19 x
#d b48(x) 48 x
#d a64(x) x 64
#d b66(x) 66 x
#d bcb(x) ]x
#d bch(x) char x
#d bcm(x) ,x
#d acm(x) x,
#d bcp(x) )x
#d beq(x) =x
#d bex(x) extern x
#d bi(x) i x
#d bin(x) int x
#d bix(x) index x
#d bj(x) j x
#d bl(x) l x
#d alt(x) x<
#d bma(x) main x
#d bob(x) [x
```

```
#d boc(x) {x
#d bop(x) (x
#d bpl(x) +x
#d app(x) x++
#d bqu(x) 'x
#d bse(x) ;x
#d bst(x) *x  bma(acp(bop(app(bcp(ai(boc(ase(bch(a16(bl(alt(bob(
ai(b66(ase(bcb(a0(bcm(aeq(bst(acb(bj(a64(bse(aob(bin(al(bi(aeq(bs
e(ai(bex(aop(bch(afo(bst(ase(bix(())))))))))))))))))))))))))))))))
))))))))))
bl(ai(bob(aob(bi(al(bcb(aop(beq(apl(b13(a13(bpl(aeq(bop(acb(bl(bo
b(a32(bi(bpl(apl(b16(bcb(ai(beq(b19(aob(bpl(bop(1))))))))))))))))
)))))))))))))
bpl(acp(b48(acp(asi(bcb(aop(beq(age(bop(aeq(bi(ai(bgt(aop(b12(aop
(bqm(awh(b12(ase(bco(acp(bi(acp(bcp(acp(bpl(aqu(bqu(A))))))))))))
)))))))))))))))))
bne(acc(bef(ase(bcp(acp(aso(bpu(acm(ai(bop(aco(bop(acb(bj(al(beq(
ami(bix(aj(axo(bop(a16(aob(bl(al(aqm(bcm(acp(acp(i))))))))))))))))
)))))))))))))))
```

Author's Analysis

"This program implements Caesar substitution however, its implementation is quite different than the usual form. It relies on **index** (better known as **strchr**) to find if the character is in the set **A-Za-z**. **1** is an array that gets filled with:

"nopqrstuvwxyzzzzabcdefghijklmmmmNOPQRSTUVWXYZZZZABCDEFGHIJKLMMMM"

"If **index** says the character is in the alphabet, then X-OR the offset with 16 to translate, and output, otherwise pass it unchanged.

"To obscure the algorithm, the program is written via preprocessor **defines**. The result is an exercise in *token pasting*. The idea of token pasting got started in 1988 or 1989, when a bunch of people (myself included) were discussing in **comp.-lang.c** how to create a **ctrl** macro for C that would allow you to say:

```
printf("this is a carriage return: %c", ctrl(m));
```

without the need for quotes around the **m**. With a little trial and error, I finally devised the following:

```
#define before_quote(x) 'x
#define after_quote(x) x'
#define ctrl(x) after_quote(before_quote(x))
```

"In this program, things like **#define b12(x) 12 x** means that at some point in the source, a **12** is followed by the compressed nested **#defines**. The **b12** gets the previous compression as an argument and prepends the **12**, thus making another step in the re-creation of the source.

"Amusingly, my preprocessor did not have enough internal space to support writing main as a single C statement. Thus, I had to break it into four separate lines, as you see at the end of the listing."

Best of Show (Grand Prize)

Adrian Mariano <adrian@u.washington.edu>
University of Washington
Mercer Island, Washington

```
#include <stdio.h>
#include <math.h>
#define X
#define Y {}
#define C  }
#define o {
#undef main
char m[500][99],v[99],R;
int*a,b,n,i,j,W,A;
float Q,G,D,M,T,B,O,U,V,N,y,e();
P(g,R,u)float*g,R,u;{int  c;for(*g=1,c=u;c--;*g*=R);}
X
K(g,R,u)float*g,u;char R;
o
if(R=='+')*g+=u;
if(R=='-')*g-=u;
if(R=='*')*g*=u;
if(R=='/')*g/=u;
if(R=='^')P(g,*g,u);
C
w(g,R,u)float*g,u;char R;
/**/{int b,f;A=atoi(*++a);b=atoi(*++a);while((f=A+b)<15000){\
                                printf("%d\n",f);A=b;b=f;}}
main(A,a)int A;char*a[];
o o
if(!strcmp(*++a,"-r"))S();
D=atof(*++a);
T=atof(*++a);
B=atof(*++a);
M=atof(*(4+(a-=3)));
C
while(D<T)
o
U=e((G=B/2,*a),D,M,a);
V=e(*a,Q=D+G,M+G*U,a);
/*/
z;/*/
N=2*e(*a,Q,M+G*V,a);
M+=B*V/3+B*N/6+B*e(*a,D+=B,M+G*N,a)/6+G*U/3;
```

```
printf("%f %f\n",D,M);
C
while(T=0)
;
W=D=1;
;
while(W!=1)
o o
strcpy(j+m,v);
o
if((j-=W)<W)break;
strcpy(j+m,m+j-W);
C
while(strcmp(m+j-W,v)>0)
j=i;
strcpy(v,i+m);
C
for(i=(W/=3)-1;++i<n;)
;
C
do
;
while(0);
for(W=1;(W=W*3+1)<n;);
C
float e(f,D,M,a)char*f,*a[];float D,M;
o
#define main L
O=0;
R='+';
for(;*f;f++)
if(*f=='y')K(&O,R,M);
else if((*f>='0')&&(*f<='9'))K(&O,R,(float)*f-'0');
else if(*f=='x')K(&O,R,D);
else if(1)R=*f;
if(1);
return O;
for(j=0;j<n;puts(j++[m]));
e("",O,&O,a);
n=j-(O=1);
while(gets(j++[m]));
if(!strcmp(*++a,"-r"))S();
C
/**/main(A,a)int A;char*a[];
Y
S(){while(gets(b++[m]));for(b--;b--;puts(b[m]));exit();}
char*f,m[500][99],R,v[99];
int b,W,n,i,j,z;
float Q,G,D,M,T,O,B,U,V,N,e();
#define Y
```

```
#define X {}
#define o }
#define C {
#include <stdio.h>
#include <math.h>
```

This program does four entirely different things. It must be recompiled appropriately for each:

1. It solves differential equations of the type $y'=f(x,y)$, which can use the operators +−*/^. The five arguments are the function, interval start and end, step size, and initial value (y1).

2. It reverses lines in a file when given the argument: `-r 0 0 0 0`

3. If you reverse the program (using the function previously described), it becomes a sort program. Interestingly, if you sort the sort program in reverse (`-r`), it goes back to solving differential equations.

4. If you sort the differential-equation program, the result produces Fibonacci numbers.

5. The Ginsu knife is $10 extra.

Author's Analysis

"I was very surprised to win the contest with my entry. To me, it seems rather prosaic, and its functions seem crystal clear compared to some of the other entries over the years. Perhaps this is merely an indication that I worked on it too long.

"I do not know the source of my inspiration for the main ideas behind my program. Many of the obfuscation techniques I employed are standard tricks which have appeared in previous years' winners. Before I wrote my program, I had examined all the previous winners.

"I started with the idea of a program that would compile both backwards and forwards. I don't know where this initial notion came from. The next step was to decide what two tasks the program would execute. At the time I was working with differential equations, so the idea of a Runge-Kutta differential equation solver came to mind. Sorting was a completely different kind of task than solving differential equations, so I decided it would be a suitable counterpart. Both sorting and solving differential equations are easy to do, so I expected little difficulty with the code-size limit.

"I took a program I had already written in good C to solve n differential equations simultaneously, and started making changes necessary for reverse compilation.

"Obviously I (and other people foolish enough to try and run my program) would need a way to reverse the source code, so I wrote in the '`-r`' reversing option. Once I got it working in that direction, I reversed the code and inserted the sorting code. I was careful to make minimal use of `#define`s and to avoid comments. Once the sort was working, I reversed it again and adjusted the code so that the differential equations part worked.

"My program now worked both forwards and backwards, so I began obfuscating the program. I reduced all the variables to meaningless single letters, made sure that I declared as few variables as possible and made other confusing changes.

"Unfortunately, the program was about 1700 bytes and the contest rules required programs of 1536 bytes or smaller. Regretfully, I changed the Runge-Kutta differential equation code to solve only a single differential equation. This put me comfortably below the 1536-byte limit.

"I was almost done when I realized that the program would reverse itself and the reversed code would compile, but if it sorted itself, the sorted code would not compile. Obviously I would have to repair such a glaring omission.

"Fibonacci numbers leapt to mind as a simple thing to calculate that I might be able to do within the source code size limit, so I added the necessary fixes for the sorted code. I allowed myself to use comments here, since I couldn't possibly do it otherwise.

"The code is littered with other minor obfuscation techniques. I inserted assignment expressions into other assignment expressions, and used things like `i[m]` where `i` is integer and `m` is an array. Lack of indentation and short, meaningless variable names go a long way toward producing incomprehensible code.

"I must admit that I am surprised people are so impressed by the program. At the time, I didn't think it was particularly hard to write. There is little in the way of actual obfuscating involved. I certainly did not expect to win . . . .

"Here is the program with comments. This version will still compile forwards and backwards, but the sorting is broken.

```
#include <stdio.h>
#include <math.h>
#define X
#define Y {}
#define C  }
#define o {

#undef main          /* This is needed for the sorted version */

char m[500][99],v[99],R;
int*a,b,n,i,j,W,A;
float Q,G,D,M,T,B,O,U,V,N,y,e();

/* The function P() is used to calculate powers.  I tried to use
pow(), the library function, but at the time, I didn't know about
the UNIX -lm option to include the math library, and I couldn't
get my entry to compile under some of the UNIX systems.
Note that this function is entirely contained in one line, so it
is legal both forwards and backwards.  Also, the loop test in-
cludes an operation, and the *g* looks rather strange, but takes
advantage of the precedence rules. */
```

```
P(g,R,u)float*g,R,u;{int c;for(*g=1,c=u;c--;*g*=R);}

X   /* This is nothing when going forward, but it becomes a {} */
    /* going backwards, so that K becomes a null function then. */
K(g,R,u)float*g,u;char R;
o               /* the o is a { when going forwards, and a } when */
if(R=='+')*g+=u;    /* going backwards. */
if(R=='-')*g-=u;
if(R=='*')*g*=u;    /* This function is responsible for applying */
if(R=='/')*g/=u;    /* appropriate binary operation to operands */
if(R=='^')P(g,*g,u);
C   /* This is a } when going forwards, and a { going backwards */

/* The next function w() is attached to the fibonacci number code
right now.  If compiled in reverse, it gets what is presently the
K function.  Note the comment in front of the fibonacci code. This
causes sort to put this line in a special place.
A and a are both global variables when compiled forwards.  When
compiled backwards, they are the args to main - also the case when
this section is executed. */

w(g,R,u)float*g,u;char R;
/**/{int b,f;A=atoi(*++a);b=atoi(*++a);while((f=A+b)<15000){
printf("%d\n",f);A=b;b=f;}}

/* This is the first version of main.  When compiled in reverse,
this functions is L(). */

main(A,a)int A;char*a[];

o o     /* Note extra layer of braces here */

if(!strcmp(*++a,"-r"))S();   /* invoke the reverse code? */
D=atof(*++a);   /* argv[2]:  x1 -- start of interval to solve in */
T=atof(*++a);   /* argv[3]:  x2 -- end of interval to solve on */
B=atof(*++a);   /* argv[4]:  h  -- stepsize for the solve */
M=atof(*(4+(a-=3))); /* argv[5] while resetting a to point to */
                /* argv[1] */
        /*              y1 -- initial value of y at x1 */


C       /* End of extra layer of braces.  This extra layer makes
           the upcoming while legal in both directions */

/* Main body of differential equation solver.
Here is equivalent code in unobfuscated C.  (This isn't the code
the program was written from.) */

/* k1 = f(x,y); */
```

```
/* k2 = f(x + 0.5 * h, y + .5 * h * k1 ); */
/* k3 = f(x + 0.5 * h, y + .5 * h * k2 ); */
/* k4 = f(x + h, y + h * k3 ); */
/* x += h; */
/* y += h * (k1 + 2*k2 + 2*k3 + k4 ) / 6; */
/* printf("%f %f\n",x,y); */

/* e() will be defined later to evalute the function. D was ini-
tialized to be the start of the interval.  It is used as x in the
code fragment above, and of course T is the end of the interval.
The explanation below refers to variables as they appear above */

while(D<T)
o
U=e((G=B/2,*a),D,M,a);  /* Get k1.  Note assignment G=B/2 slipped
       in with , operator.  This has no effect on this expr.*/

V=e(*a,Q=D+G,M+G*U,a);  /* Here k2 is calculated.  I use G which I
       defined above as h/2, and now use an assignment as an arg. */

                /* Interlude:  This breaks up the Runge-Kutta */
/*/
z;/*/          /* It is for the sorted version of the program. */
               /* z is only declared at end.  This makes use of */
               /* fact that a variable is a legal C expr itself. */

N=2*e(*a,Q,M+G*V,a);     /* Get 2*k3. */

/* Finally, put it all together.  The call to e() gets k4, and
other exprs are combined to get new value for y. Note D+=B slipped
in to do increment x+=h from the code above. */

M+=B*V/3+B*N/6+B*e(*a,D+=B,M+G*N,a)/6+G*U/3;
printf("%f %f\n",D,M);
C                 /* End of Runge-Kutta code */

while(T=0) /* This assignment is always false.  This while will */
;          /* never be evaluated - important for reversed code.
              When going forward, the important thing is the
              assignment.  The loop is empty. */
W=D=1;
;
while(W!=1)      /* W was just assigned to one, so this loop is */
o o             /* skipped */
strcpy(j+m,v);
o
if((j-=W)<W)break;
strcpy(j+m,m+j-W);
C
while(strcmp(m+j-W,v)>0)
```

```
j=i;
strcpy(v,i+m);
C
for(i=(W/=3)-1;++i<n;)
;
C                              /* Here is the end of the skipped loop. */

do                      /* Do nothing */
;
while(0);

for(W=1;(W=W*3+1)<n;);   /* n hasn't been init'd, but should be
    autoinit'd to 0.  If not, this statement might run for a
    while, but it will terminate eventually. */
C                   /* End of main() */

/* Code just finished is e() rather than main when reversed.  When
forward, e() evalutes the expression in f, with y=M and x=D.  The
"algorithm" is simply to start with an initial value and keep ap-
plying the results of the new operation and operand.  Order of
eval is strictly left to right. */

float e(f,D,M,a)char*f,*a[];float D,M;
o

#define main L            /* Wouldn't want to have two mains */

O=0;                      /* Initalize value, and the operation */
R='+';

for(;*f;f++)             /* Scan through the string */
if(*f=='y')K(&O,R,M);    /* Evalute if we find a y */
else if((*f>='0')&&(*f<='9'))K(&O,R,(float)*f-'0');/* Eval if
digit */
else if(*f=='x')K(&O,R,D);           /* Evalute if x */
else if(1)R=*f;          /* Else, assume it's an operator */
if(1);                   /* Makes this if chain legal in reverse */
return O;                /* Quit this function */
for(j=0;j<n;puts(j++[m]));
e("",O,&O,a);
n=j-(O=1);
while(gets(j++[m]));
if(!strcmp(*++a,"-r"))S();
C
/* Above stuff becomes main when reversed.  Also, comment in front
of main is for sorting the code */
/**/main(A,a)int A;char*a[];/* main is defined into L() now */
Y                         /* becomes {} when compiled forward */

 /* Here's the reversing function.  Notice that b is an int */
```

```
S(){while(gets(b++[m]));for(b--;b--;puts(b[m]));exit();}

char*f,m[500][99],R,v[99];
int b,W,n,i,j,z;
float Q,G,D,M,T,O,B,U,V,N,e();
#define Y
#define X {}
#define o }
#define C {
#include <stdio.h>
#include <math.h>
```

"Here is the reversed program with some comments:

```
#include <math.h>
#include <stdio.h>
#define C {
#define o }
#define X {}
#define Y
float Q,G,D,M,T,O,B,U,V,N,e();
int b,W,n,i,j,z;
char*f,m[500][99],R,v[99];
S(){while(gets(b++[m]));for(b--;b--;puts(b[m]));exit();}
Y   /* This is now superfluous.  It is defined as nothing */

/**/main(A,a)int A;char*a[];   /* Here's main */
C
if(!strcmp(*++a,"-r"))S();   /* Check for the reverse flag */
while(gets(j++[m]));          /* Load stdin into array m.  j is an
    int and m is char m[500][99].  This clearly imposes a limit
    on line length and count */
n=j-(O=1);                /* Slightly confusing initialization */
e("",O,&O,a);             /* e() does all the sorting */

for(j=0;j<n;puts(j++[m]));/* Now print out sorted version */
return O;                 /* Done.  Return from main().  This */
      /* statement is executed both backwards and forwards.*/
if(1);
else if(1)R=*f;
else if(*f=='x')K(&O,R,D);
else if((*f>='0')&&(*f<='9'))K(&O,R,(float)*f-'0');
if(*f=='y')K(&O,R,M);
for(;*f;f++)
R='+';
O=0;
#define main L
o
```

```
#if 0
/* The function e() contains a shellsort.  I had the code sitting
on my disk, and don't remember where it came from.  This is the
actual pre-obfuscation code.  (Looks rather confusing already.)*/

shellsort()
{
    int i,j,h;
    char v[80];

    h = 1;
    do
        h = 3*h+1;
    while ( h < n);
    do {
        h = h / 3;
        for (i=h;i<n;i++) {
            strcpy(v,a[i]);
            j = i;
            while (strcmp(a[j-h],v)>0) {
                strcpy(a[j],a[j-h]);
                j -= h;
                if (j < h) break;
            }
            strcpy(a[j],v);
        }
    }
    while (h!=1);
}
#endif 0

float e(f,D,M,a)char*f,*a[];float D,M;
C

for(W=1;(W=W*3+1)<n;);   /* All of loop body has been put in the
test */

while(0);/* This was a do...while going forward.  Now a null */
;          /* while, followed by non-empty do containing body of */
do         /* the sort.  I've added indentation below to */
           /* make loop nesting clearer.  This indentation is */
           /* not, of course, present in the final version */
  C
  ;
  for(i=(W/=3)-1;++i<n;)   /* Double assignment in the init, and */
                           /* increment moved to loop test */
    C
    strcpy(v,i+m);         /* i is an int, m is char m[][] */
    j=i;
    while(strcmp(m+j-W,v)>0)
```

```
        C
        strcpy(j+m,m+j-W);
        if((j-=W)<W)break;   /* Combined assignment and test */
        o
    strcpy(j+m,v);
  o o
while(W!=1)        /* End of do loop */

;
W=D=1;
;
while(T=0)        /* This is never true */
C
printf("%f %f\n",D,M);
M+=B*V/3+B*N/6+B*e(*a,D+=B,M+G*N,a)/6+G*U/3;
N=2*e(*a,Q,M+G*V,a);
z;/*/
/*/
V=e(*a,Q=D+G,M+G*U,a);
U=e((G=B/2,*a),D,M,a);
o                    /* End of the bogus while loop */

while(D<T)        /* D == 1 && T == 0, so this is never true */
C
M=atof(*(4+(a-=3)));
B=atof(*++a);
T=atof(*++a);
D=atof(*++a);
if(!strcmp(*++a,"-r"))S();
o o                    /* End of loop, and end of e() */

Vmain(A,a)int A;char*a[];   /* main has been defined to L */
/**/{int b,f;A=atoi(*++a);b=atoi(*++a);while((f=A+b)<15000){-
printf("%d\n",f);A=b;b=f;}}
w(g,R,u)float*g,u;char R;
C
if(R=='^')P(g,*g,u);
if(R=='/')*g/=u;
if(R=='*')*g*=u;
if(R=='-')*g-=u;
if(R=='+')*g+=u;
o
K(g,R,u)float*g,u;char R;
X
P(g,R,u)float*g,R,u;{int c;for(*g=1,c=u;c--;*g*=R);}
float Q,G,D,M,T,B,O,U,V,N,y,e();
int*a,b,n,i,j,W,A;
char m[500][99],v[99],R;
#undef main
#define o {
```

```
#define C  }
#define Y {}
#define X
#include <math.h>
#include <stdio.h>
```

"The sorted version is omitted, since there's not much to say about it. The three lines with comments on them get put first, and I arranged it so that the `/*/` would open a comment that includes all the code. The `z;  /*/` line gets sorted last, so it closes off the comment to end the program."

## CHAPTER 35

Implementing Software Timers

This chapter describes a set of functions to implement software timers. What are software timers and why do you need them? Software timers make up for inherent limitations in hardware timers. For example, while most computers have clock hardware, you can typically have the clock trigger an interrupt for only one time in the future.

When running multiple tasks, you will want to have the clock keep track of multiple timers concurrently so that interrupts can be generated correctly even if the time periods overlap. Operating systems do this all the time.

An excellent article by Robert Ward [1] discusses the related problem of building a general purpose scheduler. In the "Additional Ideas" section, Robert described the usefulness of a timer scheduling queue: "Events can specify the timing of other events by putting a timer programming request in a special queue." That is exactly what the software in this chapter will do.

The code in this chapter has other uses as well. For example, you can use it to simulate multiple timers in environments such as UNIX, which only allows each process one software timer. Even if you aren't interested in software timers, I think you will find this an intriguing chapter. Using simple techniques and data structures, this C code produces very powerful results. The code was very tricky to get right, and my commentary should be interesting if only as providing more practice in reading and writing C code.

Timers

By implementing the timers as a separate piece of software, we can reduce the complexity of the scheduler. Some people like this kind of modularization and some don't. Similarly some operating systems do this, and some don't. I like it. It makes the code easier to write, to read, and to correct (oops!).

The basic idea of timers is that they allow tasks to be run at some time in the future. When the appropriate times arrive, tasks are scheduled to be run. The responsibility of actually running them is then turned over to someone else, such as the scheduler. In order to communicate with the scheduler, we'll set up a common data structure called a `timer` (see below). I've also included a few other miscellaneous definitions that will be needed later on. For instance, `Time` is a `typedef` used to declare all relative time variables. You can complete this definition based on your needs.

```
#include <stdio.h>

#define TRUE    1
#define FALSE   0

#define MAX_TIMERS  ...    /* number of timers */
typedef ...   Time;        /* how time is actually stored */
#define VERY_LONG_TIME  ...   /* longest time possible */

struct timer {
    int inuse;              /* TRUE if in use */
    Time time;              /* relative time to wait */
    char *event;            /* set to TRUE at timeout */
} timers[MAX_TIMERS];       /* set of timers */
```

Each timer will be represented by a `struct timer`. The set of timers will be maintained in an array, `timers`. The first element of each timer declares whether the timer is in use. The second element of a timer is the amount of time being waited for. As time passes, this will be periodically updated. `event` is a pointer whose value is initially set to 0. When it is time to run the task, `*event` is set to 1. We can imagine that the scheduler also keeps a pointer to the same flag. Every so often, the scheduler reexamines the values. When the scheduler finds a value has been set to 1, it knows that the timer has expired and the associated task can be run.

Notice how simple this is. Other schedulers or other scheduler data structures could enable runnability, without worrying or even knowing about timers.

The following code initializes the timers. It runs through the array setting each `inuse` flag to `FALSE`. This `for` loop will become idiomatic to you by the end of this chapter.

```
void
timers_init() {
    struct timer *t;

    for (t=timers;t<&timers[MAX_TIMERS];t++)
        t->inuse = FALSE;
}
```

Now we can write the routines to schedule the timers. First, I'll show `timer_undeclare`. It is a little simpler than its counterpart, `timer_declare`.

There are a variety of ways to keep track of the timers. Machines that don't have sophisticated clock hardware usually call an interrupt handler at every clock tick. The software then maintains the system time in a register, as well as checking for timer entries that have expired.

More intelligent machines can maintain the clock in hardware, only interrupting the CPU after a given time period has expired. By having the clock interrupt only when an event is waiting, you can get a tremendous speedup. This technique is also common in software simulations and thread implementations.

Reading the clock may require an operating system call, but for our purposes we will assume the variable `time_now` to be automatically updated by the hardware for just this purpose. `volatile` indicates that the variable's value should not be cached but read from storage each time.

```
volatile Time time_now;
```

We will define several variables for shorthands. `timer_next` will point to the timer entry that we next expect to expire. `time_timer_set` will contain the system time when the hardware timer was last set.

```
struct timer *timer_next = NULL;   /* timer we expect to */
                                   /* run down next */
Time time_timer_set;       /* time when physical timer set */

void timers_update();      /* see discussion below */

void
timer_undeclare(t)
struct timer *t;
{
      disable_interrupts();
      if (!t->inuse) {
            enable_interrupts();
            return;
      }

      t->inuse = FALSE;

      /* check if we were waiting on this one */
      if (t == timer_next) {
            timers_update(time_now - time_timer_set);
            if (timer_next) {
                  start_physical_timer(timer_next->time);
                  time_timer_set = time_now;
            }
      }
      enable_interrupts();
}
```

Undeclaring Timers—Why and How?

`timer_undeclare` does just what its name implies, it *undeclares* a timer. Undeclaring timers is actually an important operation in some applications. For example, network code sets timers like crazy. In some protocols, each packet sent generates a timer. If the sender does not receive an acknowledgment after a short interval, the timer forces it to resend a packet. If the sender does receive an acknowledgment, it undeclares the timer. If things are going well, every single timer declared is later undeclared.

`timer_undeclare` (see the listing above) is performed with interrupts disabled. This is necessary because we are going to have an interrupt handler that can access the same data. Because this data is shared, access must be strictly controlled. I've shown the interrupt manipulation as a function call, but you must use whatever is appropriate to your system. This is very system dependent.

`timer_undeclare` starts by checking the validity of the argument as a timer entry. We will see later that the system clock can implicitly undeclare timer entries. Thus we must make a reasonable attempt to assure ourselves that a timer to be undeclared is still declared. Notice that interrupts have to be disabled just to make this check. If we made the check and *then* disabled interrupts, someone could sneak in just after the check but before the disabling, and change the value of `t->inuse`.

Once assured the timer is valid, `timer_undeclare` marks the entry "not in use." If the timer happens to be the very one next expected to expire, the physical timer must be restarted for the next shorter timer. Before doing that, all the timer entries have to be updated by the amount of time that has elapsed since the timer was last set. This is done by `timers_update`, which also calculates the next shortest timer. Looking for the shortest timer in that function is a little obscure, but it happens to be very convenient since `timers_update` has to look at every timer anyway.

`timers_update` (below) goes through the timers, subtracting the given time from each. If any reach zero this way, they are triggered by setting the event flag. Any lag in the difference between when a timer was requested and when `timers_update` is called is accounted for by basing the latency against `time_now` and also collecting timers that have "gone negative" in `timers_update`. (Why might a timer go negative?) Finally, we also remember the lowest nonzero timer to wait for by saving it in `timer_next`.

`timer_last` is just a temporary. It is a permanently non-schedulable timer that will only show up when no other timers remain active.

```
/* subtract time from all timers, enabling any that run */
/* out along the way */
void
timers_update(time)
Time time;
{
    static struct timer timer_last = {
        FALSE,                  /* in use */
        VERY_LONG_TIME,         /* time */
        NULL                    /* event pointer */
    };

    struct timer *t;

    timer_next = &timer_last;
```

```
    for (t=timers;t<&timers[MAX_TIMERS];t++) {
        if (t->inuse) {
            if (time < t->time) { /* unexpired */
                t->time -= time;
                if (t->time < timer_next->time)
                    timer_next = t;
            } else { /* expired */
                /* tell the scheduler */
                *t->event = TRUE;
                t->inuse = 0;          /* remove timer */
            }
        }
    }

    /* reset timer_next if no timers found */
    if (!timer_next->inuse) timer_next = 0;
}
```

Declaring Timers

`timer_declare` (see listing below) takes a time and an **event** address as arguments. When the time expires, the value that **event** points to will be set. (This occurs in `timers_update` under the comment `/* tell the scheduler */`.) `timer_declare` returns a pointer to a timer. This pointer is the same one that `timer_undeclare` takes as an argument.

```
struct timer *
timer_declare(time,event)
Time time;                  /* time to wait */
char *event;
{
    struct timer *t;

    disable_interrupts();

    for (t=timers;t<&timers[MAX_TIMERS];t++) {
        if (!t->inuse) break;
    }

    /* out of timers? */
    if (t == &timers[MAX_TIMERS]) {
        enable_interrupts();
        return(0);
    }

    /* install new timer */
    t->event = event;
    t->time = time;
    if (!timer_next) {
```

```
                  /* no timers set at all, so this is shortest */
                  time_timer_set = time_now;
                  start_physical_timer((timer_next = t)->time);
            } else if ((time + time_now)
                        < (timer_next->time + time_timer_set)) {
                  /* new timer is shorter than current one */
                  timers_update(time_now - time_timer_set);
                  time_timer_set = time_now;
                  start_physical_timer((timer_next = t)->time);
            } else {
                  /* new timer is longer than current one */
            }
            t->inuse = TRUE;
            enable_interrupts();
            return(t);
      }
```

As with its counterpart, interrupts are disabled in `timer_declare` to prevent concurrent access to the shared data structure. The first thing `timer_declare` does is to allocate a timer. If none are available, a **NULL** is returned so that the caller can fail or retry later. Once a timer is allocated and initialized, we must check whether the physical timer must be changed. There are three cases:

1. There are no other timers.

    In this case, we go ahead and start the physical timer with the time of this timer.

2. There are other timers, but this new one is the shortest of all.

    In this case, we must restart the physical timer to the new time. But before we do that, we must update all the other timers by the amount of time that has elapsed since the physical timer was last set.

3. There are other timers, and this new one is not the shortest.

    There is nothing to do in this case. However, for legibility it is broken into its own case, which contains only a comment. That way it is clear what is going on when the previous `else-if` test fails.

Before enabling interrupts and returning, the timer's `inuse` flag is set. The reason it is done afterward rather than with the earlier timer settings is that this prevents `timers_update` from updating it with a time period that occurred before it was even declared.

Handling Timer Interrupts

The only remaining routine is the interrupt handler, which is called when the physical clock expires. When the interrupt handler is called, we know that the time described by `timer_next` has elapsed.

```
void
timer_interrupt_handler()
{
    disable_interrupts();
    timers_update(time_now - time_timer_set);

    /* start physical timer for next shortest time if */
    /* one exists */
    if (timer_next) {
        time_timer_set = time_now;
        start_physical_timer(timer_next->time);
    }
    enable_interrupts();
}
```

Each time the interrupt handler is called, a timer has expired. By calling `timers_update`, all the timers will be decremented and any timers that have expired will have their event flags enabled. This will also set up `timer_next` so that the physical timer can be restarted for the next timer we expect to occur.

Let's examine one special case. Suppose we have only one timer set up. Now imagine that we have called `timer_undeclare` and just as interrupts are disabled, the physical clock ticks down all the way. Since interrupts are disabled, the interrupt will be delivered immediately after interrupts are enabled. But they will be enabled after the timer has been deleted. Here we see a situation where an interrupt will be delivered for a timer that no longer exists. What occurs in the interrupt handler?

`timers_update` is called. It finds nothing to update. As a consequence of this, `timer_next` is set to 0. The remainder of the interrupt handler already handles the case of no remaining timers, and the handler returns normally.

This is an example of the kind of thing you have to keep in mind when writing the code. (In fact, my first implementation didn't handle this right, and it was painful to debug. Debuggers don't work very well when fooling around with interrupts!)

Incidentally, I've written the interrupt handler so it suspends interrupts while it is active. Some environments do this automatically, so it may be unnecessary for you. If another subroutine is executing at the same time as an interrupt is being served, the subroutine will temporarily block if it reaches a `disable_interrupts` of its own.

Conclusion

I have presented an implementation of timers. The code is carefully designed so that it is relatively free of special demands placed on a scheduler. For example, it doesn't prevent the scheduler from using a different kind of timer at the same time.

One question that may have occurred to you while reading this is why the timers are maintained as an array rather than say, a linked list. Using a linked list would avoid the overhead of stepping through arrays (which can be almost entirely empty).

Keeping the list sorted by time would make the `timers_update` function much simpler.

On the other hand, a linked list would complicate the other functions. For example, `timer_undeclare` would either require you to use a doubly-linked list, or to search the entire list from the beginning each time. Another point is that real-time systems typically avoid dynamic structures to begin with. For example, using `malloc/free` from a process-wide heap can cost an indeterminate amount of time that is difficult to estimate. If I were to recode this using linked lists, I would use a `malloc` implementation from a small pool of timer-only buffers, which in effect is very similar to what I've done here with arrays. There would be a trade-off in space and time, which you might prefer or not depending on your application.

If you decide to recode or just modify my implementation, be very careful. Always imagine the worst thing that can happen when two processes attempt to access the same data structure at the same time. Happy interruptions!

Thanks

Debugging timing routines is very different than debugging other code because unrelated events in the computer can make your programs behave differently. Even putting in `printf` statements can change critical execution paths. It is extremely aggravating when problems disappear only when you are debugging. Furthermore, most debuggers do not work well when interrupts are disabled. Ed Barkmeyer was of great help in debugging the timer code and teaching me to persevere when I saw code behaving in ways that had to be impossible. Thanks to Sarah Wallace and Randy Miller, who debugged this chapter and also forced me to make all the explanations much clearer.

References

[1]   Robert Ward, "Practical Schedulers for Real-Time Applications," *The C Users Journal*, April 1990.

## CHAPTER 36

Expect

Earlier, I discussed the embeddable language Tcl (Tool Command Language), written by John Ousterhout at the University of California at Berkeley (see p. 291 in Chapter 33). In that chapter, I described how to build tools using Tcl and mentioned one I built called *Expect*. Expect has become quite popular, and I thought it would be fun to share some of the internals of it with you.

Briefly, Expect can play the role of a user in an interactive program. In effect, it can force an interactive program to be non-interactive! The first problem we applied Expect to was (of course) a game: `rogue`.

Automating Rogue

Rogue is an adventure game that presents you with a player who has various physical attributes such as a strength rating. Most of the time the strength is 16, but every so often—maybe one out of 20 games—you get an unusually good strength of 18. Many people know this, but no one in their right mind restarts the game 20 times to find those really good configurations. Well, the following Expect script can do it for you.

```
for {} 1 {} {
        spawn rogue
        expect "Str: 18" break \
               "Str: 16"
        close
    }
interact
```

The script works as follows: Inside a `for` loop, `rogue` is started by using the `spawn` keyword. Then we look to see if the strength is either 18 or 16. If it is 16, the next statement in the script is executed, closing the connection and effectively sending an `EOF` to `rogue`, which goes away. The loop is then restarted, and a new game of `rogue` is run. When a strength of 18 is found, we break out of the loop and drop down to the bottom of the script, executing the next line (`interact`). This passes control back to the real user, allowing them to play this particular game.

If you run this script, you'll actually see 20 to 30 initial configurations fly across your screen in less than a second, finally stopping with a great game for you to play. The only way to play `rogue` better is under the debugger!

The Expect Command Described

I'm not going to explain all of Expect, but the rogue script should give you enough of a taste. Instead, I'm going to focus on the most interesting part: the expect command itself. It illustrates a number of concepts, and it is real code that you might like to plug into your application, with or without the rest of the Expect program.

The expect command reads from the output of another process. The output is examined for a pattern that matches any of the patterns supplied as arguments to the command itself. expect takes arguments as pattern-action pairs. When any of the patterns match, the corresponding action is executed. Actions are just Tcl statements (such as a send, or even another expect command). As in C, compound statements may be grouped by enclosing them in braces.

In the script above, there are two patterns. When "str: 18" is seen, the break statement is executed. When "str: 16" is seen, nothing (the null action) is executed. (The game doesn't produce any other strengths at startup.)

One other feature not illustrated by the script is that the keywords eof and timeout are special patterns. If an end-of-file appears in the stream, the action paired with the eof pattern (if there is one) is executed. Similarly, if a certain time period expires without matching any patterns, the timeout action is executed.

The Expect Command Implemented

Expect follows the usual Tcl calling conventions (see below). The first argument is a programmer-supplied pointer (unused here, hence the ARGSUSED comment for lint's sake). The second is a pointer to an interpreter instance (always the same here). The third and fourth arguments are the command arguments that the script supplied, presented in argc/argv style.

```
/*ARGSUSED*/
int
cmdExpect(clientData, interp, argc, argv)
ClientData clientData;
Tcl_Interp *interp;
int argc;
char **argv;
{
```

Immediately upon entry (see below), the arguments are checked for correct usage. In this case, all we have to do is check for at least one pattern. Expect assumes a final missing action is just the null statement. This means you can write statements like "expect foo", which just delays until "foo" or EOF appears, or the timeout occurs.

```
if (argc < 2) {
    tcl_error("usage: expect [pattern action] ... \
                            pattern [action]");
    return(TCL_ERROR);
}
```

`tcl_error` is a function that saves a message to be passed back to the interpreter evaluating each Tcl statement. The interpreter will fetch and print out the message when it sees `TCL_ERROR` returned.

Next, the stream is selected. The script can switch between streams by setting the Tcl variable `spawn_id` (also set by the `spawn` command). Similarly, the timeout period is specified by setting the Tcl variable `timeout`. The code below shows how we retrieve and use these values from Tcl. (The third argument indicates scoping, but will not be further explained here.) These values are not passed as parameters because they are expected to change infrequently. Thus, they are changed by giving an explicit command (e.g., `set timeout 60`).

```
stream = atoi(Tcl_GetVar(interp,"spawn_id",0));
timeout = atoi(Tcl_GetVar(interp,"timeout",0));
```

One other variable is controlled by the script. `match_max` defines the number of characters that `expect` guarantees it will use to match patterns. The default is 2000. If patterns must match more than 2000 bytes, the script must raise this value explicitly. We don't automatically use a very large value, since that can needlessly slow down the pattern matching process (more on this later).

Fetching and resetting the buffer is shown in the following listing. `realloc` is called with the presumption that if the buffer shrinks, the probability is high that it will efficiently just return the same buffer. Similarly, if it grows back it will extend the buffer in place if possible. The code actually allocates space that is twice what the script asked for so that we can avoid dealing with matching output that straddles two buffers.

```
s = Tcl_GetVar(interp,"match_max",0);
if (buf_size != (new_size = 2*atoi(s))) {
    if (0 == (new_buf = realloc(buf,new_size+1))) {
        tcl_error("failed to grow match buf to %d bytes",
                                        new_size);
        return(TCL_ERROR);
    }
    buf_size = new_size;
    buf = new_buf;
}
```

The next step is to massage the patterns and actions into a more usable form. The code below does just this, picking up the original arguments and placing them into a structure called `pair`.

```
typedef struct {
        char *pattern;
        char *action;
        enum {keyword, pattern} type;
} pair;

pairs_inuse = argc/2;              /* number of patterns */
if (0 == (pairs=(pair *)malloc(pairs_inuse*sizeof(pair)))) {
    tcl_error("malloc(%d pairs)",pairs_inuse);
    return(TCL_ERROR);
}

timeout_action = eof_action = 0;
for (i = 1, p = pairs;i<argc;i+=2,p++) {
    if (!(strcmp(argv[i],"timeout"))) {
        p->type = keyword;
        timeout_action = argv[i+1];
    } else if (!(strcmp(argv[i],"eof"))) {
        p->type = keyword;
        eof_action = argv[i+1];
    } else {
        p->type = pattern;
        p->pattern = argv[i];
        p->action = argv[i+1];
    }
}
```

At this point, we can begin looking for patterns. The following code does this. It begins by zeroing buf, the buffer that accumulates incoming bytes. Then the code loops. Basically, the loop consists of the following steps:

1. Read as much new data as is available, blocking if none is available.

2. Break out of the loop if any patterns match or an end-of-file was read or a timeout occurred.

Naturally, the implementation is a little more complicated than that! The first thing to do in the loop is to make sure there is space in the buffer for incoming data. (rc is the number of characters in the buffer.) To guarantee that matches can occur on data of a minimum length (match_max), we copy the second half over the first if the buffer is full. (This is why we doubled the original request earlier.)

Next the function i_read is called. The arguments to i_read are the stream, where in the buffer to put new bytes, how many to read, and how long to wait for them. Internally, i_read starts an alarm and then begins reading. If the read completes, the alarm is canceled and i_read returns the numbers of characters read. Otherwise, the alarm interrupts the read, and i_read returns –2 to denote that. (–1 is returned for other errors, and 0 is returned for EOF.) Hence i_read is an *interruptible read*. I discussed various implementations of routines like i_read earlier (see p. 152 in Chapter 18).

The result of i_read is used to decide whether an EOF or timeout occurred, or some other abnormal event happened. In all of these cases, we break out of the loop.

If any characters were read, the buffer end is updated. The new characters are echoed to stdout, if desired (the script has control over this via the C variable loguser, which is mapped to a Tcl function).

At this point, all that is left is to check whether the output matches the patterns. A slight problem presented by Tcl is that it uses the C convention of null-terminating strings. Thus, we must remove any nulls by calling rm_nulls (which returns the numbers of nulls removed). rm_nulls is not shown here, but it is trivial to write. Notice that this step is done after the write to stdout, because it is likely that the nulls are involved in screen formatting operations.

The last operation is to compare the patterns against the input. This is done by calling the patternmatch function, which understands the "usual" wildcards and C escapes. Like i_read, the implementation of patternmatch is not relevant here. If a pattern matches, we abort the loop. Notice that goto is used to break out of two for loops. This is one of the few acceptable reasons to use goto in a C program; without it, the code would be harder to read.

Finally, notice that the keyword cases are skipped when looking for keywords.

```c
buf[0] = '\0';

for (;;) {
    if (rc == buf_size) {
        memcpy(buf,buf+buf_size/2,buf_size/2);
        rc = buf_size/2;
    }

    cc = i_read(stream,buf+rc,buf_size-rc,timeout);

    if (cc == 0) {          /* normal EOF */
        eof = TRUE;
        fclose(stream);
        break;
    } else if (cc == -1) {/* abnormal EOF */
        if (i_read_errno == EBADF) {
            /* process died earlier? */
            tcl_error("bad spawn_id");
        } else {
            tcl_error("i_read(spawn_id=%d): %s",
                            stream,sys_errlist[errno]);
            fclose(stream);
        }
        error = TRUE;
        break;
    } else if (cc == -2) break;    /* timed out */
```

```
        oldrc = rc;
        rc += cc;

        if (loguser) {
            fwrite(buf+oldrc,1,cc,stdout);
            fflush(stdout);
        }

        rc -= rm_nulls(&buf[oldrc],cc);
        buf[rc] = '\0';

        for (p=pairs;p<&pairs[pairs_inuse];p++) {
            if (p->type == keyword) continue;
            if (patternmatch(buf,p->pattern)) {
                match = TRUE;
                goto done;
            }
        }
    }
```

If the loop terminates, we have timed out, or have seen a pattern or end-of-file, or some error has occurred. In the last case, we simply clean up and return an error indication to the caller. Otherwise, we select the appropriate action, pass it to **Tcl_Eval** for execution, and return the result of **Tcl_Eval** to our caller. (This allows Tcl to automatically handle statements like **break** in the **rogue** script.) The input buffer is also made available in the Tcl variable **expect_match**. Using this, the script can find out what matched a pattern (or what failed to match after a time-out).

Finally, the pattern-action structure is freed, and the result is returned.

```
    done:
        if (error) result = TCL_ERROR;
        else {
            char *action;

            if (match) action = p->action;
            else if (eof) action = eof_action;
            else action = timeout_action;

            if (action) result = Tcl_Eval(interp,action,0,
                                          (char **) NULL);
            else result = TCL_OK;

            Tcl_SetVar(interp,"expect_match",buf,0);
        }

        free((char *)pairs);

        return(result);
```

More Details

I have made some simplifications in the code, primarily for readability. For instance, patterns can actually be lists of patterns, permitting multiple patterns to trigger the same action. Two entirely different pattern matchers are supported, and they both are buffered so that you can partially match output and then return later to match the rest of it.

Other interesting capabilities are that `expect` can match on multiple patterns across multiple programs simultaneously. To aid in this, `expect` supports additional commands to allow patterns to be associated with every `expect` command implicitly.

I also removed some logging code. The logging code can record the interaction, which is primarily useful in debugging. `expect` can also treat the user as a source of input and output, in which case it should not echo the input since the user is already seeing it (having just typed it). This makes the logging code even more complex.

Note also that some initialization must occur before `cmdExpect` is ever executed. For instance, we guarantee that the Tcl variables `timeout` and `spawn_id` have values by setting them initially ourselves.

Although I have omitted most of the declarations, they should be obvious. One that I must comment on is the declaration for a stream. It is a `FILE *`. This is of interest because the script may change it by accessing the Tcl variable `spawn_id`. Nothing else can be done with it. To the script, it serves only as a magic cookie that can be used to select which process to interact with. In the script's world, it appears as a rather odd string; but inside Expect, it becomes a perfectly usable stream! (Actually, it is a magic cookie as far as we are concerned too, albeit of a different flavor. We can pass it to a limited set of functions, but nothing else.)

Conclusion

I hope you've enjoyed this exploration of a very interesting function of a very real program. This particular function draws together a large number of techniques to accomplish a powerful result in a coherent way. Whether you decide to incorporate a function like this one in your code, or just use some of the techniques (such as Tcl), you have seen one way of going about it. Being production code, this also shows you the tiny little details that have to be taken into account.

Source Code

The disk accompanying this book includes the source and documentation for Expect. A Usenet newsgroup exists for discussion of the Tcl language and its applications. Called "`comp.lang.tcl`", this is a good place to discuss or ask questions about Expect, too.

A requirement of Expect is that your operating system must be multitasking. This is necessary because Expect is a process that controls other processes, and therefore you must be able to run multiple processes simultaneously. If the version of Expect on the disk does not run on your multitasking system, follow the directions in the README file to get the most recent version of Expect. While I cannot promise anything in the way of support, I may be able to help you port Expect to new systems.

Expect is in the public domain.

## CHAPTER 37

Implementing a Trap Command

Almost everyone has written programs for interpreters (such as UNIX shell scripts or DOS .BAT files). If you've ever tried to make them bulletproof, you've had to handle signals. Oh no, not signals! Yes, signals.

The UNIX Bourne shell lets the user dictate actions by using the trap command. Many other interpreters do similar things. For example, the C-shell calls it onintr. dBASE calls it on error and on key. All of these commands work similarly.

Even though they have different names, the idea is the same: in the event of a signal (e.g., error), you get a chance to clean up (say, by removing temporary files) before exiting. In this chapter, I'll show how to implement a trap-like command for your own interpreter.

The trap command I'm going to create has the following syntax:

```
trap [action] [list of signals]
```

The action is a statement in the language of the interpreter. Early UNIX shells only accepted signal numbers, but modern shells (like GNU's bash) accept the actual signal macro names as defined in signal.h. Not only is this easier on the user, but it's more portable as well.

As an example, if you write a bash script that has the line

```
trap "echo ouch" SIGABRT
```

and the interpreter calls abort (which raises the SIGABRT signal), the interpreter will print "ouch".

Implementing Trap—It's Obvious!

To implement a trap routine, you must call signal with the appropriate signal translated from its macro name. Unfortunately, the rest is not so simple. The second argument to signal requires a C function, and there is no way for the script programmer to pass the action (which must be coded in the language of the interpreter) this way.

```
signal(SIGABRT, ????);
```

How do you make the association between C code and an interpreter statement? First, assume that the interpreter statement is stored in a character array (called sigabrt_action). Then you can call `signal` with a pointer to a function, say `sigabrt_handler`, that evaluates the interpreter statement.

```
void
sigabrt_handler(sig)
int sig;
{
        eval(sigabrt_action);
}
```

Here, `eval` is presumed to evaluate the string containing the statement the user originally associated with this signal via `trap`. We need to add a few things to `sigabrt_handler`. We need to check that `sigabrt_action` has been set before passing it as an argument, and if not, perform a default action.

A Better Solution

To finish this implementation, we will have to write an `x_handler` and `x_action` for each possible signal `x`, ending up with `sigabrt_handler`, `sigfpe_handler`, `sigill_handler`, and so on. Although Standard C only defines six signals, some implementations define dozens, and because the code is going to be so similar, perhaps we can do better than a completely separate function for each signal.

We can. When a signal handler is executed, it is passed the signal number as its argument. This means that all of those functions can be replaced with a single generic signal handler:

```
/* define NSIG to be the number of signals in your system */
char *actions[NSIG];

void
sig_handler(sig) {
     eval(actions[sig]);
}
```

The complete implementation of the `trap` command follows:

```
int
cmd_trap(action,list,count)
char *action;        /* eval upon signal */
int *list;           /* list of sigs */
int count;           /* how many sigs */
{
        int i;

        for (i=0;i<count;i++,list++) {
             actions[*list] = action;
             signal(*list,sig_handler);
        }
}
```

```
void
init_trap()
{
    int i;

    for (i=0;i<NSIG;i++) actions[i] = 0;
}
```

There is no such thing as an exit signal in Standard C, but it is common and convenient to associate one with the value 0. This allows one to write:

```
trap "echo exiting" 0
```

so that the script will write `exiting` when it exits, no matter how it exits. (This is analogous to the `atexit` function in C.) Since `actions[0]` already exists, supporting signal 0 doesn't cost anything except that the interpreter must call `sig_handler(0)` at termination.

Below is a rewritten signal handler that does the other things I mentioned earlier. I've added a few useful things to `sig_handler`. The first is an `assert` verifying that the delivered signal is defined. This protects us against accessing outside the action array.

Next, we check whether `actions[sig]` is defined. If it isn't, it doesn't make sense that `sig_handler` could have even been called, except for the case where `sig == 0`. The 0 case occurs because `sig_handler(0)` is always called at interpreter exit whether or not a user action has been defined. Once the signal is verified, `signal` is called to reinstall the signal handler for systems that require this.

```
jmp_buf env;
int valid_env = 0;

void sig_handler(sig)
int sig;
{
    assert(sig >= 0 && sig < NSIG);

    if (!actions[sig]) {
        /* always an error except when sig == 0 */
        if (sig == 0) return;
        fprintf(stderr,
            "unexpected signal (%d) received\n",sig);
    } else {
        eval(actions[sig]);
    }
    if (valid_env) longjmp(env,1);
}
```

Finally, a `longjmp` is executed just in case we have defined a valid environment to jump to. For example, we might protect a call to `func` with the code below. While the `trap`'s signal handler forces `setjmp` to return 1 (thereby restarting `func`), other signal handlers could have `setjmp` return other values, allowing `func` to be aborted. As an aside, it is very odd that C does not allow `longjmp` to have `setjmp` return 0. There is no good reason for it!

```
if (1 >= setjmp(env)) {
        valid_env = TRUE;
        func();
}
valid_env = FALSE;
```

The Final Version

Now, I'll present the final version of the procedures to implement the `trap` command. In order to support a few "features" (which I'll explain in a moment), signal information will be stored in the following array of `struct`s, one per signal.

```
struct {
    char *action;
    void (*defaultX) PROTO((int sig));
    char *name;
} signals[NSIG];
```

`action` is the interpreter statement to execute when the signal arrives. If none has been defined, `action` equals 0 and `defaultx`, a C function, is executed. (I put the "x" at the end because `default` is a keyword!) `name` is the word by which the user will know the signal, and is equivalent to the C macro name.

Initializing this array is a little painful (see the following listing), but makes the rest of the code easy. First, the signal names are initialized. The first six are defined by the Standard C. The next one (signal 0) is my convention for `atexit` that I mentioned earlier. After these are several nonstandard (but common) signals. By using `#ifdef`s, the code is portable and yet supports extensions if they are present. Feel free to augment this list of signals. I've provided only a few to give you the idea.

The last part of `init_trap` saves the default actions. Because `signal` does a destructive read, we have to call it twice, the second to rewrite the original value. If you want to provide a default action, you should register it with `signal` before `init_trap` is run. Then, if the user ever sets the signal to `SIG_DFL`, it will be set to your default, not the system's.

```
void
init_trap() {
    int i;

    for (i=0;i<NSIG;i++) {
        signals[i].name = 0;
    }

    /* defined by C standard */
    signals[SIGABRT].name = "SIGABRT";
    signals[SIGFPE ].name = "*SIGFPE";
```

```
        /* "*" means reserved to us - see below */
        signals[SIGILL ].name = "SIGILL";
        signals[SIGINT ].name = "SIGINT";
        signals[SIGSEGV].name = "SIGSEGV";
        signals[SIGTERM].name = "SIGTERM";

        /* our own extension */
        signals[0].name = "ATEXIT";

        /* nonstandard but common */
#if defined(SIGHUP)              /* hangup */
        signals[SIGHUP ].name = "SIGHUP";
#endif

#if defined(SIGALRM)             /* alarm clock */
        signals[SIGALRM].name = "SIGALRM";
#endif

#if defined(SIGPWR)              /* imminent power failure */
        signals[SIGPWR ].name = "SIGPWR";
#endif

#if defined(SIGIO)               /* input/output signal */
        signals[SIGIO  ].name = "SIGIO";
#endif

    for (i=0;i<NSIG;i++) {
        signals[i].action = 0;
        signals[i].defaultX = signal(i,SIG_DFL);
        signal(i,signals[i].defaultX);
    }
}
```

Now we're ready to look at the final `cmd_trap`. I'll explain how it is to be used as I step through the code.

```
#include <stdio.h>
#include <signal.h>
#include <assert.h>
#include <setjmp.h>
#include <string.h>
#include <stdlib.h>

#define streq(x,y)       (0 == strcmp(x,y))

/* reserved to us if name begins with asterisk */
#define SIG_RESERVED(x)(signals[x].name[0] == '*')

void sig_handler();
void print_signal();
```

```
enum cmd_status {CMD_OK, CMD_ERROR};

enum cmd_status
cmd_trap(argc,argv)
int argc;
char **argv;
{
     enum cmd_status rc = CMD_OK;
     char *action = 0;
     int len;              /* length of action */
     int i;

     if (argc == 1) {
         for (i=0;i<NSIG;i++) print_signal(i);
         return(rc);
     }

     if (-1 == string_to_signal(argv[argc-1])) {
         action = argv[argc-1];
         argc--;
     }

     for (i=1;i<argc;i++) {
         int sig = string_to_signal(argv[i]);
         if (sig < 0 || sig >= NSIG) {
             fprintf(stderr,"trap: invalid signal %s",
                                          argv[i]);
             rc = CMD_ERROR;
             break;
         }

         if (!action) {
             print_signal(sig);
             continue;
         }

         if (SIG_RESERVED(sig)) {
             fprintf(stderr,"trap: cannot trap (%s)",
                                          argv[i]);
             rc = CMD_ERROR;
             break;
         }

         if (signals[sig].action)
             free(signals[sig].action);

         if (streq(action,"SIG_DFL")) {
             if (sig != 0)
                 signal(sig,signals[sig].defaultX);
             signals[sig].action = 0;
```

```
        } else {
            len = 1 + strlen(action);
            if (0==(signals[sig].action = malloc(len))) {
                fprintf(stderr,"trap: malloc failed");
                if (sig != 0)
                    signal(sig,signals[sig].defaultX);
                rc = CMD_ERROR;
                break;
            }
            memcpy(signals[sig].action,action,len);
            if (sig == 0) continue;
            if (streq(action,"SIG_IGN")) {
                signal(sig,SIG_IGN);
            } else signal(sig,sig_handler);
        }
    }
    return(rc);
}
```

First, notice that arguments are passed using the **argc/argv** convention. Even though this is not a **main** routine, the convention is a simple way of handling differing arguments that are all of type **char ***. (Compare this to using varargs.)

If no signals are provided as arguments, **trap** just lists the signals for which it has actions defined by calling **print_signal**. If signals are passed as arguments with no action supplied, **trap** lists the actions for just the named signals. **signal_to_string** is a trivial procedure that returns an appropriate printable string describing the given signal. Here are the definitions of **print_signal** and **signal_to_string**.

```
char *
signal_to_string(sig)
int sig;
{
    if (sig < 0 || sig > NSIG) {
        return("SIGNAL OUT OF RANGE");
    } else if (!signals[sig].name) {
        return("SIGNAL UNKNOWN");
    } else return(signals[sig].name + SIG_RESERVED(sig));
}

void
print_signal(sig)
int sig;
{
    if (signals[sig].action) printf("%s (%d): %s\n",
        signal_to_string(sig),sig,signals[sig].action);
}
```

The function `string_to_signal` converts signal names or numbers to the `int` form required by `signal`. `string_to_signal` (below) first tries to interpret the argument as a signal number, then as a signal name. It even tries it without the prefix "`SIG`". If the last element of `argv` isn't a signal, we assume it is an action. Fortunately, the likelihood of an action looking exactly like a signal is remote.

```
/* given signal index or name as string, */
/* returns signal index or -1 if bad arg */
int
string_to_signal(s)
char *s;
{
    int sig;
    char *name;

    /* try interpreting as an integer */
    if (1 == sscanf(s,"%d",&sig)) return(sig);

    /* try interpreting as a string */
    for (sig=0;sig<NSIG;sig++) {
        name = signals[sig].name;
        if (SIG_RESERVED(sig)) name++;
        if (streq(s,name) || streq(s,name+3))
            return(sig);
        }
    return(-1);
}
```

The remainder of `cmd_trap` loops through the signals, defining or printing them as appropriate. Any signal names prefaced by an asterisk are reserved to the interpreter and cannot be set by the user. As an example, in `init_trap`, I reserved `SIGFPE` this way.

In order to set the signal, `sig_trap` discards the old action and saves the new action, allocating and freeing space if necessary. The reason an entirely new copy of the action is saved rather than just a pointer to it is that we must assume the interpreter can throw away the `argv` strings after a command returns. For example, the action string was probably sitting in an input buffer that will be overwritten when the command interpreter reads the next line.

Finally, we call `signal`. Two special actions are recognized. If the action is `SIG_IGN`, the signal is ignored. If the action is `SIG_DFL`, our default signal handler is used. In this case, the action is set to 0 so that signals will not appear in listings, just as when the program begins.

`sig_handler` requires a few minor changes to support the new signal structure. The new version follows:

```
jmp_buf env;
int valid_env = 0;

void
sig_handler(sig)
int sig;
{
    assert(sig >= 0 && sig < NSIG);

    if (!signals[sig].action) {
        /* unexpected except when sig == 0 */
        if (sig == 0) return;
        fprintf(stderr,
            "unexpected signal delivered - %s (%d)\n",
                signal_to_string(sig),sig);
    } else {
        /* avoid reinstalling signal 0 which isn't real */
        if (sig != 0) {      /* reinstall signal handler */
            signal(sig,sig_handler);
        }
        eval(signals[sig].action);
    }

    if (valid_env) longjmp(env,1);
}
```

Caveats

Standard C states that the only thing you can do portably inside a signal handler is set a variable of type `sig_atomic_t`, an integer type. This restriction is severe. My code above violates it, as do many programs. The committee had little choice—they knew that most programs cannot abide by these restrictions, yet they had to recognize how little was truly portable amidst C environments. As P.J. Plauger says in *The Standard C Library*, "no portable use for functions declared in <signal.h> can be defined with complete safety . . . . Any time your program handles signals, accept the fact that you limit its portability."

If you restrict your quest for portability to a particular environment you can do much better. For example, POSIX allows a variety of functions to be called from a signal handler. This extends Standard C's guarantee, because the environment is more narrowly defined.

If you have the choice, of course, you should stick to what's portable, but for many programs this causes tremendous problems. It's probably not something to lose sleep over.

Conclusion

These routines provide a solid implementation of a complete and flexible signal-trapping command for a typical command interpreter. One thing that could be added is a little more error checking. In particular, signal can return `SIG_ERR` upon failure. I'll leave you with the task of integrating this into the code, and thinking about when `signal` could possibly fail. (Don't you just hate when that happens?!)

CHAPTER 38

A Heap of Errors

This chapter solves a common problem with a rarely-used data structure, the heap.

I've found that when most C programmers need to sort something, they turn to `qsort`.[1] That's understandable. It is relatively simple to use, usually fast, and is the only sort routine defined by Standard C or found in traditional C environments. In fact it has excellent characteristics. Its expected performance is O(Nlog$N$) which cannot be beat by any other comparison sort.[2] `qsort` can perform badly (O(N^2)), but this rarely happens.

The notation O(x) is read *"order x"*. O(x) means that the time an algorithm takes to run is proportional to data of size x. This is, in a sense, a measure of how good the implementation is. You could throw in a constant factor. But in reality, significantly large data sets always overwhelm any constant factor. Thus, a superb bubble-sort (which is O(N^2)) will eventually take more time than an unoptimized `qsort` as the amount of data to be sorted is increased. (Compare the two functions *time = 1000N*log*N* vs. *time = 3N²*. When *N* gets large enough, the constant factors 1000 and 3 cease to be important.)

The reason why I found myself looking at other sorts was that I had been asked to speed up a compiler. I discovered that a significant amount of time was being spent processing errors. This didn't seem sensible. Upon closer inspection, I saw that the compiler wrote all its errors to a file, then sorted the file (to reorder errors emitted by multiple passes) and printed the file. To save coding, the sort was done externally to the program with the following code:

```
system("sort errorfile");
```

At first I thought this was very clever. Then I realized that that was exactly the reason why the program was slow—the system had to find space to load the sort program, load it, run it, and then swap back in the compiler. In fact, `system` is traditionally implemented by running yet another program—the command processor—which in turn runs the sort program. Ugh!

I resolved to do the sorting internally to the program, thus saving the creation of the two extra processes. I also wanted to avoid using dynamic memory allocation, or

---

1. Neither Classic C nor Standard C requires it, but `qsort` implementations invariably use Quicksort.
2. In this chapter, all logs are assumed to be base 2.

even consuming arbitrary amounts of stack space—after all, I might have ended up in the error handler specifically because space had run out!

Heapsort is an excellent solution for this problem—much better than `qsort`. Heapsort can run in a fixed amount of data and stack space. And unlike `qsort`, Heapsort is O(*N*log*N*) even in the worst case. I'll explain later exactly how we know this.

Heap

A heap is a binary tree with data stored at every node. It is weakly ordered—the only constraint is that parent nodes are smaller than their children. (The ordering can be reversed, of course.) Below is an example of a heap. It is not sorted in any usual sense. There is no simple way to print the nodes in sorted order, such as a depth-first or breadth-first traversal.

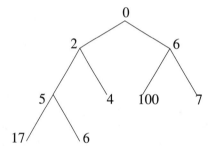

Notice how each number is smaller than the two directly below it. That's the heap constraint. The only remaining restriction is that the tree remain balanced. In particular there can be a difference of at most one level between any two leaves, and leaves must be added to the heap from left to right. Each level must be completely filled before adding leaves at a new level. In the tree above, a new node would be created as the left-hand child of node 4. For example, suppose we need to add a 1.

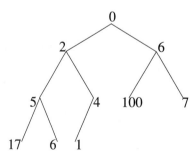

Adding a 1 to the end of the tree causes the heap constraint to be violated, but it is easy to fix things up. Because the 1 is smaller than the 4, we must swap them. Although this fixes the local problem, it creates another problem. Namely, the 2 is larger than the 1. We can swap the 1 and 2 in the same way, leaving us with a tree that again satisfies the heap constraint.

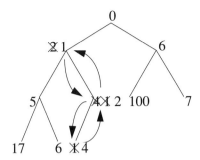

In this way, we can continue adding elements. The number of swaps that each additional element may require is at most the height of the tree (minus 1) or log$N$. Since there are N items to be added, we can build the heap in Nlog$N$ time.

Sorting the Heap

In the compiler I described, every error message generated gets put on the heap. At the end of the program (or when we've run out of heap memory), we want to print out the messages in order. Interestingly, it is not necessary to sort the heap in order to do this.

All we need to do is somehow be handed each entry in the heap in order. We do it as follows. The first number is easy—it is always at the top of the heap. If we remove it, we need to shift things around. If we can massage the N-1 elements of the heap into a new heap, then we can repeat this procedure for every entry in the heap.

To fix the heap and leave it a balanced tree at the same time, first move the final element (right-most bottom leaf) to the root of the tree. I've reproduced the tree above after removing the old root (0) and moving the final element (4) to the root.

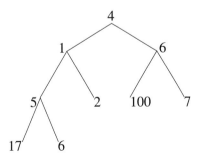

Because the 4 is bigger than its left child, we must swap the 4 and the 1. That leaves the 4 as the parent of 2, a smaller element. These must be swapped also, leaving the tree as a heap.

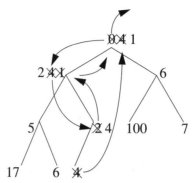

Again, it takes time at most log$N$ (the height of the tree) to retrieve the smallest element and reestablish the heap constraint. Since there are N elements to remove, we can remove them all in Nlog$N$ time.

We can enter elements into the heap in eNlog$N$ time and delete them in dNlog$N$ time, where e and d are constants defining how long it takes to manipulate a node while entering and deleting. All together this means the algorithm requires $(d+e)N$log$N$ time. The (d+e) is an example of a constant factor, as I mentioned earlier. A good compiler can easily lower the constant, but it can't do anything about the Nlog$N$ part. Thus, we just call the algorithm O(Nlog$N$) and leave it at that.

An implementation based on a literal interpretation of what I've described would use a binary tree and a lot of calls to `malloc`. However, there is a faster way of implementing a heap. And it will turn out to be simpler, too.

Observe that a binary tree can be stored in an array in breadth-wise order. In the diagram below, the nth array element is the node in the tree with the corresponding label. A convenient property of this representation is that the parent of node i is node i/2, and the children of node j are nodes k*2 and k*2+1. The math is simpler when counting from 1, so element 0 in the array is simply ignored.

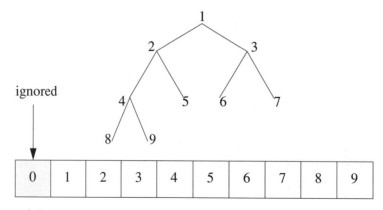

Elements of the array must contain space for a pointer to an error message and a line number. The array can be declared as follows:

```
#define ERROR_MAX    100

static struct heap_element {
     int line;
     char *msg;
} heap[ERROR_MAX+1];

static int error_count = 0;
```

error_count is the number of errors in the array.

To make the heap relatively transparent to the application, I've written a function eprintf, which is just like printf except that output is buffered in the heap. The first argument is a printf-like format string. The second argument is always a line number. This is used to sort the messages, of course. I've chosen to have the error routine itself prefix all messages with a standardized line number format, so there is no need to embed a %d in the format for the line number.

For instance, if lineno had the value 17, and varname had the value "foo", the statement:

```
eprintf("undeclared variable: %s",lineno,varname);
```

would produce the following output:

```
line 17: undeclared variable: foo
```

It is easy to modify this format if you wish.

Now, I'll go through the implementation; it takes surprisingly little code. There are two halves to the code. The top half is called each time you want to print an error. The bottom half is called to do the final printing in sorted order.

eprintf is defined below by a function that takes a variable number of arguments using the varargs conventions (see p. 131 in Chapter 16). After separating the first two arguments (which are always the format and line number), a new node is added to the heap. error_count contains the number of errors generated so far, which is also useful as an index to the end of the heap. We now begin the procedure of installing the new error at the end of the heap and swapping it upwards to its rightful spot.

Part of the swapping isn't physically necessary. Since the new error is always going to be one of the nodes to be swapped, we can just remember to install it after all the other movement is done. What's left is to move all the larger values down and out of the way. This is accomplished by the while loop with the inner assignment heap[child] = heap[parent]. Notice that this is a structure assignment; we are assigning both the line number and error message at the same time. I could have used pointers, but since it is only two small elements per struct, it didn't seem worth the trouble.

```
/* 1st arg is format, 2nd is line #, other args are whatever is */
/* demanded by the format */
/* Standard C */                    /* Classic C */
void                                void
eprintf(char *fmt, int line, ...)   eprintf(va_alist)
                                    va_dcl
{                                   {
    int child, parent;                  int child, parent;
                                        char *fmt;
                                        int line;
    va_list arg;                        va_list arg;

    va_start(arg,line);                 va_start(arg);
                                        fmt = va_arg(arg,char *);
                                        line = va_arg(arg,int);

    /* remainder is common to both Classic C and Standard C */
    child = ++error_count;
    parent = child/2;
    while (parent) {
        if (line < heap[parent].line) {
            heap[child] = heap[parent];
        } else break;
        child = parent;
        parent = child/2;
    }
    heap[child].line = line;
    heap[child].msg = error_string;

    vsprintf(error_string,fmt,arg);
    error_string += strlen(error_string) + 1;

    if (error_string + ERROR_MAX_STRLEN >
                    error_string_base + ERROR_MAX_SPACE
        || error_count == ERROR_MAX) {
        eflush();
    }

    va_end(arg);
}
```

Finally, the new error is installed in its rightful position. All that is left is to copy the string into a new buffer and link that to the actual heap. I have chosen to store all the error messages in one large chunk of space. `error_string_base` is a pointer to the base of this memory, and `error_string` is a pointer to the unused part of it. In `eprintf`, it is simply moved to the end of the new error message by adding the length of the message (plus 1 for the 0 byte at the end) to itself.

This static allocation allows us to avoid the problems of running out of space and not being able to print any errors at all. A large buffer is hardly necessary. Even 4K would be impressive for a typical C compiler. You can do this at the beginning of your program as follows:

```
#define ERROR_MAX_SPACE          4000
static char error_string_base[ERROR_MAX_SPACE];
static char *error_string = error_string_base;
#define ERROR_MAX_STRLEN         200
```

I've added the definition `ERROR_MAX_STRLEN`, which is the length of the largest string that could appear as an error. This will prevent writing past the end of the `error_string_base` array. It is used as follows: after inserting an error into memory, if the space remaining is less than `ERROR_MAX_STRLEN`, the errors are flushed immediately.

The error flushing routine, `eflush`, is shown below. It follows the idea sketched out earlier on how to print the heap. First, the top of the heap is printed. This is always the smallest remaining element, and it is always at `heap[1]`.

This element is replaced with the last element in the heap, called `replace` in the code. It then percolates down into the heap, finding its appropriate spot. All that is necessary is to iterate, finding the smaller of the children at each node, and then comparing to see whether the `replace` node is still greater than the smallest child.

As with the top half `eprintf` function, there is no need to actually swap values because `replace` is always going to be overwritten until the final movement. Thus, nodes appear to bubble upward until the final statement when `replace` overwrites the last node that was less than it.

This restores the heap condition so that the next outer iteration will continue the process properly, printing the lowest remaining entry.

```
void
eflush()
{
    while (error_count) {
        struct heap_element *replace;
        int parent, child;

        fprintf(stderr,"line %d: %s\n",heap[1].line,
                                    heap[1].msg);

        replace = &heap[error_count--];

        child = 1;
        while (1) {
            parent = child;
            if (child > error_count) break;
            if (child+1 <= error_count) {
                    if (heap[child].line > heap[child+1].line)
                        child++;
            }
```

```
            if (replace->line <= heap[child].line) break;
            heap[parent] = heap[child];
        }
        heap[parent] = *replace;
    }
}
```

Conclusion

To recap, the runtime of this implementation is O(*N*log*N*). I haven't analyzed the constant factor, but I'll mention that Quicksort is usually considered to have a constant factor that is half that of Heapsort. However, in this application, Heapsort does extremely well. It avoids dynamic memory allocation, recursion, and excess function calls, easily beating out any `qsort` implementation. Plus, there is no fear of running out of stack space, which is an important concern in an error handler.

At the beginning of this chapter, I said that Heapsort was a rarely-used algorithm. Well, that's not entirely true. It's very common in operating systems for maintaining priority lists such as scheduler and I/O queues, and is an important building block in many advanced data structures and algorithms.

Nevertheless, it is often given short shrift by C programmers simply because `qsort` is a sort routine provided by the standard library, which you can plug in with little thought. Nonetheless, `qsort` isn't the best answer to all sorting needs. I've shown only one alternative here, but perhaps you'll add it to your bag of techniques and feel inclined to investigate some of the other sorting possibilities as well.

## CHAPTER 39

The 1991 Obfuscated C Code Contest

This chapter contains the final installment of the winners (so far) of the annual Obfuscated C Code Contest. I'd like to congratulate all the winners and encourage everyone to participate again in future years.

And now the 1991 winners. (*Drum roll.*) The envelope please . . .

Best Utility

Anthony C Howe <ant@mks.com>
Mortice Kern Systems Inc.
Waterloo, Ontario, Canada

```
#include <ctype.h>
#include <curses.h>
#define T isspace(*(t=Z(p)))&&
#define V return
#define _ while
int d,i,j,m,n,p,q,x,y;char*c,b[BUF],*f,*g=b,*h,k[]="hjklHJKL[]tbixWRQ",*t;
char*Z(a){if(a<0)V b;V b+a+(b+a<g?0:h-g);}P(a)char*a;{V
a-b-(a<h?0:h-g);}S(){p=0;}bf(){n=p=P(c);}Q(){q=1;}C(){clear();Y();}
G(){t=Z(p);_(t<g)*--h= *--g;_(h<t)*g++= *h++;p=P(h);}B(){_(!T b<t)--p;_(T
b<t)--p;}M(a){_(b<(t=Z(--a))&&*t-'\n');V
b<t?++a:0;}N(a){_((t=Z(a++))<c&&*t-'\n');V
t<c?a:P(c);}A(a,j){i=0;_((t=Z(a))<c&&*t-'\n'&&i<j){i+= *t-'\t'?1:8-(i&7);++a;}
V
a;}L(){_{0<p&&--p;}R(){_{p<P(c)&&++p;}U(){p=A(M(M(p)-1),x);}
D(){p=A(N(p),x);}H(){p=M(p);}E(){p=N(p);L();}
J(){m=p=M(n-1);_(0<y--)D();n=P(c);}K(){j=d;_(0<--j)m=M(m-1),U();}
I(){G();_((j=getch())-'\f'){if(j-'\b')g-h&&(*g++=j-'\r'?j:'\n');else
b<g&&--g;p=P(h);Y();}}X(){G();p=h<c?P(++h):p;}
F(){j=p;p=0;G();write(i=creat(f,MODE),h,(int)(c-h));close(i);p=j;}W(){_(!T
t<c)++p;_(T
t<c)++p;}int(*z[])()={L,D,U,R,B,J,K,W,H,E,S,bf,I,X,F,C,Q,G};
Y(){m=p<m?M(p):m;if(n<=p){m=N(p);i=m-P(c)?d:d-2;_(0<i--)m=M(m-1);}
move(0,0);i=j=0;n=m;_(1){p-n||(y=i,x=j);t=Z(n);if(d<=i||c<=t)break;
if(*t-'\r')addch(*t),j+= *t-'\t'?1:8-(j&7);if(*t=='\n'||COLS<=j)
++i,j=0;++n;}clrtobot();++i<d&&mvaddstr(i,0,"<< EOF >>");move(y,x);
refresh();}main(u,v)char**v;{h=c=b+BUF;if(u<2)V
2;initscr();d=LINES;raw();noecho();idlok(stdscr,1);if(0<(i=open(f= *++v,0))){
g+=read(i,b,BUF);g=g<b?b:g;close(i);}S();_(!q){Y();i=0;j=getch();
_(k[i]&&j-k[i])++i;(*z[i])();}endwin();V 0;}
```

This program implements a small yet fast and complete full-screen editor. While the author wants it to be known that he does not normally write obfuscated code, he professed spending 10 months writing the unobfuscated version upon which this program is based. While the program has many of the usual obfuscations, the author claims that much of the credit for being able to implement a real editor in such a small program goes to choosing the right algorithms. The critical algorithm for the program is called the Buffer Gap Scheme and is described here courtesy of Stephen Trier of Case Western Reserve University.

Analysis

"The idea is to divide the file into two sections at the cursor point, the location at which the next change will take place. These sections are placed at opposite ends of the buffer, with the *gap* in between them representing the cursor point. For example, here's a sixteen-character buffer containing the words `The net`, with the cursor on the letter `n`:

```
The --------net
```

(The "–" is used to represent the spaces making up the gap.)

"If you want to insert a character, all you must do is to add it into one end or the other of the gap. Conventional editors that move the cursor left as you type would insert at the top edge of the gap. For example, if I wanted to change the word `net` to `Usenet`, I would start by typing the letter `U`, and the editor would change the buffer to look like this:

```
The U-------net
```

"This represents the string `The Unet`, with the cursor still on the `n`. Typing an `s` followed by an `e` produces the following two snapshots:

```
The Us------net
The Use-----net
```

"Changing the phrase from `The Usenet` to `The Usenix` requires moving our cursor to the right one spot, so we don't waste time retyping an `n`. To move the cursor point back and forth through the file, we must move letters *across* the gap. In this case, we're moving the cursor toward the end of the phrase, so we move the `n` across the gap, to the top end.

```
The Usen-----et
```

"Now we're ready to delete the `e` and the `t`. To do this, we just widen the gap at the bottom edge, wiping out the appropriate character. After deleting the `e` and then the `t`, the buffer looks like these snapshots:

```
The Usen------t
The Usen-------_
```

(Note that the gap now extends all the way to the edge of the buffer. This means that the file now reads `The Usen`, with the cursor at the very end.) Backspacing works out to be something very similar to delete, with the gap widening at the top instead of the bottom.

"Adding the letters **i** and **x** gives the following snapshots after each key is pressed:

```
The Useni-------_
The Usenix------_
```

"Moving the cursor back to the top of the file means moving the characters across the buffer in the other direction, starting with the **x**, like this:

```
The Useni------x
```

"Finally, after doing this once for each of the letters in the buffer, we're at the top of the file, and the buffer looks like this:

```
------The Usenix
```

"Of course, there are many details yet to consider. Real buffers will be much larger than this, probably starting at 64K and stopping at whatever size is appropriate for the machine at hand. In a real implementation, line breaks have to be marked in some way. Moving the cursor between lines can get complicated, and virtual memory must be considered when the data to be stored is larger than the gap. Finally, there's the question of making the screen reflect the contents of the buffer.

"For more information on the Buffer Gap Scheme, read Craig A. Finseth in 'Theory and Practice of Text Editors or A Cookbook For An EMACS' (TM-165, MIT Laboratory for Computer Science)."

The unobfuscated code to the program shown here is indeed small. For example, moving the cursor to the left is simply decrementing an index as long as it is not 0.

```
void
left()
{
        if (0 < index) --index;
}
```

Moving to the right is only slightly more complicated. Here **pos** computes the true end of the buffer (**ebuf**) by subtracting the space used by the gap.

```
void right()
{
        if (index < pos(ebuf)) ++index;
}
```

The author is being extremely efficient. Rather than move the gap around (as the theory suggests), he waits until there is actual editing. Until then, cursor motion is just a matter of changing a single variable.

Here is **delete**, which enlarges the gap as described above and updates the cursor position. Since a change has been made to the buffer, **movegap** is called to synchronize the gap and the trivial manipulations that were done by **left** and **right**.

```
void delete()
{
        movegap();
        if (egap < ebuf) index = pos(++egap);
}
```

Of course, after each operation the screen is updated (courtesy of curses, a popular library for character-graphics applications). This and some other machinery is not shown but is also quite small. Combining the usual gamut of obfuscation plus lots of free time led to this incredibly small implementation.

Best of Show

Daniel J. Bernstein <brnstnd@nyu.edu>
New York University
New York, New York

```
#include <stdio.h>
#define D define
#D H(x,y,z)  f(p){--p;c=x-_+1];f(c>0){y+1]=z[c];z[c]=y];y]=y+1];}}
#D O(x,y)  F(x,int U;int T=0;d=M(U=1);W{f(c==y)b g[T++]=c;f(T==U)g=real-
loc(g,U<<=1);}g[T]=0;)
#D W  Y((c=k?K[--k]:getchar())-EOF)
#D S  i[q
#D F(w,z)  f(c==w){z h}
#D f  if
#D P  p>1&&(c=u,
#D _  s[p
#D C  =G
#D g  S]
#D J(x,y)  F(I[x],y)
#D Q  P e
#D Y  while
#D b  break;
#D u  _--]
#D m  p&&
#D R  char*
#D l  Z[c]
#D L  strlen
#D d  i[++q]
#D G  c)
#D h  ;continue;
#D N  s[++p]
#D e  _]
#D j  x;{R r=M(L(
#D v  return
#D w  [256]
#D V  f(k>o||p>o||q>o)v 2;
R I="I'd love ta win: the most useful !$>%'/#<&*|^ _OBFUSCATED_ utility.
Pleez?";U(y,x)R y;R*j*x)+L(y)+1);sprintf(r,"%s%s",*x,y);*x=r;}R T(x)R j
x)+1);strcpy(r,x);v
```

```
r;}R(i w);static R(Z w);K w;main(a,A)int a;R*A;{int s
w,p=0,q=0,n=0,c,k=0;W{V
f(c>='0'&&c<='9'){f(!n)N=0;n=1;e=10*e+(c-'0')h}n=0;J(39,m
sprintf(d=M(13),"%d",e))
J(37,q&&puts(g))J(34,q&&printf("%s",g))J(27,H(p,_,s))O('[',']')J(56,f(p
){c=e;N=c;})J(2,m--p)J(10,N=a)J(4,f(q){N=L(g);X(S--
]);})J(1,f(q){S+1]=T(g);++q;})J(53,m
e>=0&&e<a&&(d=T(A[u])))
J(54,q>1&&(--q,U(S+1],i+q)))J(5,q&&p>1&&(_-1]=open(g,_-1],e),--p,X(S--
])))J(47,m
close(u))
J(26,m(e=dup(e)))O('"','"')J(51,H(q,S,i))J(49,N=fork())J(12,wait(&N)+1|
|(e=-1))J(68,{++p;pipe(s+p++)==-1&&(e=-1);})F('q',v
0)
F('=',W{R x;f(m u)f(x=1){k+=n=L(x);V;Y(*x)K[--k]=*x++;k+=n;n=0;}b})-
J(15,f(q)W{1&&X(1);l=T(g);b})J(33,f(c=q){*i=g;g=0;Y(--q&&**(i+q))g++;-
f(q){N=execvp(*i,i+q+1);q=c;}})J(38,P
c&&(e/C))
J(35,Q=e>G)F('+',Q+C)J(42,Q*C)J(41,Q=~(e&G))J(57,m(e=-e))J(3,)F('\n',)-
putchar(c);puts(73+I);}}
```

This program defines a new language: SORTA. It's got features sorta from C, sorta from Forth, and sorta from Ada. It's sorta a joke, but the author has crammed in 20 different stack operations and enough basic system calls to do some useful things. The author says,

> SORTA lets you manipulate files and spawn programs easily, has bitwise operators, and gives you absolutely brilliant error messages like "?" (that's the C bit). SORTA programs work with a stack (that's the FORTH bit)—actually two stacks, one for integers and one for strings. And all SORTA operations are strongly typed, detect practically any failure, and garbage-collect (that's the Ada bit).

Perhaps the highlight of the implementation is the string embedded in the program that evidently helped get it selected as a winner. The value of I ("I'd love ta win ...") while seemingly a plea to the judges, is actually used by the program as a map of command names to actions.

A sample piece of obfuscated code looks like this:

```
J(39,m sprintf(d=M(13),"%d",e))
```

which, after some twisted macro expansions, becomes:

```
if (c == I[39]) {
    p && sprintf (i[++q] = M (13), "%d", s[p]);
    continue;
}
```

Character 39 in the I array is a # which is defined in SORTA as "make top of i stack non-destructively in ASCII, push result onto s stack." As mentioned above, the program uses a separate stack for integers and strings. Naturally, they are reverse-named, as we can see in the fragment above. The M is a call to `malloc` (defined outside the program), here arbitrarily allocating 13 bytes for every integer.

Most Useful Label

Christian Dupont <cdupont@ensl.ens-lyon.fr>
Ecole Normale Superieure de Lyon
Laboratoire d'Informatique Parallele
Lyon, France

```
    /* common sense  to nohonest programmer */
#include <stdio.h>
main(){int x   ,gi=4,i,f,ri=1,httxkbl=1,m=012;long cd=0x5765248d,n;
    char u[0x50][032];FILE *ind;
       ind=fopen(s,t); for(i=0; i<0x1a; i++){goto daswjhkls;vhjsgfdylllgjhd:;}
/*borntorun.*/goto cOgO;cOgO:i=0;fclose(ind);cOgO:
x=  u [gi][m]; sorryfor_this_unused_but_very_needed_label:
    if(  m==gi){x=0x70;f=0x68;}else goto cOgO ; b:putchar(x); if(
!(n-httxkbl++))
#define yank putchar('
  {httxkbl=1;         yank ');goto
   hxi;}goto bl;
            /* hardlyundrstandable, but
likely to be missed if removed */
    daswjhkls:    fgets(u[i], 0120, ind);
  /*obfuscated, eh? */goto
   vhjsgfdylllgjhd;
          cOgO : n=cd&0x40000000L>>0x1e;
 goto         cOgO;    g6w:
              if(x!=0x2e){i++;goto cOgO;}else /*
injail*/yank\n');goto vhjsgfdylllgjhd;
cOgO :
f=u[m][gi];goto b;bl:m=(i+1)*(4*
x+3*f)%032;gi=(i+1)*(x+2*f)%0x1a; goto g6w;
  hxi:cd^=        n=  cd&(7<<3*(014-++ri));
n >>=3*(12-ri); goto bl;vhjsgfdylllgjhd:;}
```

This program must be compiled with the option `-Ds="cdupont.c"` and `-Dt="r"` where `cdupont.c` is the name of the program itself. When run the program says:

```
    f u cn ndrstnd ths u cn gt gd jb n cmptr scnc.
```

Analysis

This program reads its own source into an array and then proceeds to derive the output string from the source. Characters in certain positions tell the program what to output and where to look next for new characters. Whitespace is introduced depending on values encoded in one of the constants at the beginning of the program.

The program has numerous labels but these are not so much for producing hard-to-follow control flow as they are for providing data as the program itself is being read. In fact, one label isn't even the target of any `goto`. It is apologetically named `sorryfor_this_unused_but_very_needed_label`. Placing the right character in the right position probably wasn't a fun task for the author. Fortunately, he could create new identifiers, rename old ones, insert whitespace, and add `hardlyun-drstandable` comments to make the characters fall exactly where they were needed.

Best X11 Graphics

David Applegate <david+@cs.cmu.edu>
School of Computer Science, Carnegie Mellon University
Pittsburgh, Pennsylvania

Guy Jacobson <guy@ulysses.att.com>
AT&T Bell Laboratories
Murray Hill, New Jersey

```
#define _ define
#_ u unsigned
#_ w char*
#_ j(x)(*(*(x*)&T)++)
#_ H j(short*)
#_ K j(w)
#_ e j(u*)
#_ r register u
#_ R(b)write(A,T=h,4*b);
#_ S (u*)sbrk(Q*4+U*8)+U
#_ E(a,b,c)a=c&1<<31|b/2;c=c*2|b&1;
#_ V q= *L;L+=F;E(d,q,x)E(f,d,s)g=f&q;f^=q
#_ W while(
#_ Z q=I&f;M|=q&c;c^=q;I^=f;M|=g&c;c^=g
#_ Y W(F= *s++)&16)*T=10**T+F-'0';T++
#_ D(q,s)c);W q>s)G= *--q,*q= *s,*s++=G;
#_ P if(i^z){x=Q+(n=D(x,n)
#_ C if(i){q=Q*4+(s=(w)D(q,s)
u A,U,Q,J,X[9999];main(a,b)w*b;{r*c,*d,y,f,g,F,G,I,M,N,z,*x,*n,i;w q,*h=(w)X,*
T,*s=".slo.-W00,tmhw.W/";T=h;if(a>1){H=2;K=23;K=112;s=b[1];Y;Y;Y;Y;}else{H=1;W
*s)K=1+*s++;}connect(A=socket(a,1,0),T=h,24-a*4);H=17004;H=11;e=0;e=0;i=66==*h
;R(3)read(A,h,8);e;H;read(A,h,4*H);T=h;e;F=e;e;e;I=11+H;f=H-6;K;U=K;i^=K;z=!K;
T+=I/4*4+8*U;I=e;T+=16;U=H/32;J=H/30*30;T+=14;M=K;f/=U;T=h;K=55;K;H=4;e=F;e=I;
e=0;R(4)N=F+8192;K=53;K=M;H=4;e=N;e=I;H=U*32;H=J;R(4)K=2;K;H=4;e=I;e=1;e=N;R(4
)Q=J*U;c=S;d=S;L(c);W 1){P}C}y=0;W y<J){K=72;K=0;g=J-y;H=6+U*(g>f?g=f:g);e=N;e
=F;H=U*32;H=g;H=0;H=y;K=0;K=1;R(6)write(A,c+y*U,g*U*4);y+=g;}K=61;K=0;H=4;e=I;
e=0;e=0;R(4)C}P}v(c,d);}}L(A)r*A;{r*T=A+Q,X=getpid();W A<T)*A++=X=3*X^X/2;}v(n
,O)u*n,*O;{r*A,F=U,*L=n-F,*G=L+Q,I,c,d,M,f,g,N,q,i=0,X,T,v,s,x,*y,*z;W L<n){*L
= *G;G++[F]=L++[F];}W i<J){z=O+i*F;y=n+i*F-F;i+=30;L=y-1;A=L+U*32;W L<A){L+=F;
E(X,*L,x)E(q,X,s)}X=0;W X++<F){L=y++;G=z++;V;c=g|f&d;I=f^d;V;W L<=A){M=0;Z;N=d
;T=f;v=g;V;Z;c^=I&d;*G=c&~M&(I^d|N);G+=F;c=v|T&N;I=T^N;}}}z=0;y=n;I=J;W--I!=-1
){f= *z>>31;G=z+F;L=y+F;W G>z){M= *--G;*--L=(M*2)+f;f=M>>31;}z+=F;y+=F;}}
```

This program plays Conway's game of Life on an X window server. It actually draws on the root window so that if you have other windows doing things, they won't be disturbed. The program can be called as:

```
davidguy ip-address:server.screen
```

where IP address is a dotted quad address such as `127.0.0.1`. Amusingly, if you rename the program `guydavid`, it runs in reverse video. (The actual code to make this decision just looks at the least-significant-bit of the first character in the name.)

Authors' Analysis

"The program starts by setting the background to random bits, and then plays Life, with one cell for each pixel of the screen. In the game of Life, a cell survives to the next round if 2 or 3 of its 8 neighbors are also alive, and a cell is born if exactly 3 of its neighbors are alive. A cell dies of exposure if it has only 0 or 1 neighbors, and dies of overcrowding if it has 4 or more neighbors.

"The algorithm used to compute the next generation is based on the observation that a cell's state in the next generation is a Boolean function of its current state, and the states of its 8 neighbors (i.e., a Boolean function from 9 bits to 1 bit). This function can be computed by a Boolean circuit. In addition, intermediate values computed by the circuit can be shared between neighboring cells, reducing the number of gates per cell required. These ideas have been used before, to compute the next generation through a series of bitblits. Instead of doing this, we map values in the circuit to bits in registers, so that the next generation can be computed efficiently within registers, minimizing memory accesses. As a result, the computation of the next generation is performed with about 1.6 instructions per life cell, consisting of 0.125 memory accesses, 0.17 shifts, and 1.3 logic operations. The net result is that the time to transfer the bits to the X server, and for the X server to draw them on the screen, dominates the time to compute the next generation.

"We think the program is interesting for these reasons:

1. It implements an extremely efficient algorithm for the computation it performs. One cool feature of the algorithm (at least as far as this contest is concerned) is that its obscurity is fundamentally necessary for its efficiency. In other words, even if we took steps to present the algorithm clearly, relating the computation performed to the specification of what the program was supposed to do would still be hard to understand.

2. It belongs to a class of programs that programmers make the following complaints about: they require a mountain of code to implement even the simplest program, and they must be linked with giant libraries of hard-to-understand functions. In contrast to these complaints (made by wimps, in our humble opinion), our program fits in under 1536 bytes, doesn't need any external functions except for a few system calls, and doesn't need to include any header files."

This is hardly a fair comparison. The authors have ruthlessly sacrificed readability, and after expanding the preprocessor directives, the program is actually 5.5K. Even at that length, it is difficult making even the slightest change since everything is hard-coded at the lowest level.

Most Well-Rounded Confusion

Diomidis Spinellis <dds@doc.ic.ac.uk>
Imperial College of Science, Technology and Medicine
University of London
London, England

```
#include <stdio.h>
#define Q r=R[*p++-'0'];while(
#define B ;break;case
char*s="Qjou!s\\311^-g\\311^-n\\311^-c\\::^-q-ma%mO1JBHm%BQ-aP1J[O1HB%[Q<nbj\
o)*|gps)<<*txjudi)m*|aQdbtf!::::;sfuvso<aQefgbvmu;aQ<m,,a%CQ<csfbla%bQ<aN2!Q\
\ndbtf!aP2Q;m>aP2Q<a%!D12J!JGJHJOJQJFJSJJJMHS%HD12D12N3!N4\nJUJT%UQm>aP4HC%T\
Qs\\q,,^>m,2<m>aP4HC%SD12N1\nJNQm>s\\..q^aHC%NHb%GN1!D32P3%RN1UP1D12JPQUaP1H\
R%PN4\nQ<g\\(aP3Q(^>aP2Q,2<n\\(aP3Q(^>aP4Hb%OD12D12N2!N3\nJVP3Q,,<jg)aP3Q=>n\
\\(aP3Q(^*m>g\\(aP3Q(^<fmtf!m,,aHC%QN1!N1\nJ#Qqsjoug)#&e]o#-aP1Q*aHb%#Qqvut)\
aP1Q*aHb%FN1\nQm>::::aHC%VP3Q>bupj)hfut)c**aHb%JD12JON1!Qjg)a%LN1UP1D12JIQUa\
P1HL%IQ*m>aN2!N2\nP2Q<fmtf!m,,aHC%MN1!N2>P2Q>aN2\nP2Hbdd!b/d";k;char R[4][99]
;main(c,v)char**v;{char*p,*r,*q;for(q=s;*q;q++)*q>' '&&(*q)--;{FILE*i=fopen(v
[1],"r"),*o=fopen(q-3,"w");for(p=s;;p++)switch(*p++){B'M':Q(k=fgetc(i))!=EOF
&&k!=*p)*r++=k;if(k==EOF){fputs("}}\n",o);fclose(o);return system(q-6);}*r=0
B'P':while(*p!='')fputc(*p++,o)B'O':Q*r)fputc(*r++,o);p--B'C':k=0;Q k<*p-'0'
)(*r++=fgetc(i),k++);*r=0 B'I':k= *p;if(**R==k)goto G B'G':k= *p;G:p=s;while(
*p!='$'||p[1]!= k)p++;p++B'N':R[*p-'0'][0]++;}}}
```

This entry nicely complements the author's winner from the previous year, a BASIC interpreter. This winning entry is a BASIC compiler!

Author's Analysis

"Having a problem at hand, I started designing the system. A compiler translates code from the source language into executable code of the target machine. This means that the compiler implementer (i.e., me) would need to know the target machine architecture and instructions. This would make the compiler unportable as it would work only for a specific machine architecture (e.g., VAX, Sun3, or SPARC). A recent trend that overcomes this difficulty is to have the compiler produce C code instead of target machine assembly language. After the compiler finishes, it executes the system C compiler, which then translates the C code into native code. Thus C is treated as a portable assembly language. Some compilers that are implemented using this technique are the original AT&T C++ compiler, along with the Eiffel and Sather compilers.

"Mapping BASIC into C was easy:

- Variables remain the same. At the top of the C file all are declared:

```
int A,B,C,D,E,F,G,H,I,J,K,L,M,N,O,P,Q,R,S,T,U,V,W,X,Y,Z;
```

  Expressions can therefore be converted directly to C code.

- Line number sequencing is implemented by a **switch** statement within an endless loop:

```
for (;;)
```

```
switch (line) {
case 10: line = 10; /* Code for line 10 */
case 20: line = 20; /* Code for line 20 */
...
case 9999: return;
default: line++;
}
```

When a line does not exist, the **default** case is executed. This increments the line pointer until a suitable line is found. When the last line is executed, the line pointer is incremented up to 9999 and the program terminates. Control is normally transferred by falling through from one **case** statement to the other (i.e., no **break** statement is provided).

- All statements that change the flow of control (GOTO, GOSUB, RETURN, IF, FOR, NEXT) are simply implemented by assigning to the line number variable and executing **break**. GOSUB is handled by pushing the calling line number into a small integer array stack and RETURN by popping it out. FOR stores the line number where it was executed and the maximum limit into an array indexed by the variable number. Examples:

```
GOTO 70              becomes    line = 70;

GOSUB 500            becomes    stack[pointer++] = line;
                                line = 500;

RETURN              becomes    line = stack[--pointer];

IF A > 30 THEN 80    becomes    if (A > 30) line = 80;

FOR I = 1 TO 10      becomes    I = 1;
                                forline['I'] = line + 1;
                                limit['I']= 11;

NEXT I               becomes    I++;
                                if (I <= limit['I'])
                                        line = forline['I'];
```

- PRINT is converted into **printf** or **puts** and INPUT into **atoi(gets(buffer))**.

"As an example, the following is a naive prime number calculation program in BASIC and its translation into C by the compiler:

```
10 REM Calculate prime numbers up to 30000
20 REM By Diomidis Spinellis.
25 PRINT "0, 1, 2"
30 FOR I = 3 TO 30000
40    FOR J = 2 TO I - 1
50     IF (I / J) * J == I THEN 80
60    NEXT J
```

```
70    PRINT I
80 NEXT I
90 END

int r[200],f[200],m[200],b[99],p,l,
A,B,C,D,E,F,G,H,I,J,K,L,M,N,O,P,Q,R,S,T,U,V,W,X,Y,Z;
main(){for(;;)switch(l){case 9999:return;default:;l++;break;
case 10:l=10;;
case 20:l=20;;
case 25:l=25;puts("Prime numbers:");
case 30:l=30;I = 3 ;f['I']=30+1;m['I']= 30000;
case 40:l=40;J = 2 ;f['J']=40+1;m['J']= I - 1;
case 50:l=50;if((I / J) * J == I )l=80;else l++;break;
case 60:l=60;J++;if(J<=m['J'])l=f['J'];else l++;break;
case 70:l=70;printf("%d\n",I);
case 80:l=80;I++;if(I<=m['I'])l=f['I'];else l++;break;
case 90:l=90;l=9999;break;}}
```

"The next step in the design was the definition of a suitable language for implementing the compiler. The language had to be easy to interpret, yet powerful enough to enable a concise implementation of the compiler. After some thought, I designed the COGMIP$ abstract machine, named after its six instructions. An abstract machine is simply the description of a machine that does not actually exist as hardware. These machines have a number of theoretical and practical advantages and uses. A famous abstract machine is the Turing machine, a computer science artifact for describing all possible problems such as whether a program that finds if a program terminates can be written (this is known as the Halting Problem). Other abstract machines have been actually implemented as interpreters, and are used for executing exotic programming languages such as Prolog (with the Warren Abstract Machine), functional languages (with the SECD or G machines), and Smalltalk.

"The COGMIP$ machine has four registers (like variables) and six instructions: Copy, Output, Goto, Match, If, Print. The registers are numbered from 0-3. The specification of the machine is the following:

`$l`	: Label l
`Ic`	: If first character of register 0 is c branch to label c
`P...`` `	: Print string up to `
`Or`	: Output register r
`Mrc`	: Read input up until character c is matched into register r
`Crn`	: Copy n input characters into register r
`Gl`	: Branch to label l
`Nr`	: Increment register r

(Architecture purists will notice that this is a complex and non-orthogonal [register 0 has special meaning] instruction set.) The code for the machine is read by a small assembler. The assembler reads the code that was split into lines, and includes comments and packs it into a very long character string. To make matters a bit more complicated, it encodes the string by adding 1 to the value of every character. This is a part of the output string:

```
m>aP4HC%TQs\\q,,^>m,2<m>aP4HC%SD12N1\nJNQm>s\\.
```

"The assembler was implemented as a Perl script. (Perl is a language designed and implemented by Larry Wall, another OCCC winner.)

"By now you have probably become confused by the number of languages that are being used together, so I will summarize. The BASIC source is converted into C by a program written in COGMIP$. The resulting C source is compiled into an executable program by the C compiler. The COGMIP$ program is interpreted by a C program. COGMIP$ is translated from its source format into an encoded bytestring used by the COGMIP$ assembler. The COGMIP$ assembler is written in Perl. The Perl code for the COGMIP$ assembler follows:

```perl
# Bytecode compiler
open(FO, ">bac.h");
print FO "char*s=\"";
while (<>) {
# Remove lines containing block C comments
if (/\/\*/) { next; }
# Remove assembly comments
s/^;.*//;
s/\t;.*//;
# Remove white space
s/[ \t\n]//g;
# Actual space is represented by _.  Convert it.
s/_/ /g;
# Check the Print command
if (/^P[^`]$/) {
print STDERR "$ARGV[0]i($.): Unfinished P command\n";
}
$s = '';
# Add one to all elements of the string apart from \n
for ($i = 0; $i < length($_); $i++) {
$c = substr($_, $i, 1);
$s2 = substr($_, $i, 2);
if (!/printf/ && $s2 eq "\\n") {
$s .= "\\n";
$i++;
} else {
$s .= pack('c', ord(substr($_, $i, 1)) + 1);
}
}
# Escape the \n and the "
$s =~ s/\\([^n])/\\\\$1/g;
$s =~ s/"/\\\"/g;
print FO $s;
}
print FO "\";\n";
```

"At this point you are ready to delve into the innards of the BASIC compiler. Here are excerpts of the COGMIP$ source:

```
; The BASIC compiler written in COGMIP$ bytecode
;
; Initialise vars (return stack for lines, limits and chars)
Pint_r[200],f[200],m[200],b[99],p,l`
; Print ,A,B, ... ,Z
; Set R0 to A (with no assignment instruction!)
$1                      ; Loop for counting up to A
N0                      ; Increment R0
IA                      ; Have we reached A ?
G1                      ; No; loop
$A                      ; R0 contains A
P,`
O0                      ; Print it
IZ                      ; Is it the last one?
N0                      ; No; increment it
GA                      ; Do the next one
$Z                      ; Z was printed
P;main(){for(;;)switch(l){`
Pcase_9999:return;`
Pdefault:`
P;l++`
$B                      ; Loop here for breaking commands
P;break`
$a                      ; Loop here for normal commands
P;`
; Line parsing starts here
M1_                     ; R1 = Line number
P\ncase_`
O1                      ; Print line number
P:l=`                   ; Set line number variable
O1
P;`                     ; case L: l = L;
$_
C01                     ; Get first command character
I_                      ; Skip spaces
IF                      ; Check for FOR
IG                      ; Check for GOTO or GOSUB
IN                      ; Check for NEXT
IP                      ; Check for PRINT
IE                      ; Check for END
IR                      ; Check for RETURN or REM
II                      ; Check for IF or INPUT
IL                      ; Check for LET
GR                      ; Else throw the line away
;;;;;;;;;;;;;;;;;;;;;;;;;;;
; GOTO E or GOSUB E
$G                      ; GOTO or GOSUB
C01
```

```
C01                     ; Get third character into R0
M2_                     ; Skip to space
M3\n                    ; Get line number
IT                      ; GOTO
IS                      ; GOSUB
;;;;;;;;;;;;;;;;;;;;;;;;
; GOTO R3
$T
P/* GOTO */\n`
Pl=`
O3                      ; L = E
GB                      ; Print ;break; and Loop
;;;;;;;;;;;;;;;;;;;;;;;;
; GOSUB R3
$S
P/* GOSUB */\n`
Pr[p++]=l+1;l=`
O3                      ; r[p++] = 1; 1 = R3
GB                      ; Print ;break; and Loop
;;;;;;;;;;;;;;;;;;;;;;;;
; RETURN or REM
$R
C01
M0\n                    ; Get rest in R0
IM                      ; Check for REM
;;;;;;;;;;;;;;;;;;;;;;;;
; RETURN
P/* RETURN */\n`
Pl=r[--p]`
GB                      ; Print ;break; and Loop
;;;;;;;;;;;;;;;;;;;;;;;;
; REM
$M
P/* REM */\n`
Ga
;;;;;;;;;;;;;;;;;;;;;;;;
; Compile instruction and file name; accessed via offset
; calculated from end of compiled string (i.e. -3 and -6)
cc_a.c
```

"The COGMIP$ interpreter was easy to implement. No special obfuscation techniques were used other than standard source code space compression tricks. This is the commented version of it:

```c
/* Basic Compiler - (C) Copyright 1991 Diomidis Spinellis */
/* All rights reserved. */
#include <stdio.h>
#include "bac.h"     /* The COGMIP$ instructions */
char R[3][20];       /* The COGMIP$ registers */

/* Set the r variable to the instruction register */
```

```
#define RD r = R[*p++ - '0'];

main(argc, argv)
char **argv;
{
    char *p = s - 1, *r;
    int k;
    /* Open input and output files */
    FILE *fi = fopen(argv[1], "r"), *fo = fopen("a.c", "w");

    for (;;) {
        /* COGMIP$ interpreter main loop.  p is the COGMIP$
           instruction pointer and points to the current
           instruction. */
        p++;
        switch(*p++) {
        case 'M':        /* Mrc Match into r up to character */
            RD
            while ((k = fgetc(fi)) != EOF && k != *p)
                *r++ = k;
            /* If end of file is reached, add closing braces,
               compile and exit. */
            if (k == EOF) {
                fputs("}}\n", fo);
                fclose(fo);
                system("cc -g a.c");
                return;
            }
            *r = 0;
            break;
        case 'P':            /* Ps` Print string up to ` */
            while (*p != '`') fputc(*p++, fo);
            break;
        case 'O':            /* Or Output r */
            RD
            while (*r) fputc(*r++, fo);
            p--;
            break;
        case 'C':            /* Crn Copy into r n characters */
            RD
            for (k = 0; k < *p - '0'; k++) *r++ = fgetc(fi);
            *r = 0;
            break;
        case 'I':            /* Il if r0 == 1 goto l */
            k = *p;
            if (**R == k) goto G;
            break;
        case 'G':            /* Gl goto l */
            k = *p;
        G:/* Used by If */
```

```
                    p = s;
                    while (*p != '$' || p[1] != k) p++;
                    p++;
                    break;
            case '$':                /* Label; do nothing */
                    break;
            default:
                    printf("Internal error %c(%d)\n", p[-1], p-s);
                    return;
            }
        }
    }
}
```

"The final task was putting the interpreter and the encoded COGMIP$ code together into a 1133-character-long source file. Approximately the first half of the source is the COGMIP$ code and the second half its interpreter."

Best Output

Sean Barrett <buzzard@eng.umd.edu>
University of Maryland
Hyattsville, Maryland

```
#include <stdio.h>
#define X(s) (!(s&3)-((s&3)==2))
#define W while
char Z[82][82],A,B,f,g=26;z(q){return atoi(q);}m(d,1){return
Z[   B       +   X     (  f    +
3) * d+1 *X(f+ 2 )][ A+X ( f ) * d +
1* X          (      f    + 3 ) ] ;}int
h= 0;D(p,s)char*s; {W(h>>3<p>> 3 ) {putchar('\t'
);        h =      (      h   +8
)&~7 ;}W(h < p ){putchar(' ');++h; }(void)printf(
"%s"    ,   s          )    ;h+=strlen(s);}main(x,a)char **a; {
# define P(x)  (x?(5-(x))*(6-(x ))/2:11)
int b; { char b[256],i,  j=0;  FILE*F;F=fopen(x-1?a[1]:"buzzard.c","r");W(
fgets( b ,256 ,F)){for(i=0;b[ i];++ i)
Z[j][i ] =( b [    i   ]      ==' '?1:2*(b[i]==(x>2?*a[2]:'\\')));++j;}fclose
(F);}A   =4 ; B = 3 ; f = 1;x >3? A=z(a[3]),B=z(a[4]):0;b='\n';do{if(b=='\n'
){int y ,      s , d , p    , q        ,i;for
(y=-11; y<= 11;++ y){ for(s = 1 ,d=0;s+3;s-=2){for
(;d!=2    +    3 * s   ;    d+=s){
if(m(d,0) !=1 ){p=P (d) ;if (abs( y )
    <p&&  !   m     (      d  , 0 )||abs(y)>p)break;for
(i  =-p;i<p;++i)D(g+i*2,"--");D(0,"\-");break;}if(d==5)continue;
p=P(d+1);q=P(d);if
(abs(y)      >q)continue;if
(abs(y)      <p)D(g-s*(2*p+1),"|");else if(m(d,s)){if
(abs(y)      <=p)for(i=(s==1?-q:p);i!=(s==1?-p:q);
(abs(y)      ),++i)D(g+2*i+(s==-1),"--");}else if
(abs(y)      ==p)D(g-s*(2*p+1),"|");else D(g-
(abs(y)      *s*2),(s==1)^(y>0)?"\\":"/");}d-=s;}puts(
"");h=0;}}f+=(b=='r')-(b=='l');f&=3;if(b=='f'){if(!(m(1,0))continue;
A+=X(f);B+=X(f-1);}}W((b=getchar())!=-1&&m(0,0)==1);return 0;}
```

Yet another maze program, but with a twist. It allows you to traverse through the maze with a graphical display. Here is an example of the game in progress:

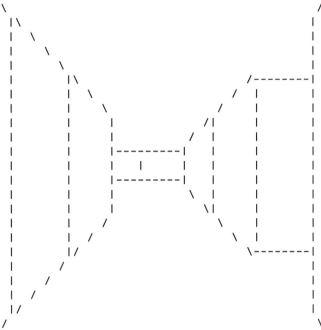

Author's Analysis

"I think my maze program really isn't obfuscated in any interesting ways. The prize that it won was for what it displayed, not how it was obfuscated. I guess no one had ever thought to draw a first-person view of a maze using character graphics.

"I'm not sure where the inspiration to do this came from. I do know that it partially derived from a contest for which I had written a 10-line BASIC program (each 120 characters long, so similar in length to the OCCC length) which drew a maze in first-person perspective graphically. There were in fact two versions of that program; one had the maze embedded as data, and the other generated it on the fly.

"Once I had the basic idea, that is, to do a character-based first-person-perspective maze, most of the rest was trivial. I sketched out in my mind how the code would work if I wrote it the natural way: you scan through the maze, starting from the eye location and moving in the direction the eye is facing, and draw the walls as you get to them. I considered using a screen-handling package like curses to do the drawing for me. I also considered keeping a matrix to represent the screen, drawing into that, and then dumping the screen from top to bottom, which would allow display on 'dumb' terminals (even printing terminals).

"Then I realized I could just throw CPU at the problem, and go through the whole above process once for every line, and only record what appeared on that line. In the end, the algorithm didn't really need to waste much CPU. It consists of one main loop:

```
for every line y
        draw the left half of this line
        draw the right half of this line
```

"Given an eye represented by '>', meaning someone facing right, consider this maze situation drawn from above.

```
123456
>     7
DCBA98
```

"To 'draw the left half of this line,' we have to consider the walls (or non-walls) numbered 1..7, and for the right half, the walls numbered 7..D. As it turns out, anything displayed with wall 1 is displayed before (that is, to the left of, which when we're printing from left to right must happen 'before') wall 2, and wall 2 before wall 3, etc. all the way around to C before D.

"That means the primary loop amounts to

```
for every line y
        walk through the walls on the left from near to far
        walk through the walls on the right from far to near
```

"Actually, because of obfuscation this came out as

```
for every line y
        for direction one of left..right
                for depth=start..end as appropriate for direction
```

"The actual decisions for where to draw which joint derive from the old BASIC programs. The spacing to simulate perspective is handled by the macro P. Normally, the spacing is inversely proportional to the distance, something like this:

```
spacing_between_lines_at_this_distance = 100 / (distance+1)
```

"However, at the low resolution I was using, I was forced to tweak this somewhat.

"The join-drawing algorithms do not correctly handle a case like

```
    XXX
XX
>   XX
XXXX
```

which gets displayed as if it was

```
XX X
>   X
XXXX
```

"In general, in fact, they don't ever handle multiple open spaces, like

```
XX  XX
>     X
XXXXXX
```

which will get drawn as if the two open squares have a division between them.

"The original program which was submitted to the OCCC was hard-coded to read itself as a data file; the program was modified by me for official release with the extra options it has now. I did these modifications directly to the obfuscated code, and was forced to rejuggle the self-coded maze arrangement.

"The function D keeps track of cursor position on a line and draws a string at a certain horizontal position, using appropriate combinations of spaces and tabs to get there. I thought it was a nice touch to support tabs.

"The function m is critical for deciphering the gory details of the algorithm. m(a,b) returns the value of the maze square which is located a away from where you're facing (a down the hall, that is), and b to the left. (Or is it to the right?) b only ever takes on the values 1, 0, or −1, so it's used to scan the walls in front of you and to each immediate side as you scan down the hall.

"I believe that covers algorithms, now on to obfuscation. The largest obfuscation in the program is just the fact that the algorithms to decide what sort of line/character to draw at a given depth are gory ad hoc algorithms with no helpful comments or variable names. I suspect it would be difficult to predict what it will do when run, since it is very difficult to figure out quite how it does do what it does.

"I actually left some names vaguely mnemonic, figuring that what was going on was unclear enough anyway. (A,B) is your location, and f is the direction you're facing. D is the routine that does displays, and the macro P helps with perspective. I myself don't see much obfuscation in it, beyond my unmodularization and some 'traditional' OCCC obfuscations. I had read through past entries pretty thoroughly."

Best One-Liner

Thomas A. Fine <fine@cis.ohio-state.edu>
J Greely <jgreely@cis.ohio-state.edu>
Ohio State University, Dept. of Computer and Information Science
Columbus, Ohio

```
main(a,b){while((a=getchar())+1)putchar((b=64^a&223)&&b<27?a&96|(b+12)%26+1:a);}
```

This program performs Caesar substitution by changing each character in place.

Author's Analysis

"The logical algorithm is to read a character, twiddle it, and print. It's the twiddling that's interesting. Note that in the explanation, I refer to bits as 76543210 from high to low.

The 1991 Obfuscated C Code Contest

388 ·

1. Get the character in variable **a**. Note the fun way we check for end-of-file.

2. Reverse bit 6, and strip bit 5. Bit 6 determines (mostly) whether or not this
    character is a letter. Bit 5 would determine case if we cared. Assign this value
    to variable **b**. (We need to save it, since we need to make two comparisons and
    maybe one operation with this value.) We can't abuse our first variable, since it
    saves the bits we're changing.

3. Check this value to see if it is a letter. If it is zero, then we have either the at-
    sign (64) or the backquote (96). It also must be less than 27. This checks the
    range for letters, as well as implicitly checking the value of bit 6 (if it was orig-
    inally clear, it is set now, so **b** would be too big).

4. If it is not a letter, the conditional expression inside of the **putchar** returns the
    original character (**a**). Otherwise, it returns a really messy expression that per-
    forms the actual Caesar rotation and fixes the fifth and sixth bits:

5. Step A: Subtract 1 to get into the range 0–25 (for the modulo operation). Step
    B: Add 13 to the character. Steps A and B are combined. Step C: Take this
    modulo 26 to make the addition wrap around. Step D: Fix bits 5 and 6, based
    on **a**. Step E: Add 1 back in (we took it out in step A.) This is okay to do *after*
    step D, because we know the addition won't trickle up past the fourth bit (**b**
    would have to be 31 for this to happen).

"Incidentally, I've often done these same tricks in low-level graphics code, or when
working with assemblers and disassemblers (although it is a bit more readable).
Obfuscation is largely a measure of what you're not used to."

Best Game

James "Rince" Bonfield <rince@cs.warwick.ac.uk>
University of Warwick
Wrestlingworth, Sandy Beds, England

```
#include <curses.h>
#define R break
#define U M[h][f]
#define W M[g][e]
#define T M[y][x]
#define B(a) "A"#a"A",
#define A "AAAAAAAAAAAAAAAAAAAAAAA"
#define z(a) case a:if(U=='B')U=W,x=e,y=g,u--;
#define Z(a,b) else if(U==a&&d==b)U=W='B';R;
#define K(a) a##a##a
#define k(a) #a#a#a#a#a"\0"
#define V " \0"
#define S " \0/----\\\0_/  \\_"
int u=484,X[]={-1,0,0,1},Y[]={0,1,-1,0},x,y,D,i,j,a;char o,m,*t,*O="MNOH"
,*k="hjkl",*s=K(k(#))V V V" ___ \0 /  \\\0 \\___/\0 ___ \0 /@@@\\\0 "
"\\@@@/\0| | /\\\0----||\0   \\\/\0 /--\\\0  \\\/ \0 ==| \0 ==| \0 "
" /\\ \0  \\--/\0 /0__o\0 \\___/\0 /_\\_ \0"K(" << \0")V k(v)V V k(^)V"
" /\\  \0 < > \0 \\\/ \0o__o\\ \0\\___/ \0 _/_\\ \0 0__o"S"\0 ^__^"S,
M[12][22]={A,B(LCABBBBBBBABBCBBCABB)B(CCABAKAAABAFBABABAEB
```

```
)B(BBBBABBIBBBBBEEABACL)B(CCBNIBBAAAAGALBBBABC)B(AAAAAAJACBABBCABAABC
)B(LLAACCBACBAAALLCABBB)B(BDLAAABABCAAAALCABBL)B(BCBIBBBBBBBAAAAACBB
)B(BCCAABBADBBBBDBDBDBC)B(LBBACCCCDBCABBBDBBBB)A};main(){initscr();clear();
noecho();cbreak();x=y=4;D=39,o='M';m=T;while(D&&u){for(i=j=a=0;j<7;!(mvaddstr(
j*3+a,i*6,s+(((M[((y-1)/5)*5+j][((x-1)/10)*10+i]-'A')*3+a++)*7)),a^3)&&(a=0,!
(++i^12))&&(a=i=0,j++));refresh();T='B';if(t=(char*)strchr(k,getch())){int e=
x,g=y,f=x,h=y,d=t-k;o=O[d];f=(e=x+X[d])+d[X];h=(g=y+Y[d])+d[Y];switch(W){case
'B':x=e;y=g,u--;R;z('C')else if(U=='C')U=W='L';R;z('D')R;case'L':x=e;y=g,u--;D
--;R;z('E')Z('I',0)z('F')Z('J',1)z('G')Z('K',2)}}m=T;T=o;}clear();mvaddstr(12
,31,u?"Well done!":"Too many moves");move(23,0);refresh();endwin();return 0;}
```

This program presents you with a delightful little puzzle. Using curses to draw the graphics, you direct a creature around a maze, salvaging and occasionally making diamonds from the rubble. The puzzle seems very simple and almost crude, yet every move has side-effects that force you to reconsider the simplest action.

Here is a snapshot of the opening screen:

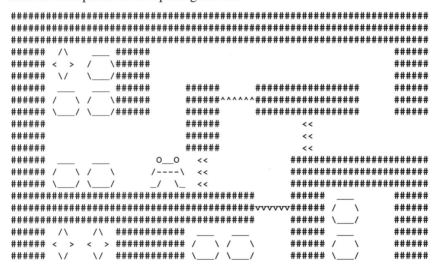

You're the funny-looking creature near the middle (which actually changes shape as it moves), surrounded by the puzzle walls and lots of other good stuff. The four thin walls to the right are doors to be unlocked, for which you have to find keys elsewhere.

While the puzzle is deceptively tricky, the author managed to squeeze the graphics and maze (which is much bigger than shown here) into a very small program. The author claims that he really didn't try to obfuscate the program. It is simply "well-compacted." Leaving it as written, here is his explanation.

Author's Analysis

"I had previously found an archive of obfuscated programs and was quite interested in them. However, it wasn't until I'd written this game (unobfuscated) that I realized quite how short it was—even with all the silly little bits that weren't essential to game play. So I decided to see how short I could make it. It was a real challenge to get it below the 1.5Kb limit.

"The initial `#define`s were added at the very end of the program development—their main use is to shrink the program. Scrutinizing for the ideal `define`s to compress the program is a puzzle in itself, and always leaves programs more obscure.

"The `K` and `k` macros use # (quote a string) and ## (concatenate strings) directives defined by Standard C. Hence, `K(a)` will be `aaa` and `k(a)` will be `"a""a""a""a""a""a""\0"`. This should generate a string equivalent to `"#""#""#""#""#""#""\0""#""#""#""#""#""#""\0""#""#""#""#""#""#""\0"` which is equivalent to `"######\0######\0######\0"`. Several Standard C compilers got confused by `K(k(#))` on line 15, which uses the # and ## directives on a # symbol. (Fortunately I had `gcc`, which worked fine.)

"The interesting global variables are `s`, the array of graphical figures, and `M`, the maze, which uses a macro `B` to shrink things. The use of all capital letters makes the whole thing a bit harder to read.

"Now we come to `main`. I shall *attempt* to describe the algorithm—I'm a bit unsure myself now as I don't have the original unobfuscated code lying around anymore!

"Before entering the main loop, we initialize curses. The program could never have been as small without extensive use of prewritten libraries. (I'll skip further mention of curses.) Then we proceed to iterate the following body:

```
for(i=j=a=0;j<7;!(mvaddstr(j*3+a,i*6,s+(((M[((y-1)/
5)*5+j][((x-1)/10)*10+i]-'A')*3+a++)*7)),a^3)&&(a=0,!(++-
i^12))&&(a=i=0,j++));
```

"I have trouble understanding this myself now, but it should display the 12x8 map. (`i`,`j` are the `x`,`y` coordinate pointers). I'll try and explain why it looks so horrible. When using a `for` statement as in:

```
for (i=0; i<100; i++) func(i);
```

we can write this simply as   `for (i=0; i<100; func(i),i++);`

"We can also rewrite   `if (func1(i)) func2(i);`

as   `func1(i) && func2(i)`

"The `for` statement has the usual components, but only the final test is interesting:

```
for (i=j=a=0;j<7;!(mvaddstr(j*3+a,i*6,s+(((M[((y-1)/5)*5+j]
[((x-1)/10)*10+i]-'A')*3+a++)*7)),a^3)&&(a=0,!(++i^12))&&
(a=i=0,j++));
```

"Using the techniques already mentioned, it draws a single sprite with:

```
mvaddstr(j*3+a,i*6,s+(((M[((y-1)/5)*5+j][((x-1)/10)*10+i]-
'A')*3+a++)*7)),a^3
```

"The `y` coordinate is `j*3+a` (sprites are 3 deep, `a` is the current line in the 3 high sprite we're drawing) and the `x` coordinate is just `i*6` (sprites are 6 wide). The string is a section from the sprite array, `s`. The sprite to draw (starting at `'A'`) is:

```
M[((y-1)/5)*5+j][((x-1)/10)*10+i]
```

"This is odd because it has to take into account our `xy` coordinates to work out which 'screen' we're on (if you imagine it as a 2x2 block of screens) and our sprite to draw in the screen (from `i` and `j`).

"We can then subtract `'A'` from this character to get a zero-based sprite number. Multiplying by 21 (sprites are 3x7) and `a*3` (current line) will tell us where the offset into the sprite array is (i.e., `&s[offset]` which is equivalent to `s+offset`). Note that `a` (current line of 3 line sprite) is incremented in this `mvaddstr`. Anyway, that's the biggest chunk done. This `mvaddstr` is grouped (using the comma operator) with `a^3` (i.e., false when `a` is 3) to produce a true value when `a` is 3 (entire sprite is drawn). Then we can reset `a`, and increment the `i` coordinate. Similarly when `i` is 12, reset it and `a`, then proceed to the next row (`j++`). Fairly simple, eh?

"At this point `refresh` draws the screen. A few interesting points remain. `T='B'` blanks out the square we're on, enabling the effect of eating diamonds.

```
if (t=(char*)strchr(k,getch())) {
```

reads a character and finds its offset in the key array. In this manner, the direction to move next is determined.

```
o=O[d]; f=(e=x+X[d])+d[X]; h=(g=y+Y[d])+d[Y];
```

sets `o` to be the sprite corresponding to the new direction. `e` and `g` become coordinates of the next sprite in the direction we pressed, and `f` and `h` the coordinates of the next sprite in that direction, too. Then we can make use of two macros (`W` and `T`) for these two sprites. `W` is the one nearest to us.

"A large `switch` based on the sprite we just tried to walk onto has cases with different actions on the sprite (`T`) we just tried to push another one onto. This is the main algorithm for how the game works and can be shrunk enormously via `define`s (such as `z` and `Z`). I won't describe this—it's quite obvious if you examine the postprocessed source. But note that this same code does the updating of our `x` and `y` coordinates, decrements diamonds left, moves left, and updates the map upon collisions.

"At loop termination, an appropriate message is printed . . . and the user is free to play again!"

Grand Prize

Brian Westley (Merlyn LeRoy) <merlyn@digibd.com>
DigiBoard, Inc.
St. Paul, Minnesota

```
           a(X){/*/X=-              a(X){/*/X=
           -1;F;X=-                 -1;F;X=-
           -1;F;}/*/                -1;F;}/*/
char*z[]={"char*z[]={","a(X){/*/X=-","-1;F;X=-","-1;F;}/*/","9999999999  :-| ",
"int q,i,j,k,X,O=0,H;S(x)int*x;{X+=X;O+=O;*x+1?*x+2||X++:O++;*x=1;}L(n){for(*",
"z[i=1]=n+97;i<4;i++)M(256),s(i),M(128),s(i),M(64),N;X*=8;O*=8;}s(R){char*r=z",
"[R];for(q&&Q;*r;)P(*r++);q&&(Q,P(44));}M(m){P(9);i-2||P(X&m?88:O&m?48:32);P(",
"9);}y(A){for(j=8;j;)~A&w[--j]||(q=0);}e(W,Z){for(i-=i*q;i<9&&q;)y(W|(1<<i++&",
"~Z));}R(){for(k=J[*J-48]-40;k;)e(w[k--],X|O);}main(u,v)char**v;{a(q=1);b(1);",
"c(1);*J=--u?O?*J:*v[1]:53;X|=u<<57-*v[u];y(X);K=40+q;q?e(O,X),q&&(K='|'),e(X",
",O),R(),O|=1<<--i:J[*J-48+(X=O=0)]--;L(q=0);for(s(i=0);q=i<12;)s(i++),i>4&&N",
";s(q=12);P(48);P('}');P(59);N;q=0;L(1);for(i=5;i<13;)s(i++),N;L(2);}",0};
           b(X){/*/X=-              b(X){/*/X=-
           -1;F;X=-                 -1;F;X=-
           -1;F;}/*/                -1;F;}/*/
int q,i,j,k,X,O=0,H;S(x)int*x;{X+=X;O+=O;*x+1?*x+2||X++:O++;*x=1;}L(n){for(*
z[i=1]=n+97;i<4;i++)M(256),s(i),M(128),s(i),M(64),N;X*=8;O*=8;}s(R){char*r=z
[R];for(q&&Q;*r;)P(*r++);q&&(Q,P(44));}M(m){P(9);i-2||P(X&m?88:O&m?48:32);P(
9);}y(A){for(j=8;j;)~A&w[--j]||(q=0);}e(W,Z){for(i-=i*q;i<9&&q;)y(W|(1<<i++&
~Z));}R(){for(k=J[*J-48]-40;k;)e(w[k--],X|O);}main(u,v)char**v;{a(q=1);b(1);
c(1);*J=--u?O?*J:*v[1]:53;X|=u<<57-*v[u];y(X);K=40+q;q?e(O,X),q&&(K='|'),e(X
,O),R(),O|=1<<--i:J[*J-48+(X=O=0)]--;L(q=0);for(s(i=0);q=i<12;)s(i++),i>4&&N
;s(q=12);P(48);P('}');P(59);N;q=0;L(1);for(i=5;i<13;)s(i++),N;L(2);}
           c(X){/*/X=-              c(X){/*/X=-
           -1;F;X=-                 -1;F;X=-
           -1;F;}/*/                -1;F;}/*/
```

This program plays tic-tac-toe. Did you guess that already? Well, you couldn't guess how bizarre a tic-tac-toe game can be until you've seen this program! It plays tic-tac-toe *on* itself. The code is written as a tic-tac-toe grid; moves are carried out within the source code. As if that wasn't enough, this program gets better over time as it plays, by producing improved copies of its own source code!

(Note that the *initial* compile line is: `-DP=putchar -DN="P(10)" -DQ="P(34)"` `-DF="S(&X)" -DJ=z[4]-DK=J[14] -DH="w[]={146,7,292,73,448,56,84,` `273,325,297,108,324,22,40,48,40,17,325}" westley.c -o westley`. String constants in the code must be writeable.) In the following discussion, tic-tac-toe positions are numbered 1 to 9, row-wise from upper left-hand corner to lower right. For example, 2 refers to the top row, center column.

Author's Analysis

"The program, when run, reproduces itself with both the player's move (X) and the computer's move (0) added. Recompile *this* program (using the same compile line) and repeat until the game is finished.

"As an example, in response to '`westley 3`' (remember that 3 refers to the upper-right corner), the program prints:

```
            a(X){/*/X=-               a(X){/*/X=-
            -1;F;X=-                  -1;F;X=-              X
            -1;F;}/*/                 -1;F;}/*/
char*z[]={"char*z[]={","a(X){/*/X=-","-1;F;X=-","-1;F;}/*/","3999999999  :-| ",
"int q,i,j,k,X,O=0,H;S(x)int*x;{X+=X;O+=O;*x+1?*x+2||X++:O++;*x=1;}L(n){for(*",
"z[i=1]=n+97;i<4;i++)M(256),s(i),M(128),s(i),M(64),N;X*=8;O*=8;}s(R){char*r=z",
"[R];for(q&&Q;*r;)P(*r++);q&&(Q,P(44));}M(m){P(9);i-2||P(X&m?88:O&m?48:32);P(",
"9);}y(A){for(j=8;j;)-A&w[--j]||(q=0);}e(W,Z){for(i-=i*q;i<9&&q;)y(W|(1<<i++&",
"-Z));}R(){for(k=J[*J-48]-40;k;)e(w[k--],X|O);}main(u,v)char**v;{a(q=1);b(1);",
"c(1);*J=--u?O?*J:*v[1]:53;X|=u<<57-*v[u];y(X);K=40+q;q?e(O,X),q&&(K='|'),e(X",
",O),R(),O|=1<<--i:J[*J-48+(X=O=0)]--;L(q=0);for(s(i=0);q=i<12;)s(i++),i>4&&N",
";s(q=12);P(48);P('}');P(59);N;q=0;L(1);for(i=5;i<13;)s(i++),N;L(2);}",0};
            b(X){/*/X=-               b(X){/*/X=-
            -1;F;X=-                  -1;F;X=-
            -1;F;}/*/                 -1;F;}/*/
int q,i,j,k,X,O=0,H;S(x)int*x;{X+=X;O+=O;*x+1?*x+2||X++:O++;*x=1;}L(n){for(*
z[i=1]=n+97;i<4;i++)M(256),s(i),M(128),s(i),M(64),N;X*=8;O*=8;}s(R){char*r=z
[R];for(q&&Q;*r;)P(*r++);q&&(Q,P(44));}M(m){P(9);i-2||P(X&m?88:O&m?48:32);P(
9);}y(A){for(j=8;j;)-A&w[--j]||(q=0);}e(W,Z){for(i-=i*q;i<9&&q;)y(W|(1<<i++&
-Z));}R(){for(k=J[*J-48]-40;k;)e(w[k--],X|O);}main(u,v)char**v;{a(q=1);b(1);
c(1);*J=--u?O?*J:*v[1]:53;X|=u<<57-*v[u];y(X);K=40+q;q?e(O,X),q&&(K='|'),e(X
,O),R(),O|=1<<--i:J[*J-48+(X=O=0)]--;L(q=0);for(s(i=0);q=i<12;)s(i++),i>4&&N
;s(q=12);P(48);P('}');P(59);N;q=0;L(1);for(i=5;i<13;)s(i++),N;L(2);}
            c(X){/*/X=-               c(X){/*/X=-
            -1;F;X=-          0        -1;F;X=-
            -1;F;}/*/                 -1;F;}/*/
```

"If the computer wins, the face in the upper right-hand corner (:-|) will smile (:-)). If it is a draw, the face does not change. If the computer loses, it changes to a sad face (:-(). If this happens, the whole board should replace the original program; the computer changes its play and will continue to do so until it no longer loses games.

"If you want a program that never loses, replace the string 9999999999 :-| with 9883857753 :-| .

"The vertical 'bars' of the grid are identical functions, with the name of the function as a, b, or c. After each function is called, the global variables x and o contain bit masks of where all the x's and o's are placed. The statement:

```
        X=-   <char>   -1;
```

evaluates to 1, –1, or –2 when x is 1 and <char> is one of 'x', 'o', or ' '. The function s(&X) sets the appropriate bits in (global variables) x and o and resets the value of &x to 1. This is how the current position is computed.

"The player's move is ORed into the x mask, and (if it is the opening move) the strategy string's first character is set to the player's first move (or 5 if the computer moves first).

"The evaluation function y(M) checks if the mask has a winning pattern (any of the first eight bit masks of the w array), and sets the variable q to 0 if it does.

"The player's move is evaluated to see if the human has won. The face is set as described above, and if the human has won, the digit in the strategy string is decremented to change the computer's play for next game.

"If the human has not won, the e(N,M) function evaluates if any move not in mask N can produce a win in mask M. The first evaluation e(X,O) checks if o can make a legal winning move. If so, the computer has a winning move and makes it. If not, the face is reset, and a non-winning move is generated.

"A non-winning move first checks if X can win in one move; if so, this move is selected, blocking the win. Otherwise, a move is generated by looking down the list of *move templates* (see below). The first move template that generates a move not already occupied by an **x** or **o** is returned.

"The move templates are static tic-tac-toe positions that generate possible moves by making the **e** function return *winning* moves, e.g., the template:

```
.  .  .
o  ,  o    (this is the value 40; 2³ + 2⁵)
.  .  .    ("o"s are 1 bits, "." and "," are 0 bits)
```

will make the **e** function return a center move, as this is the only move that produces three in a row. Notice that the computer does not consider which cells contain **x**'s and **o**'s when making a template move, only which cells are empty and not-empty. This makes for unusual play.

"The templates are carefully chosen to eventually block all traps that **x** can try by just blundering in the way. Also note that the winning and strategy templates are part of the compile line, making it possible to change the rules of the game by changing the compile line. The default templates are:

```
O , O     , . .     . . .     . . .     . . .
, , ,     . O .     O , O     O O ,     O , O
O , O     . . O     . . .     . . .     . . .


. , ,     O , O     , . O     O . ,     O , O
. O .     , , .     O , O     O , O     , , ,
O O ,     O . .     O . ,     , . O     O , O
```

"A digit of **9** causes the program to start with the first template, **8** starts at the second, etc. The templates are scanned until a legal move is found. A template is scanned from bottom to top, right to left (i.e., move 9 is tested first, then 8, down to move 1)."

## CHAPTER 40

C, Me, and a Few Good Books

Many of the chapters in this book were originally published as columns in magazines. Magazines can be a good way of communicating timely information, and I want to encourage you to read them and submit articles to them. I can recommend several fine magazines that specialize in C:

> *The C Users Journal*—A "fun" magazine covering C and C++ for the beginning to advanced programmer. *CUJ* supports a very large C and C++ software library.

> *The C++ Journal*—A quarterly magazine with articles catering to experienced C++ programmers.

> *The C++ Report*—A monthly magazine of tutorials and hands-on articles aimed at all levels of experience.

> *The Journal of C Language Translation*—A high-quality journal covering issues important to C implementors, including language extensions, standards interpretations, and compiler implementation techniques.

Many magazines regularly carry C columns or encourage use of C, such as *Computer Language* and *Dr. Dobb's Journal*. Many excellent computer science journals (e.g., *Communications of the ACM* and *Software—Practice & Experience*) print substantial amounts of C code in their articles.

You may be amused to learn that I actually started writing as a favor to my dad, who published and edited several computer magazines. In fact, he didn't even pay me at first. Can you believe it?[1] He knew I could express myself (especially when it came to asking for loans), and C seemed like a language that might be mildly interesting to an increasing number of his readers. The year was 1984.

Since that time, interest in C has mushroomed way beyond anyone's expectations. I had no idea that there would be dozens of companies selling C compilers, interpreters, and debuggers, or that hundreds of software houses would use C as their primary system programming language. (So why are there still bugs in my compiler?!)

---

1. Admittedly, he didn't charge me rent either.

C is truly a *lingua franca* of system programming, and has surpassed many general-purpose languages such as Pascal and Fortran. Perhaps only Ada and C++ currently stand a chance of reaching comparable popularity. As yet, however, they have not reached the necessary critical mass.

An important event in C's history was the establishment of a standard, rigorously defining the language, libraries, and host environment. The ANSI X3J11 committee worked on a C standard for six years. As is typical with standards, final resolution dragged on much longer than planned. The standard was eventually ratified in December 1989.

Shortly after that, ANSI C (an American standard) was approved as ISO C (an International standard), and then FIPS C (a U.S. government standard). Except for formatting and section-number differences, all are identical. To reduce confusion, it is common parlance to say "Standard C" when referring to any of them. Each standard may be ordered directly from its sponsoring organization (see p. 403 in the Appendix). For more info on Standard C, contact Plum Hall, Inc.

While there are as yet few fully-conforming Standard C compilers, many C compilers are moving in that direction by supporting the new Standard C features, such as function prototypes and stringizing.

The standard has made some changes and a significant number of additions to the language, although the primary work was integrating different working practices from existing C compilers. There are still some deliberate gaps in the specifications, but they have been substantively clarified and noted, so that portable coding practices are much easier than without the guarantees made by the standard. While it is therefore possible to gripe about what the X3J11 committee did or did not do, it is time to rally behind their work. The standard is a good thing.

On the other hand, reality prevents me from ignoring the fact that Classic C is alive and well and will be for many years. After all, not everyone can afford to plunk down the cash for a new compiler, especially when the old one isn't broken. Continuing sales of books based on Classic C, such as *K&R1*, attest to its health.

But the standards work is not over. X3J11 is still actively answering interpretations of the standard. And a working group of X3J11 is looking at extensions such as complex arithmetic and variably-sized arrays.

C++

Another very important development you should be aware of is C++. C++ is one of many attempts at adding modern ideas to the C programming language. C++ is particularly popular because most of C is acceptable to C++. Thus, you can use a C++ compiler with little investment in retraining, only using or experimenting with a new feature when you decide to. C++ retains much of the efficiency inherent in C and is link-compatible with it.

The more important features of C++ include:

- data abstraction including data hiding, operator overloading, and guaranteed initialization and cleanup,

- object-oriented programming including derived classes (inheritance), and

- other enhancements including scoped and type constants, in-line functions, overloaded function names, and memory-allocation operators (`new` and `delete`) understood directly by the compiler.

You can read more about the language in *The C++ Programming Language* [1] and *The Annotated C++ Reference Manual* [2].

C++ has actually been in use since 1984, and parts of Standard C were influenced by it (e.g., function prototypes). Some vendors have already begun using C++ as their primary system programming language, and it seems destined to grow in popularity. Most importantly, I see the possibility of lessened interest in revising Standard C (a ritual of standards) because C++ provides more fertile ground for impacting reality. Companies selling C++ compilers include AT&T, Borland, Microsoft, Oasys, Oregon Software, and Zortech.

C++ is not entirely a bed of roses, however. Learning to use C++ is not easy. It's a big language, and it has its share of foibles. However, once learned, it is very powerful, and you probably won't want to go back to C. Perhaps the worst aspect of C++ is that it is a language still in design. It lacks a standard. While ANSI X3J16 and ISO WG21 together are working on one, the language is still evolving.[2] There is a struggle between wanting to finish a standard for what exists now, or finish the language and then write the standard. Expect a sequence of *de facto* standards to be available for several years before an ANSI/ISO-sanctioned standard is issued.

Numerical C Extensions Group (NCEG)

Standard C does not explicitly address several issues of importance to the numerical community. This area lacked widespread existing practice to serve as a model and would have delayed the standard by years. Indeed, many people do not believe the C standard should be addressing such issues in the first place. Others believe that C has serious problems in ignoring the issues!

To address these problems, interested people formed NCEG (the Numerical C Extensions Group)—now working group X3J11.1 within ANSI—to define numerical extensions to Standard C. While not specifically chartered to create a standard, they will hopefully play a major role in establishing guidelines for future C standard revisions. Look for NCEG to publish technical reports that provide guidelines for implementors. Some of the specific areas being addressed by NCEG are:

- aliasing

- extended integer, complex, and IEEE floating-point support

---

2. According to Scott Wheeler: "C++ is so named because every time you think you've finished learning it, Bjarne adds a new feature."

- variably-sized arrays and array syntax
- exceptions and `errno`
- item parallelization
- aggregate initializers

At one time, X3J11.1 also studied parallel extensions; however, this has since been incorporated into the charter of yet another group, ANSI X3H5. (Indeed, X3J11 discussed *all* these issues while developing the current C standard. However, they exerted considerable restraint in avoiding production of a "kitchen sink" language specification. Many aspects of the standard reflect the careful consideration of these very issues, balanced against other important requirements.)

C Interpreters

Another important development in the world of C is that of C interpreters. Interpreters allow you to make a small code change and run the program without recompiling. This can sharply reduce the time spent coding. The environment these interpreters provide executes C statements as you type them. For example, I typed in the following while using CodeCenter from CenterLine.

```
1 -> struct gorp {
2 +>         int *n;
3 +>         char *name;
4 +>         struct gorp *foo;
5 +> } c,d;
6 -> set c.foo = d;
Error #543:  Illegal argument type:
        (struct gorp *) = (struct gorp)
7 -> set c.foo = &d;
(struct gorp *) 0xd972c /* d */
8 -> display c
display (1) set on expression 'c'.
9 -> int arr[10];
10 -> arr[8] = 17;
(int) 17
11 -> arr[17] = 8;
Error #166:  Illegal array index 17 into variable arr.  Max-
imum array index is 9.
12 -> d.n = arr;
(int *) 0xdc6d4 /* arr[0] */
13 -> display arr
display (2) set on expression 'arr'.
```

When I typed **display**, several windows popped up, which looked like this:

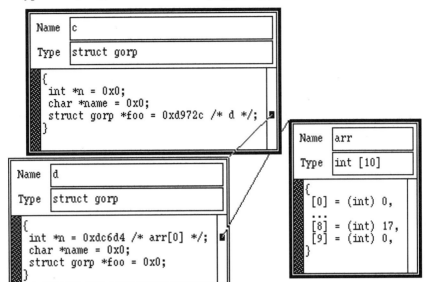

The little black squares are pointers that it will follow for you if you like. Impressive, isn't it? To assign new data, you don't even have to use C syntax. Just point to the object and type in new values!

Interpreters have some drawbacks, such as slower execution and large memory requirements. Indeed, your computer must hold in memory not only the machine instructions for your program, but the source, an intermediate form used by the interpreter, the symbol table, and the interpreter, too! But these disadvantages are greatly outweighed by their advantages.

Companies selling similarly powerful C interpreters include Borland, Catalytix, Gimpel Software, MicroPro, Microsoft, Rational Systems, and Stepstone.

GNU C and C++

The Free Software Foundation (FSF) has made available free C and C++ compilers. (**gcc** and **g++**).[3] As with other FSF products, **gcc** and **g++** are:

Very high quality—for example, optimization includes: invariant code motion out of loops, common subexpression elimination, automatic register packing, constant propagation and elimination of consequent dead code, copy propagation, elimination of dead stores, jump optimization including cross-jumping, delaying of stack adjustments after function calls, arithmetic performed in subword types when appropriate, etc.

Unsupported—strictly speaking, FSF itself offers no support although there are third-party companies such as Cygnus from which you can buy support.

---

3. "gcc" stands for "GNU C compiler." "GNU" stands for "GNU's Not UNIX."

In keeping with the price, though, there are many unofficial maintainers, plus a dedicated electronic mailing list and Usenet newsgroups such as `gnu.gcc` and `gnu.g++`. FSF records known bugs and suggested fixes.

Supplied in source form—programs are distributed in source form, so you can change them as you desire. (Also, you can fix bugs!)

Free, but not public domain—FSF places certain restrictions on the software. In particular, you can use, change, make copies, and distribute as you desire, as long as you do not charge for it or remove their restrictions of use.

As I mentioned, `gcc` and `g++` are of very high quality. Indeed, many people have discarded the compiler supplied by their vendor and turned to `gcc` or `g++` instead. Sometimes, this is because they are better compilers; another reason is they are portable to a large number of machines. If you support software that itself is portable, it is much easier to keep it running on one compiler than ten.

Furthermore, `gcc` supports many experimental extensions to C that are continually being proposed. Although some complain that this encourages nonportable coding, `gcc` tracked Standard C as it was developing more closely than any other compiler.

`gcc` also comes with some auxiliary software, such as `gdb`, the GNU debugger.

The GNU C compiler can be `ftp`'d from `prep.ai.mit.edu`. The file is called `/u2/emacs/gcc-`*version*`.tar.z` where *version* is the version number. This includes machine descriptions on existing machines supported by `gcc`, and extensive documentation on porting `gcc` to a new machine.

For more information about GNU C, contact the Free Software Foundation (see p. 403 in the Appendix).

Books

Before I end, I'm going to recommend a few books I've found to be so good that they have a permanent place on my desktop. I feel that any C programmer deserves to have these books at ready grasp. (As for *this* book? Well, consider leaving it on the coffee table alongside *Life With UNIX*.)

C: A Reference Manual by Samuel Harbison & Guy Steele, Prentice Hall, 1984.

A very readable reference to both Classic C and Standard C. Usually referred to simply as *H&S*. Several editions are in print.

ANSI X3.159 by a cast of thousands, American National Standards Institute, 1989.

This is *the* standard. Even though it may be hard to read, all other readings are only interpretations of it. Technically equivalent to *ISO/IEC Standard 9899:1990*, International Standards Organization, Geneva, 1990, except that the ANSI version includes a very useful rationale.

C++ for C Programmers by Ira Pohl, Benjamin/Cummings Publishing Co., 1989.

> An excellent introduction to C++ for skilled C programmers.

The Standard C Library by P. J. Plauger, Prentice Hall, 1992.

> Both a book and machine-readable source for an implementation of the Standard C library. Meant to be both readable and efficient, the former goal is sacrificed at times, but the result is invaluable nonetheless.

The C Programming Language by Brian Kernighan and Dennis Ritchie, Prentice Hall, 1978 (1st edition), 1988 (2nd edition).

> Two editions of *K&R* exist. The second edition is based on Standard C. It includes discussions of C language changes and a `yacc`-able grammar.

> The first edition of *K&R* will remain in print, as it differs significantly from the second, and continues to describe many of the extant C implementations. You might be amused to hear that the original expectation of the publisher was that an average of nine copies would be sold to each of the 130 UNIX sites that existed at the time the book was first published. As of 1992, over a million and a half copies had been printed!

Summary

C and its variants, such as C++, will remain the workhorses for systems programming during the next decade. Interest in and use of C continues to grow at an incredible rate.

Nonetheless, the C language is not for everyone. C is relatively low-level and not oriented toward any one specific application area—CASE and 4GLs are often more suitable and may be the future for many programming projects. Other tasks, such as rapid prototyping or real-time programming, are often more easily done in other languages. Make sure you use C when appropriate, and you will reap the benefits of the maturity and power of the language.

Oh, and one last thing—Try not to write any more obfuscated C! Please?!

References

[1]   Bjarne Stroustrup, *The C++ Programming Language*, Addison Wesley, 1986.

[2]   Margaret Ellis, Bjarne Stroustrup, *The Annotated C++ Reference Manual*, Addison Wesley, 1990.

Appendix—Addresses

This appendix contains the addresses of organizations and companies referred to throughout the book. Unless stated otherwise, addresses are in the United States.

Addison-Wesley Publishing Co.
Longman Publishing Co.
Benjamin/Cummings Publishing Co.
1 Jacob Way
Reading, MA 01867
1-800-447-2226

American National Standards Institute (ANSI)
1430 Broadway
New York, NY 10018
1-212-642-4900

AT&T Customer Information Center
P.O. Box 19901
Indianapolis, IN 46219
1-800-432-6600

Austin Code Works
11100 Leafwood Lane
Austin, TX 78750-3464
1-512-258-0785
info@acw.com

Borland International
1800 Green Hills Road
Scotts Valley, CA 95066-0001
1-408-438-8400

The C Users Journal
The C Users' Group
R&D Publications, Inc.
PO Box 3127
Lawrence, KS 66046
1-913-841-1631
cuj@rdpub.com

The C++ Journal
2 Haven Avenue
Port Washington, NY 11050-9768
1-516-767-7107
mcdhup!image!info

The C++ Report
588 Broadway
Suite 604
New York, NY 10012
1-212-274-0640

Catalytix Corporation
1 Kendall Square, Bldg 600
Cambridge, MA 02139
1-617-497-2160

CenterLine Software, Inc.
10 Fawcett Street
Cambridge, MA 02138-1110
1-617-498-3000
info@centerline.com

Cygnus Support
814 University Avenue
Palo Alto, CA 94301
1-415-322-3811
info@cygnus.com

Free Software Foundation
675 Mass Avenue
Cambridge, MA 02139
1-617-876-3296
gnu@prep.ai.mit.edu

Gimpel Software
3207 Hogarth Lane
Collegeville, PA 19426
1-215-584-4261

ISO Central Secretariat
Case postale 56
1211 Geneva 20
SWITZERLAND

Journal of C Language Translation
PO Box 380349
Cambridge, MA 02238-0349
1-617-492-3869
jclt@iecc.cambridge.ma.us

Micro/Systems Journal
c/o M&T Publishing, Inc.
411 Borel Avenue, Suite 100
San Mateo, CA 94402
1-215-358-9500

Microsoft Corp.
1 Microsoft Way
Redmond, WA 98052-6399
1-206-882-8080

National Institute of Standards and
Technology (NIST)
Computer Systems Laboratory
Gaithersburg, MD 20899
1-301-975-2822
postmaster@nist.gov

Oasys
1 Cranberry Hill
Lexington, MA 02173
1-617-862-2002

Obfuscated C Code Contest
judges@toad.com or hoptoad!judges

Oregon Software
c/o Taumetric Corp.
8765 Fletcher Parkway, Suite 301
La Mesa, CA 91942
1-619-697-7674
support@taumet.com

PC/Blue
c/o New York Amateur Computer Club
Box 3442
Church Street Station
New York, NY 10008

Plum Hall, Inc.
2L Ouli Street, Suite 261
PO Box 111333
Kamuela, HI 96743
1-808-885-6663
plum@plumhall.com

Prentice Hall, Inc.
Route 9W
Englewood Cliffs, NJ 07632
1-201-592-2000

Professional Press
101 Witmer Road
Horsham, PA 19044
1-215-957-1500

Rational Systems, Inc.
220 No. Main St.
Natick, MA 01760
1-508-653-6006
73667.1753@compuserve.com

The StepStone Corporation
75 Glen Road
Sandy Hook, CT 06482
1-203-426-1875

X3J11, Convener
Tom Plum
(see Plum Hall, Inc.)

X3J11.1 (NCEG), Convener
Rex Jaeschke
2051 Swans Neck Way
Reston, VA 22091
1-703-860-0091
rex@aussie.com

Zortech, Inc.
c/o Symantec
135 South Road
Bedford, MA 01730
1-617-275-4800
support@zortech.com

Index

Italicized page numbers denote the most definitive references.

Symbols

Numerics

A

B

C